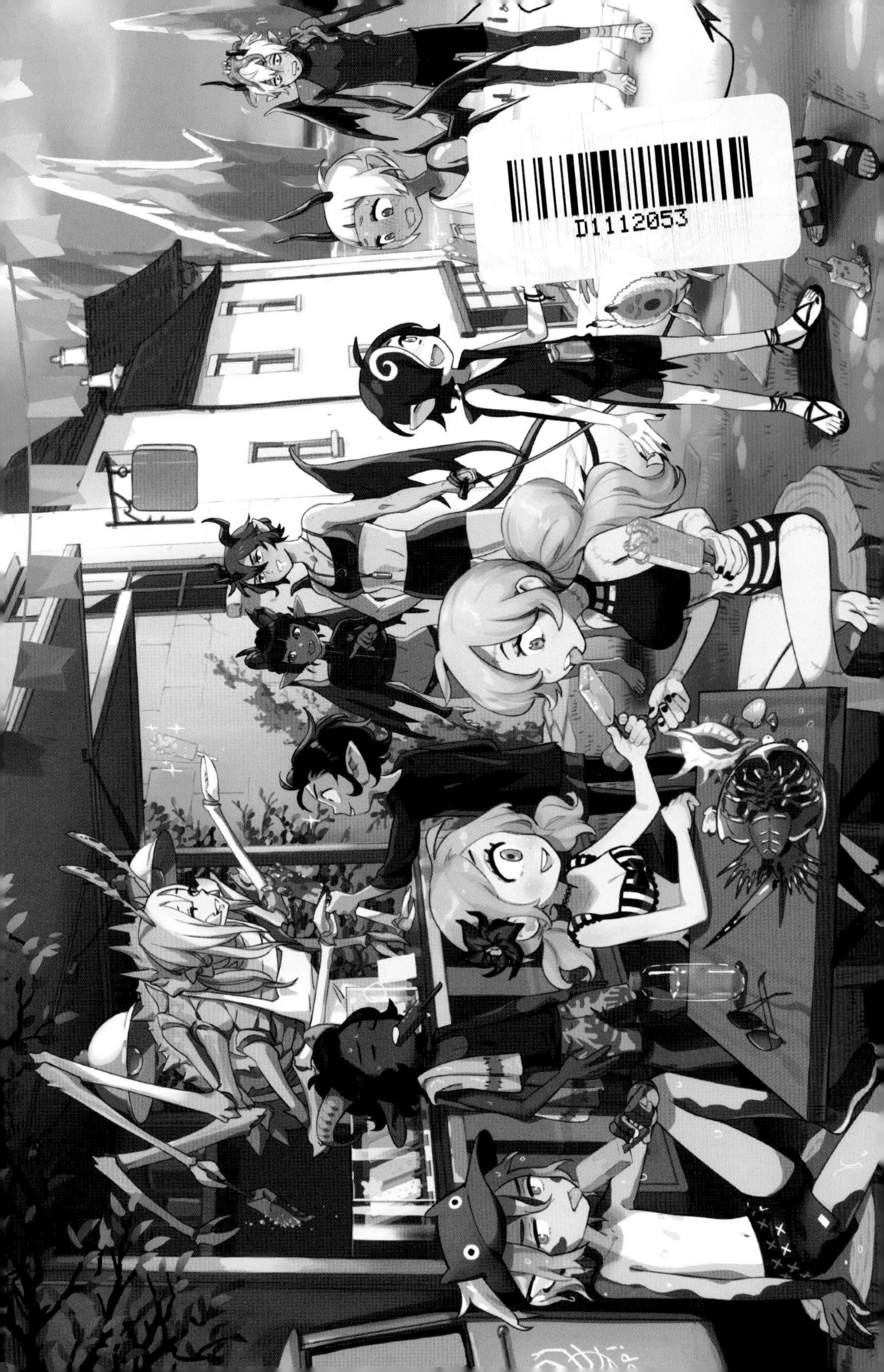

DEVIL'S CANDY

VOLUME 2

ART BY REM STORY BY BIKKURI

ORIGINALS

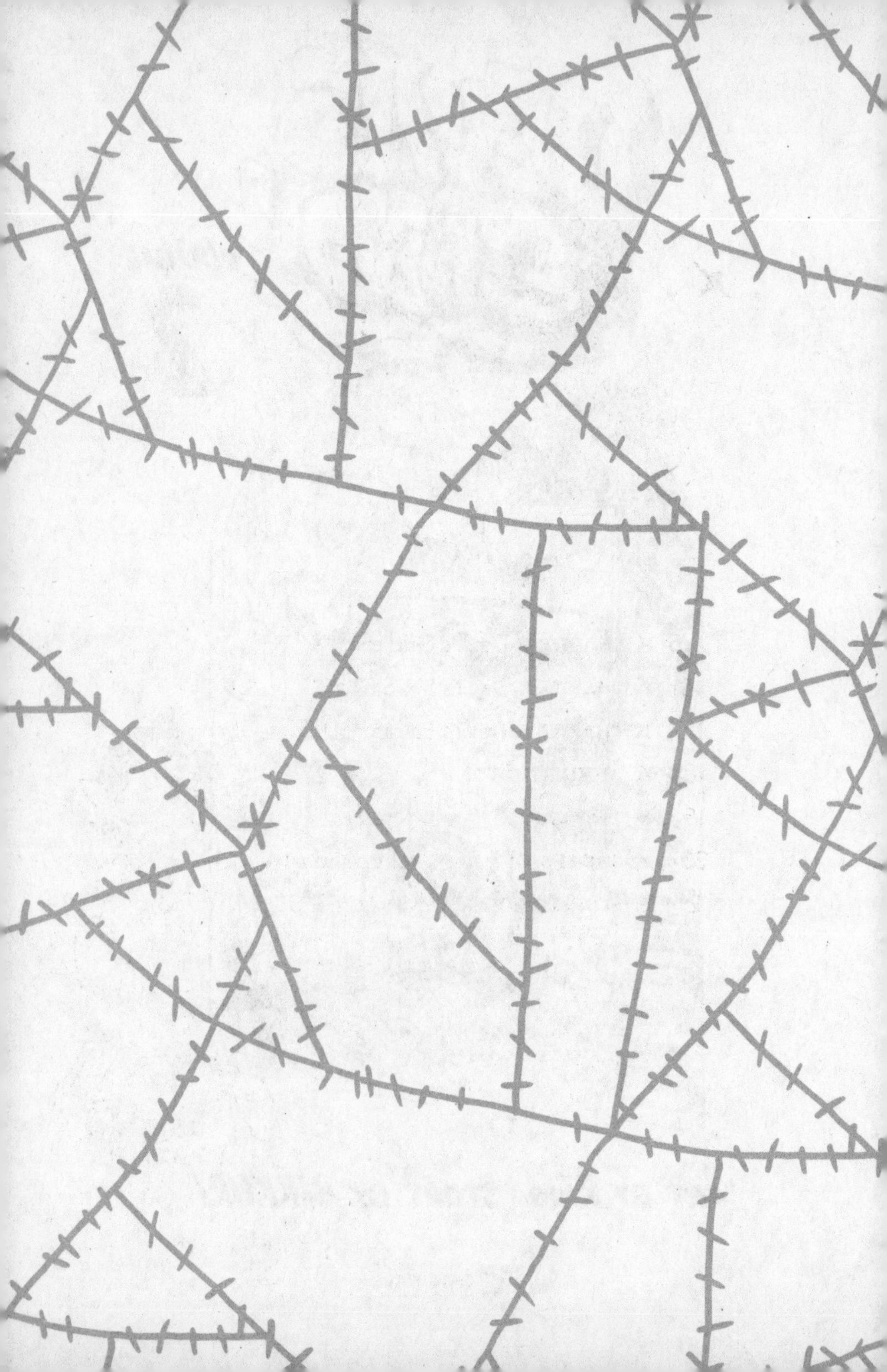

DEVIL'S CANDY

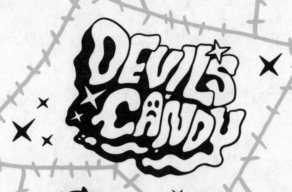

VOLUME 2

CONTENTS

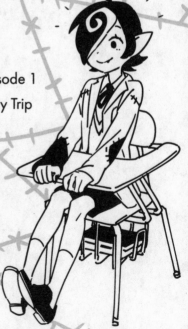

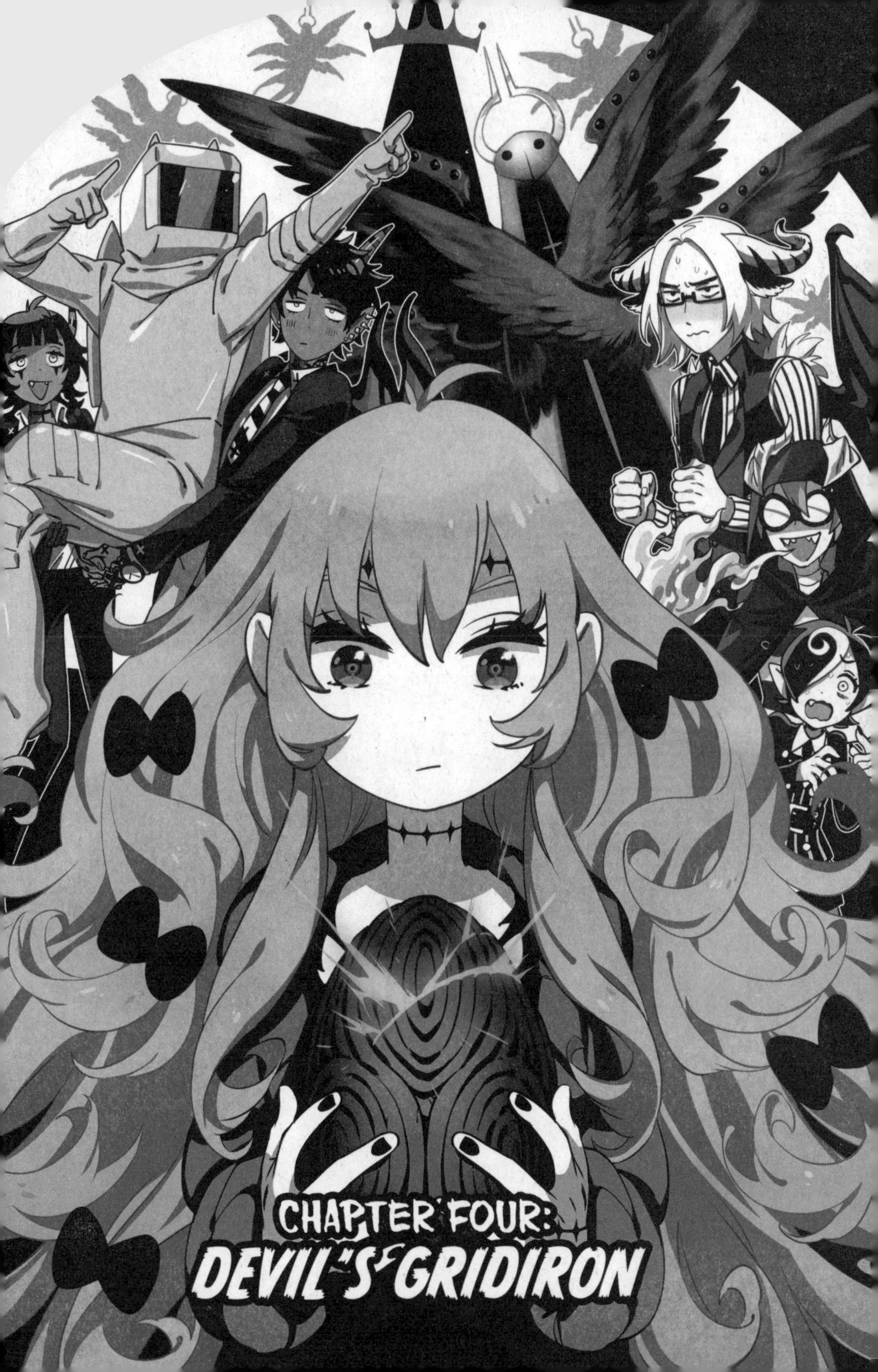
CHAPTER FOUR:
DEVIL'S GRIDIRON

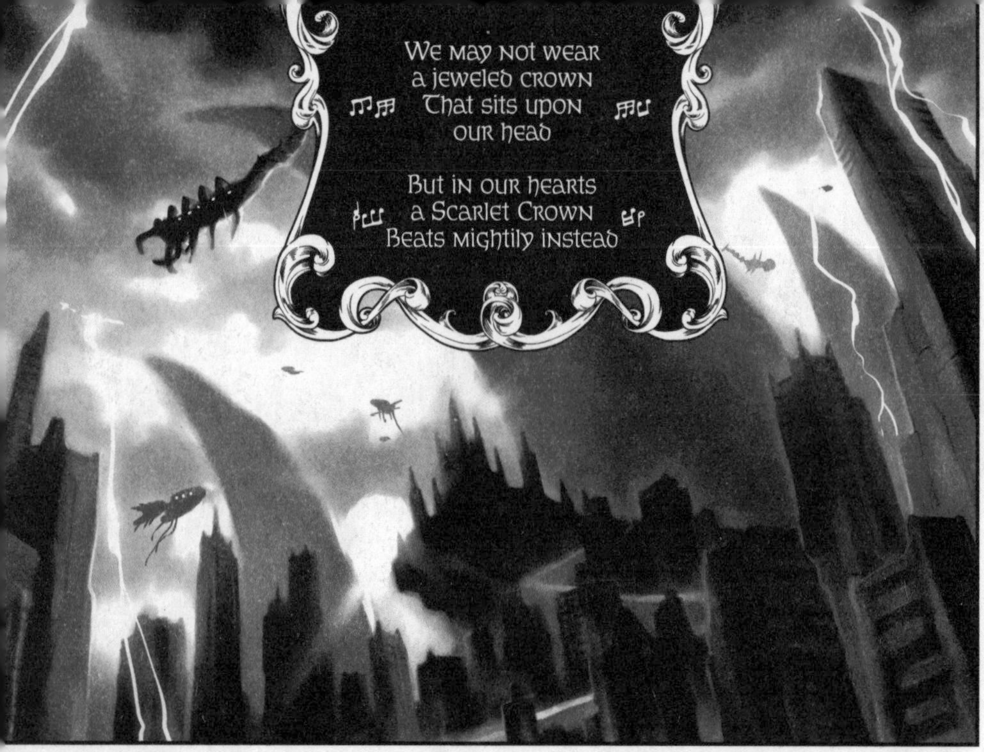
We may not wear
a jeweled crown
That sits upon
our head

But in our hearts
a Scarlet Crown
Beats mightily instead

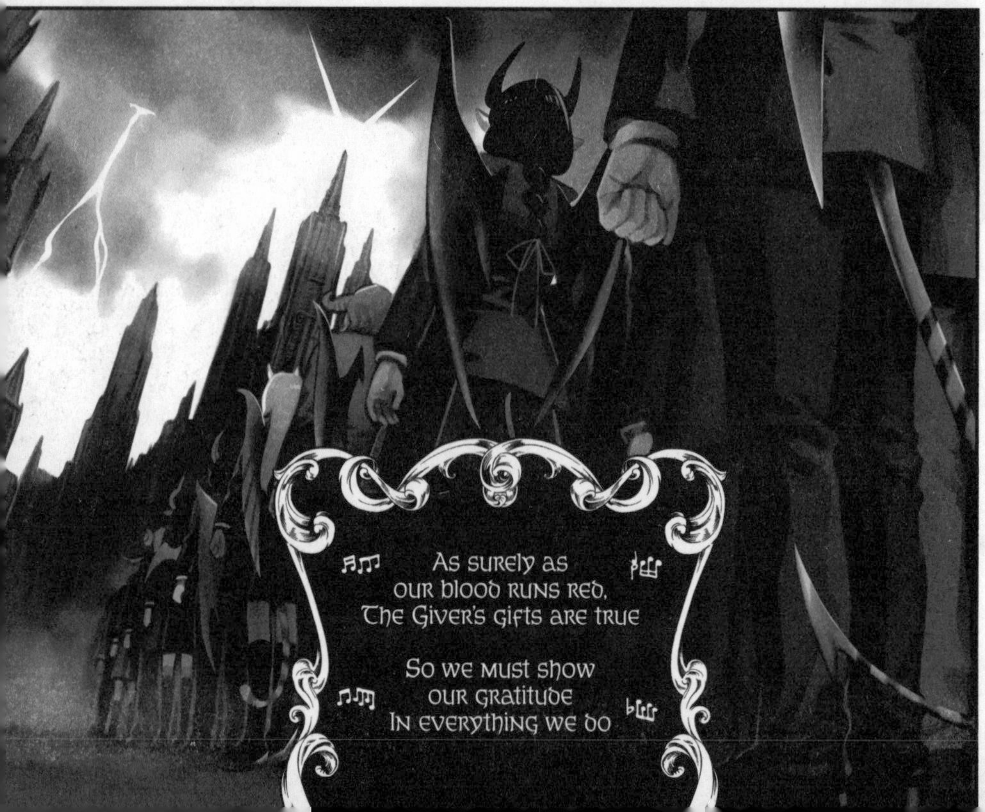
As surely as
our blood runs red,
The Giver's gifts are true

So we must show
our gratitude
In everything we do

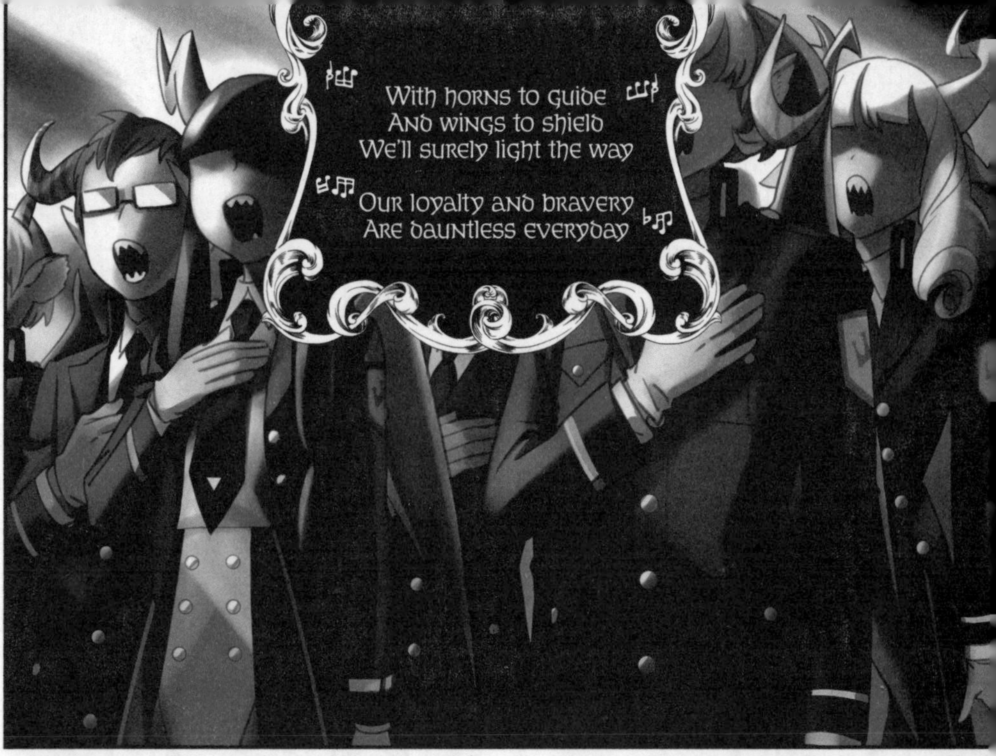
With horns to guide
And wings to shield
We'll surely light the way
Our loyalty and bravery
Are dauntless everyday
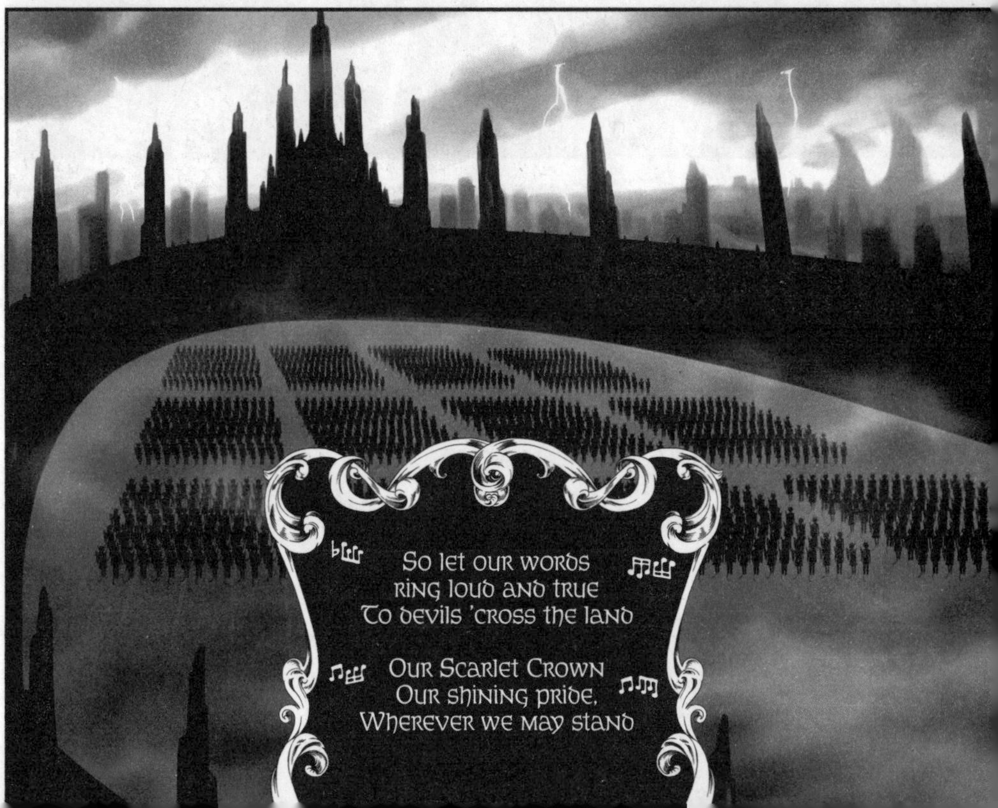
So let our words
ring loud and true
To devils 'cross the land
Our Scarlet Crown
Our shining pride,
Wherever we may stand

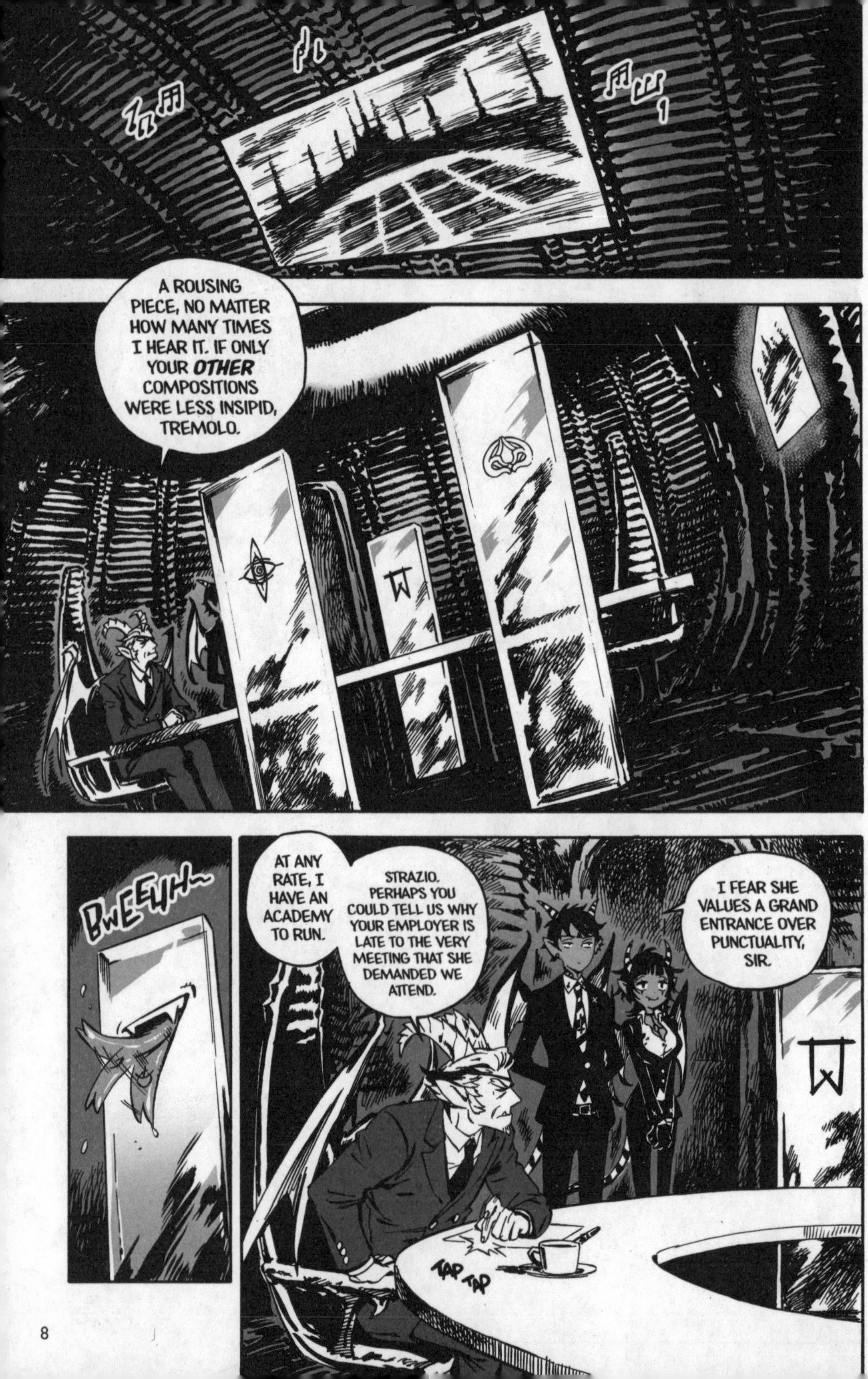
A ROUSING PIECE, NO MATTER HOW MANY TIMES I HEAR IT. IF ONLY YOUR OTHER COMPOSITIONS WERE LESS INSIPID, TREMOLO.
BWEEUH~
AT ANY RATE, I HAVE AN ACADEMY TO RUN.
STRAZIO. PERHAPS YOU COULD TELL US WHY YOUR EMPLOYER IS LATE TO THE VERY MEETING THAT SHE DEMANDED WE ATTEND.
I FEAR SHE VALUES A GRAND ENTRANCE OVER PUNCTUALITY, SIR.
TAP TAP

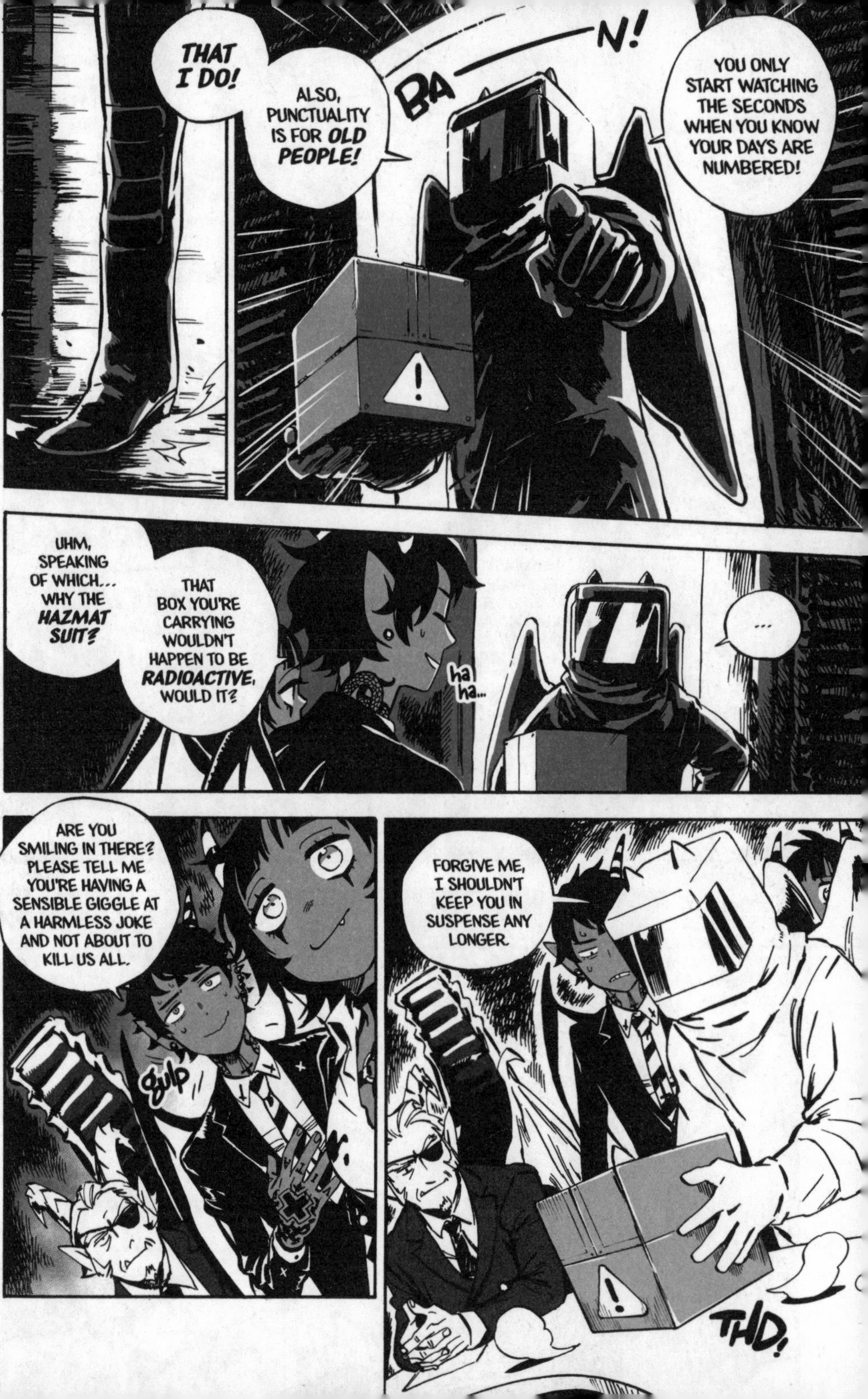
THAT I DO!
ALSO, PUNCTUALITY IS FOR OLD PEOPLE!
BA—N!
YOU ONLY START WATCHING THE SECONDS WHEN YOU KNOW YOUR DAYS ARE NUMBERED!
UHM, SPEAKING OF WHICH... WHY THE HAZMAT SUIT?
THAT BOX YOU'RE CARRYING WOULDN'T HAPPEN TO BE RADIOACTIVE, WOULD IT?
ha ha...
...
ARE YOU SMILING IN THERE? PLEASE TELL ME YOU'RE HAVING A SENSIBLE GIGGLE AT A HARMLESS JOKE AND NOT ABOUT TO KILL US ALL.
gulp
FORGIVE ME, I SHOULDN'T KEEP YOU IN SUSPENSE ANY LONGER.
THD!

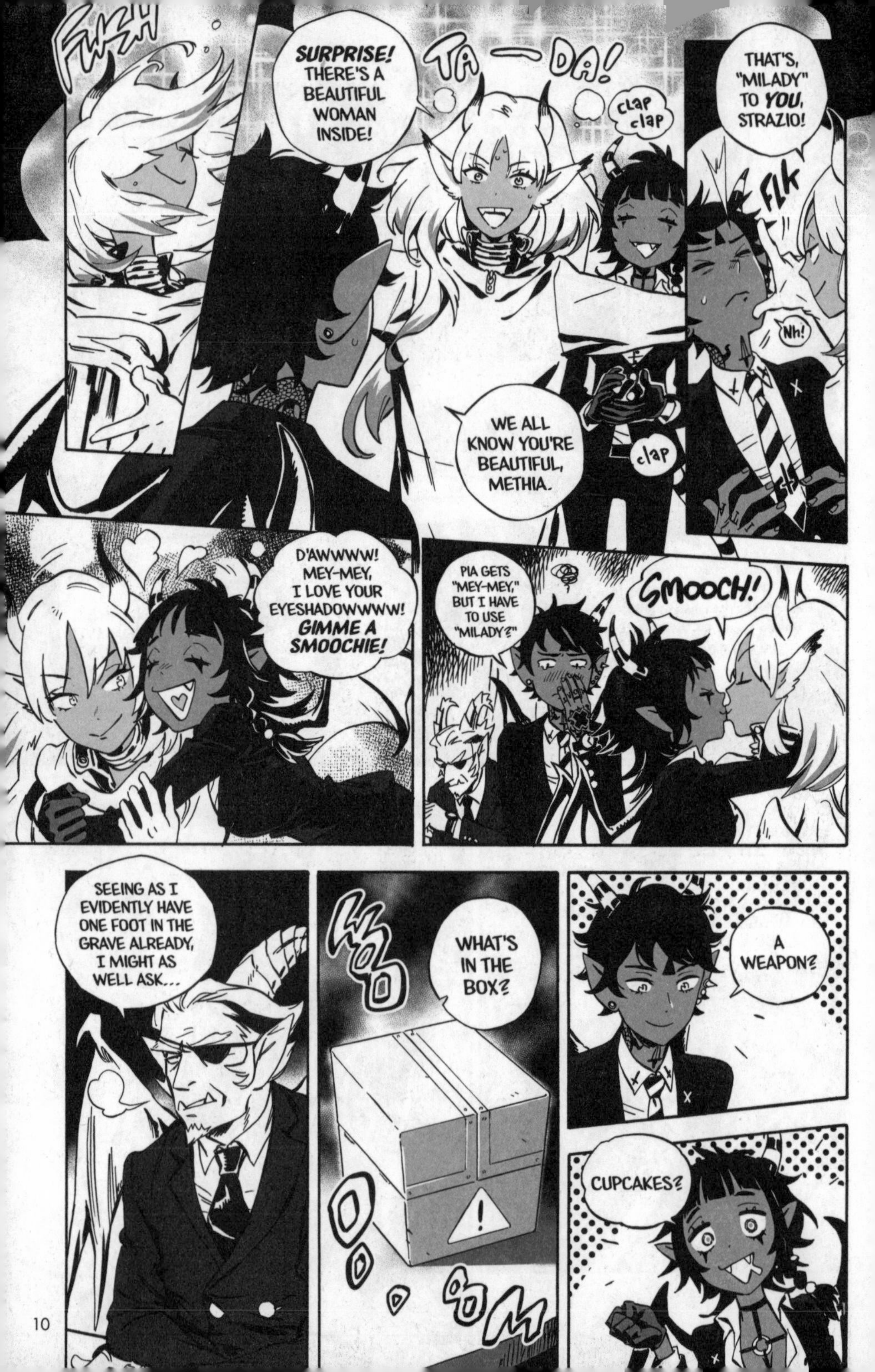
FWSH
SURPRISE! THERE'S A BEAUTIFUL WOMAN INSIDE!
TA—DA!
clap clap
WE ALL KNOW YOU'RE BEAUTIFUL, METHIA.
clap
THAT'S, "MILADY" TO YOU, STRAZIO!
FLK
Nh!
D'AWWWW! MEY-MEY, I LOVE YOUR EYESHADOWWWW! GIMME A SMOOCHIE!
PIA GETS "MEY-MEY," BUT I HAVE TO USE "MILADY?"
SMOOCH!
SEEING AS I EVIDENTLY HAVE ONE FOOT IN THE GRAVE ALREADY, I MIGHT AS WELL ASK...
WHAT'S IN THE BOX?
A WEAPON?
CUPCAKES?

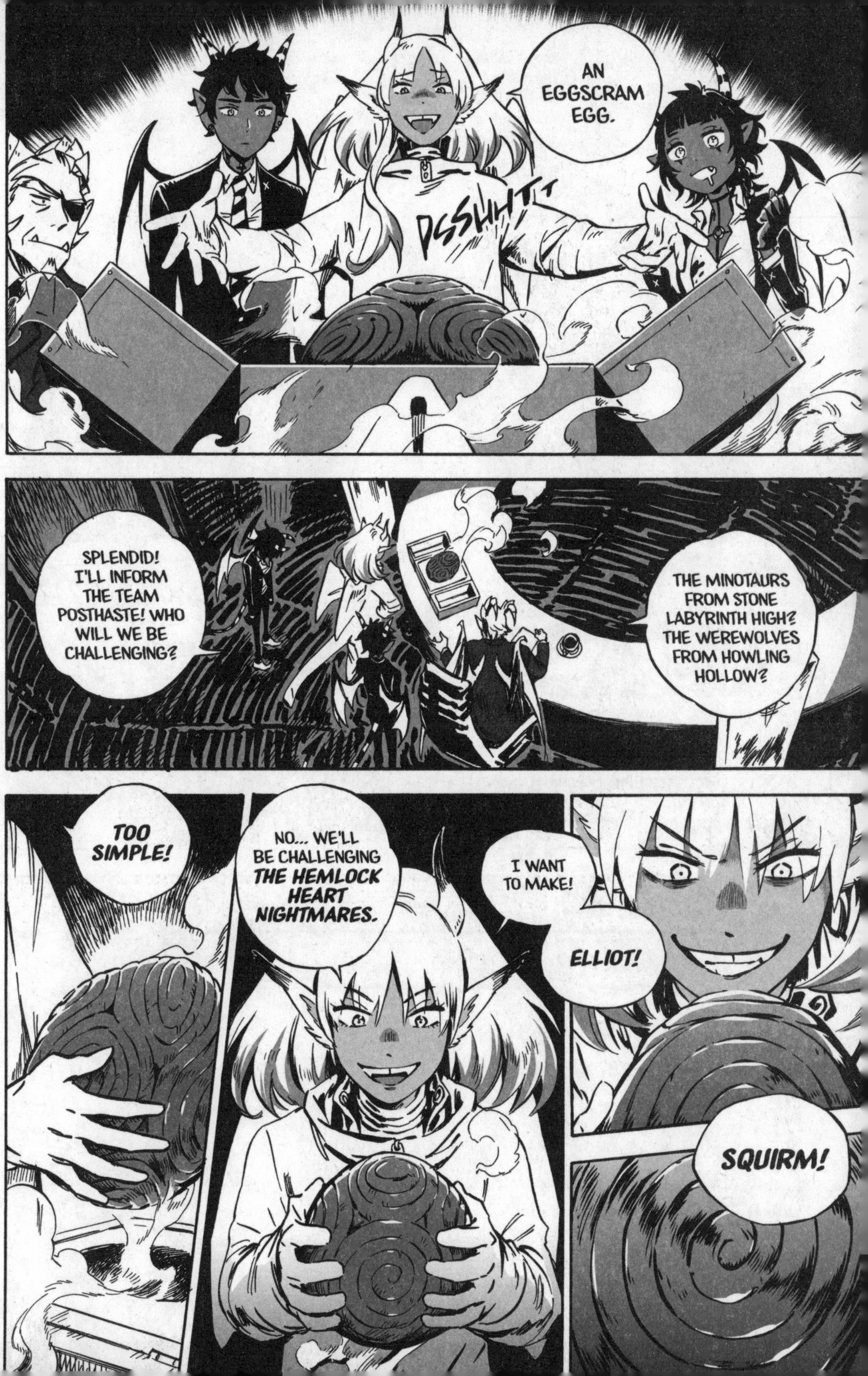
AN EGGSCRAM EGG.
PSSHHT
SPLENDID! I'LL INFORM THE TEAM POSTHASTE! WHO WILL WE BE CHALLENGING?
THE MINOTAURS FROM STONE LABYRINTH HIGH? THE WEREWOLVES FROM HOWLING HOLLOW?
TOO SIMPLE!
NO... WE'LL BE CHALLENGING THE HEMLOCK HEART NIGHTMARES.
I WANT TO MAKE!
ELLIOT!
SQUIRM!

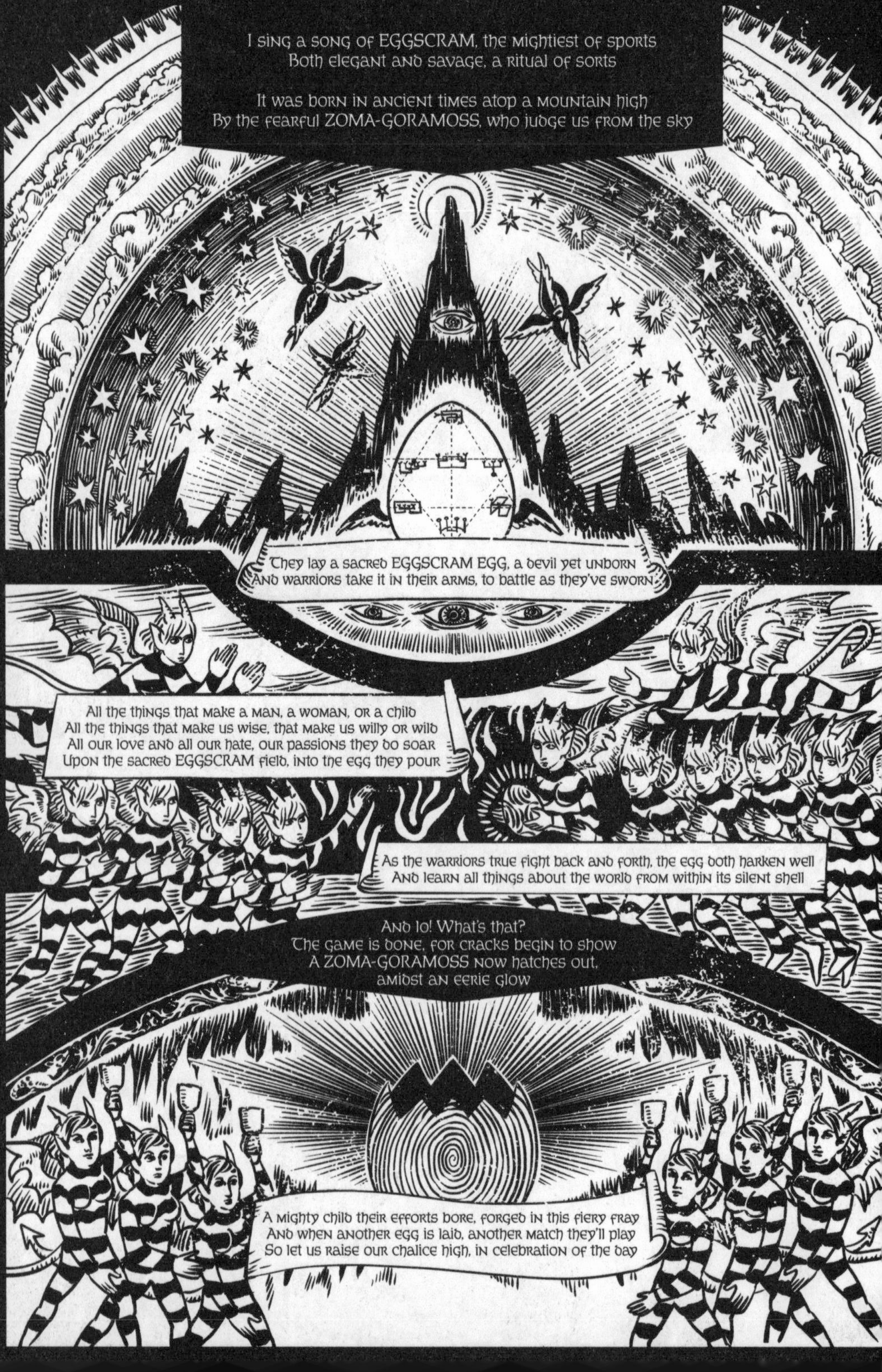
I sing a song of EGGSCRAM, the mightiest of sports
Both elegant and savage, a ritual of sorts
It was born in ancient times atop a mountain high
By the fearful ZOMA-GORAMOSS, who judge us from the sky
They lay a sacred EGGSCRAM EGG, a devil yet unborn
And warriors take it in their arms, to battle as they've sworn
All the things that make a man, a woman, or a child
All the things that make us wise, that make us willy or wild
All our love and all our hate, our passions they do soar
Upon the sacred EGGSCRAM field, into the egg they pour
As the warriors true fight back and forth, the egg doth harken well
And learn all things about the world from within its silent shell
And lo! What's that?
The game is done, for cracks begin to show
A ZOMA-GORAMOSS now hatches out,
amidst an eerie glow
A mighty child their efforts bore, forged in this fiery fray
And when another egg is laid, another match they'll play
So let us raise our chalice high, in celebration of the day

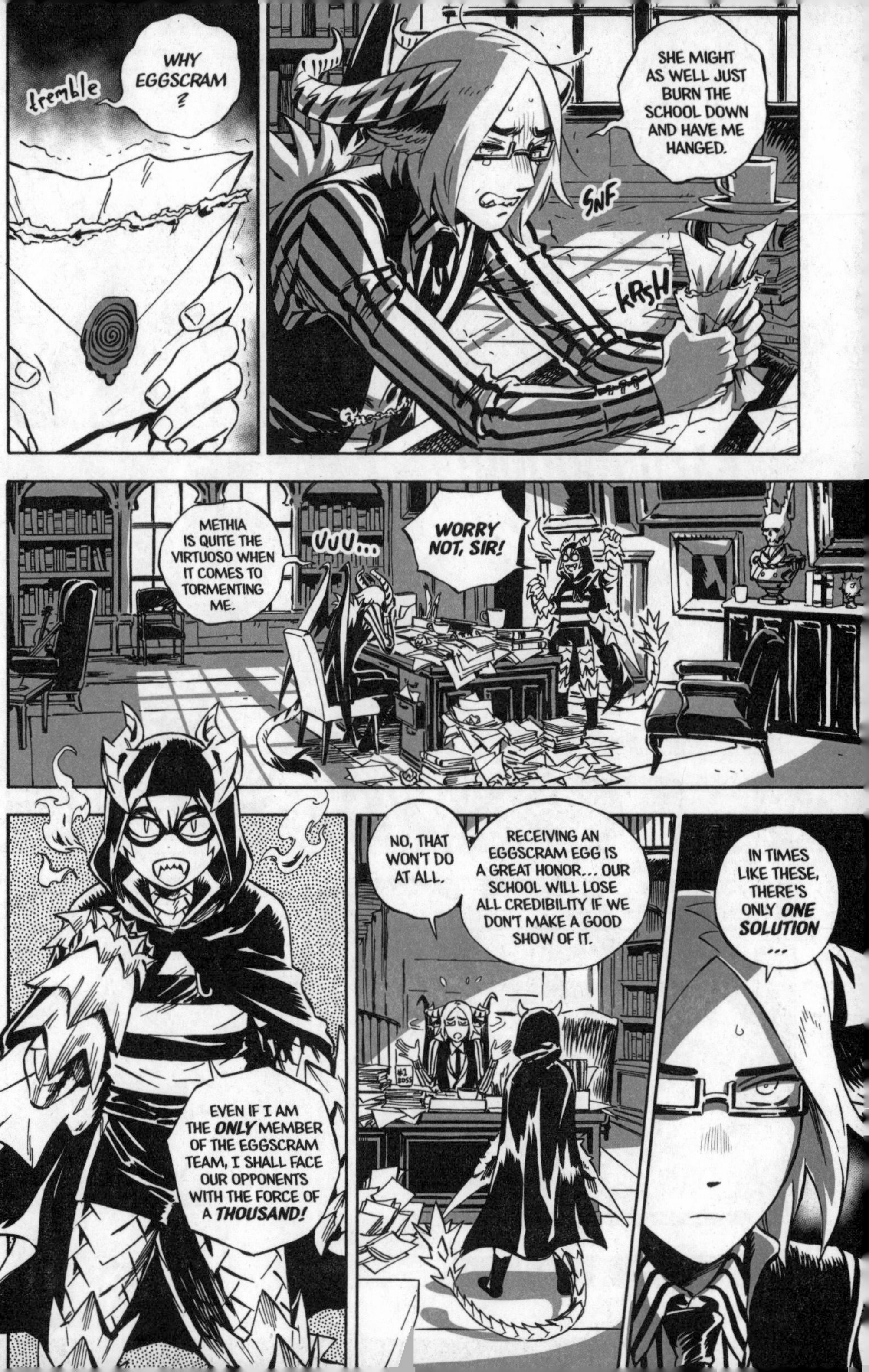
tremble
WHY EGGSCRAM?
SHE MIGHT AS WELL JUST BURN THE SCHOOL DOWN AND HAVE ME HANGED.
SNF
KRSH
METHIA IS QUITE THE VIRTUOSO WHEN IT COMES TO TORMENTING ME.
UUU...
WORRY NOT, SIR!
EVEN IF I AM THE ONLY MEMBER OF THE EGGSCRAM TEAM, I SHALL FACE OUR OPPONENTS WITH THE FORCE OF A THOUSAND!
NO, THAT WON'T DO AT ALL.
RECEIVING AN EGGSCRAM EGG IS A GREAT HONOR... OUR SCHOOL WILL LOSE ALL CREDIBILITY IF WE DON'T MAKE A GOOD SHOW OF IT.
#1 BOSS
IN TIMES LIKE THESE, THERE'S ONLY ONE SOLUTION...

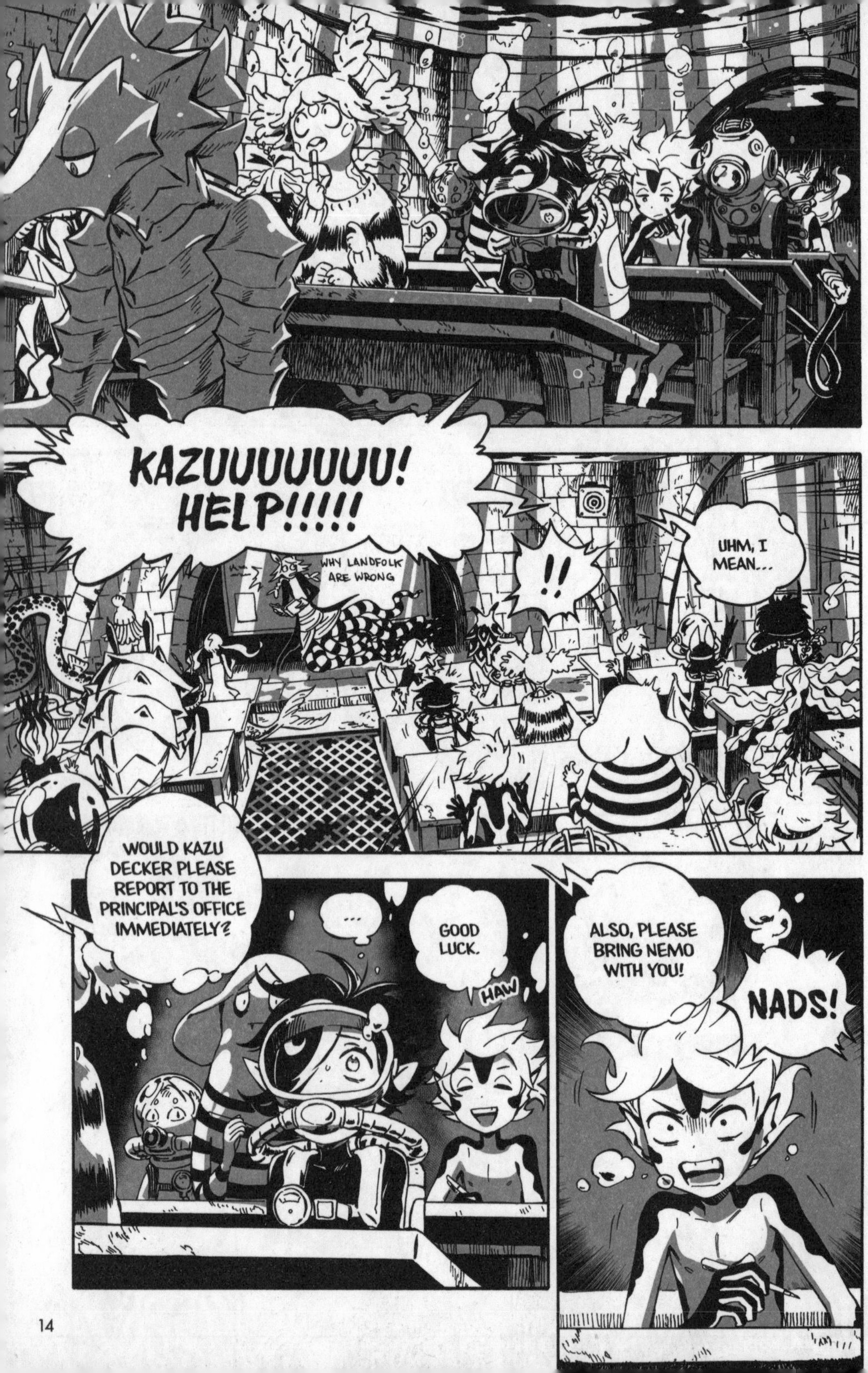
KAZUUUUUUU! HELP!!!!!
WHY LANDFOLK ARE WRONG
!!
UHM, I MEAN...
WOULD KAZU DECKER PLEASE REPORT TO THE PRINCIPAL'S OFFICE IMMEDIATELY?
...
GOOD LUCK.
HAW
ALSO, PLEASE BRING NEMO WITH YOU!
NADS!

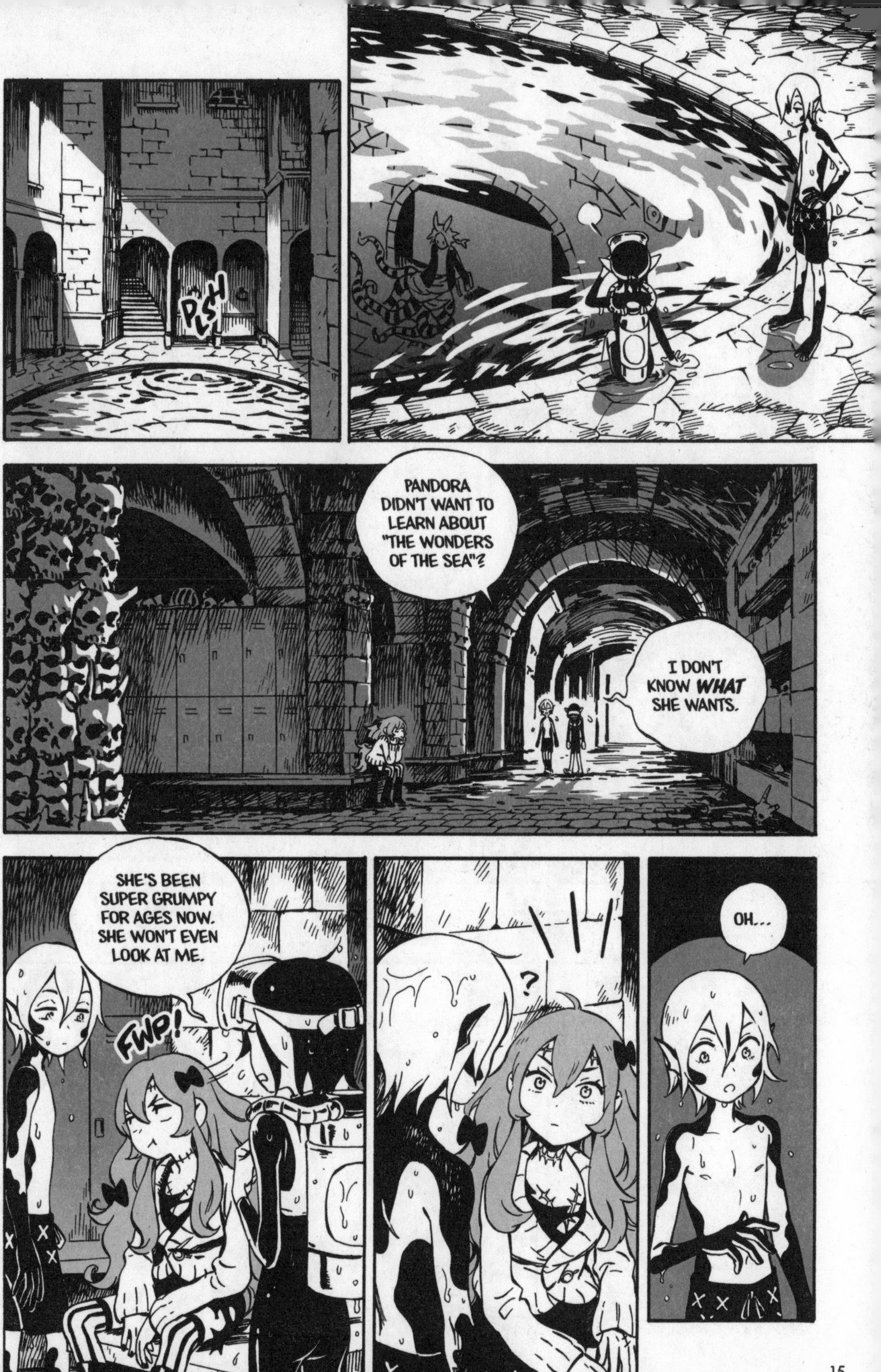
PLSH
PANDORA DIDN'T WANT TO LEARN ABOUT "THE WONDERS OF THE SEA"?
I DON'T KNOW WHAT SHE WANTS.
SHE'S BEEN SUPER GRUMPY FOR AGES NOW. SHE WON'T EVEN LOOK AT ME.
FWP!
?
OH...

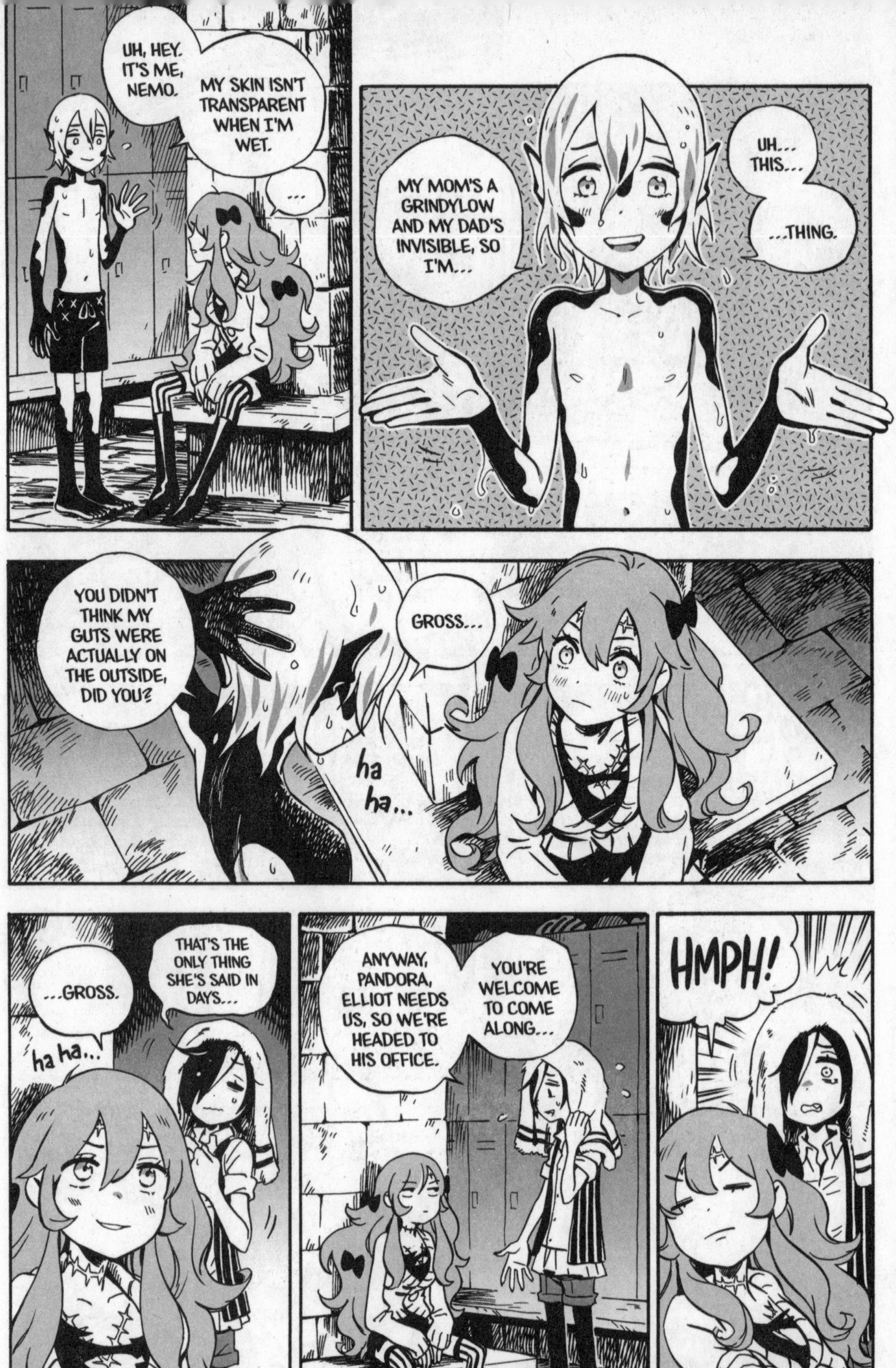

UH, HEY. IT'S ME, NEMO.
MY SKIN ISN'T TRANSPARENT WHEN I'M WET.
...
MY MOM'S A GRINDYLOW AND MY DAD'S INVISIBLE, SO I'M...
UH... THIS...
...THING.
YOU DIDN'T THINK MY GUTS WERE ACTUALLY ON THE OUTSIDE, DID YOU?
GROSS...
ha ha...
...GROSS.
THAT'S THE ONLY THING SHE'S SAID IN DAYS...
ha ha...
ANYWAY, PANDORA, ELLIOT NEEDS US, SO WE'RE HEADED TO HIS OFFICE.
YOU'RE WELCOME TO COME ALONG...
HMPH!

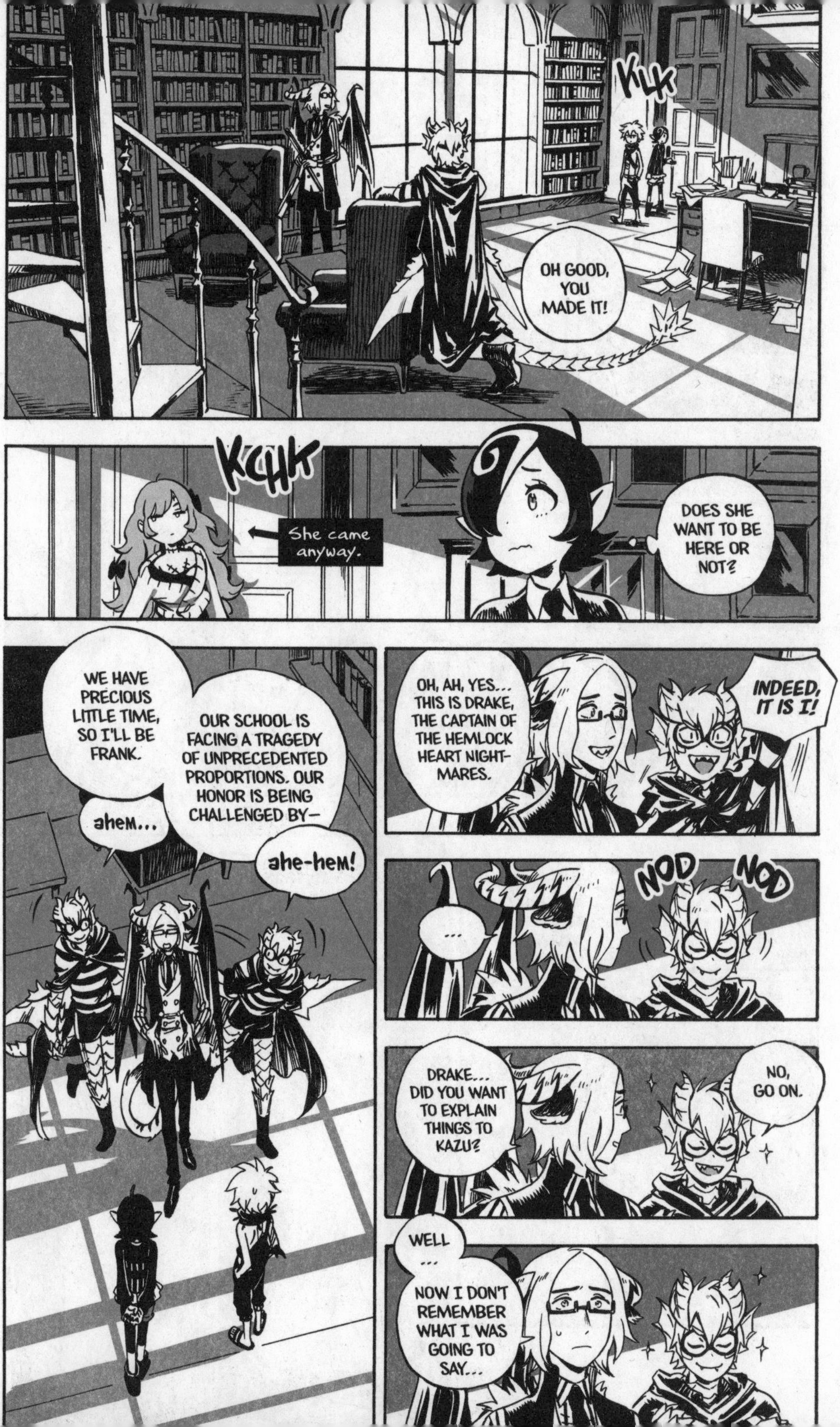
KLIK
OH GOOD, YOU MADE IT!
KCHK
She came anyway.
DOES SHE WANT TO BE HERE OR NOT?
WE HAVE PRECIOUS LITTLE TIME, SO I'LL BE FRANK.
OUR SCHOOL IS FACING A TRAGEDY OF UNPRECEDENTED PROPORTIONS. OUR HONOR IS BEING CHALLENGED BY—
ahem...
ahe-hem!
OH, AH, YES... THIS IS DRAKE, THE CAPTAIN OF THE HEMLOCK HEART NIGHT-MARES.
INDEED, IT IS I!
...
NOD NOD
DRAKE... DID YOU WANT TO EXPLAIN THINGS TO KAZU?
NO, GO ON.
WELL ...
NOW I DON'T REMEMBER WHAT I WAS GOING TO SAY...

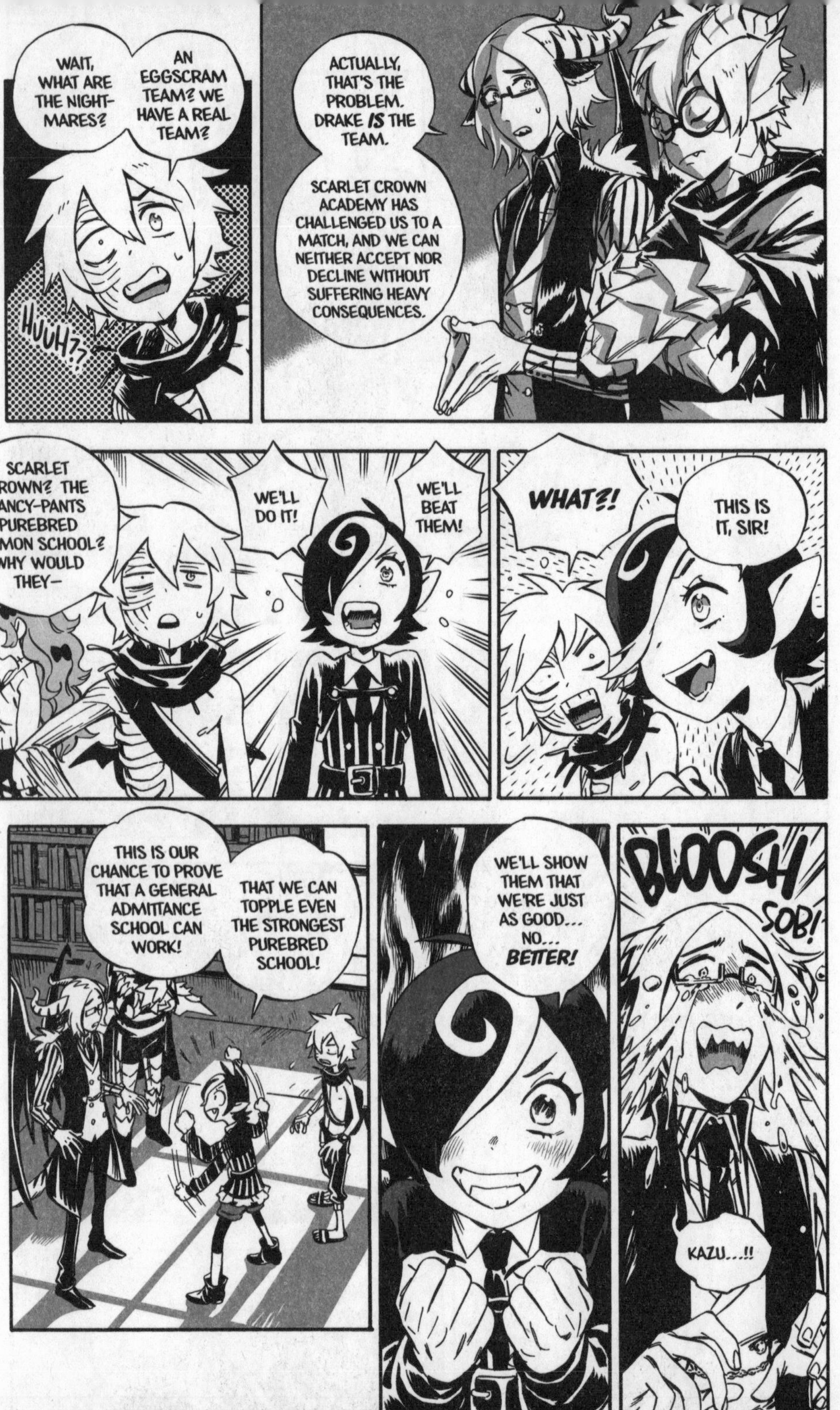
WAIT, WHAT ARE THE NIGHT-MARES?
AN EGGSCRAM TEAM? WE HAVE A REAL TEAM?
HUUH??
ACTUALLY, THAT'S THE PROBLEM. DRAKE IS THE TEAM.
SCARLET CROWN ACADEMY HAS CHALLENGED US TO A MATCH, AND WE CAN NEITHER ACCEPT NOR DECLINE WITHOUT SUFFERING HEAVY CONSEQUENCES.
SCARLET CROWN? THE FANCY-PANTS PUREBRED DAEMON SCHOOL? WHY WOULD THEY–
WE'LL DO IT!
WE'LL BEAT THEM!
WHAT?!
THIS IS IT, SIR!
THIS IS OUR CHANCE TO PROVE THAT A GENERAL ADMITTANCE SCHOOL CAN WORK!
THAT WE CAN TOPPLE EVEN THE STRONGEST PUREBRED SCHOOL!
WE'LL SHOW THEM THAT WE'RE JUST AS GOOD... NO... BETTER!
BLOOSH
SOB!
KAZU...!!

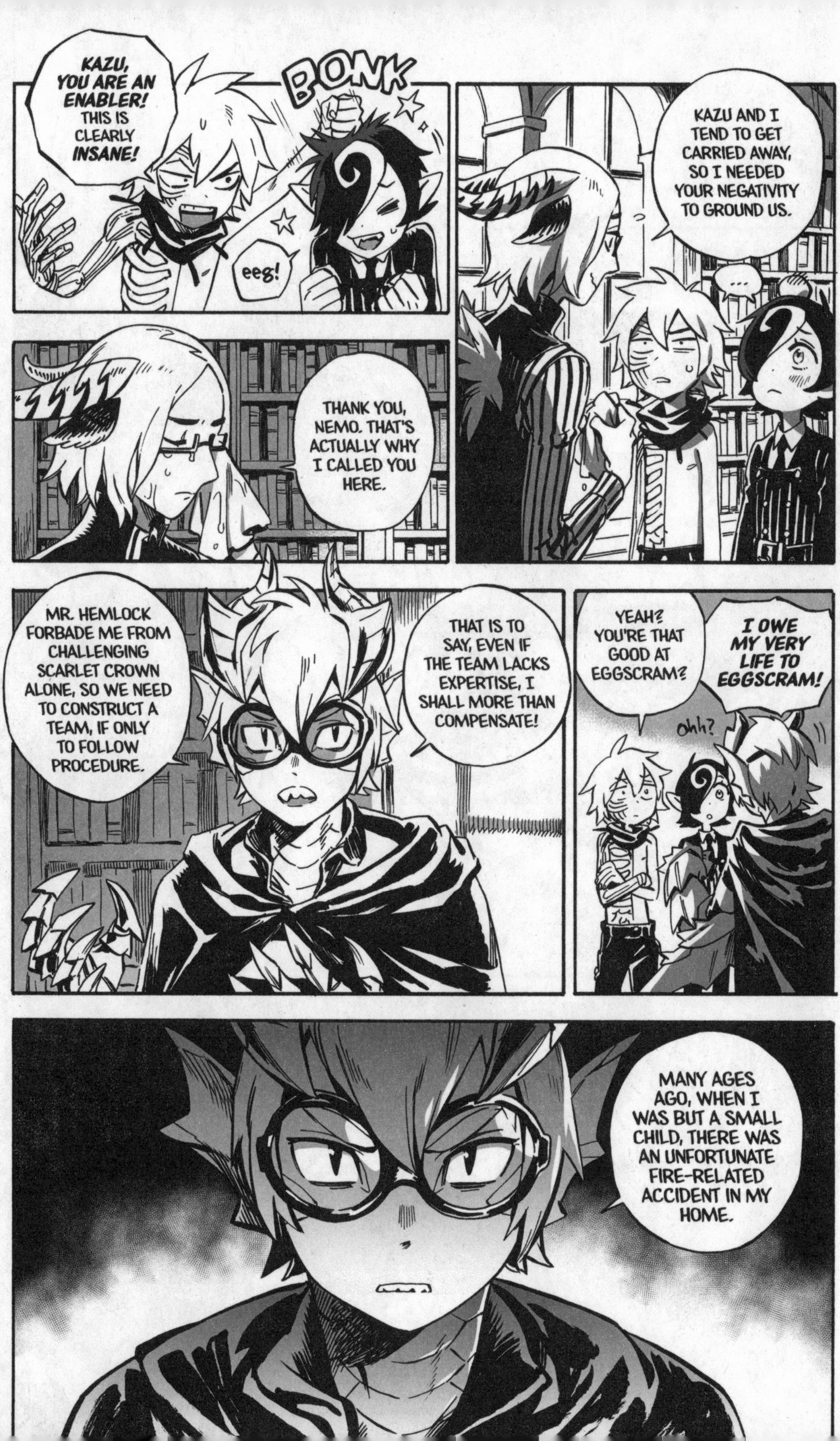
KAZU, YOU ARE AN ENABLER! THIS IS CLEARLY INSANE!
BONK
eeg!
THANK YOU, NEMO. THAT'S ACTUALLY WHY I CALLED YOU HERE.
KAZU AND I TEND TO GET CARRIED AWAY, SO I NEEDED YOUR NEGATIVITY TO GROUND US.
...
MR. HEMLOCK FORBADE ME FROM CHALLENGING SCARLET CROWN ALONE, SO WE NEED TO CONSTRUCT A TEAM, IF ONLY TO FOLLOW PROCEDURE.
THAT IS TO SAY, EVEN IF THE TEAM LACKS EXPERTISE, I SHALL MORE THAN COMPENSATE!
YEAH? YOU'RE THAT GOOD AT EGGSCRAM?
I OWE MY VERY LIFE TO EGGSCRAM!
Ohh?
MANY AGES AGO, WHEN I WAS BUT A SMALL CHILD, THERE WAS AN UNFORTUNATE FIRE-RELATED ACCIDENT IN MY HOME.

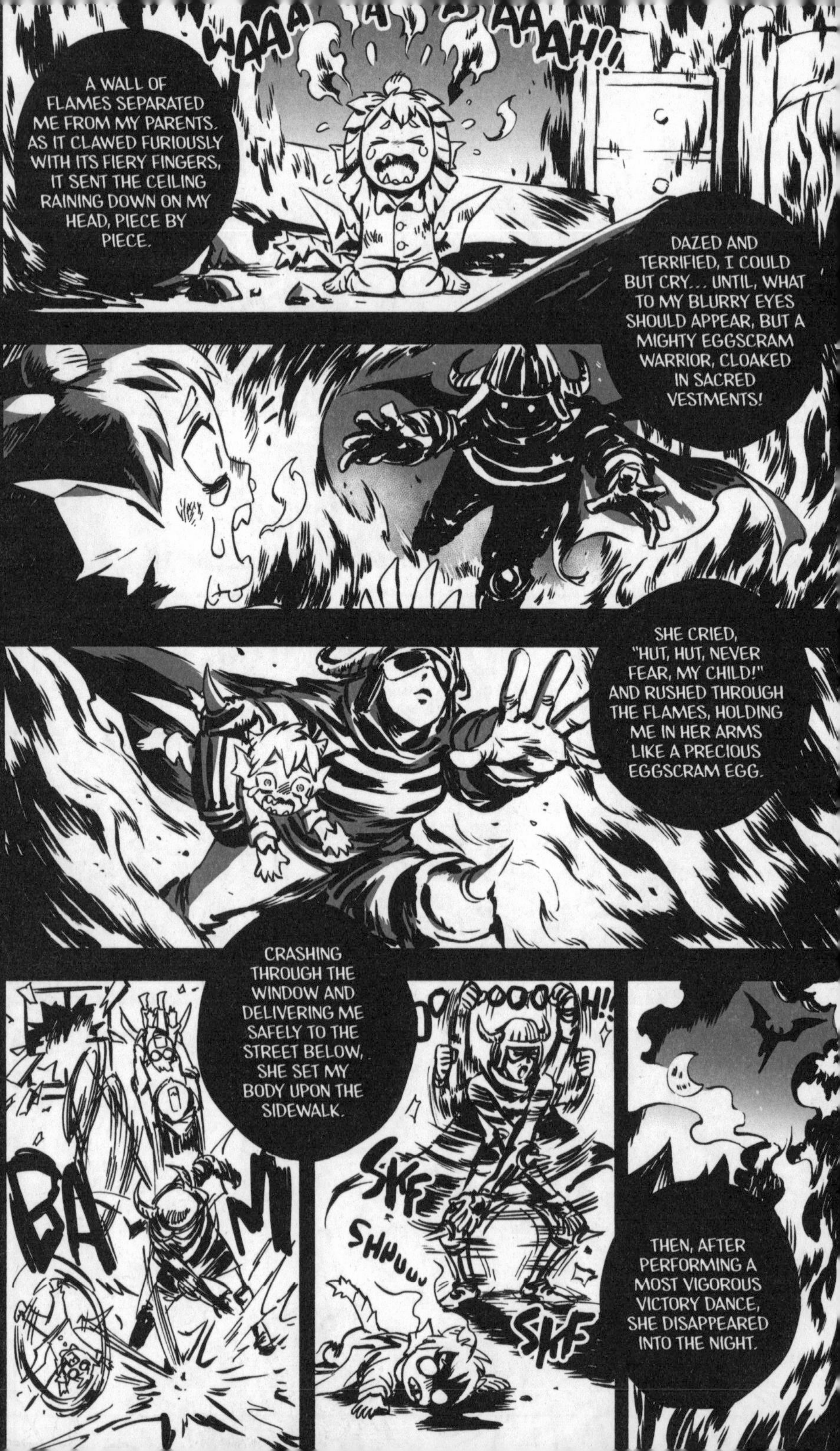
WAAAAAAAAAH!!
A WALL OF FLAMES SEPARATED ME FROM MY PARENTS. AS IT CLAWED FURIOUSLY WITH ITS FIERY FINGERS, IT SENT THE CEILING RAINING DOWN ON MY HEAD, PIECE BY PIECE.
DAZED AND TERRIFIED, I COULD BUT CRY... UNTIL, WHAT TO MY BLURRY EYES SHOULD APPEAR, BUT A MIGHTY EGGSCRAM WARRIOR, CLOAKED IN SACRED VESTMENTS!
SHE CRIED, "HUT, HUT, NEVER FEAR, MY CHILD!" AND RUSHED THROUGH THE FLAMES, HOLDING ME IN HER ARMS LIKE A PRECIOUS EGGSCRAM EGG.
BA-M
CRASHING THROUGH THE WINDOW AND DELIVERING ME SAFELY TO THE STREET BELOW, SHE SET MY BODY UPON THE SIDEWALK.
DOOOOOOSH!!
SKF
SHUUUU
SKF
THEN, AFTER PERFORMING A MOST VIGOROUS VICTORY DANCE, SHE DISAPPEARED INTO THE NIGHT.

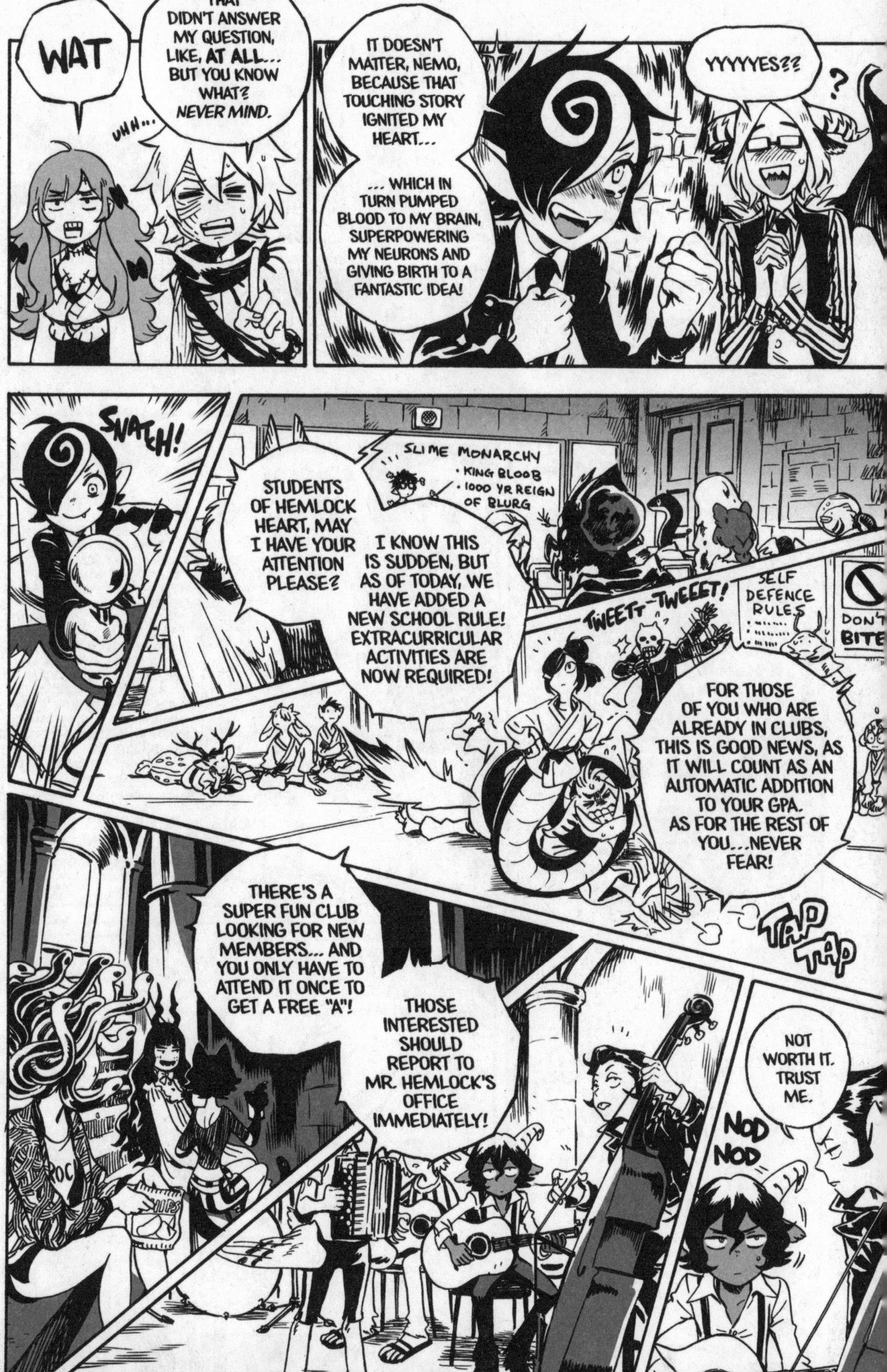
WAT
THAT DIDN'T ANSWER MY QUESTION, LIKE, AT ALL... BUT YOU KNOW WHAT? NEVER MIND.
UHH...
IT DOESN'T MATTER, NEMO, BECAUSE THAT TOUCHING STORY IGNITED MY HEART...
... WHICH IN TURN PUMPED BLOOD TO MY BRAIN, SUPERPOWERING MY NEURONS AND GIVING BIRTH TO A FANTASTIC IDEA!
YYYYYES??
?
SNATCH!
STUDENTS OF HEMLOCK HEART, MAY I HAVE YOUR ATTENTION PLEASE?
SLIME MONARCHY
• KING BLOOB
• 1000 YR REIGN OF BLURG
I KNOW THIS IS SUDDEN, BUT AS OF TODAY, WE HAVE ADDED A NEW SCHOOL RULE! EXTRACURRICULAR ACTIVITIES ARE NOW REQUIRED!
TWEETT-TWEEET!
SELF DEFENCE RULES
DON'T BITE
FOR THOSE OF YOU WHO ARE ALREADY IN CLUBS, THIS IS GOOD NEWS, AS IT WILL COUNT AS AN AUTOMATIC ADDITION TO YOUR GPA. AS FOR THE REST OF YOU...NEVER FEAR!
TAP TAP
THERE'S A SUPER FUN CLUB LOOKING FOR NEW MEMBERS... AND YOU ONLY HAVE TO ATTEND IT ONCE TO GET A FREE "A"!
THOSE INTERESTED SHOULD REPORT TO MR. HEMLOCK'S OFFICE IMMEDIATELY!
NOT WORTH IT. TRUST ME.
NOD NOD

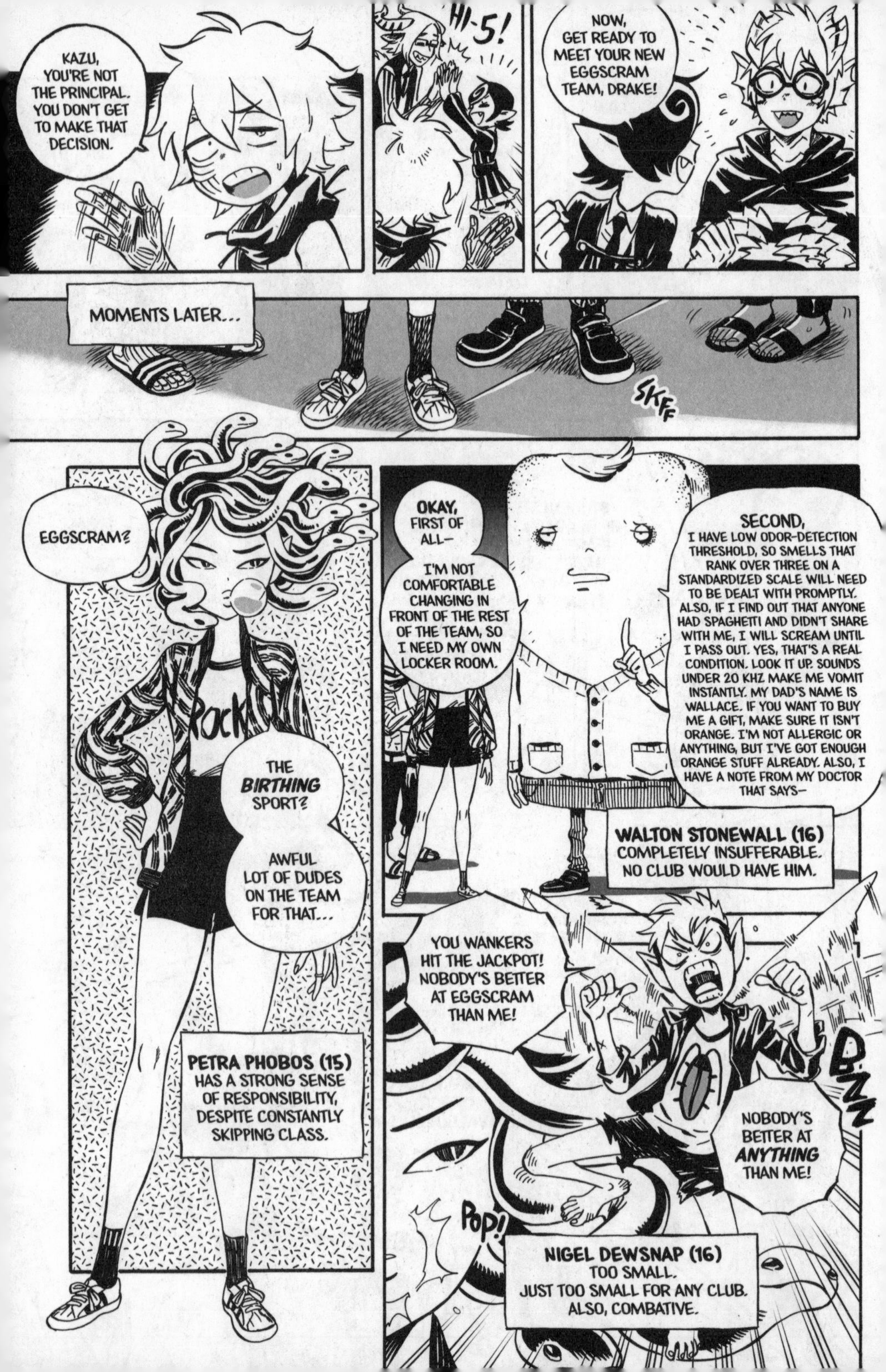
KAZU, YOU'RE NOT THE PRINCIPAL. YOU DON'T GET TO MAKE THAT DECISION.
HI-5!
NOW, GET READY TO MEET YOUR NEW EGGSCRAM TEAM, DRAKE!
MOMENTS LATER...
SKFF
EGGSCRAM?
THE BIRTHING SPORT?
AWFUL LOT OF DUDES ON THE TEAM FOR THAT...
PETRA PHOBOS (15)
HAS A STRONG SENSE OF RESPONSIBILITY, DESPITE CONSTANTLY SKIPPING CLASS.
OKAY, FIRST OF ALL—
I'M NOT COMFORTABLE CHANGING IN FRONT OF THE REST OF THE TEAM, SO I NEED MY OWN LOCKER ROOM.
SECOND, I HAVE LOW ODOR-DETECTION THRESHOLD, SO SMELLS THAT RANK OVER THREE ON A STANDARDIZED SCALE WILL NEED TO BE DEALT WITH PROMPTLY. ALSO, IF I FIND OUT THAT ANYONE HAD SPAGHETTI AND DIDN'T SHARE WITH ME, I WILL SCREAM UNTIL I PASS OUT. YES, THAT'S A REAL CONDITION. LOOK IT UP. SOUNDS UNDER 20 KHZ MAKE ME VOMIT INSTANTLY. MY DAD'S NAME IS WALLACE. IF YOU WANT TO BUY ME A GIFT, MAKE SURE IT ISN'T ORANGE. I'M NOT ALLERGIC OR ANYTHING, BUT I'VE GOT ENOUGH ORANGE STUFF ALREADY. ALSO, I HAVE A NOTE FROM MY DOCTOR THAT SAYS—
WALTON STONEWALL (16)
COMPLETELY INSUFFERABLE. NO CLUB WOULD HAVE HIM.
YOU WANKERS HIT THE JACKPOT! NOBODY'S BETTER AT EGGSCRAM THAN ME!
BZZ
NOBODY'S BETTER AT ANYTHING THAN ME!
POP!
NIGEL DEWSNAP (16)
TOO SMALL. JUST TOO SMALL FOR ANY CLUB. ALSO, COMBATIVE.

SIGHHHH...

whee~ sports...

RICKET PANTANO (14)
ESCAPING FROM DRAMA IN THE DRAMA CLUB.

EGG?

GERALDO GARCIA (17)
??????

NEMO MUST~~ER~~ (14)
~~QUIT BOWL DROP~~

I *SAID* I'M NOT PLAYING!

I'M AFRAID YOU MUST, NEMO. I'LL EXPEL YOU IF YOU DON'T PARTICIPATE.

BY THE WAY, THE TURNOUT WAS MUCH LESS THAN I EXPECTED. WHY IS THAT?

IT'S BECAUSE YOU'RE ALWAYS MAKING *EMPTY THREATS* AND EVERYONE KNOWS YOU'RE FULL OF HOT AIR!

23

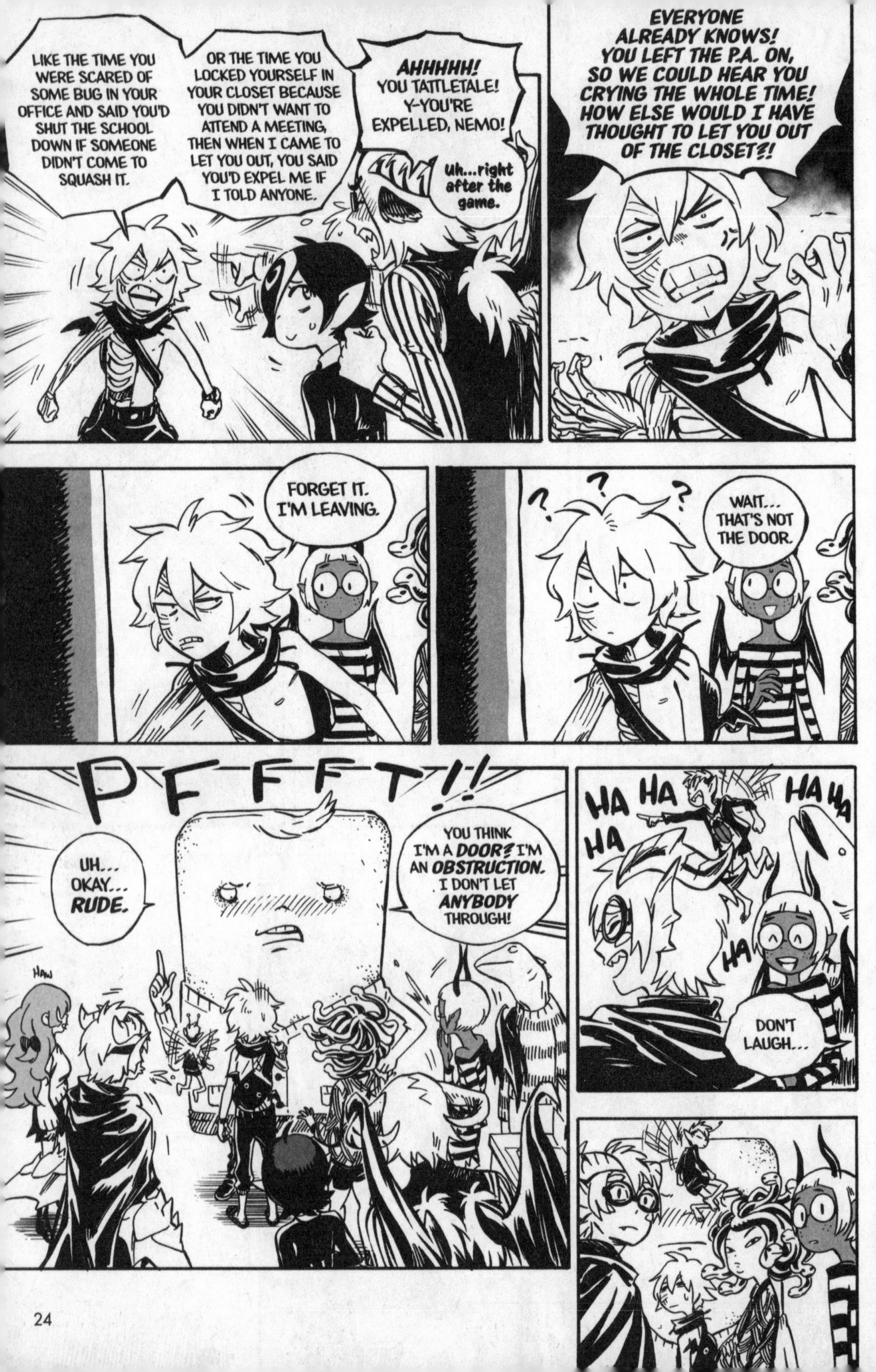

LIKE THE TIME YOU WERE SCARED OF SOME BUG IN YOUR OFFICE AND SAID YOU'D SHUT THE SCHOOL DOWN IF SOMEONE DIDN'T COME TO SQUASH IT.
OR THE TIME YOU LOCKED YOURSELF IN YOUR CLOSET BECAUSE YOU DIDN'T WANT TO ATTEND A MEETING, THEN WHEN I CAME TO LET YOU OUT, YOU SAID YOU'D EXPEL ME IF I TOLD ANYONE.
AHHHHH! YOU TATTLETALE! Y-YOU'RE EXPELLED, NEMO!
Uh...right after the game.
EVERYONE ALREADY KNOWS! YOU LEFT THE P.A. ON, SO WE COULD HEAR YOU CRYING THE WHOLE TIME! HOW ELSE WOULD I HAVE THOUGHT TO LET YOU OUT OF THE CLOSET?!
FORGET IT. I'M LEAVING.
? ? ?
WAIT... THAT'S NOT THE DOOR.
PFFFT!!
UH... OKAY... RUDE.
YOU THINK I'M A DOOR?! I'M AN OBSTRUCTION. I DON'T LET ANYBODY THROUGH!
HAW
HA HA HA HA HA HA
HA
DON'T LAUGH...

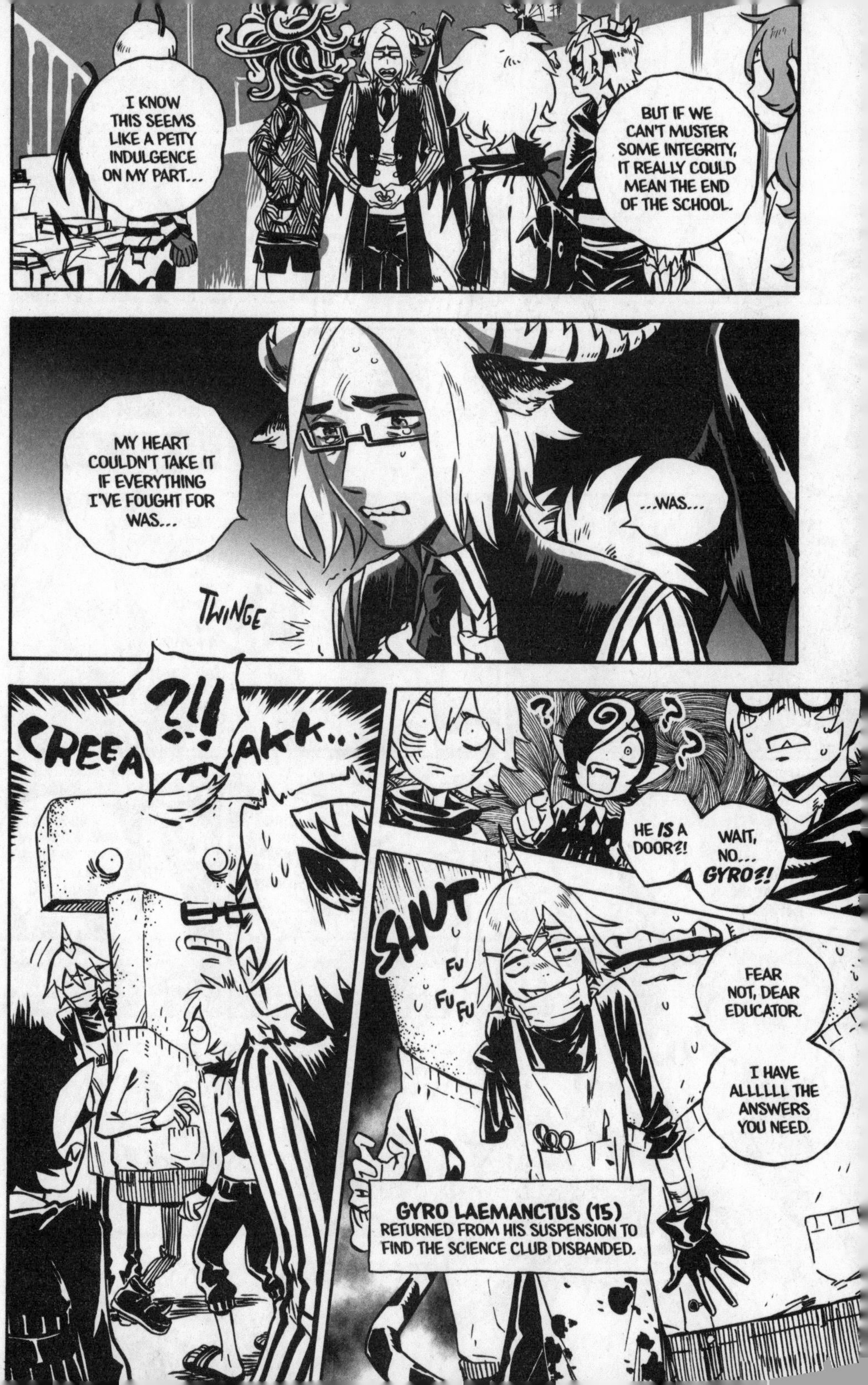
I KNOW THIS SEEMS LIKE A PETTY INDULGENCE ON MY PART...
BUT IF WE CAN'T MUSTER SOME INTEGRITY, IT REALLY COULD MEAN THE END OF THE SCHOOL.
MY HEART COULDN'T TAKE IT IF EVERYTHING I'VE FOUGHT FOR WAS...
...WAS...
TWINGE
CREEAAKK...
?!!
HE *IS* A DOOR?!
WAIT, NO... **GYRO?!**
SHUT
FU FU FU
FEAR NOT, DEAR EDUCATOR.
I HAVE ALLLLLL THE ANSWERS YOU NEED.
GYRO LAEMANCTUS (15)
RETURNED FROM HIS SUSPENSION TO FIND THE SCIENCE CLUB DISBANDED.

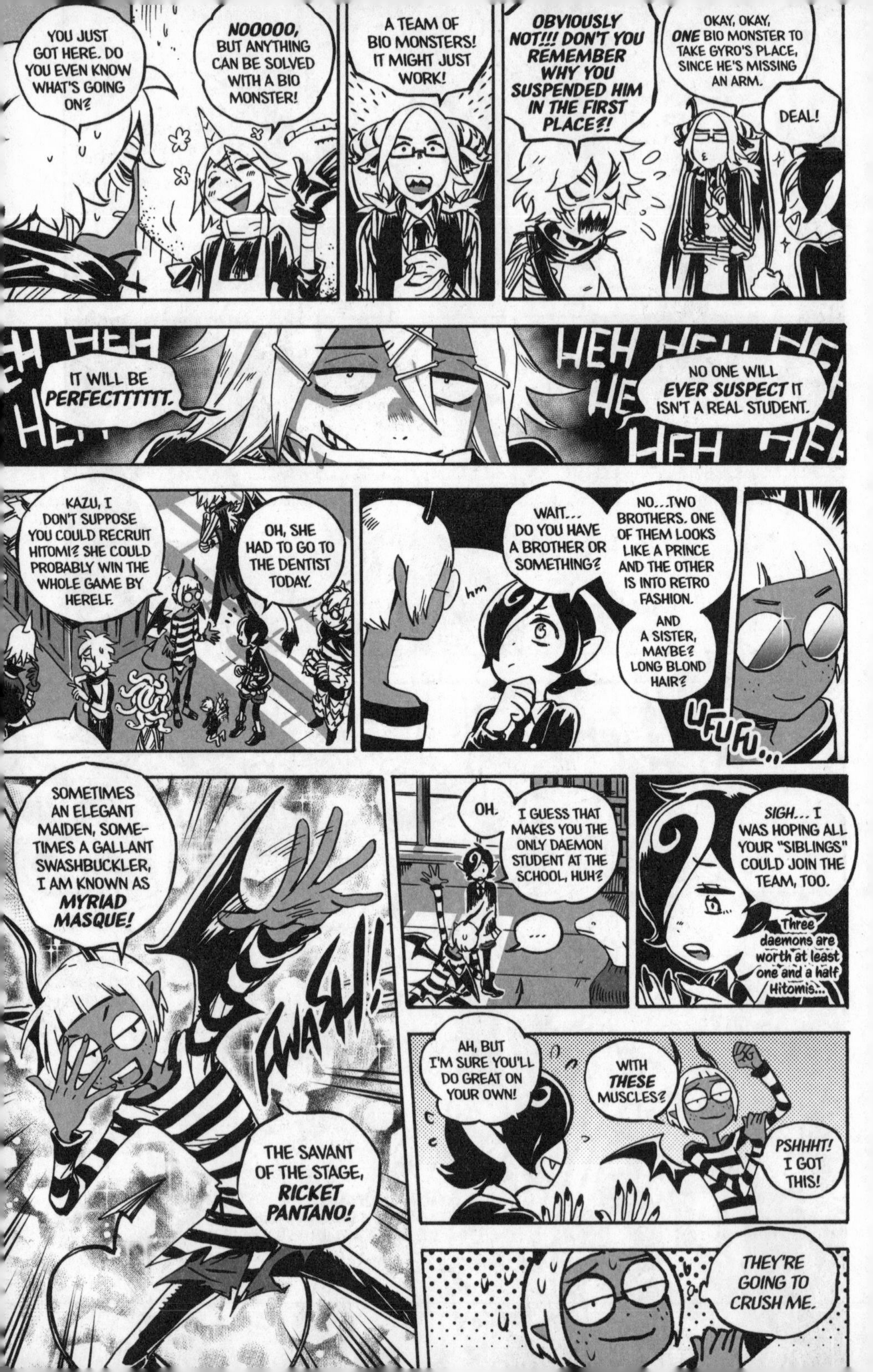
YOU JUST GOT HERE. DO YOU EVEN KNOW WHAT'S GOING ON?
NOOOOO, BUT ANYTHING CAN BE SOLVED WITH A BIO MONSTER!
A TEAM OF BIO MONSTERS! IT MIGHT JUST WORK!
OBVIOUSLY NOT!!! DON'T YOU REMEMBER WHY YOU SUSPENDED HIM IN THE FIRST PLACE?!
OKAY, OKAY, ONE BIO MONSTER TO TAKE GYRO'S PLACE, SINCE HE'S MISSING AN ARM.
DEAL!
HEH HEH
IT WILL BE PERFECTTTTTTT.
HEH HEH
NO ONE WILL EVER SUSPECT IT ISN'T A REAL STUDENT.
HEH HEH
KAZU, I DON'T SUPPOSE YOU COULD RECRUIT HITOMI? SHE COULD PROBABLY WIN THE WHOLE GAME BY HERELF.
OH, SHE HAD TO GO TO THE DENTIST TODAY.
hm
WAIT... DO YOU HAVE A BROTHER OR SOMETHING?
NO...TWO BROTHERS. ONE OF THEM LOOKS LIKE A PRINCE AND THE OTHER IS INTO RETRO FASHION.
AND A SISTER, MAYBE? LONG BLOND HAIR?
UFUFU...
SOMETIMES AN ELEGANT MAIDEN, SOMETIMES A GALLANT SWASHBUCKLER, I AM KNOWN AS MYRIAD MASQUE!
FWASH!!
THE SAVANT OF THE STAGE, RICKET PANTANO!
OH.
I GUESS THAT MAKES YOU THE ONLY DAEMON STUDENT AT THE SCHOOL, HUH?
...
SIGH... I WAS HOPING ALL YOUR "SIBLINGS" COULD JOIN THE TEAM, TOO.
Three daemons are worth at least one and a half Hitomis...
AH, BUT I'M SURE YOU'LL DO GREAT ON YOUR OWN!
WITH THESE MUSCLES?
PSHHHT! I GOT THIS!
THEY'RE GOING TO CRUSH ME.

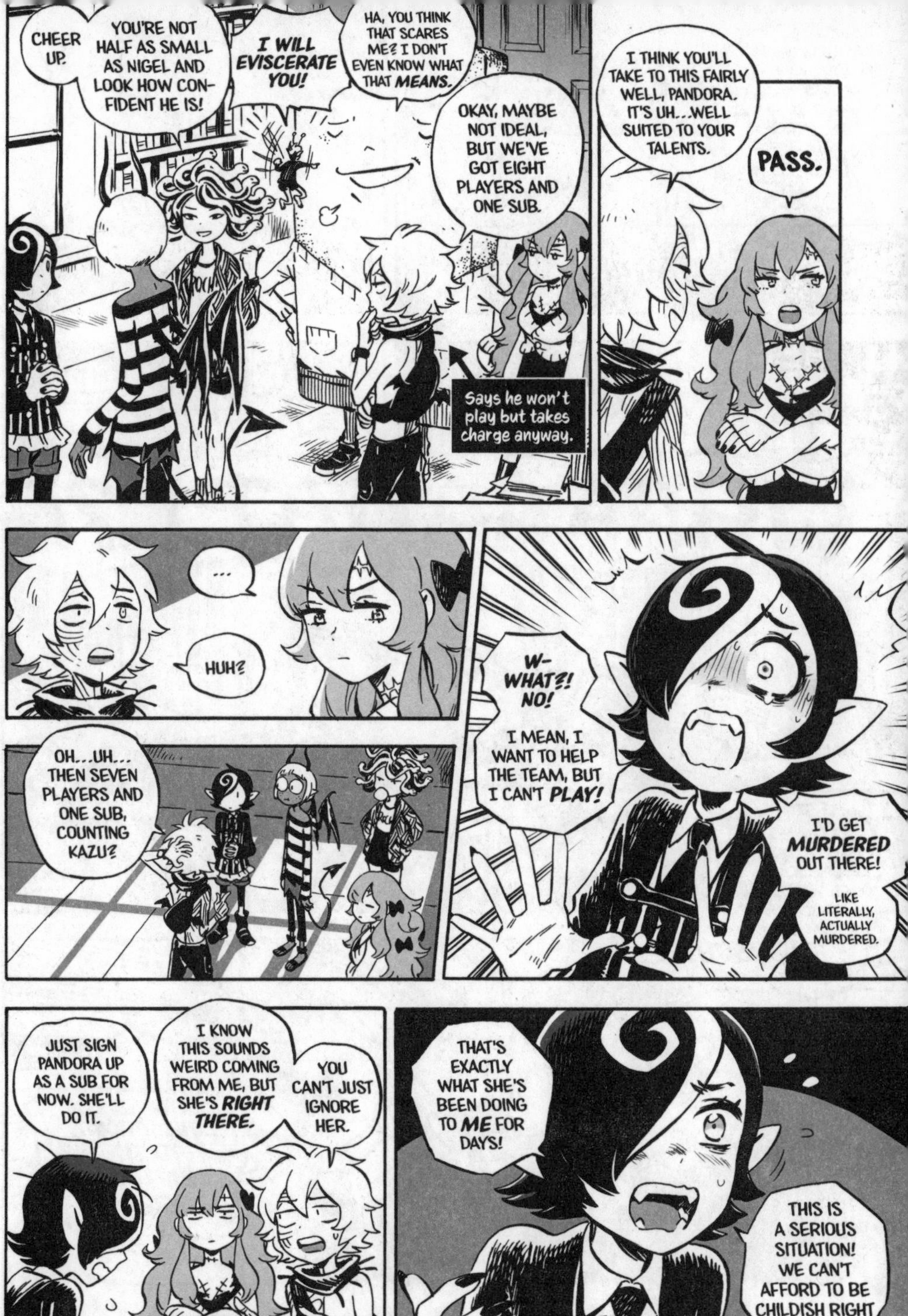
CHEER UP.
YOU'RE NOT HALF AS SMALL AS NIGEL AND LOOK HOW CON-FIDENT HE IS!
I WILL EVISCERATE YOU!
HA, YOU THINK THAT SCARES ME? I DON'T EVEN KNOW WHAT THAT MEANS.
OKAY, MAYBE NOT IDEAL, BUT WE'VE GOT EIGHT PLAYERS AND ONE SUB.
Says he won't play but takes charge anyway.
I THINK YOU'LL TAKE TO THIS FAIRLY WELL, PANDORA. IT'S UH...WELL SUITED TO YOUR TALENTS.
PASS.
...
HUH?
OH...UH... THEN SEVEN PLAYERS AND ONE SUB, COUNTING KAZU?
W-WHAT?! NO!
I MEAN, I WANT TO HELP THE TEAM, BUT I CAN'T PLAY!
I'D GET MURDERED OUT THERE!
LIKE LITERALLY, ACTUALLY MURDERED.
JUST SIGN PANDORA UP AS A SUB FOR NOW. SHE'LL DO IT.
I KNOW THIS SOUNDS WEIRD COMING FROM ME, BUT SHE'S RIGHT THERE.
YOU CAN'T JUST IGNORE HER.
THAT'S EXACTLY WHAT SHE'S BEEN DOING TO ME FOR DAYS!
THIS IS A SERIOUS SITUATION! WE CAN'T AFFORD TO BE CHILDISH RIGHT NOW!

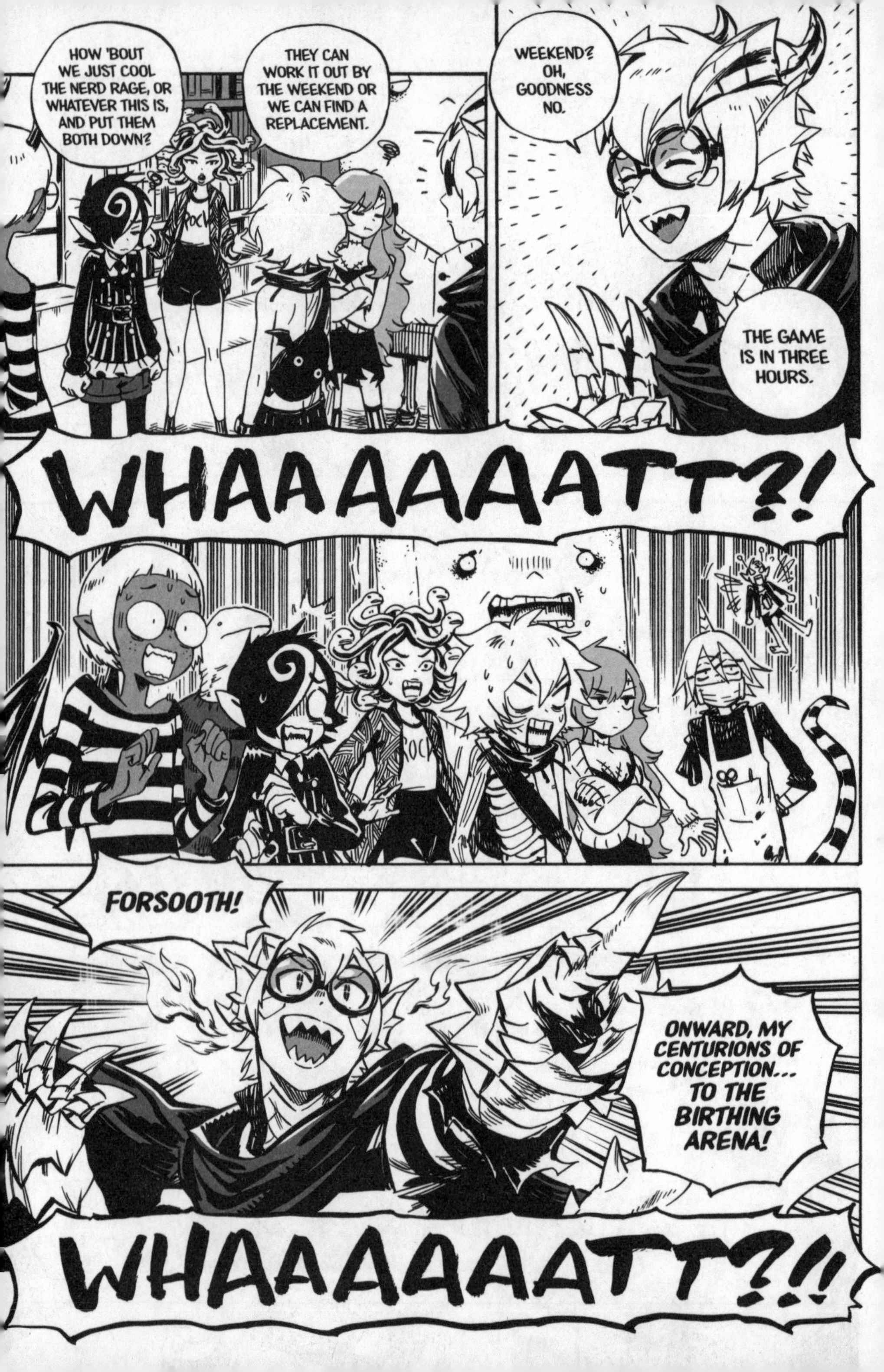

HOW 'BOUT WE JUST COOL THE NERD RAGE, OR WHATEVER THIS IS, AND PUT THEM BOTH DOWN?
THEY CAN WORK IT OUT BY THE WEEKEND OR WE CAN FIND A REPLACEMENT.
WEEKEND? OH, GOODNESS NO.
THE GAME IS IN THREE HOURS.
WHAAAAAATT?!
FORSOOTH!
ONWARD, MY CENTURIONS OF CONCEPTION... TO THE BIRTHING ARENA!
WHAAAAAATT?!!

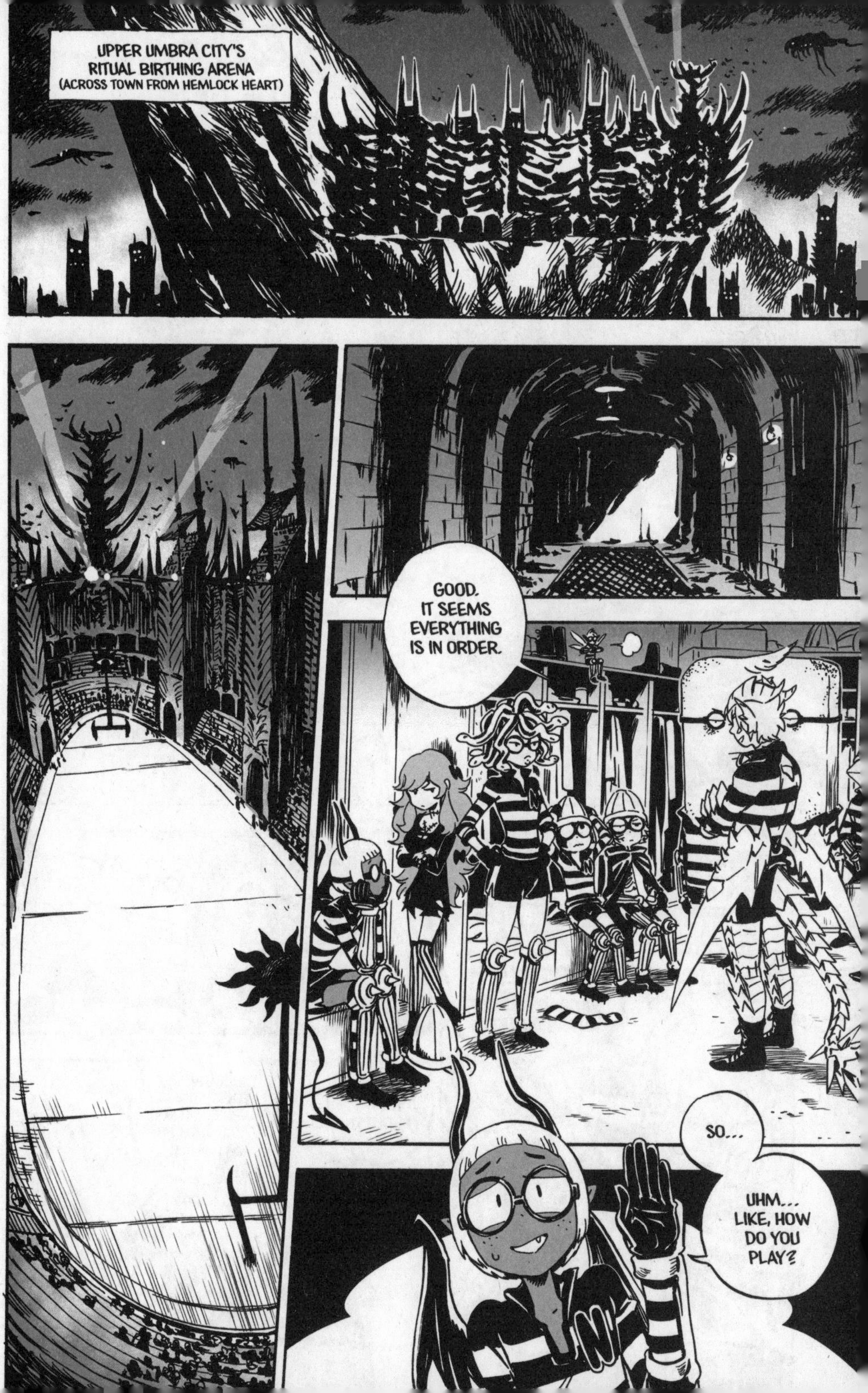
UPPER UMBRA CITY'S RITUAL BIRTHING ARENA (ACROSS TOWN FROM HEMLOCK HEART)
GOOD. IT SEEMS EVERYTHING IS IN ORDER.
SO...
UHM... LIKE, HOW DO YOU PLAY?

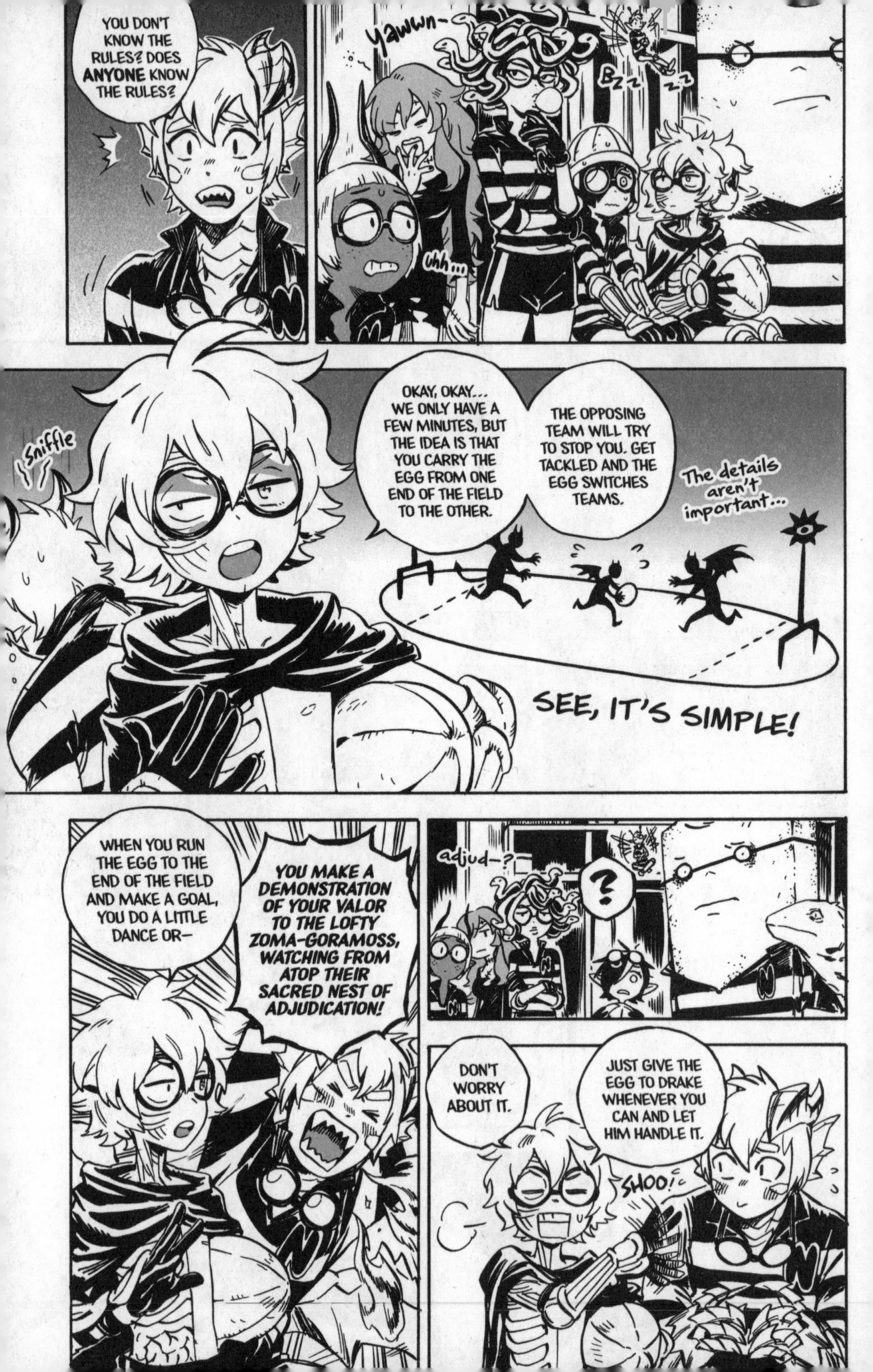
YOU DON'T KNOW THE RULES? DOES ANYONE KNOW THE RULES?
yawwn-
BZZZ ZZ
uhh...
Sniffle
OKAY, OKAY... WE ONLY HAVE A FEW MINUTES, BUT THE IDEA IS THAT YOU CARRY THE EGG FROM ONE END OF THE FIELD TO THE OTHER.
THE OPPOSING TEAM WILL TRY TO STOP YOU. GET TACKLED AND THE EGG SWITCHES TEAMS.
The details aren't important...
SEE, IT'S SIMPLE!
WHEN YOU RUN THE EGG TO THE END OF THE FIELD AND MAKE A GOAL, YOU DO A LITTLE DANCE OR-
YOU MAKE A DEMONSTRATION OF YOUR VALOR TO THE LOFTY ZOMA-GORAMOSS, WATCHING FROM ATOP THEIR SACRED NEST OF ADJUDICATION!
adjud-?
?
DON'T WORRY ABOUT IT.
JUST GIVE THE EGG TO DRAKE WHENEVER YOU CAN AND LET HIM HANDLE IT.
SHOO!

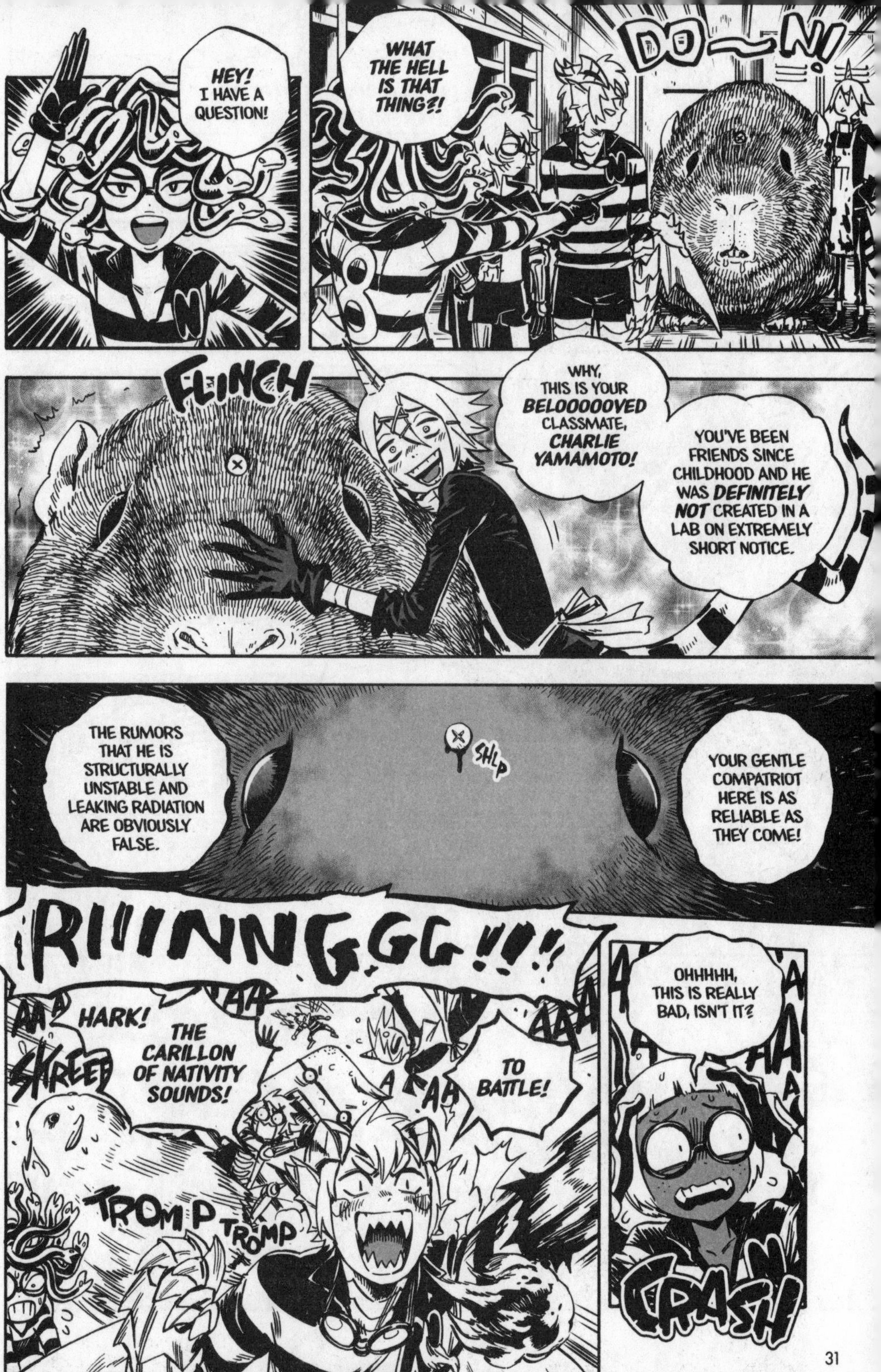
HEY! I HAVE A QUESTION!
WHAT THE HELL IS THAT THING?!
DO—N!
FLINCH
WHY, THIS IS YOUR BELOOOOOVED CLASSMATE, CHARLIE YAMAMOTO!
YOU'VE BEEN FRIENDS SINCE CHILDHOOD AND HE WAS DEFINITELY NOT CREATED IN A LAB ON EXTREMELY SHORT NOTICE.
THE RUMORS THAT HE IS STRUCTURALLY UNSTABLE AND LEAKING RADIATION ARE OBVIOUSLY FALSE.
SHLP
YOUR GENTLE COMPATRIOT HERE IS AS RELIABLE AS THEY COME!
RIIINNGGG!!!
HARK!
THE CARILLON OF NATIVITY SOUNDS!
TO BATTLE!
TROMP TROMP
OHHHHH, THIS IS REALLY BAD, ISN'T IT?
CRASH

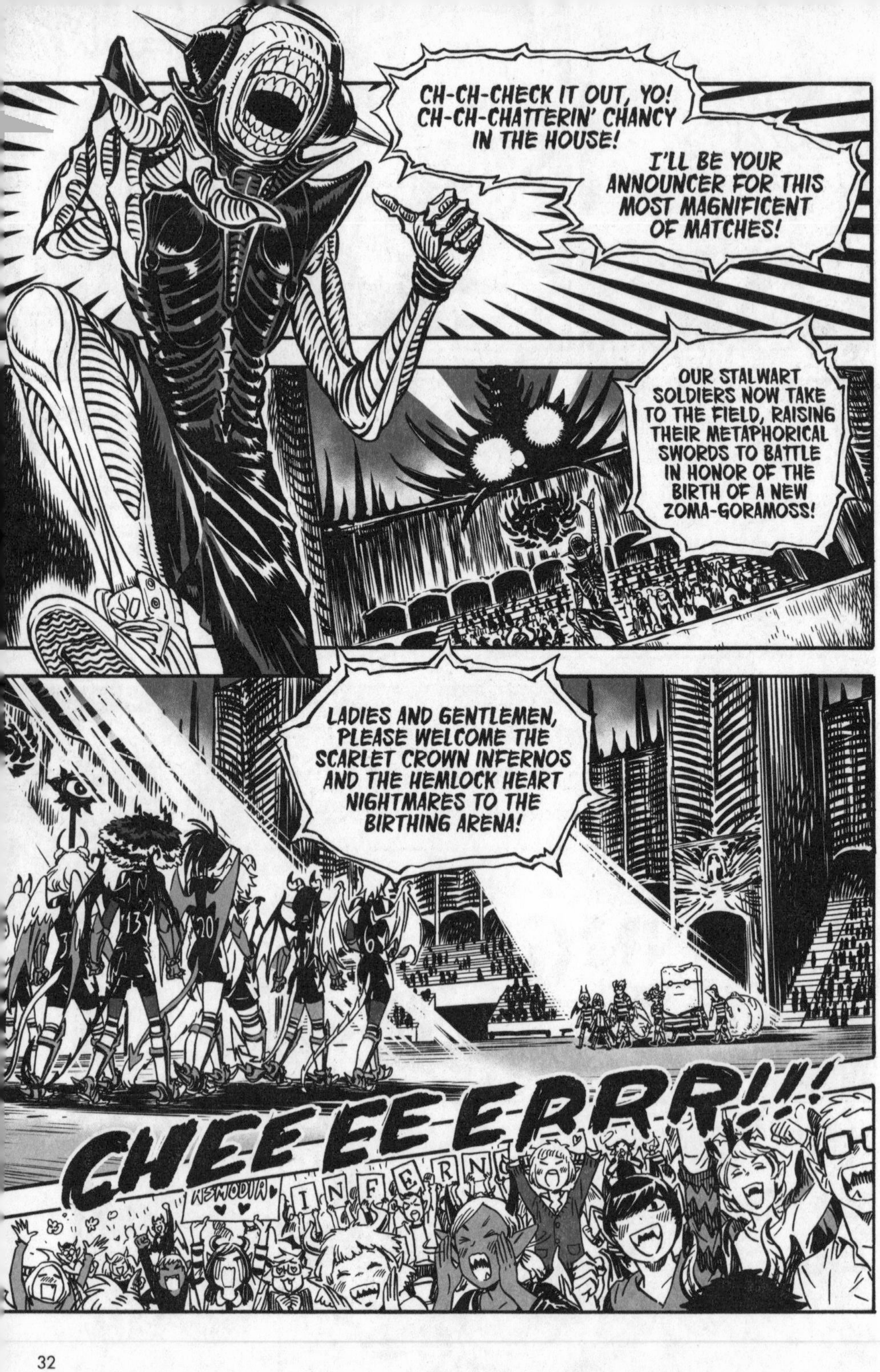
CH-CH-CHECK IT OUT, YO! CH-CH-CHATTERIN' CHANCY IN THE HOUSE!
I'LL BE YOUR ANNOUNCER FOR THIS MOST MAGNIFICENT OF MATCHES!
OUR STALWART SOLDIERS NOW TAKE TO THE FIELD, RAISING THEIR METAPHORICAL SWORDS TO BATTLE IN HONOR OF THE BIRTH OF A NEW ZOMA-GORAMOSS!
LADIES AND GENTLEMEN, PLEASE WELCOME THE SCARLET CROWN INFERNOS AND THE HEMLOCK HEART NIGHTMARES TO THE BIRTHING ARENA!
CHEEEEERRR!!!

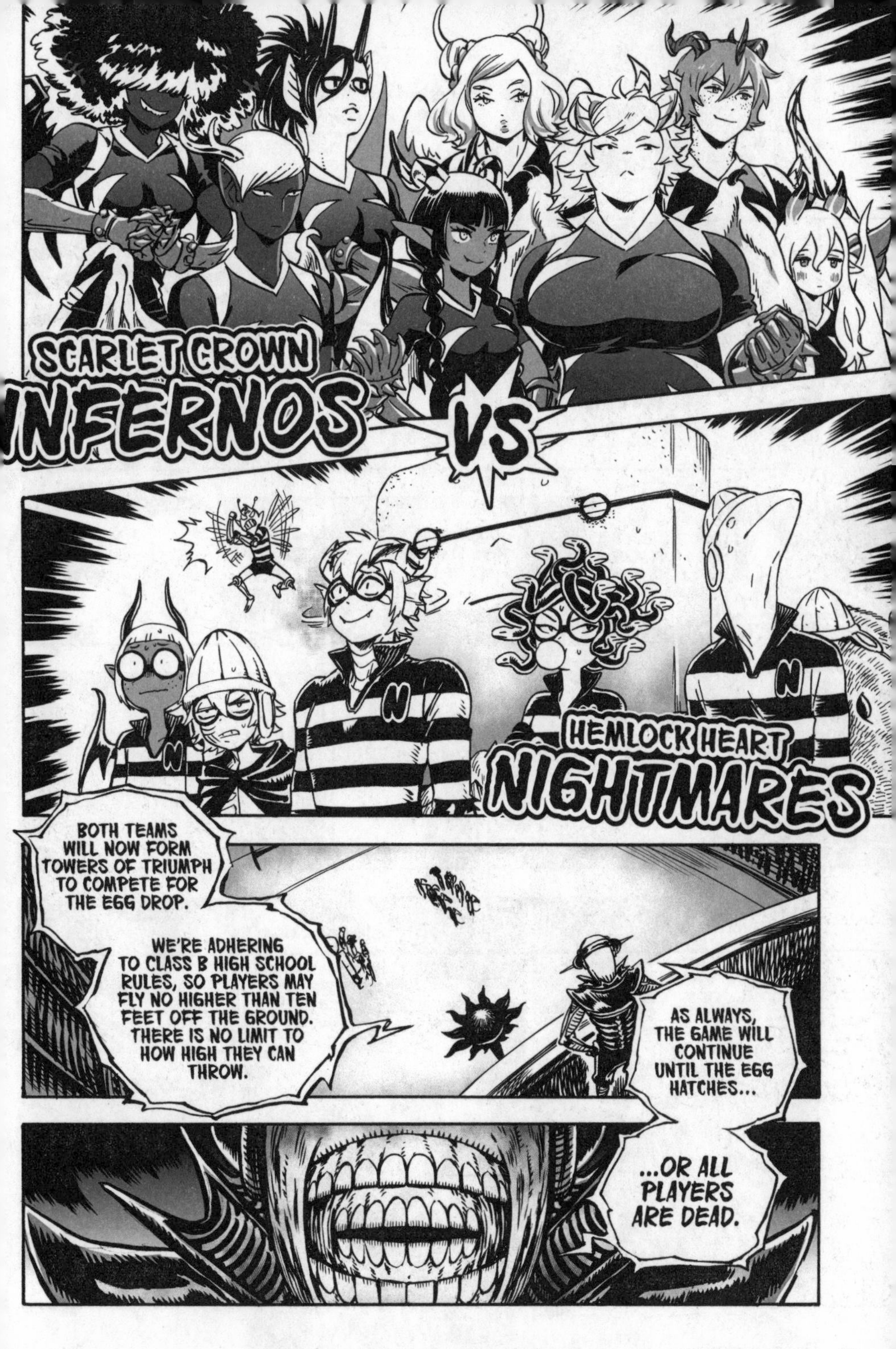
SCARLET CROWN
INFERNOS
VS
HEMLOCK HEART
NIGHTMARES
BOTH TEAMS WILL NOW FORM TOWERS OF TRIUMPH TO COMPETE FOR THE EGG DROP.
WE'RE ADHERING TO CLASS B HIGH SCHOOL RULES, SO PLAYERS MAY FLY NO HIGHER THAN TEN FEET OFF THE GROUND. THERE IS NO LIMIT TO HOW HIGH THEY CAN THROW.
AS ALWAYS, THE GAME WILL CONTINUE UNTIL THE EGG HATCHES...
...OR ALL PLAYERS ARE DEAD.

Surely there won't be too many fatalities...!

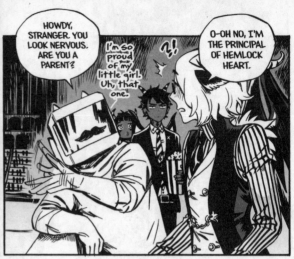

HOWDY, STRANGER. YOU LOOK NERVOUS. ARE YOU A PARENT?

I'm so proud of my little girl. Uh, that one.

?!

O-OH NO, I'M THE PRINCIPAL OF HEMLOCK HEART.

HATE TO SAY IT, PARTNER, BUT THE ODDS AIN'T LOOKIN' GOOD FOR YOUR LITTLE TYKES.

YOU REALLY THINK YOU CAN WIN THIS?

WE WON'T KNOW UNTIL WE TRY.

AH, EXCUSE ME. WHAT I MEAN IS... THERE'S NEVER BEEN A GENERAL ADMITTANCE SCHOOL BEFORE. THIS IS ALL UNCHARTED TERRITORY, SO TO SPEAK.

WE MAY STUMBLE AND WE MAY FALL, BUT I TRULY BELIEVE THAT WE'RE PAVING THE WAY TO A NEW WORLD.

...!

HAPPY TRAILS. ♥

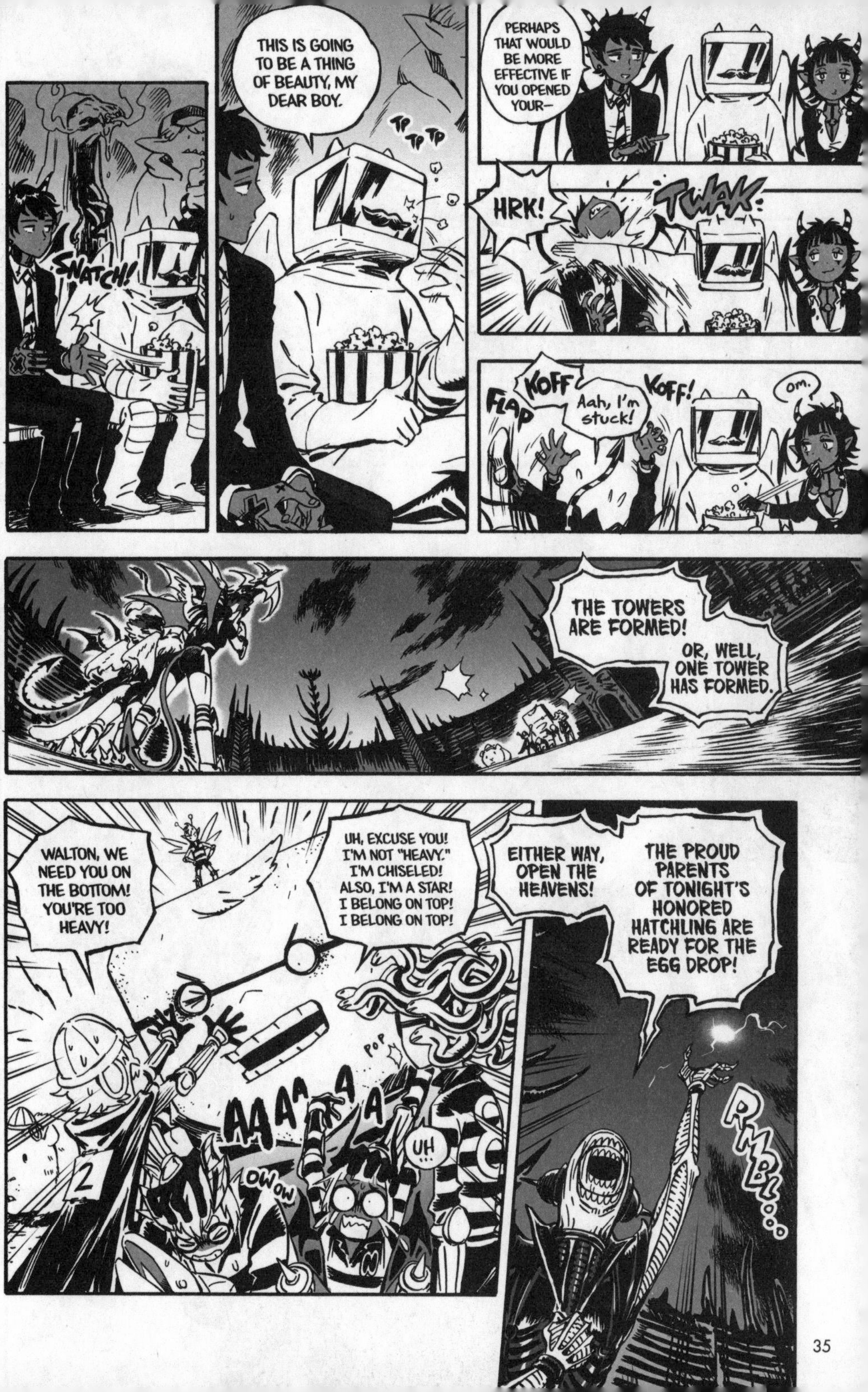
SNATCH!
THIS IS GOING TO BE A THING OF BEAUTY, MY DEAR BOY.
TP TP TP
PERHAPS THAT WOULD BE MORE EFFECTIVE IF YOU OPENED YOUR–
HRK!
TWAK
FLAP
KOFF
Aah, I'm stuck!
KOFF!
om.
THE TOWERS ARE FORMED!
OR, WELL, ONE TOWER HAS FORMED.
WALTON, WE NEED YOU ON THE BOTTOM! YOU'RE TOO HEAVY!
UH, EXCUSE YOU! I'M NOT "HEAVY." I'M CHISELED! ALSO, I'M A STAR! I BELONG ON TOP! I BELONG ON TOP!
POP
AAAAAA
UH
OWOW
2
EITHER WAY, OPEN THE HEAVENS!
THE PROUD PARENTS OF TONIGHT'S HONORED HATCHLING ARE READY FOR THE EGG DROP!
RMBL...

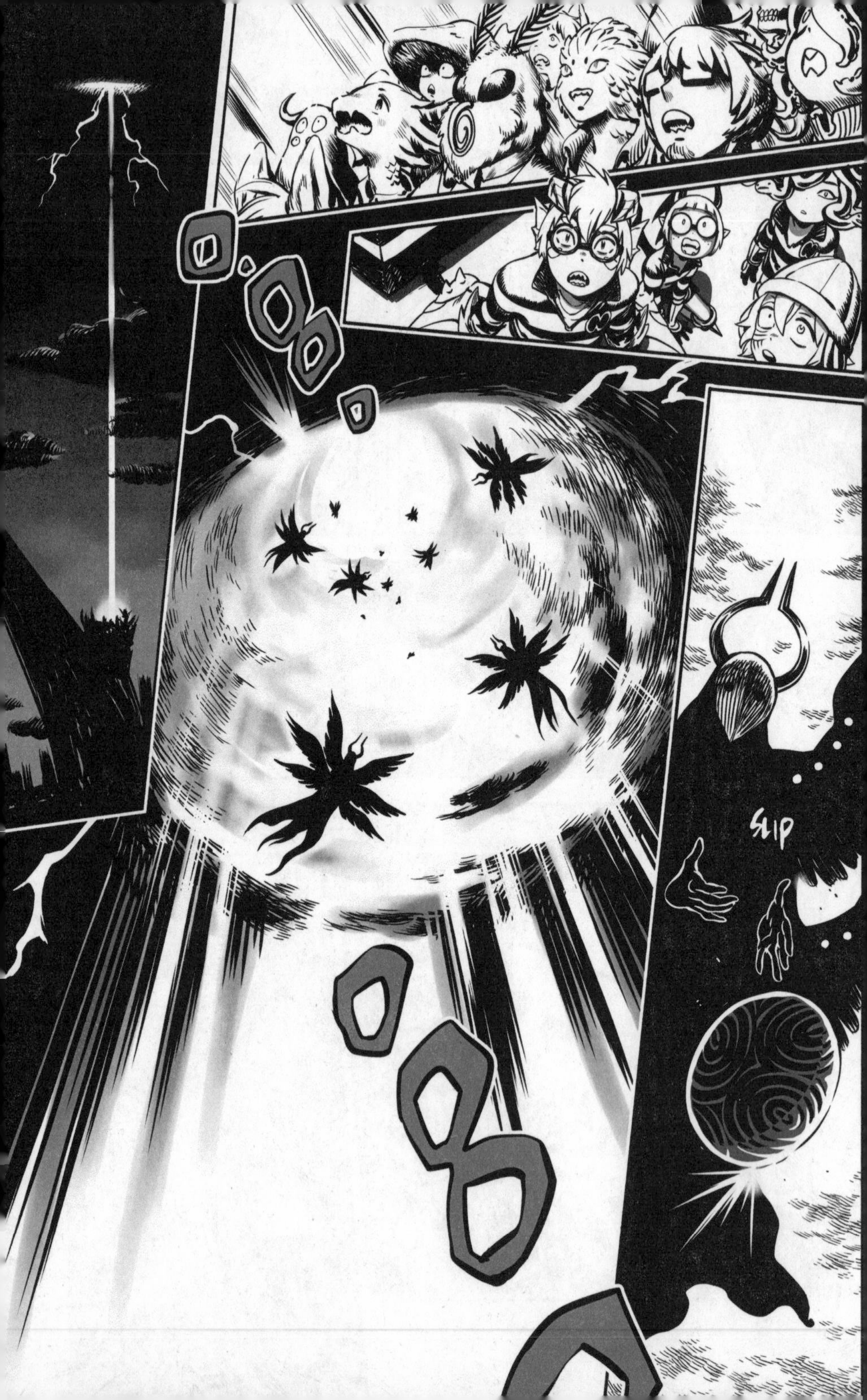
SLIP

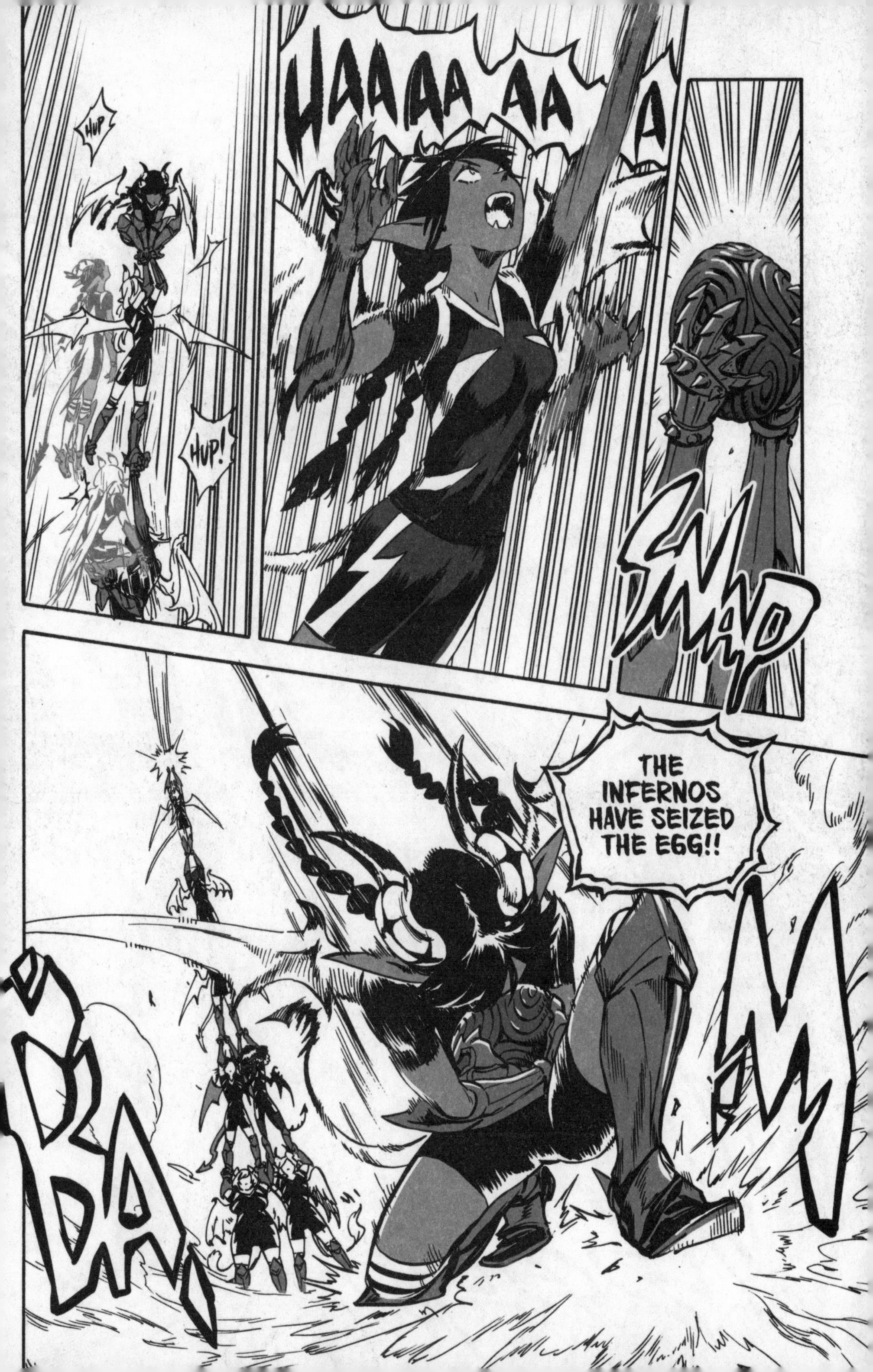
HUP
HUP!
HAAAA AA A
SNAP
THE INFERNOS HAVE SEIZED THE EGG!!
BA
DA
M

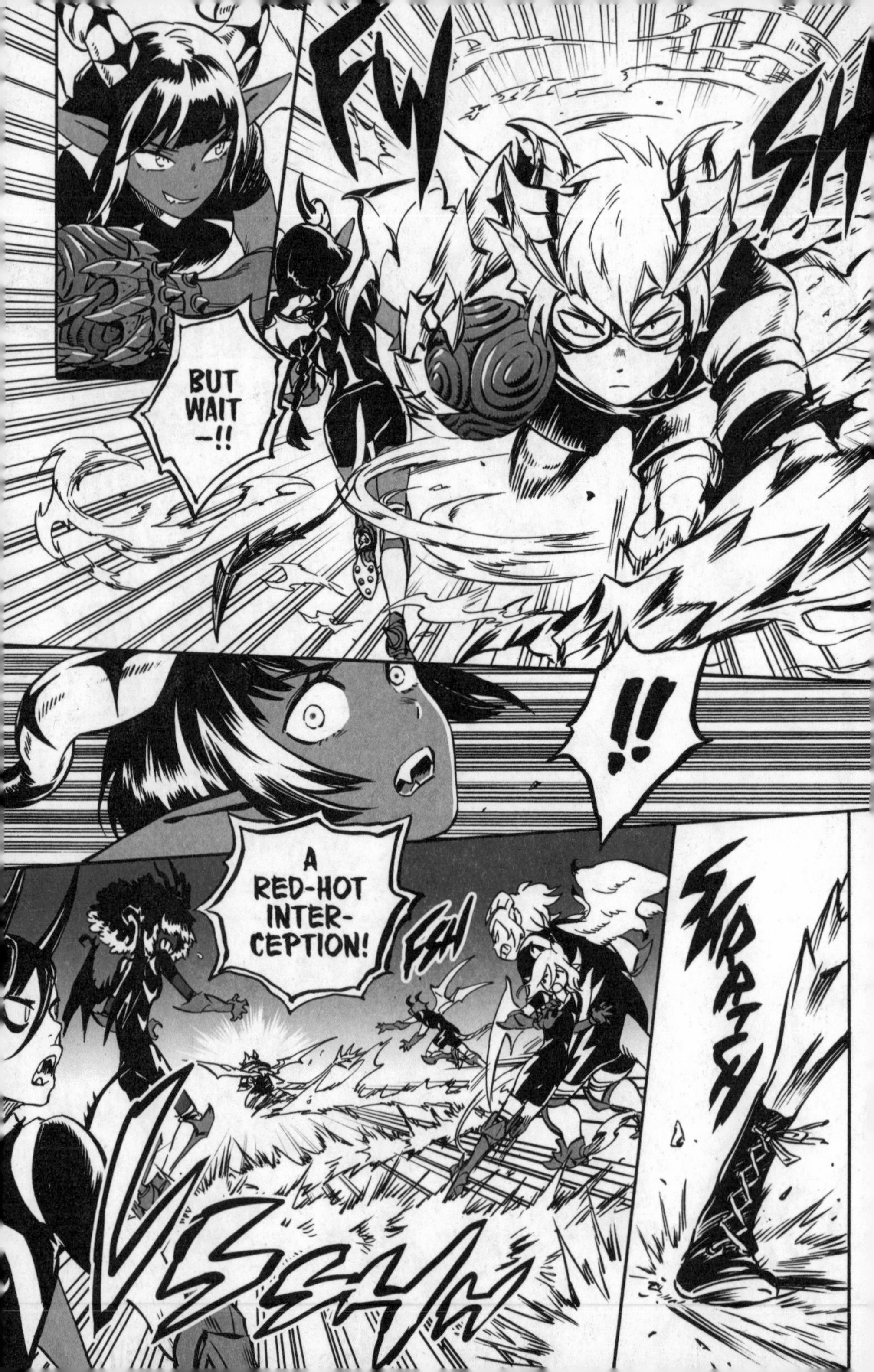
FW
SH
BUT WAIT—!!
!!
A RED-HOT INTER-CEPTION!
SH

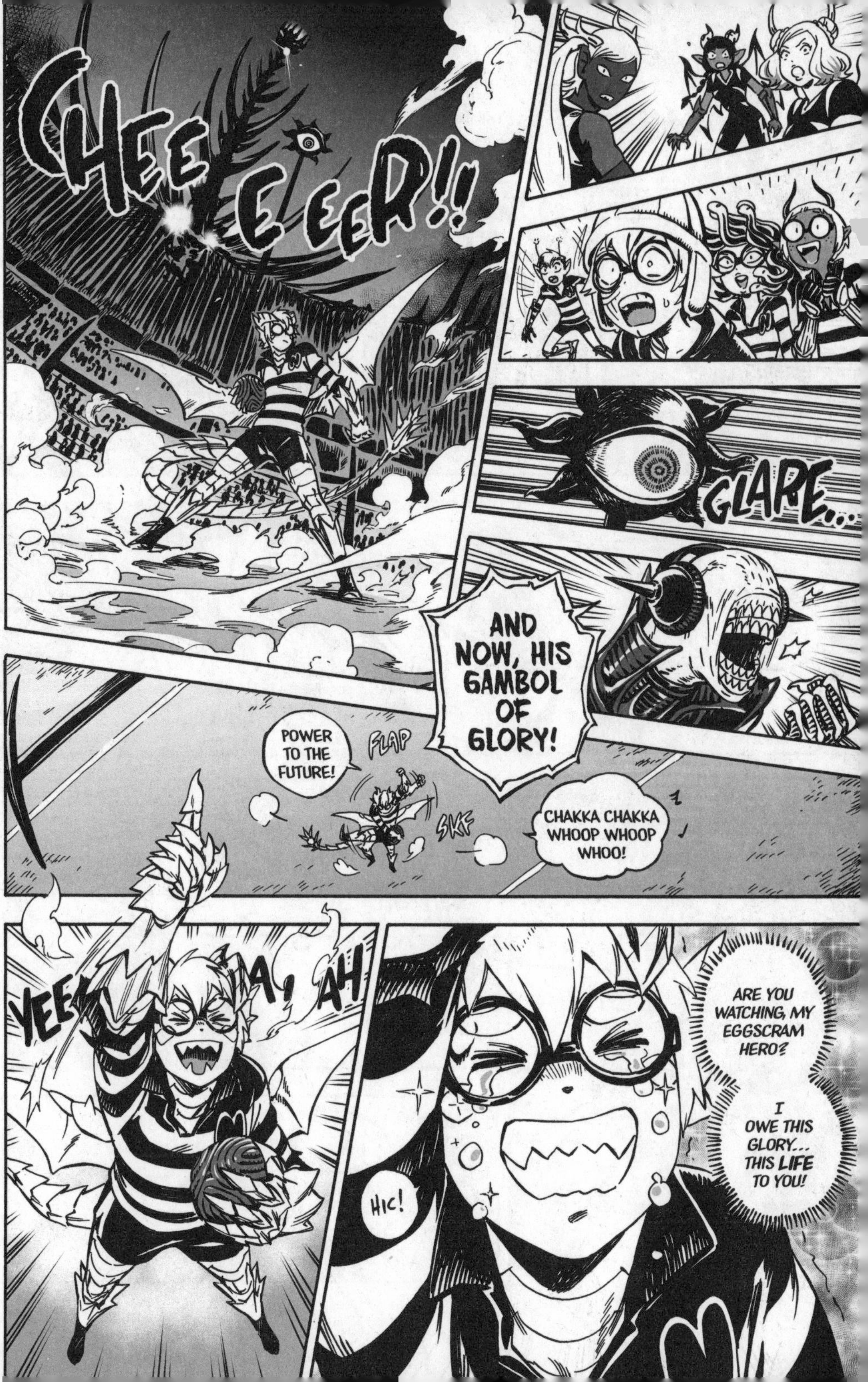
CHEEEEER!!
GLARE...
AND NOW, HIS GAMBOL OF GLORY!
POWER TO THE FUTURE!
FLAP
SKF
CHAKKA CHAKKA WHOOP WHOOP WHOO!
YEE A, AH
HIC!
ARE YOU WATCHING, MY EGGSCRAM HERO?
I OWE THIS GLORY... THIS LIFE TO YOU!

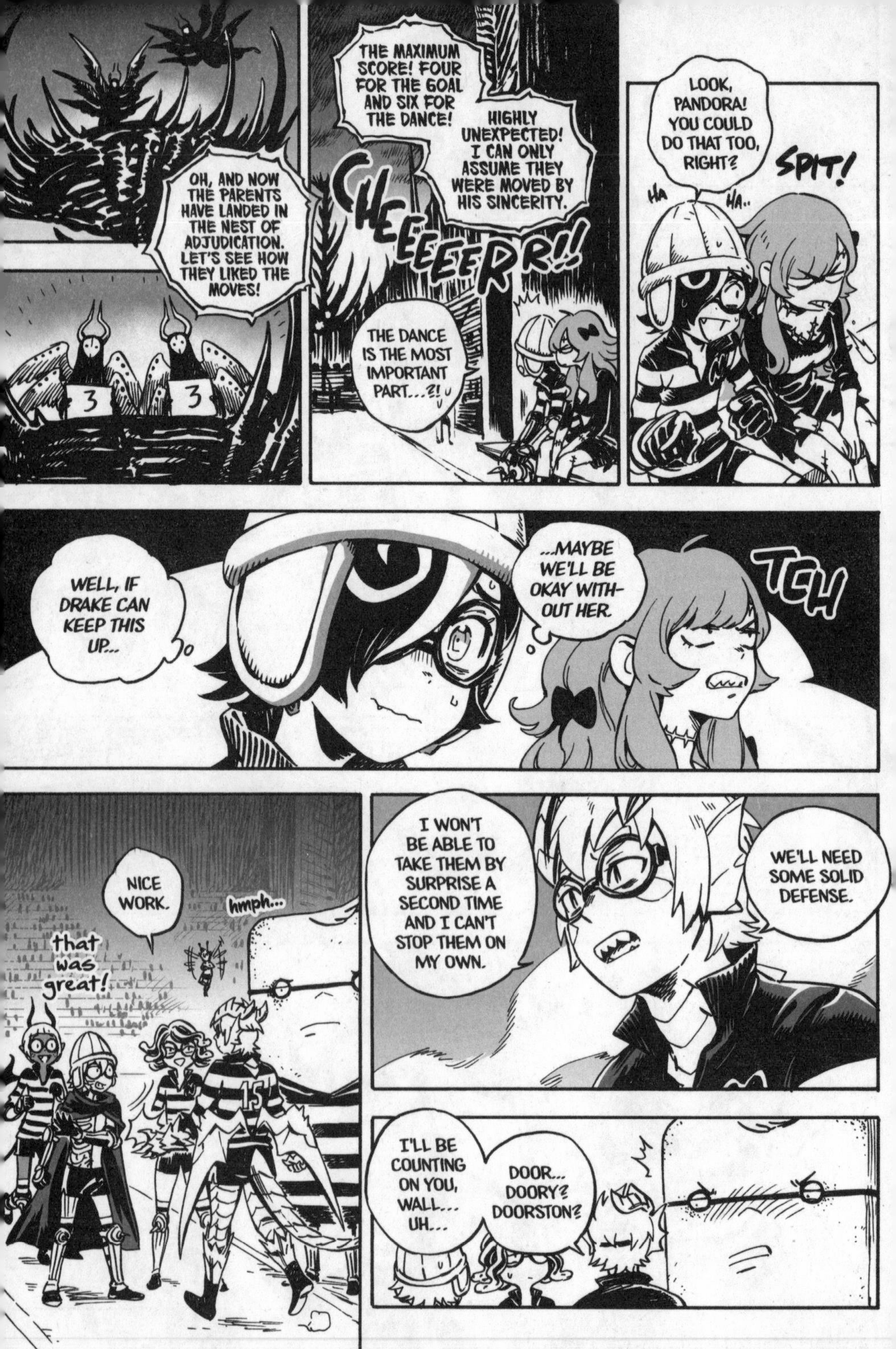
OH, AND NOW THE PARENTS HAVE LANDED IN THE NEST OF ADJUDICATION. LET'S SEE HOW THEY LIKED THE MOVES!
3
3
THE MAXIMUM SCORE! FOUR FOR THE GOAL AND SIX FOR THE DANCE!
HIGHLY UNEXPECTED! I CAN ONLY ASSUME THEY WERE MOVED BY HIS SINCERITY.
CHEEEEERR!!
THE DANCE IS THE MOST IMPORTANT PART...?!
LOOK, PANDORA! YOU COULD DO THAT TOO, RIGHT?
HA HA..
SPIT!
WELL, IF DRAKE CAN KEEP THIS UP...
...MAYBE WE'LL BE OKAY WITHOUT HER.
TCH
NICE WORK.
hmph...
that was great!
I WON'T BE ABLE TO TAKE THEM BY SURPRISE A SECOND TIME AND I CAN'T STOP THEM ON MY OWN.
WE'LL NEED SOME SOLID DEFENSE.
I'LL BE COUNTING ON YOU, WALL... UH...
DOOR... DOORY? DOORSTON?

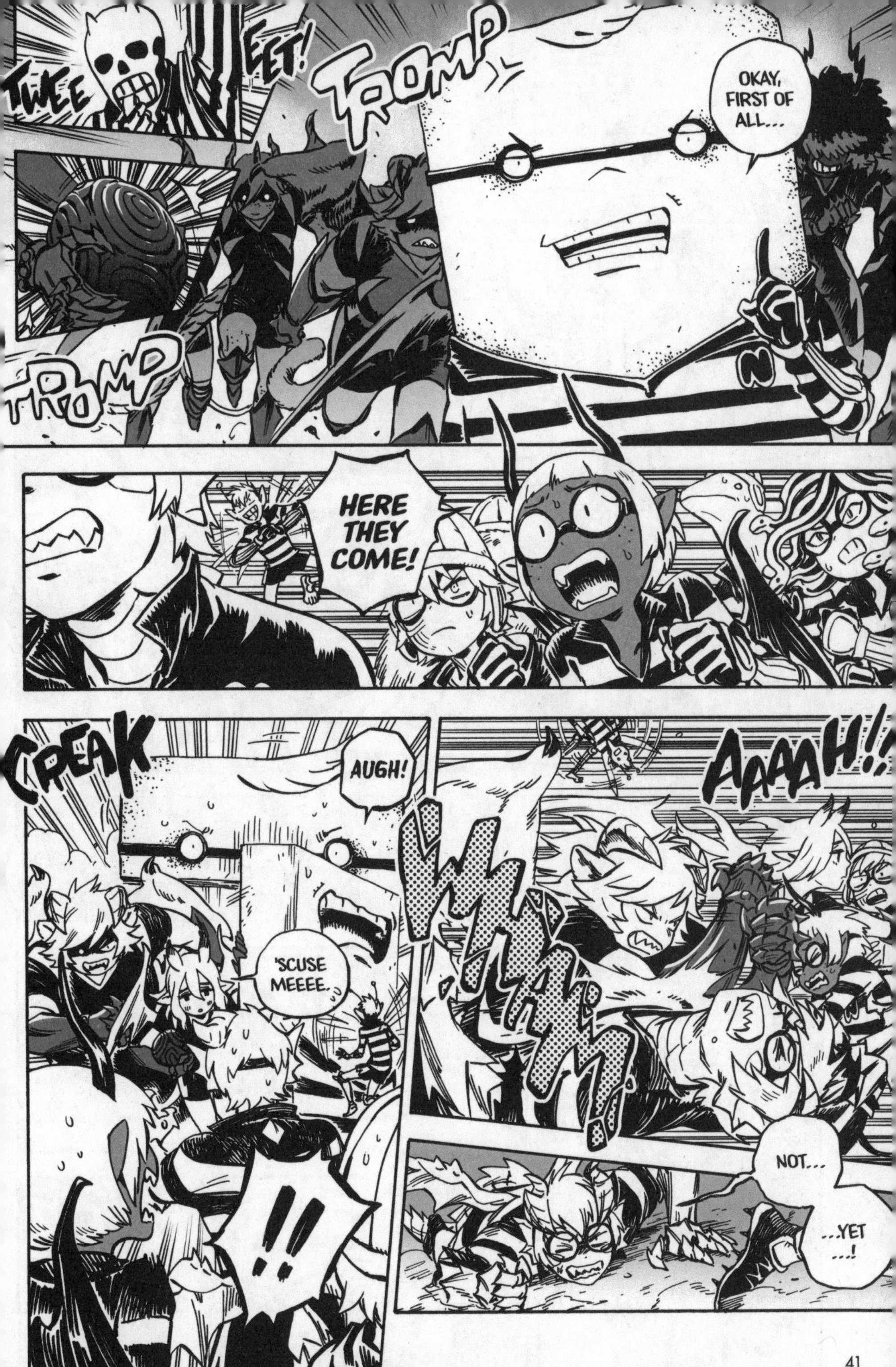
TWEEEET!
TROMP
OKAY, FIRST OF ALL...
TROMP
HERE THEY COME!
CREAK
AUGH!
'SCUSE MEEEE.
!!
AAAAH!!
NOT...
...YET...!

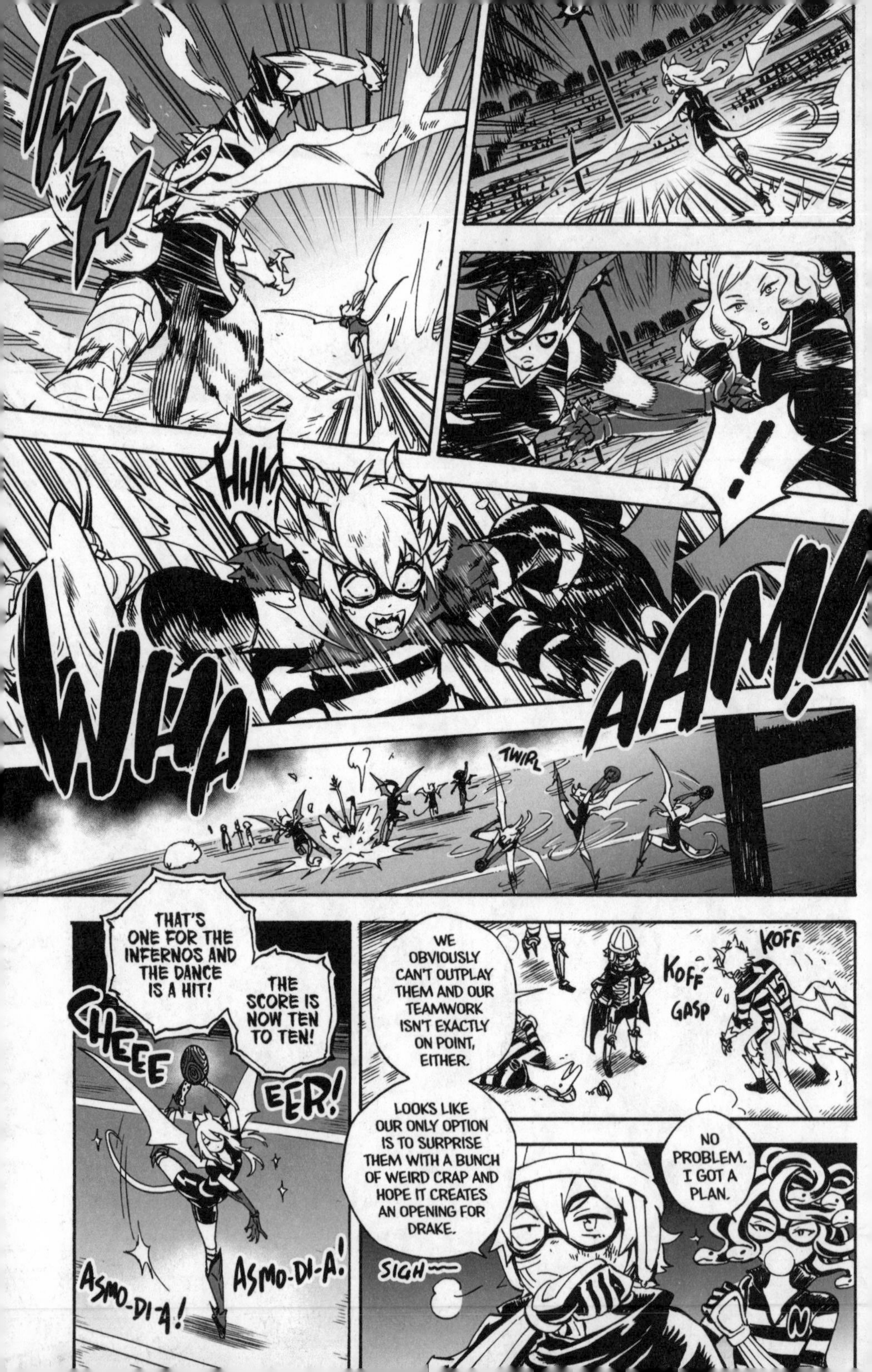
FWSH
!
THHK!
WHAAAM!!
TWIRL
THAT'S ONE FOR THE INFERNOS AND THE DANCE IS A HIT!
THE SCORE IS NOW TEN TO TEN!
CHEEEEER!
ASMO-DI-A!
ASMO-DI-A!
WE OBVIOUSLY CAN'T OUTPLAY THEM AND OUR TEAMWORK ISN'T EXACTLY ON POINT, EITHER.
KOFF
KOFF
GASP
LOOKS LIKE OUR ONLY OPTION IS TO SURPRISE THEM WITH A BUNCH OF WEIRD CRAP AND HOPE IT CREATES AN OPENING FOR DRAKE.
SIGH
NO PROBLEM. I GOT A PLAN.

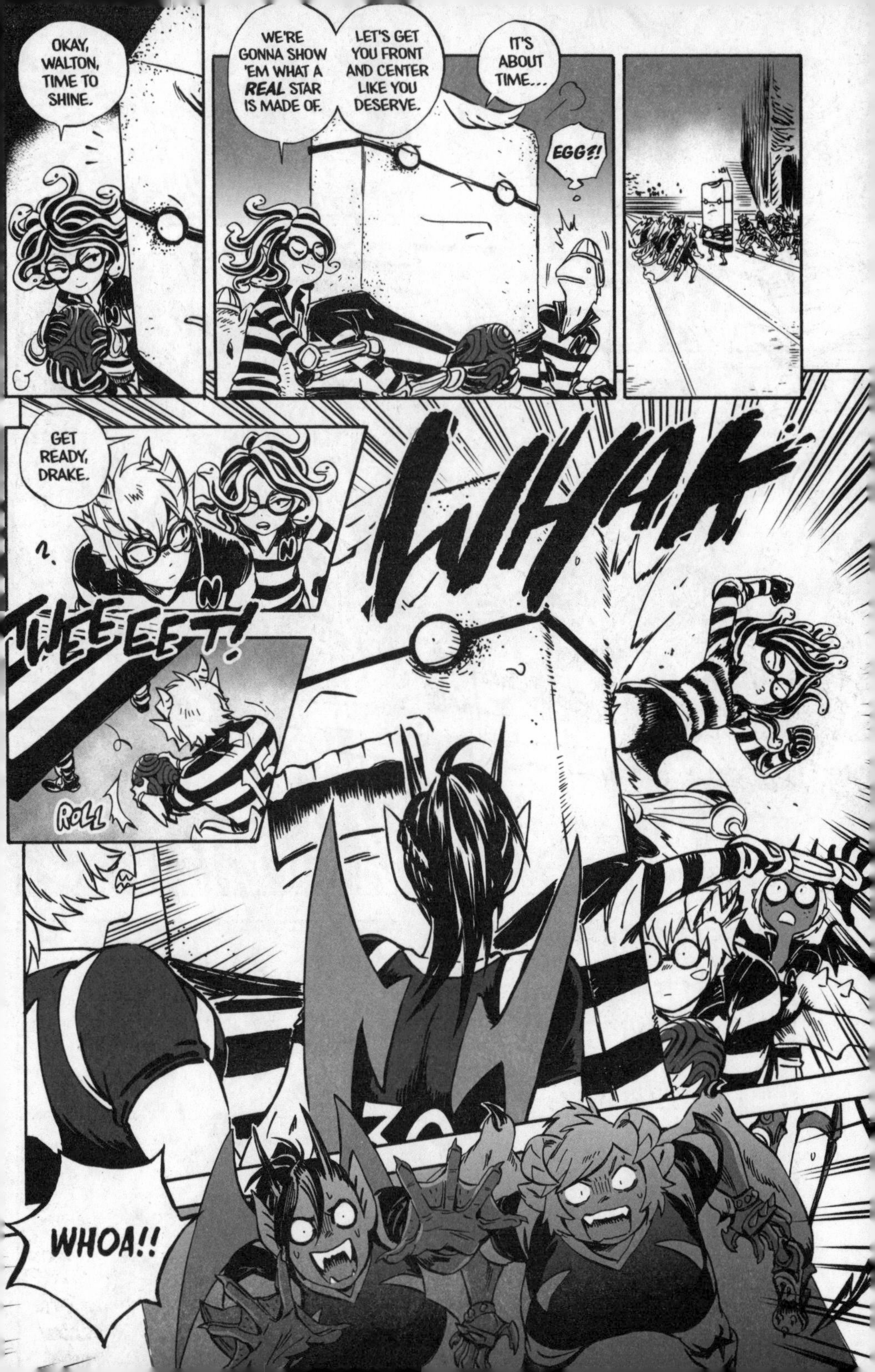
OKAY, WALTON, TIME TO SHINE.
WE'RE GONNA SHOW 'EM WHAT A REAL STAR IS MADE OF.
LET'S GET YOU FRONT AND CENTER LIKE YOU DESERVE.
IT'S ABOUT TIME...
EGG?!
GET READY, DRAKE.
WHAK!
TWEEEET!
ROLL
WHOA!!

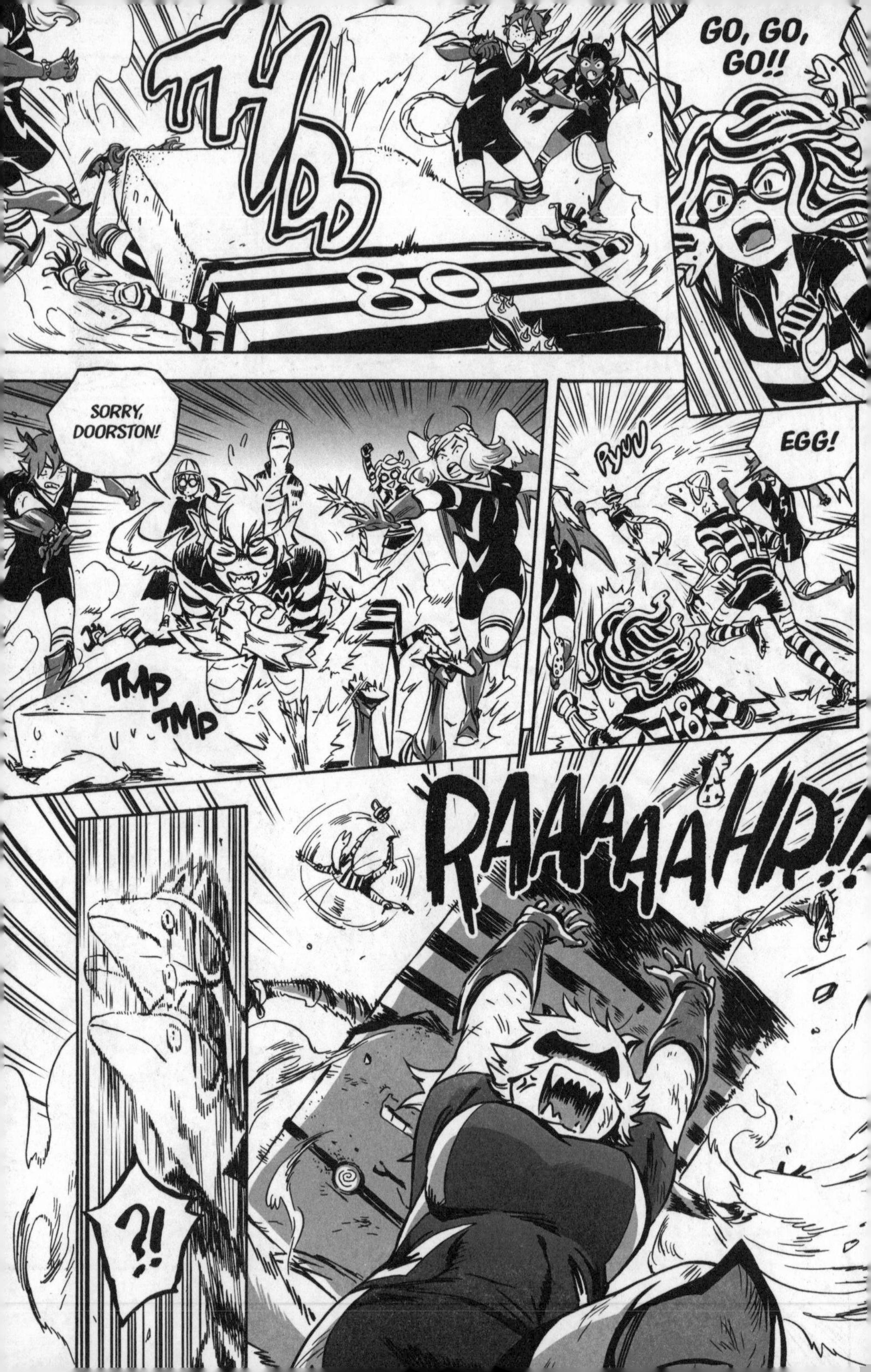
TUDD
GO, GO, GO!!
SORRY, DOORSTON!
TMP TMP
Pyuu
EGG!
RAAAAAHR!!
?!

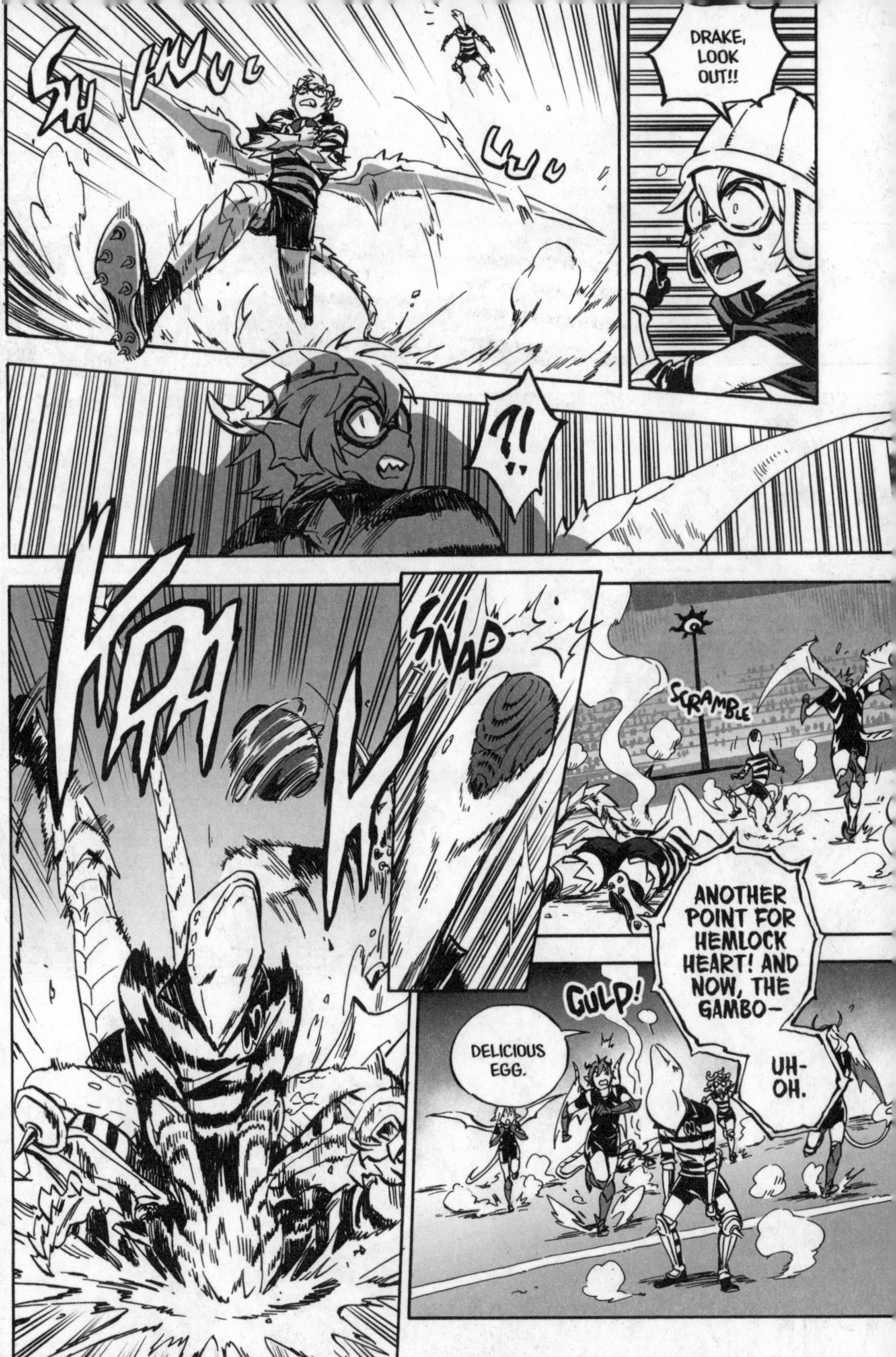
SHHHUUU
UUU
DRAKE, LOOK OUT!!
?!
KRAK
SNAP
SCRAMBLE
ANOTHER POINT FOR HEMLOCK HEART! AND NOW, THE GAMBO—
GULP!
DELICIOUS EGG.
UH-OH.

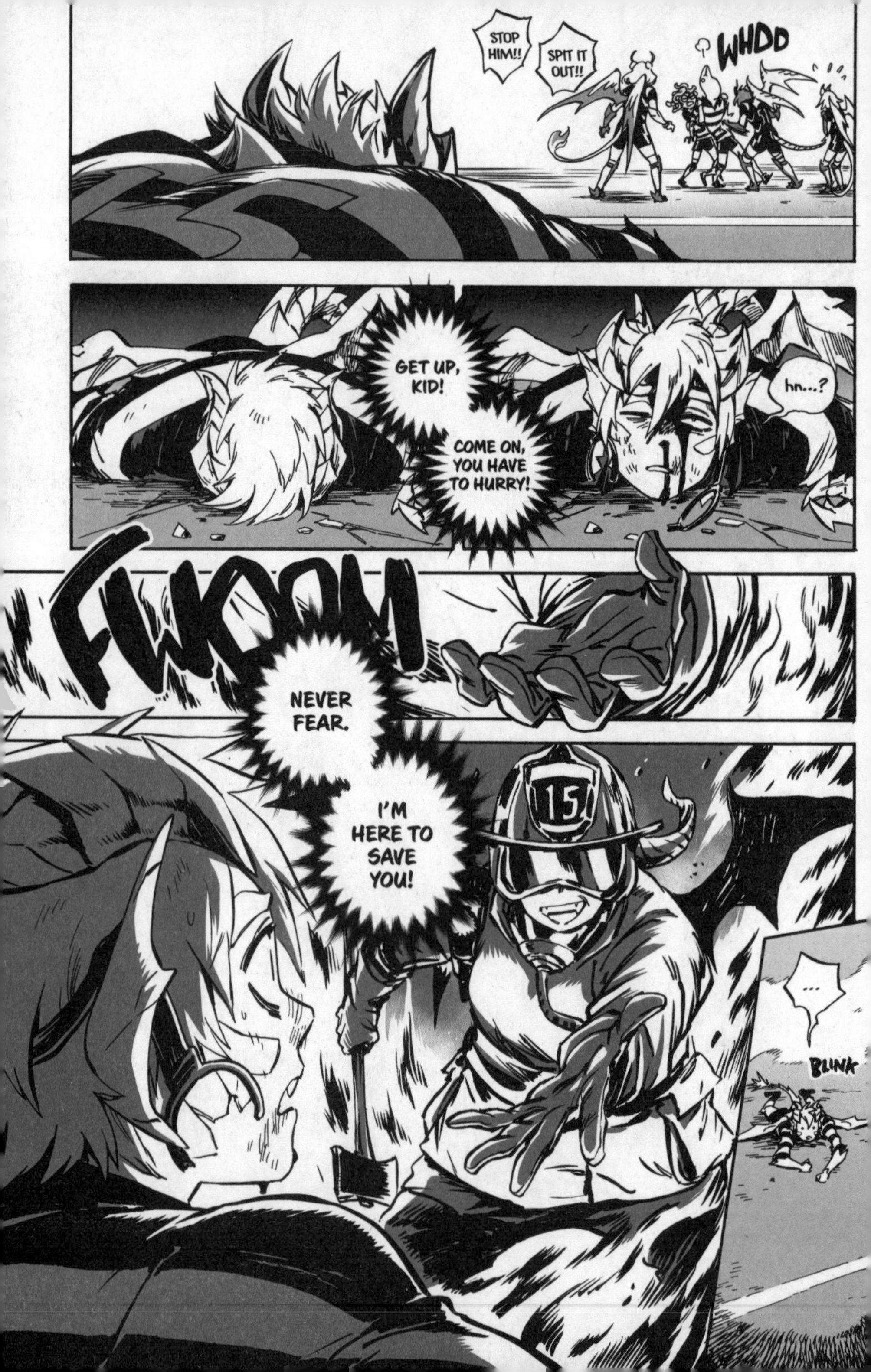
STOP HIM!!
SPIT IT OUT!!
WHDD
GET UP, KID!
COME ON, YOU HAVE TO HURRY!
hn...?
FWOOM
NEVER FEAR.
I'M HERE TO SAVE YOU!
15
...
BLINK

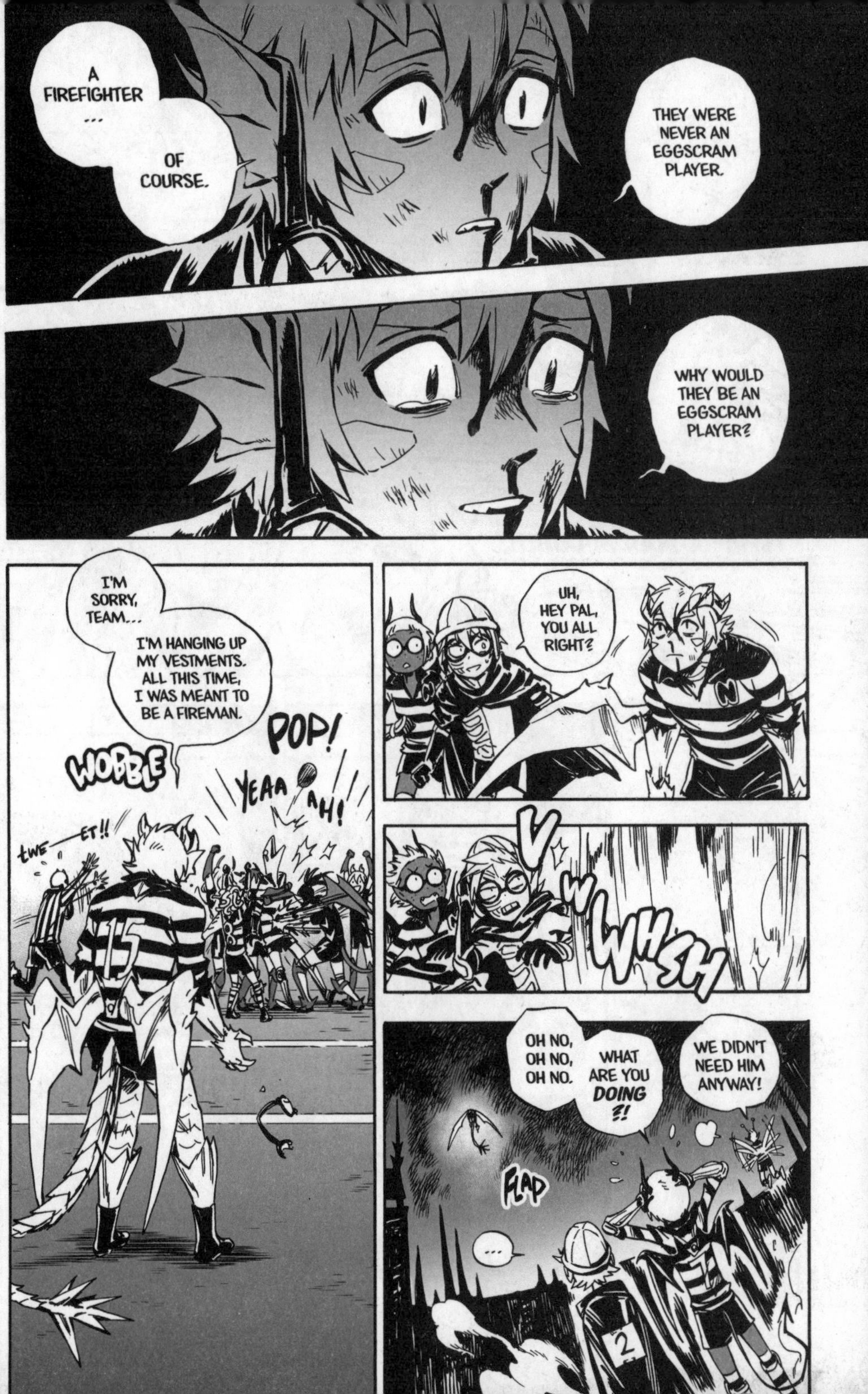
A FIREFIGHTER ...
OF COURSE.
THEY WERE NEVER AN EGGSCRAM PLAYER.
WHY WOULD THEY BE AN EGGSCRAM PLAYER?
I'M SORRY, TEAM...
I'M HANGING UP MY VESTMENTS. ALL THIS TIME, I WAS MEANT TO BE A FIREMAN.
WOBBLE
POP!
YEAA AH!
TWE—ET!!
UH, HEY PAL, YOU ALL RIGHT?
VWWHSH
OH NO, OH NO, OH NO.
WHAT ARE YOU DOING?!
WE DIDN'T NEED HIM ANYWAY!
FLAP
...

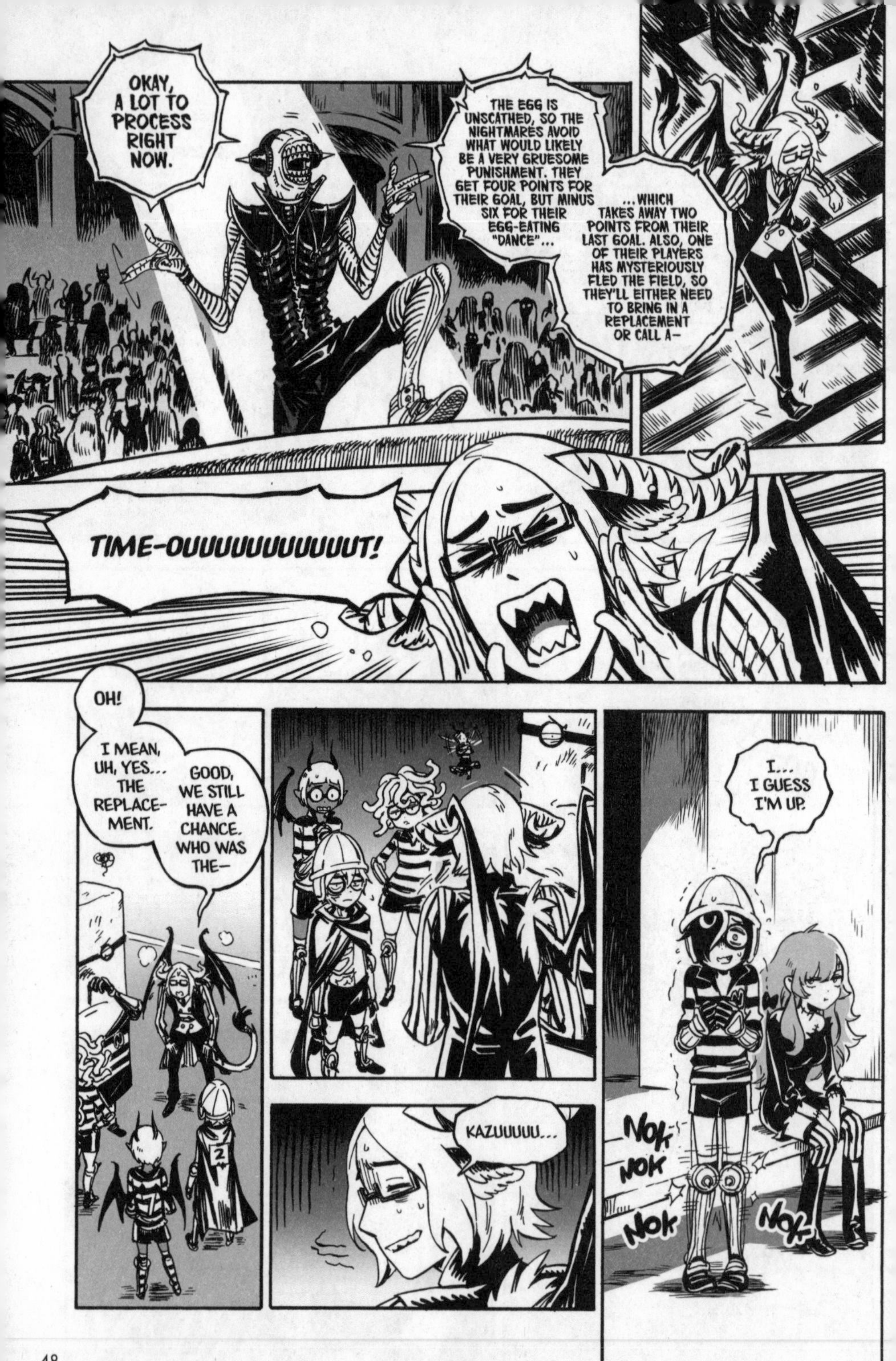
OKAY, A LOT TO PROCESS RIGHT NOW.
THE EGG IS UNSCATHED, SO THE NIGHTMARES AVOID WHAT WOULD LIKELY BE A VERY GRUESOME PUNISHMENT. THEY GET FOUR POINTS FOR THEIR GOAL, BUT MINUS SIX FOR THEIR EGG-EATING "DANCE"...
...WHICH TAKES AWAY TWO POINTS FROM THEIR LAST GOAL. ALSO, ONE OF THEIR PLAYERS HAS MYSTERIOUSLY FLED THE FIELD, SO THEY'LL EITHER NEED TO BRING IN A REPLACEMENT OR CALL A–
TIME-OUUUUUUUUUUUT!
OH!
I MEAN, UH, YES... THE REPLACEMENT.
GOOD, WE STILL HAVE A CHANCE. WHO WAS THE–
KAZUUUUU...
I... I GUESS I'M UP.
NOK NOK NOK NOK

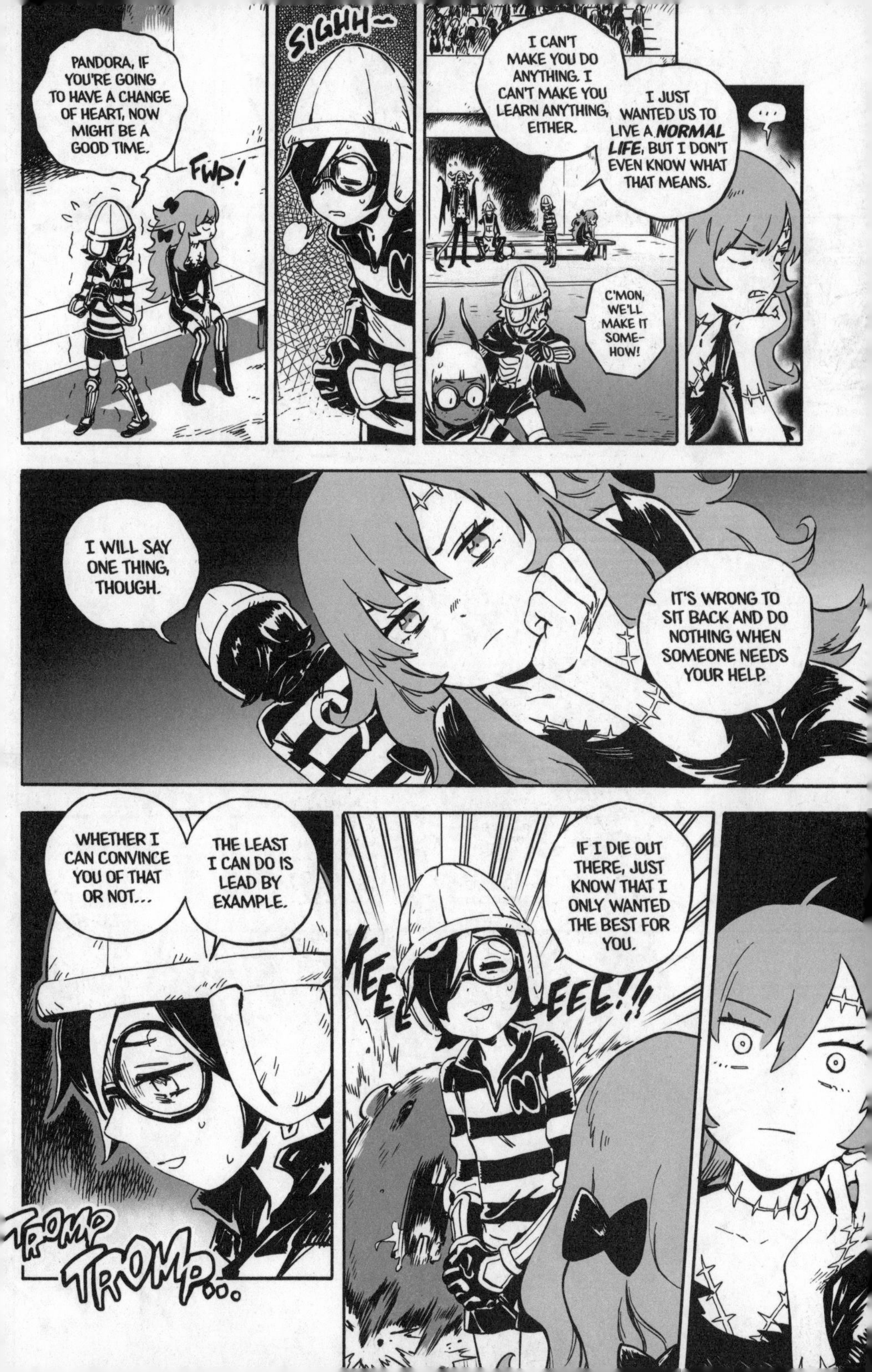
PANDORA, IF YOU'RE GOING TO HAVE A CHANGE OF HEART, NOW MIGHT BE A GOOD TIME.
FWP!
SIGHH~
I CAN'T MAKE YOU DO ANYTHING. I CAN'T MAKE YOU LEARN ANYTHING, EITHER.
I JUST WANTED US TO LIVE A NORMAL LIFE, BUT I DON'T EVEN KNOW WHAT THAT MEANS.
C'MON, WE'LL MAKE IT SOME-HOW!
...
I WILL SAY ONE THING, THOUGH.
IT'S WRONG TO SIT BACK AND DO NOTHING WHEN SOMEONE NEEDS YOUR HELP.
WHETHER I CAN CONVINCE YOU OF THAT OR NOT...
THE LEAST I CAN DO IS LEAD BY EXAMPLE.
TROMP TROMP...
IF I DIE OUT THERE, JUST KNOW THAT I ONLY WANTED THE BEST FOR YOU.
KEEEEEEE!!

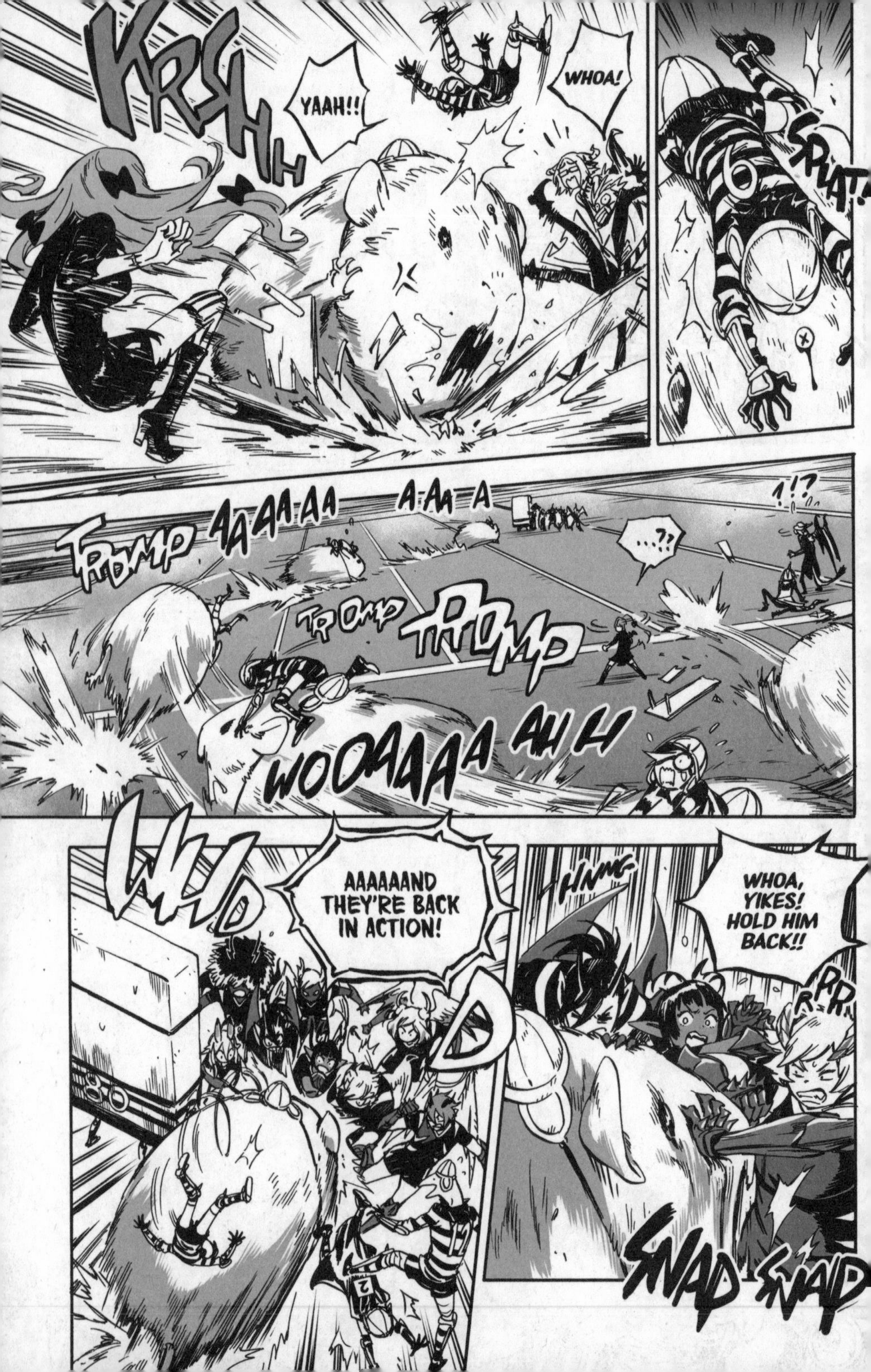
KRSHHH
YAAH!!
WHOA!
SPLAT!!
TROMP AAAAAA A-AA A
!!?
...?!
TROMP TROMP
WOOAAAA AAH
WHUD
AAAAAAND THEY'RE BACK IN ACTION!
HNNG
WHOA, YIKES! HOLD HIM BACK!!
RRR
SNAP SNAP

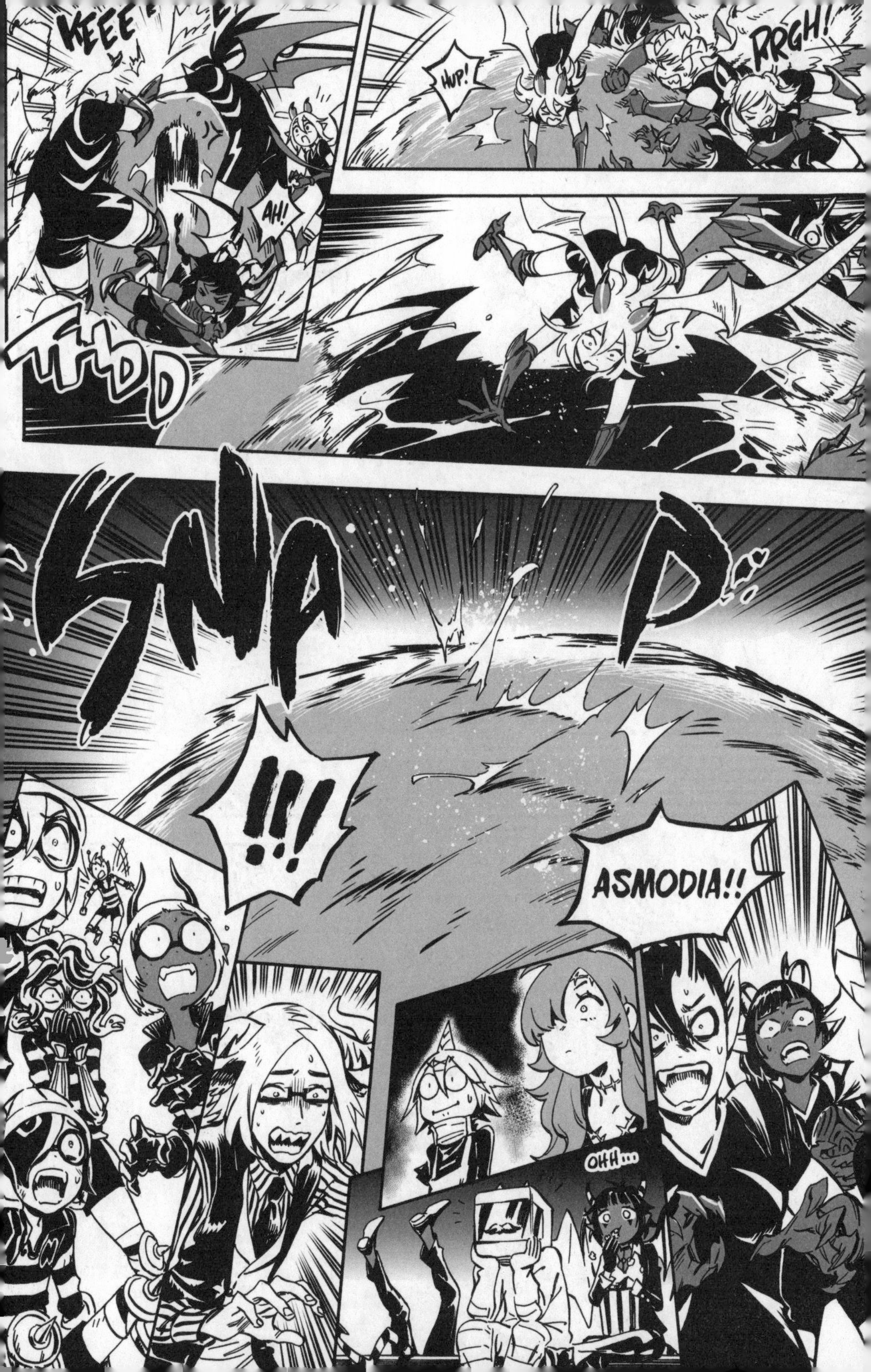
KEEE
AH!
THDD
HUP!
RRGH!
SNAP
!!!
ASMODIA!!
OHH...

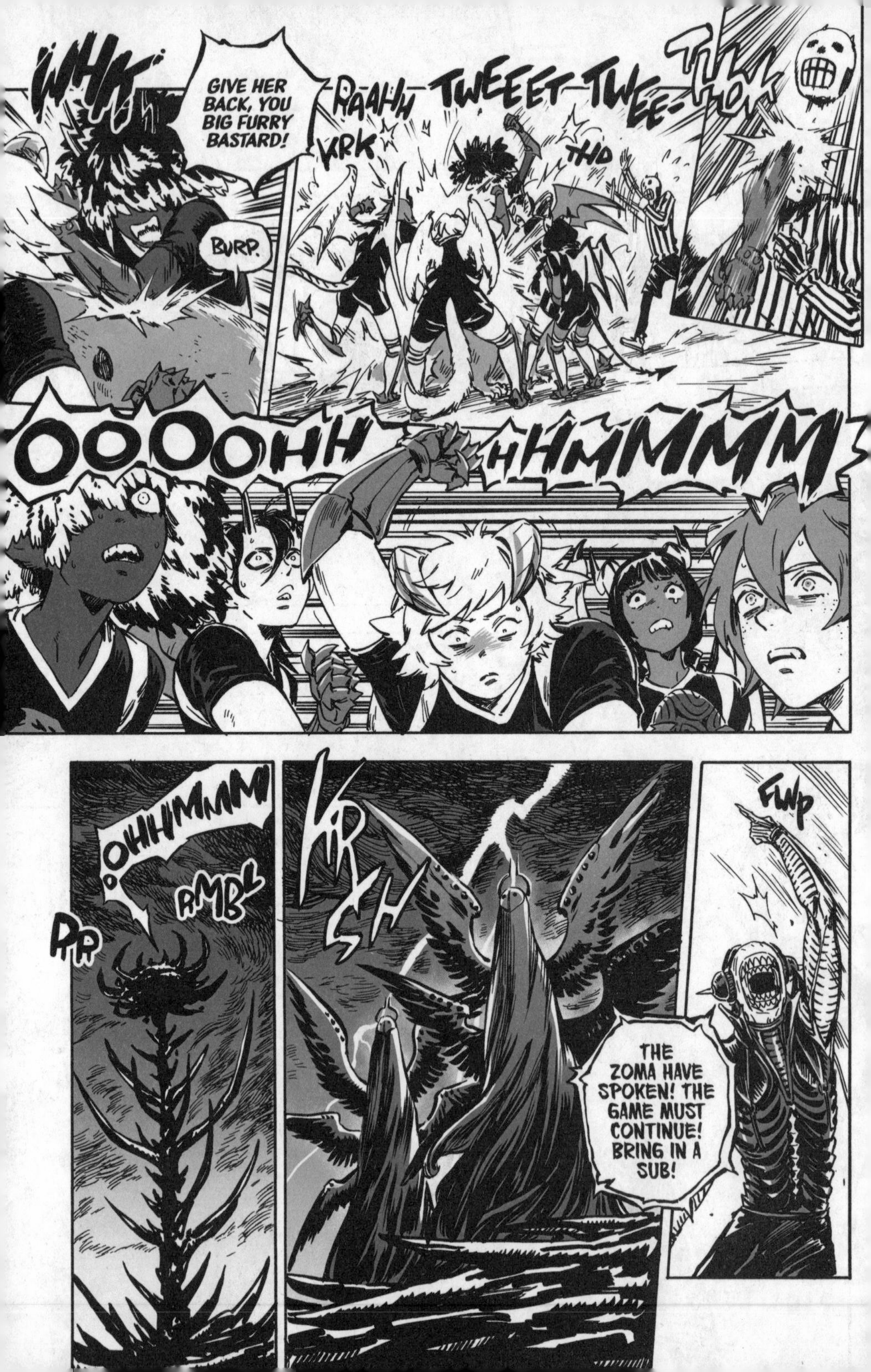
WHK
GIVE HER BACK, YOU BIG FURRY BASTARD!
BURP.
RAAHH
TWEEEET-TWEE-
KRK
THD
TI-HON
OOOOOHH HHMMMMMM
OHHMMM
RMBL
RR
KRSH
FWP
THE ZOMA HAVE SPOKEN! THE GAME MUST CONTINUE! BRING IN A SUB!

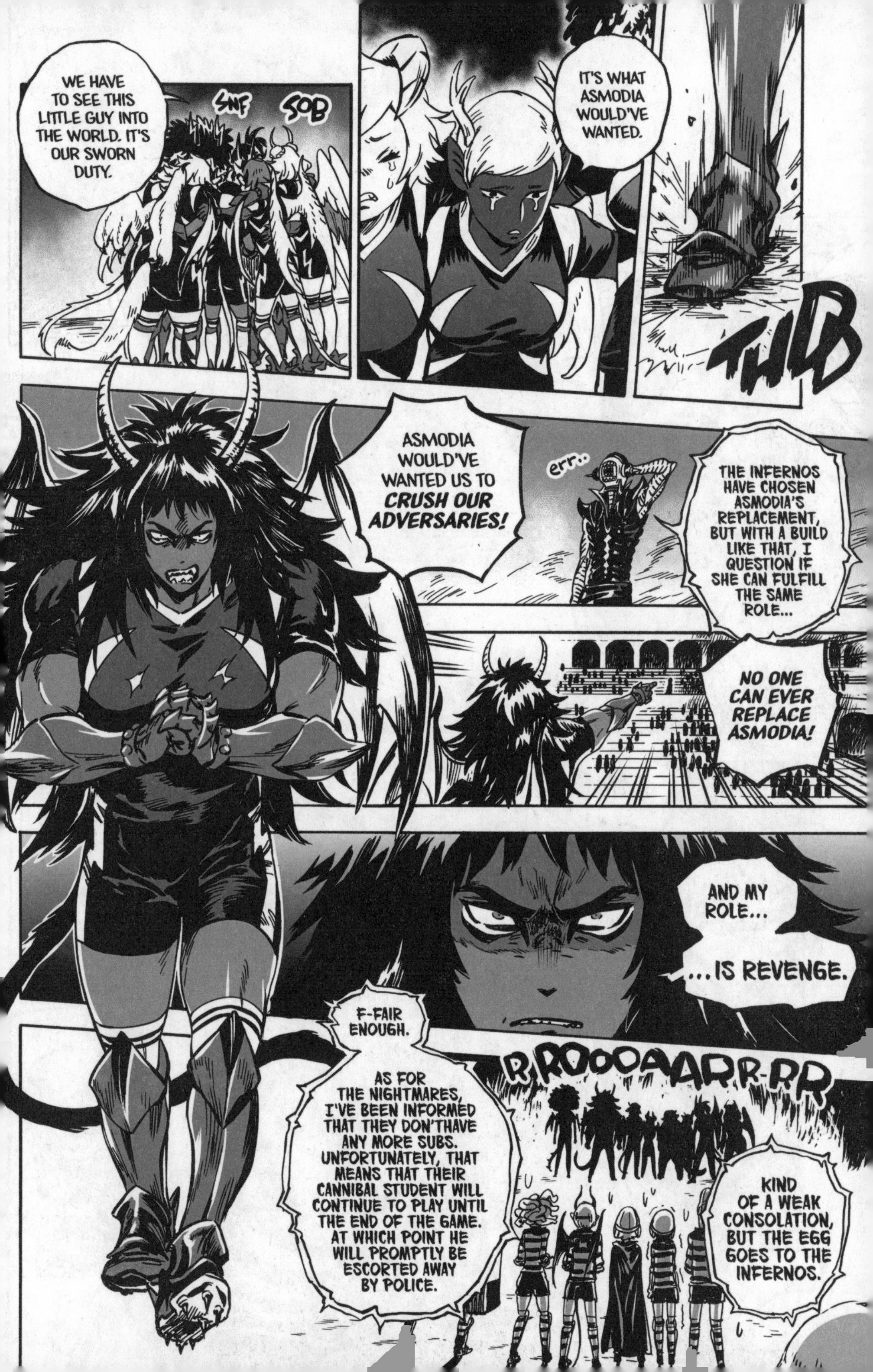
WE HAVE TO SEE THIS LITTLE GUY INTO THE WORLD. IT'S OUR SWORN DUTY.
SNF
SOB
IT'S WHAT ASMODIA WOULD'VE WANTED.
THUD
ASMODIA WOULD'VE WANTED US TO CRUSH OUR ADVERSARIES!
err..
THE INFERNOS HAVE CHOSEN ASMODIA'S REPLACEMENT, BUT WITH A BUILD LIKE THAT, I QUESTION IF SHE CAN FULFILL THE SAME ROLE...
NO ONE CAN EVER REPLACE ASMODIA!
AND MY ROLE...
...IS REVENGE.
F-FAIR ENOUGH.
RROOOAARR-RR
AS FOR THE NIGHTMARES, I'VE BEEN INFORMED THAT THEY DON'THAVE ANY MORE SUBS. UNFORTUNATELY, THAT MEANS THAT THEIR CANNIBAL STUDENT WILL CONTINUE TO PLAY UNTIL THE END OF THE GAME. AT WHICH POINT HE WILL PROMPTLY BE ESCORTED AWAY BY POLICE.
KIND OF A WEAK CONSOLATION, BUT THE EGG GOES TO THE INFERNOS.

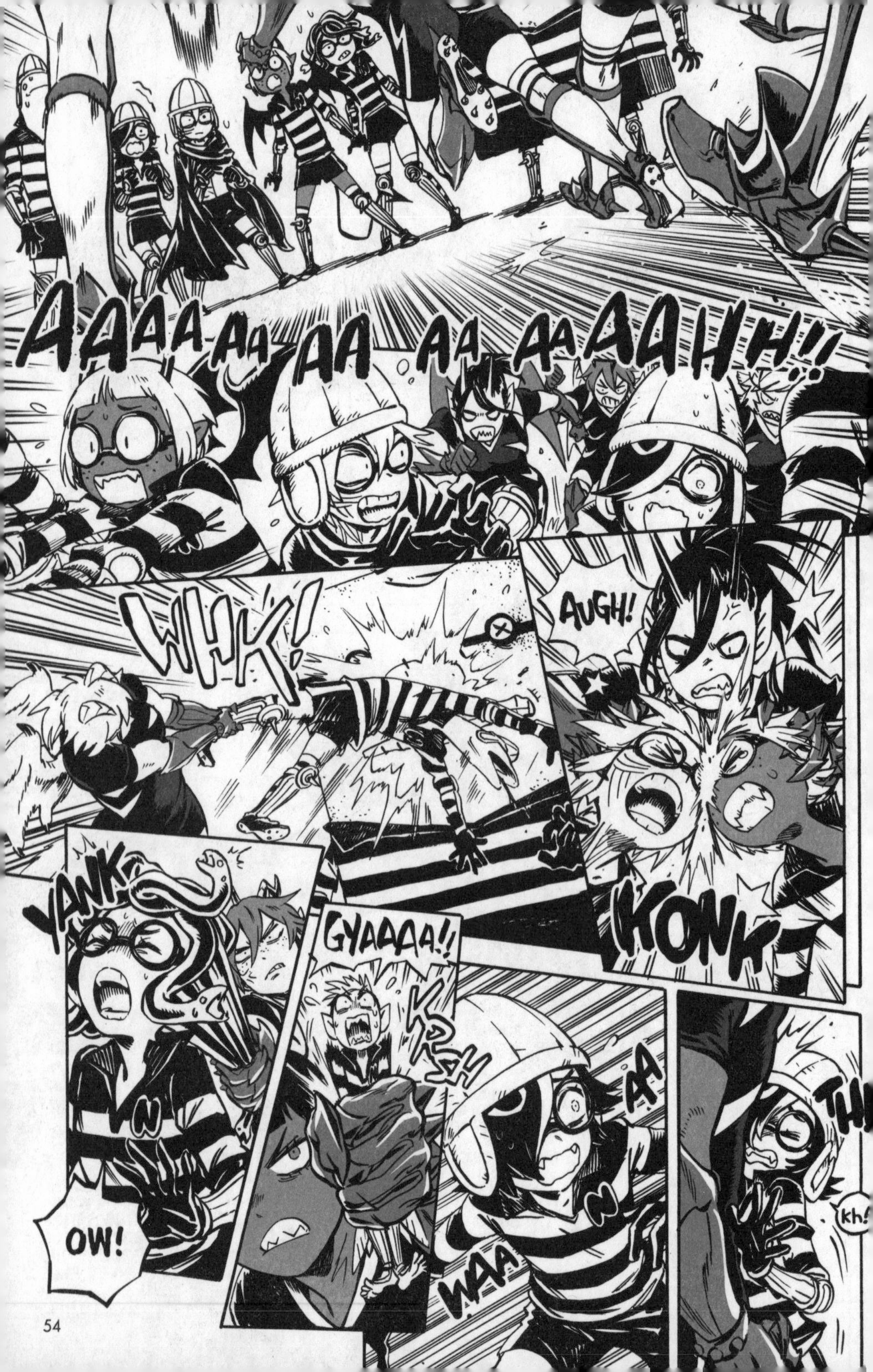
AAAAAAAAAAAAAAAAAHHH!!
WHK!
AUGH!
KONK
YANK
OW!
GYAAAA!!
KRSH
AA
WAA
TH
kh!

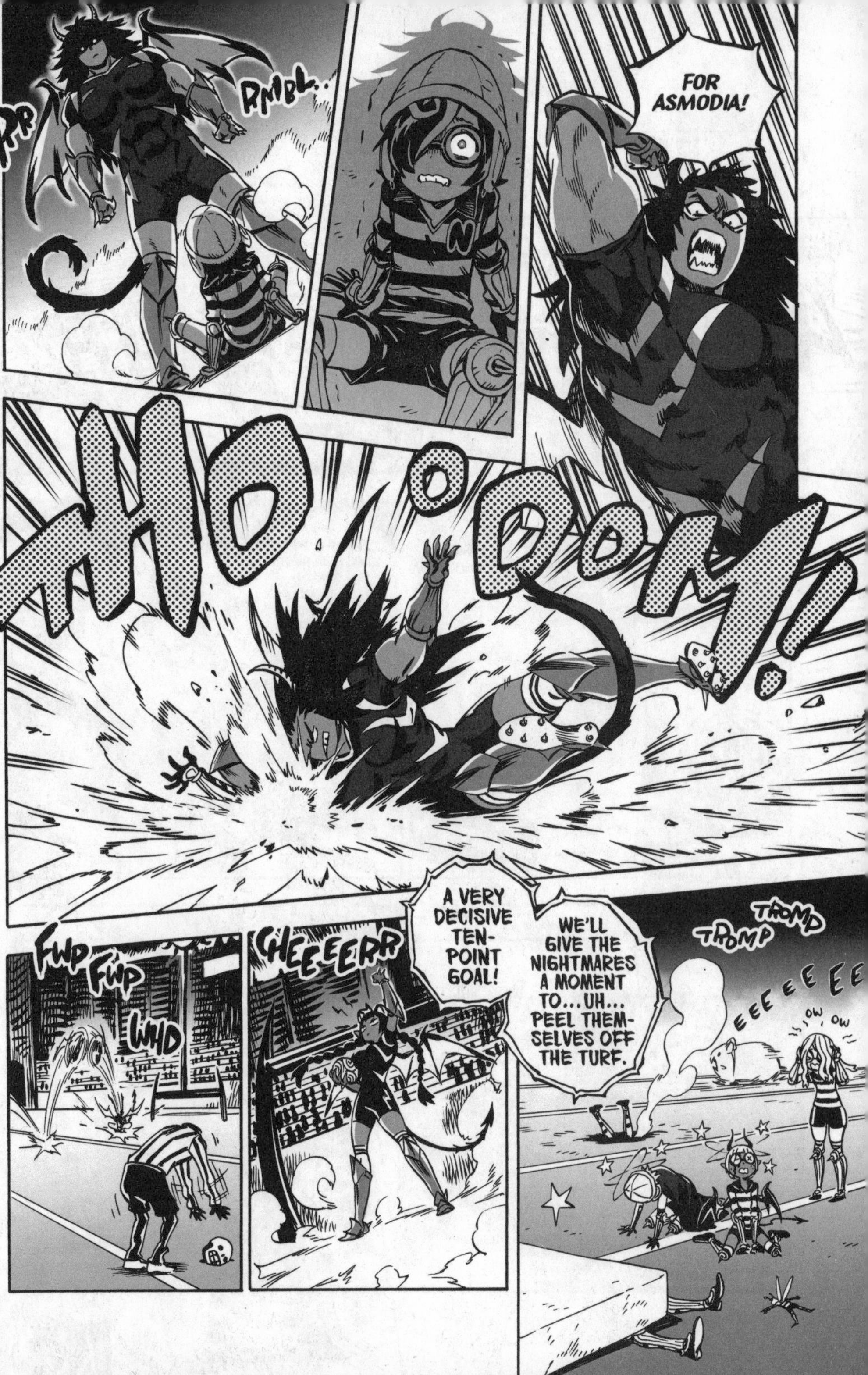
RR
RMBL...
FOR ASMODIA!
THOOOM!
FWP
FWP
WHD
CHEEEERR
A VERY DECISIVE TEN-POINT GOAL!
WE'LL GIVE THE NIGHTMARES A MOMENT TO... UH... PEEL THEM-SELVES OFF THE TURF.
TROMP
TROMP
EEEEEEE
OW, OW

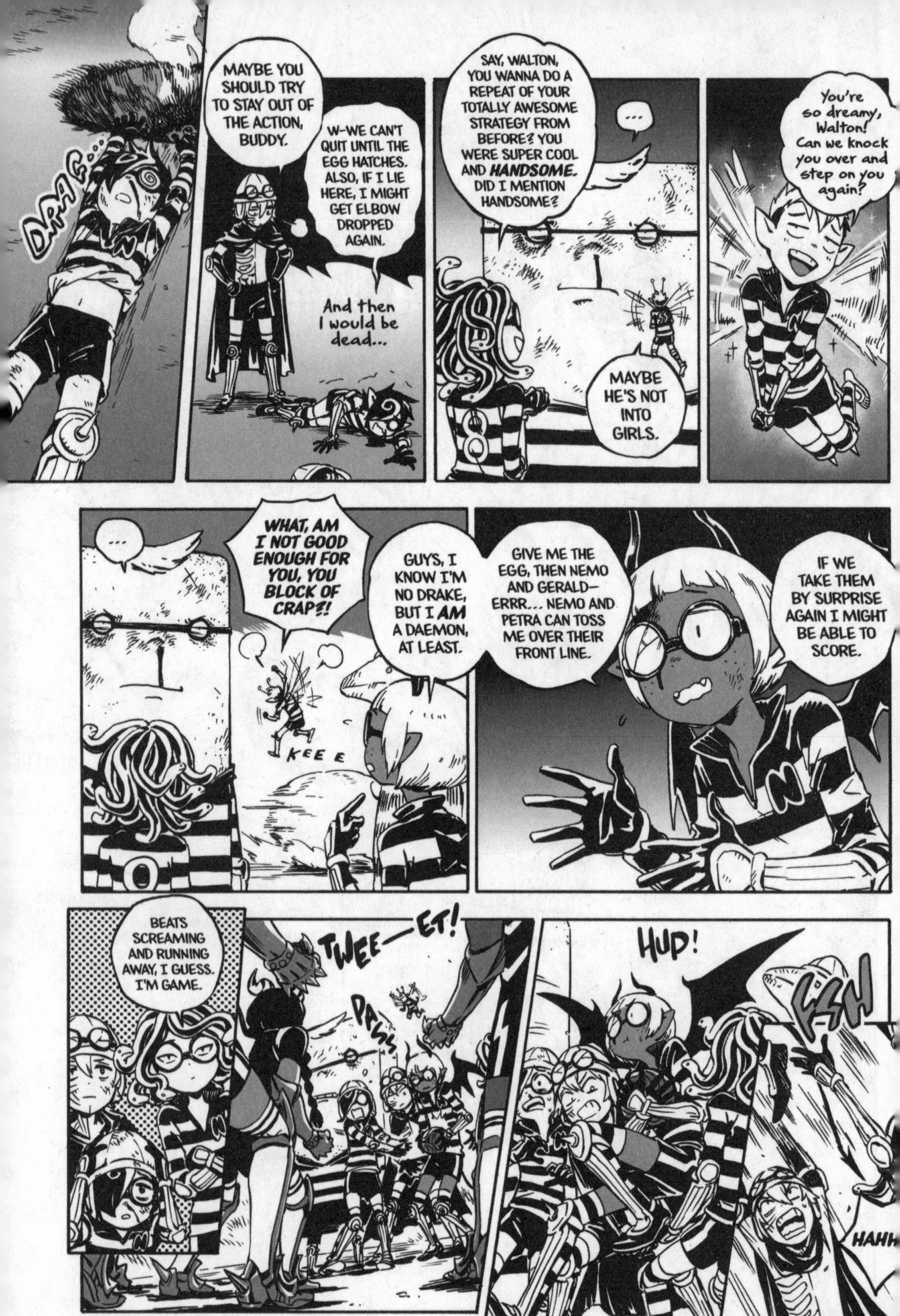
DRAG...
MAYBE YOU SHOULD TRY TO STAY OUT OF THE ACTION, BUDDY.
W-WE CAN'T QUIT UNTIL THE EGG HATCHES. ALSO, IF I LIE HERE, I MIGHT GET ELBOW DROPPED AGAIN.
And then I would be dead...
SAY, WALTON, YOU WANNA DO A REPEAT OF YOUR TOTALLY AWESOME STRATEGY FROM BEFORE? YOU WERE SUPER COOL AND HANDSOME. DID I MENTION HANDSOME?
...
MAYBE HE'S NOT INTO GIRLS.
You're so dreamy, Walton! Can we knock you over and step on you again?
...
WHAT, AM I NOT GOOD ENOUGH FOR YOU, YOU BLOCK OF CRAP?!
KEEE
GUYS, I KNOW I'M NO DRAKE, BUT I AM A DAEMON, AT LEAST.
GIVE ME THE EGG, THEN NEMO AND GERALD— ERRR... NEMO AND PETRA CAN TOSS ME OVER THEIR FRONT LINE.
IF WE TAKE THEM BY SURPRISE AGAIN I MIGHT BE ABLE TO SCORE.
BEATS SCREAMING AND RUNNING AWAY, I GUESS. I'M GAME.
TWEE—ET!
PASS
HUP!
FSH
HAHH

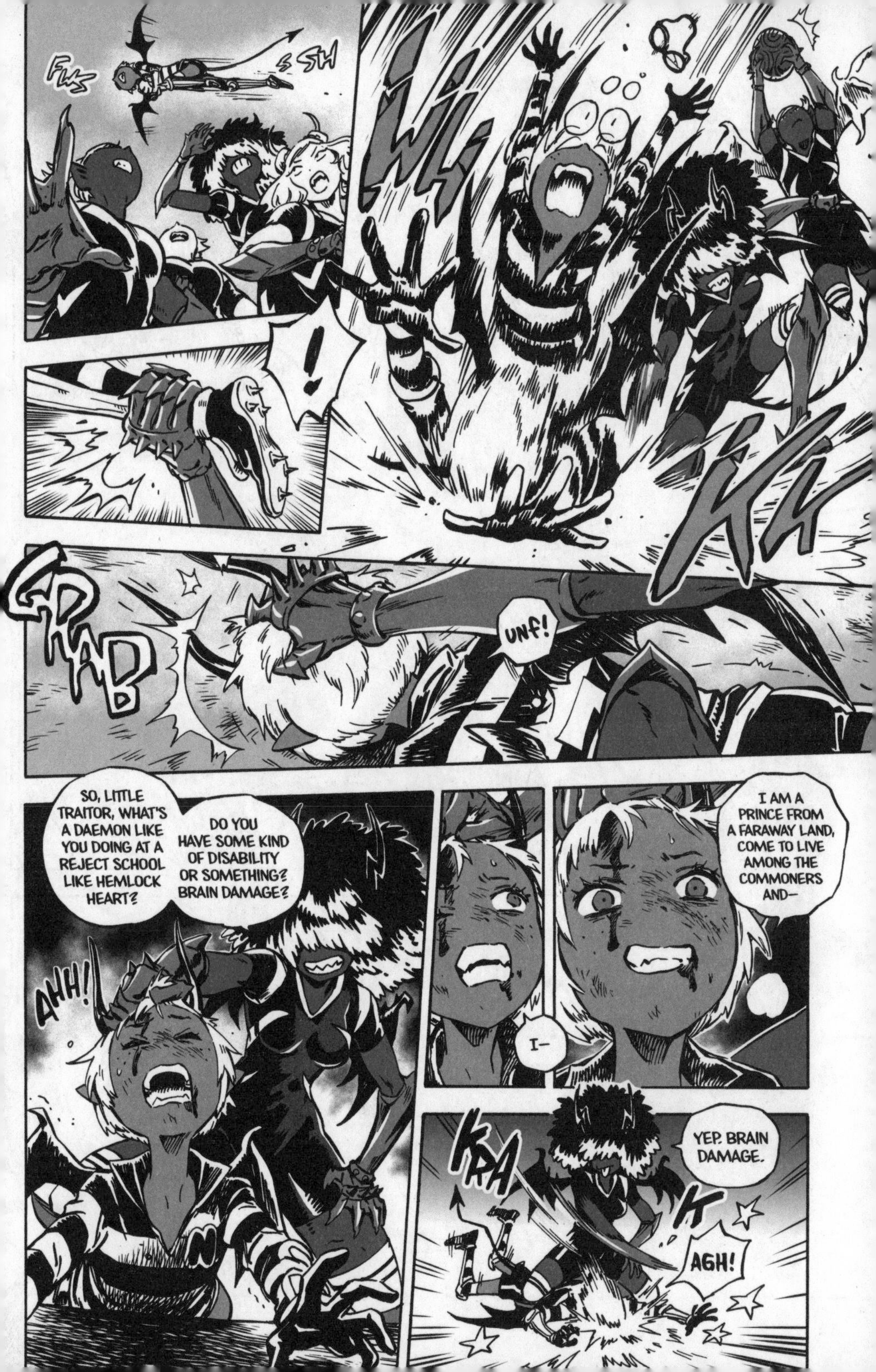
FWS
SSH
WH
!
KK
GRAB
UNF!
SO, LITTLE TRAITOR, WHAT'S A DAEMON LIKE YOU DOING AT A REJECT SCHOOL LIKE HEMLOCK HEART?
DO YOU HAVE SOME KIND OF DISABILITY OR SOMETHING? BRAIN DAMAGE?
AHH!
I—
I AM A PRINCE FROM A FARAWAY LAND, COME TO LIVE AMONG THE COMMONERS AND—
KRAK
YEP. BRAIN DAMAGE.
AGH!

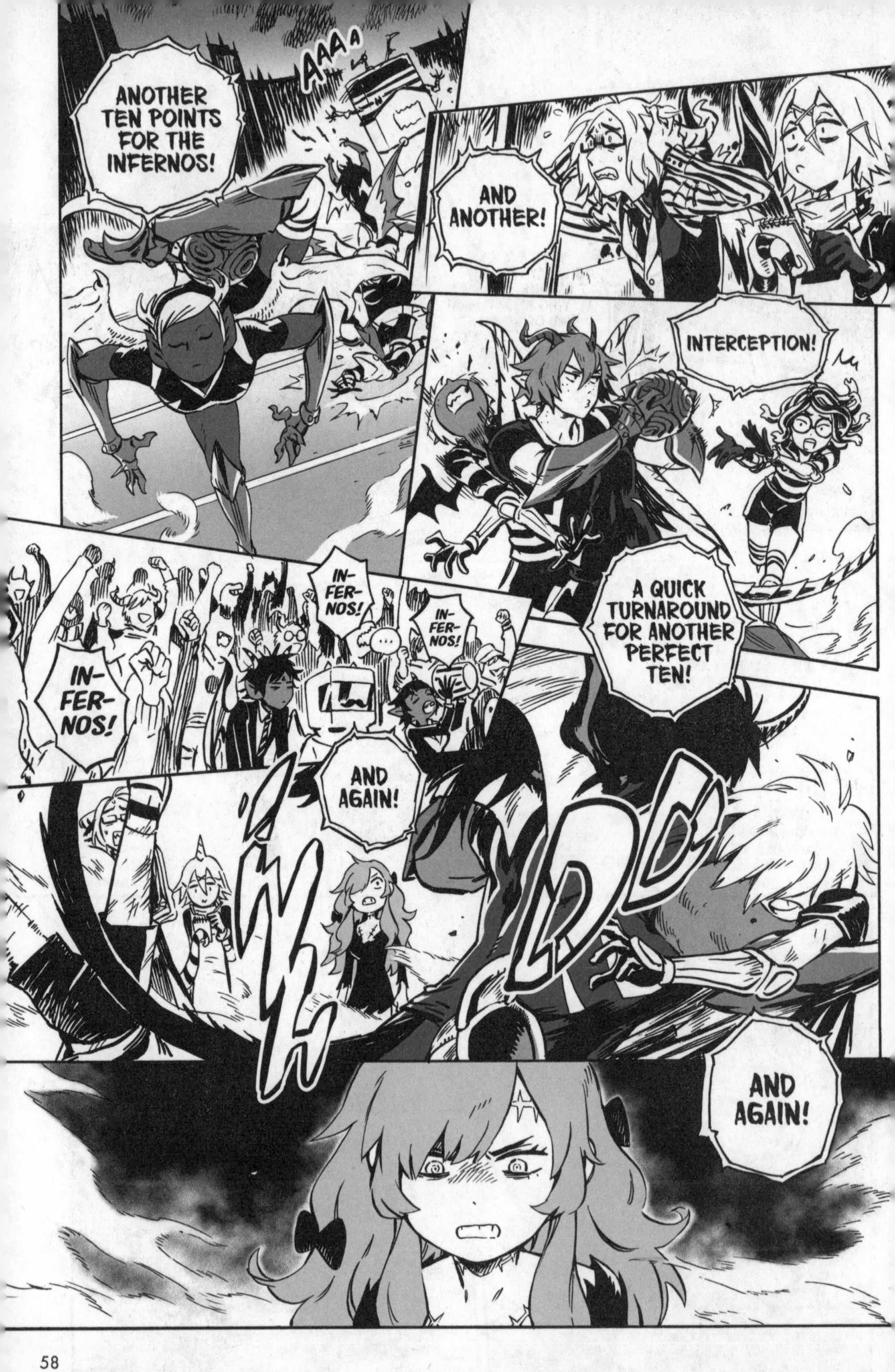

AAAA
ANOTHER TEN POINTS FOR THE INFERNOS!
AND ANOTHER!
INTERCEPTION!
A QUICK TURNAROUND FOR ANOTHER PERFECT TEN!
IN-FER-NOS!
IN-FER-NOS!
...
IN-FER-NOS!
AND AGAIN!
AND AGAIN!

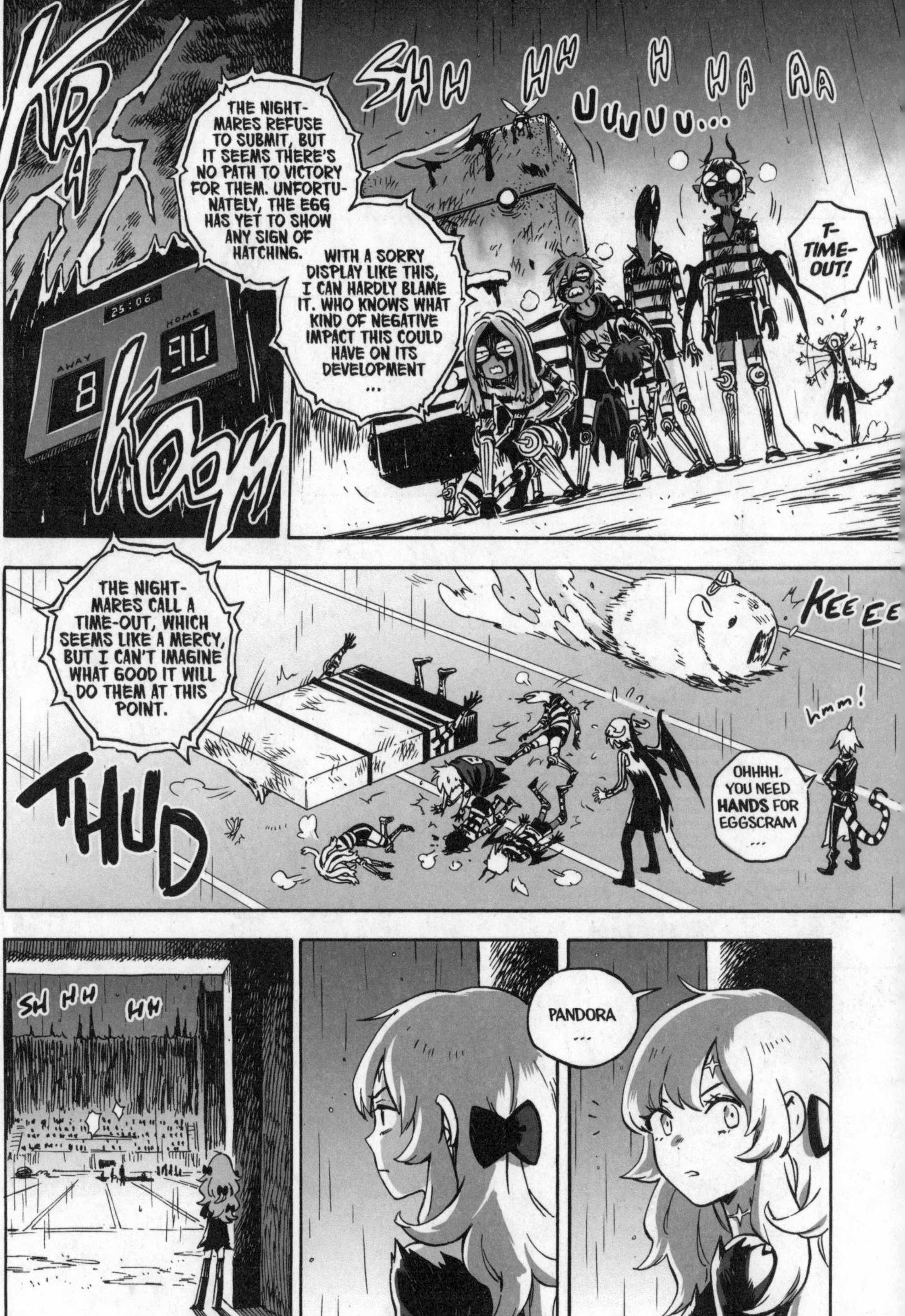
KRA-A-A
THE NIGHT-MARES REFUSE TO SUBMIT, BUT IT SEEMS THERE'S NO PATH TO VICTORY FOR THEM. UNFORTU-NATELY, THE EGG HAS YET TO SHOW ANY SIGN OF HATCHING.
25:06
HOME
AWAY
8
90
KOOM
SHH HH H HA AA
UUUUU...
WITH A SORRY DISPLAY LIKE THIS, I CAN HARDLY BLAME IT. WHO KNOWS WHAT KIND OF NEGATIVE IMPACT THIS COULD HAVE ON ITS DEVELOPMENT ...
T-TIME-OUT!
THE NIGHT-MARES CALL A TIME-OUT, WHICH SEEMS LIKE A MERCY, BUT I CAN'T IMAGINE WHAT GOOD IT WILL DO THEM AT THIS POINT.
KEE EE
THUD
hmm!
OHHHH. YOU NEED HANDS FOR EGGSCRAM ....
SH HH HH
PANDORA ...

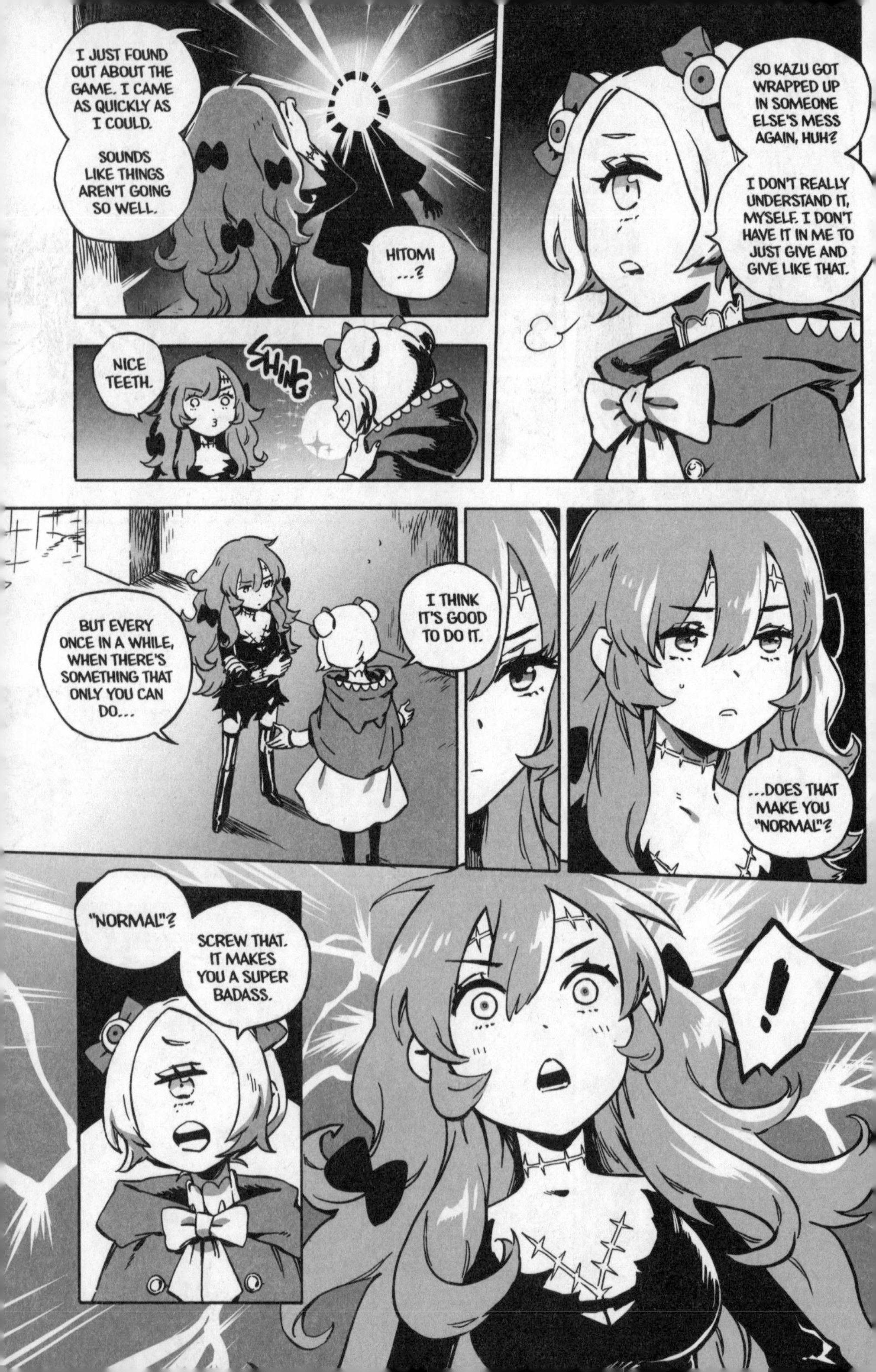
I JUST FOUND OUT ABOUT THE GAME. I CAME AS QUICKLY AS I COULD.
SOUNDS LIKE THINGS AREN'T GOING SO WELL.
HITOMI ...?
NICE TEETH.
SHING
SO KAZU GOT WRAPPED UP IN SOMEONE ELSE'S MESS AGAIN, HUH?
I DON'T REALLY UNDERSTAND IT, MYSELF. I DON'T HAVE IT IN ME TO JUST GIVE AND GIVE LIKE THAT.
BUT EVERY ONCE IN A WHILE, WHEN THERE'S SOMETHING THAT ONLY YOU CAN DO...
I THINK IT'S GOOD TO DO IT.
...DOES THAT MAKE YOU "NORMAL"?
"NORMAL"?
SCREW THAT. IT MAKES YOU A SUPER BADASS.
!

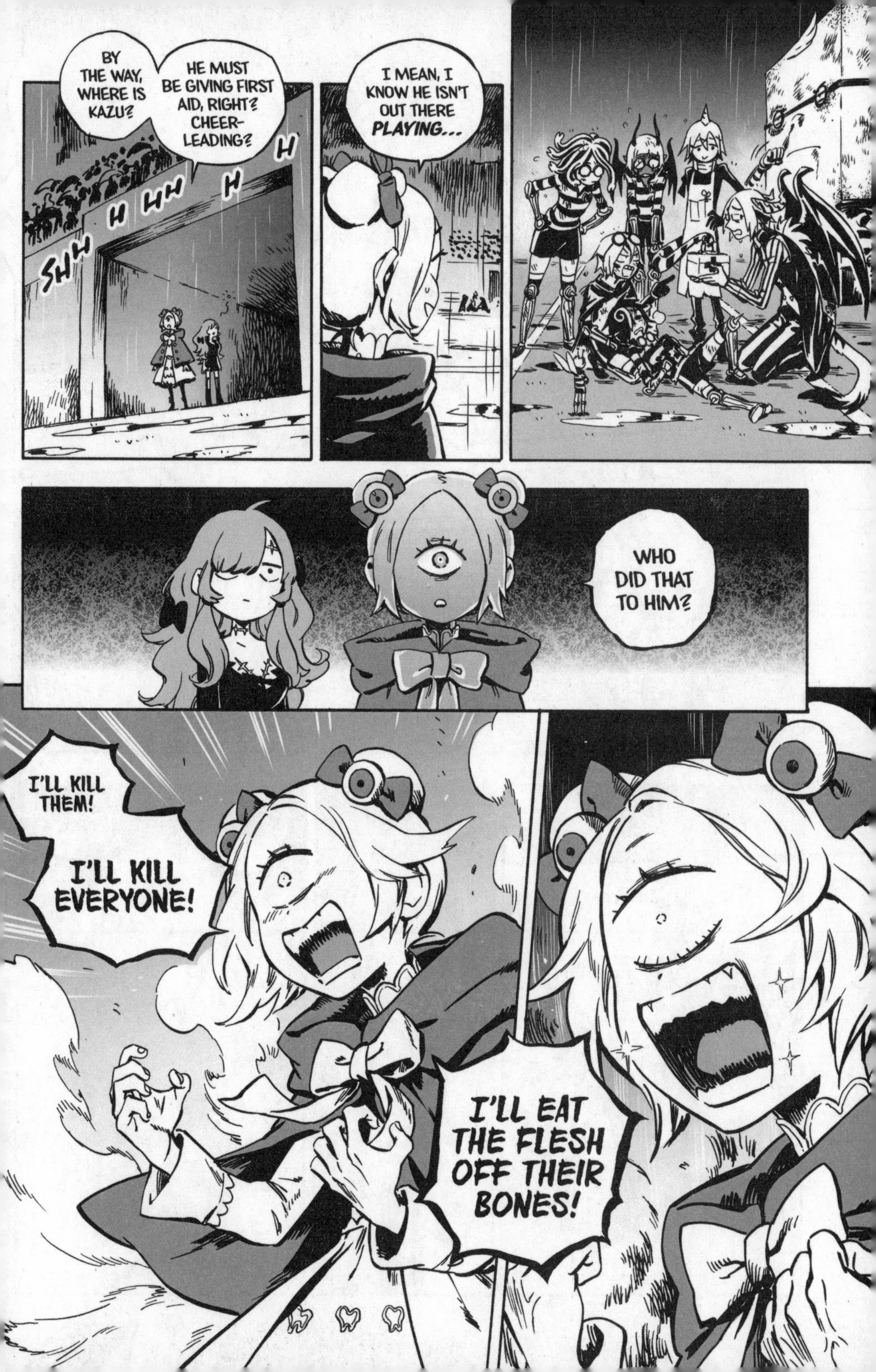
BY THE WAY, WHERE IS KAZU?
HE MUST BE GIVING FIRST AID, RIGHT? CHEER-LEADING?
SHHH H HHH H H
I MEAN, I KNOW HE ISN'T OUT THERE PLAYING...
WHO DID THAT TO HIM?
I'LL KILL THEM!
I'LL KILL EVERYONE!
I'LL EAT THE FLESH OFF THEIR BONES!

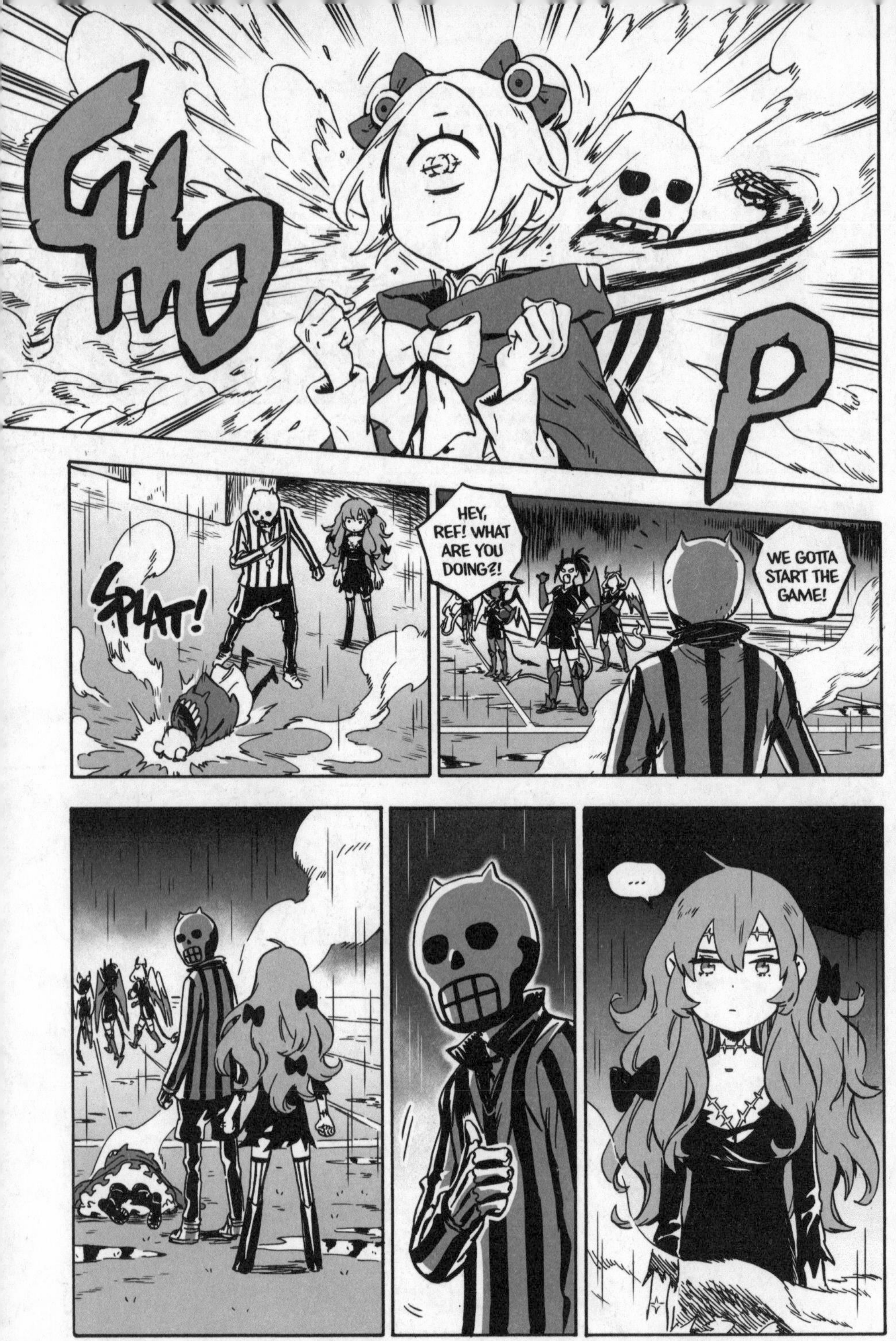
GWOP
SPLAT!
HEY, REF! WHAT ARE YOU DOING?!
WE GOTTA START THE GAME!
...

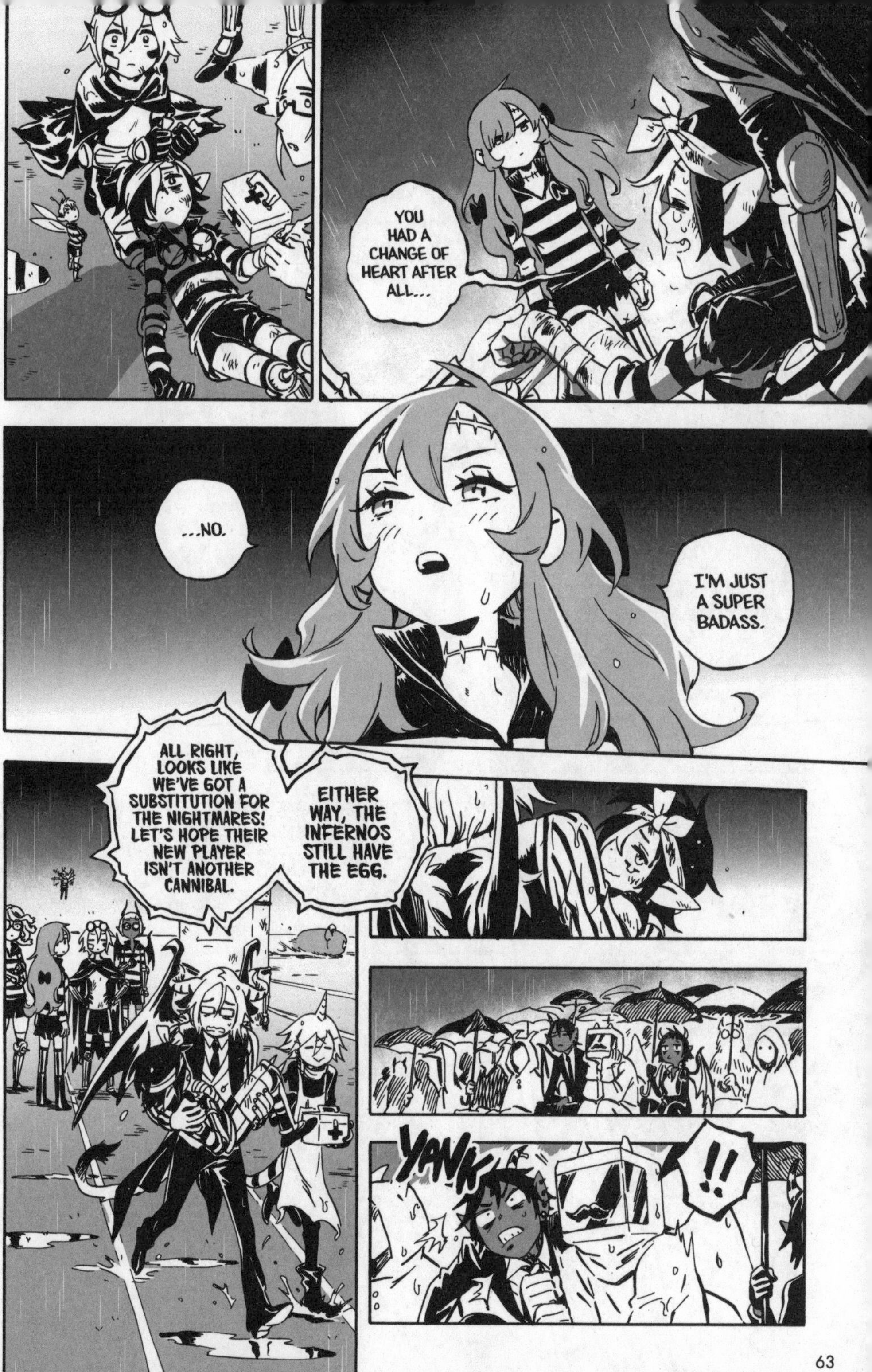
YOU HAD A CHANGE OF HEART AFTER ALL...
...NO.
I'M JUST A SUPER BADASS.
ALL RIGHT, LOOKS LIKE WE'VE GOT A SUBSTITUTION FOR THE NIGHTMARES! LET'S HOPE THEIR NEW PLAYER ISN'T ANOTHER CANNIBAL.
EITHER WAY, THE INFERNOS STILL HAVE THE EGG.
YANK
!!

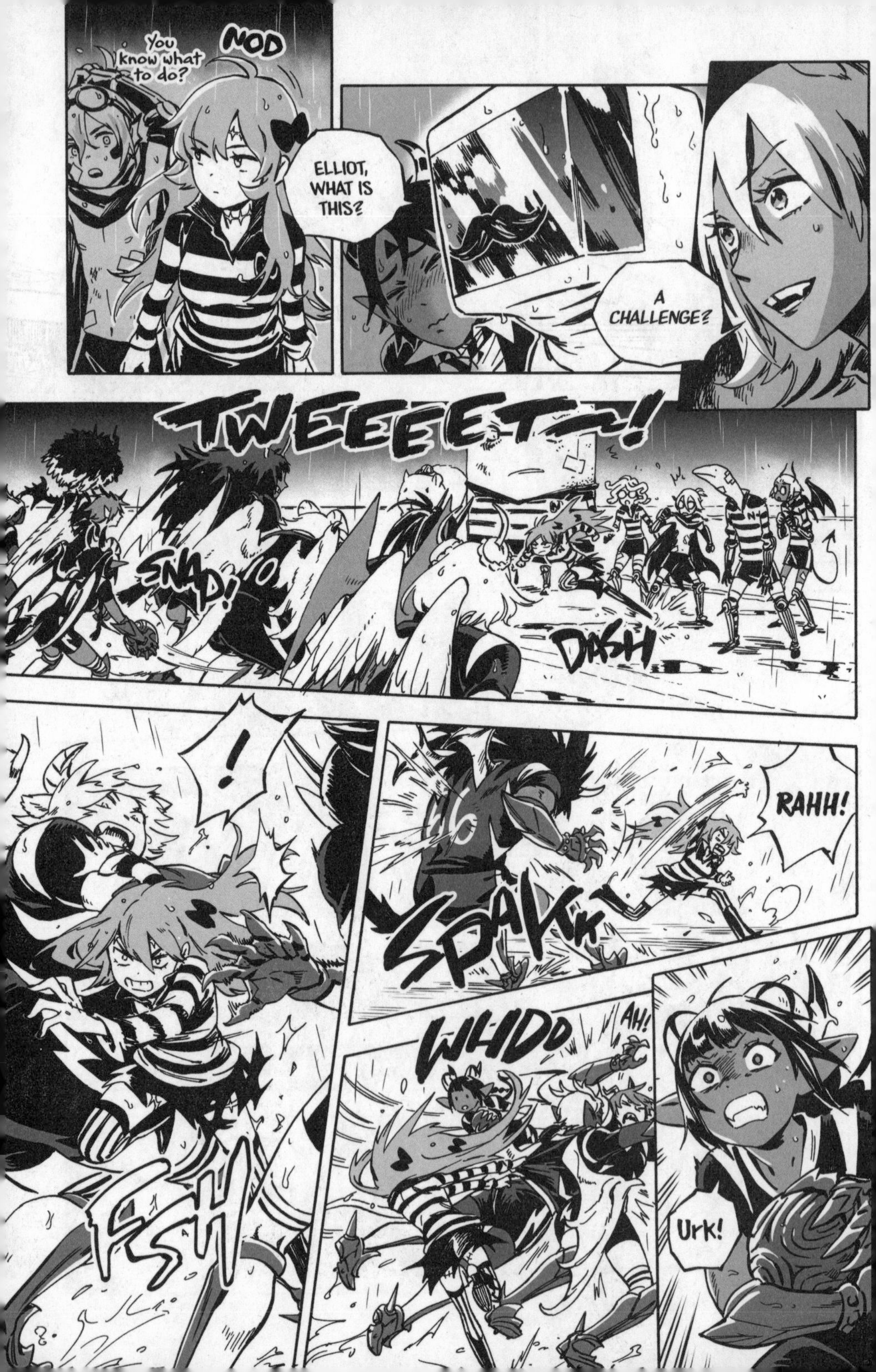
You know what to do?
NOD
ELLIOT, WHAT IS THIS?
A CHALLENGE?
TWEEEET~!
SNAP!
DASH
!
RAHH!
SPAKK
FSH
WHUD
AH!
Urk!

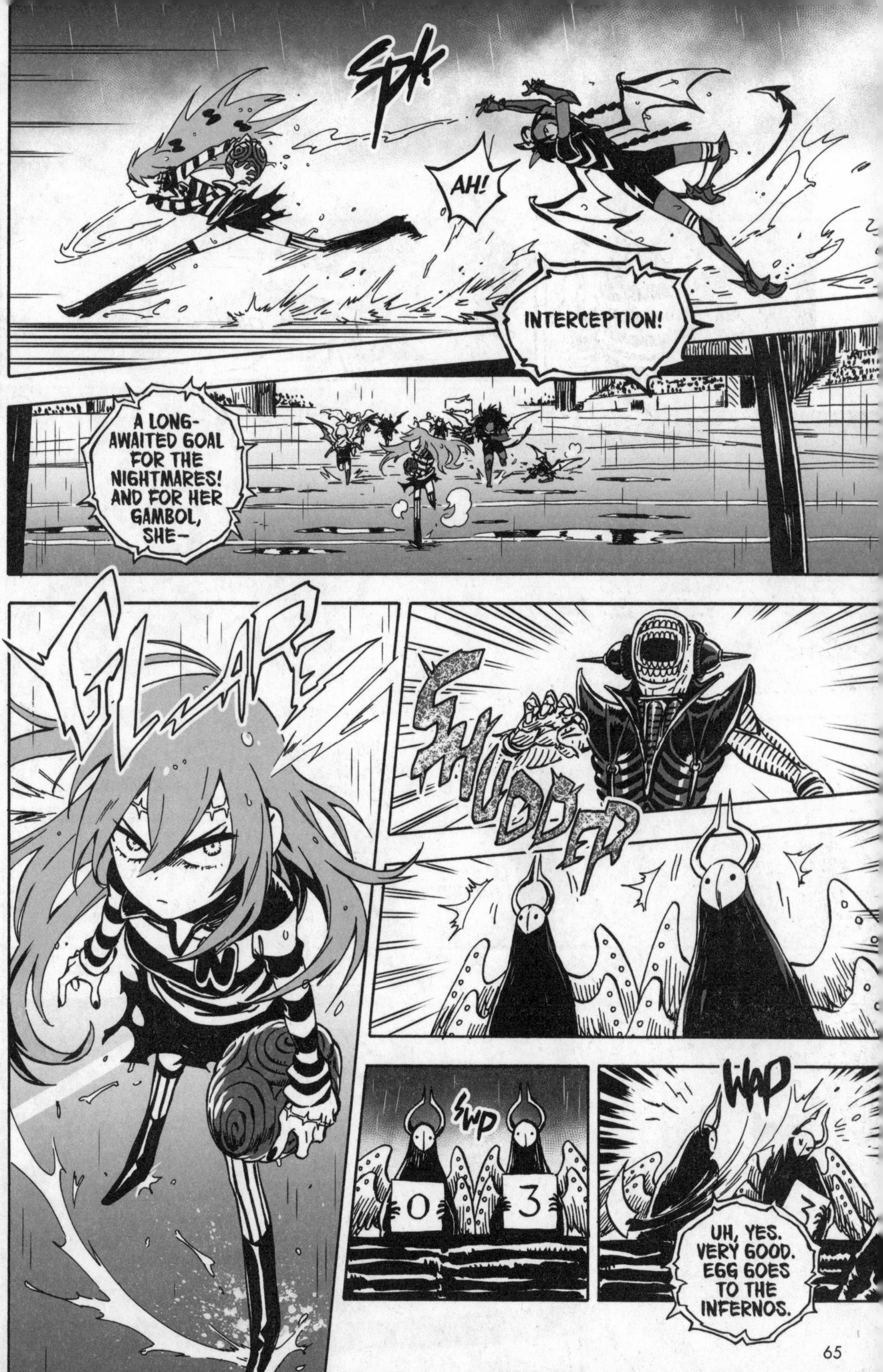
SPK
AH!
INTERCEPTION!
A LONG-AWAITED GOAL FOR THE NIGHTMARES! AND FOR HER GAMBOL, SHE-
GLARE
SHUDDER
SWP
0
3
WAP
UH, YES. VERY GOOD. EGG GOES TO THE INFERNOS.

YEAHHH!

I TAUGHT HER THAT ONE.

PUSH A LITTLE HARDER, GERALDO, AND I'LL BUY YOU AN EGG AFTER THE GAME.

I CAN HAS EGG?!

YOU SHOULD'VE TRIED THAT ONE SOONER...

WALTON, I GOT ONE PIECE OF ADVICE FOR YOU. SOMETIMES, IF YOU WANNA KEEP PEOPLE OUT, YOU GOTTA LET OTHER PEOPLE IN.

PEOPLE LIKE *ME*, WHO WANT TO HELP YOU BLOCK PEOPLE LIKE *THEM*.

B Zz z z

...

HEY! ARE YOU LISTENING TO ME, YOU *****ING MUPPET?!

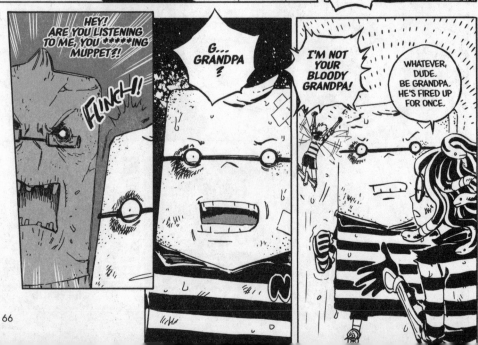

HEY! ARE YOU LISTENING TO ME, YOU *****ING MUPPET?!

FLINCH!

G... GRANDPA?

I'M NOT YOUR BLOODY GRANDPA!

WHATEVER, DUDE. BE GRANDPA. HE'S FIRED UP FOR ONCE.

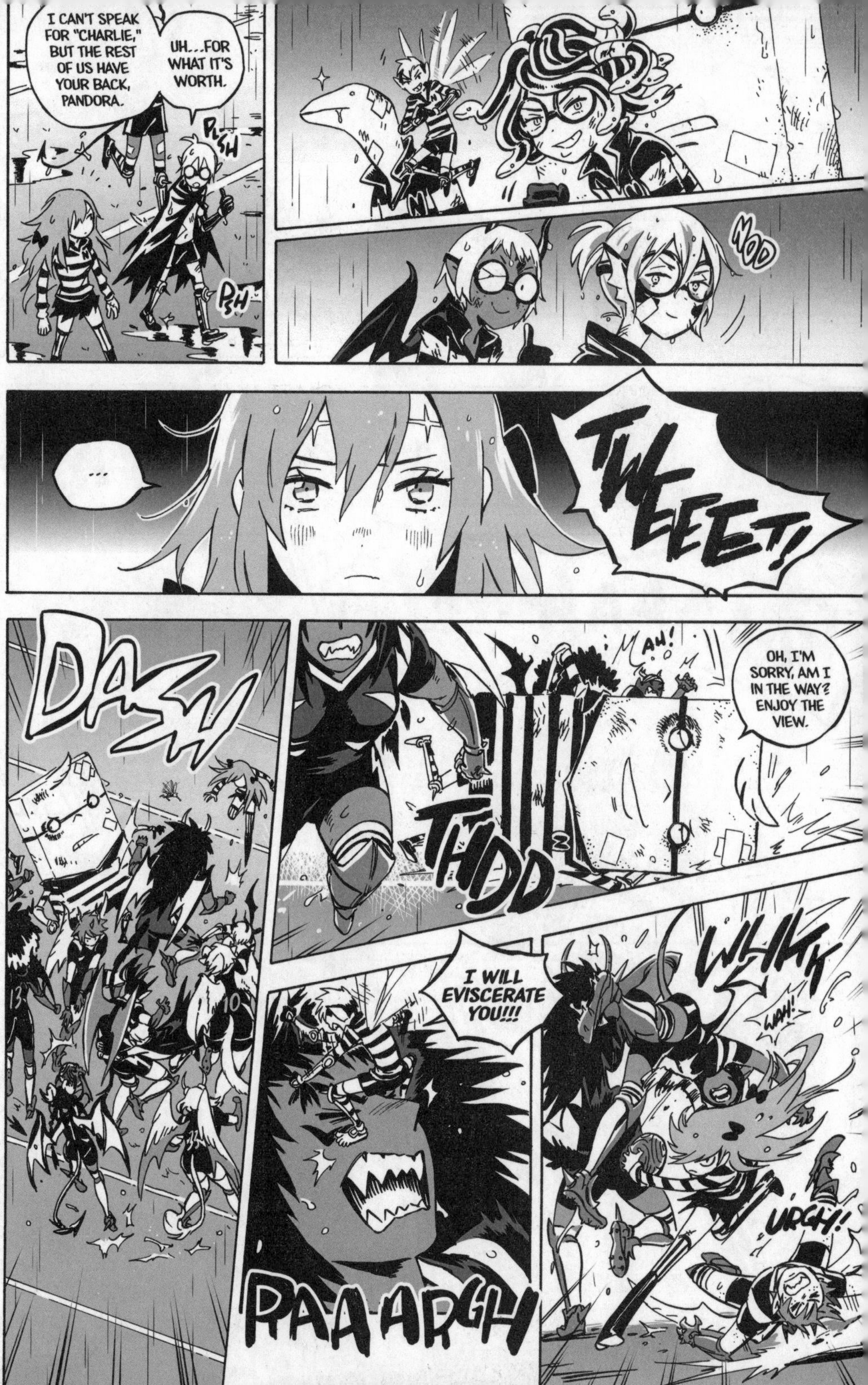
I CAN'T SPEAK FOR "CHARLIE," BUT THE REST OF US HAVE YOUR BACK, PANDORA.
UH...FOR WHAT IT'S WORTH.
PLISH
PSH
NOD
...
TWEEEET!
DASH
MAH!
OH, I'M SORRY, AM I IN THE WAY? ENJOY THE VIEW.
THDD
I WILL EVISCERATE YOU!!!
PAA ARGH
WHKK
WAH!
URGH!

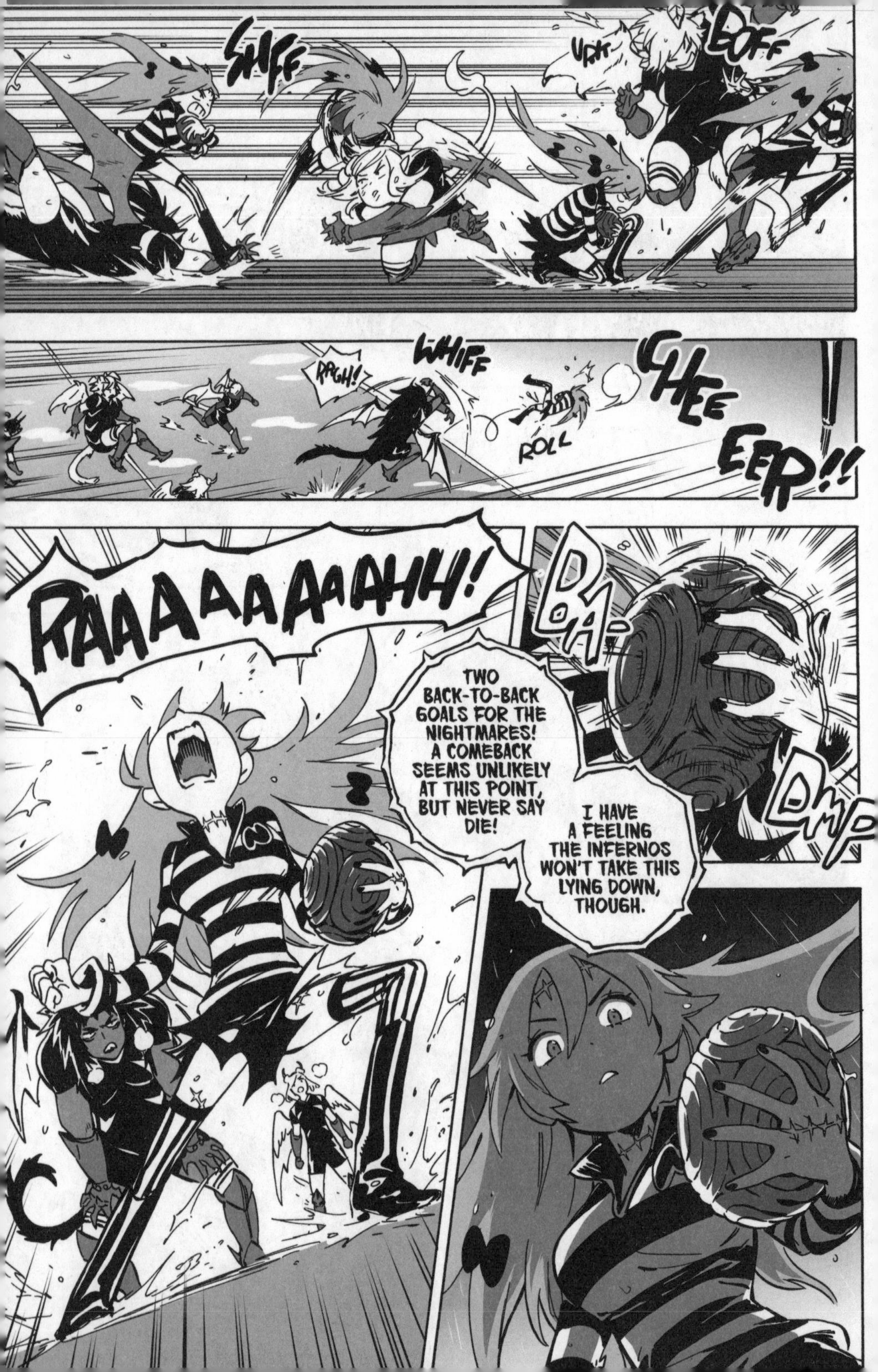
SHFF
URK
BOFF
RRGH!
WHIFF
ROLL
CHEEEER!!
RAAAAAAAAAHH!
BA-
DMP
TWO BACK-TO-BACK GOALS FOR THE NIGHTMARES! A COMEBACK SEEMS UNLIKELY AT THIS POINT, BUT NEVER SAY DIE!
I HAVE A FEELING THE INFERNOS WON'T TAKE THIS LYING DOWN, THOUGH.

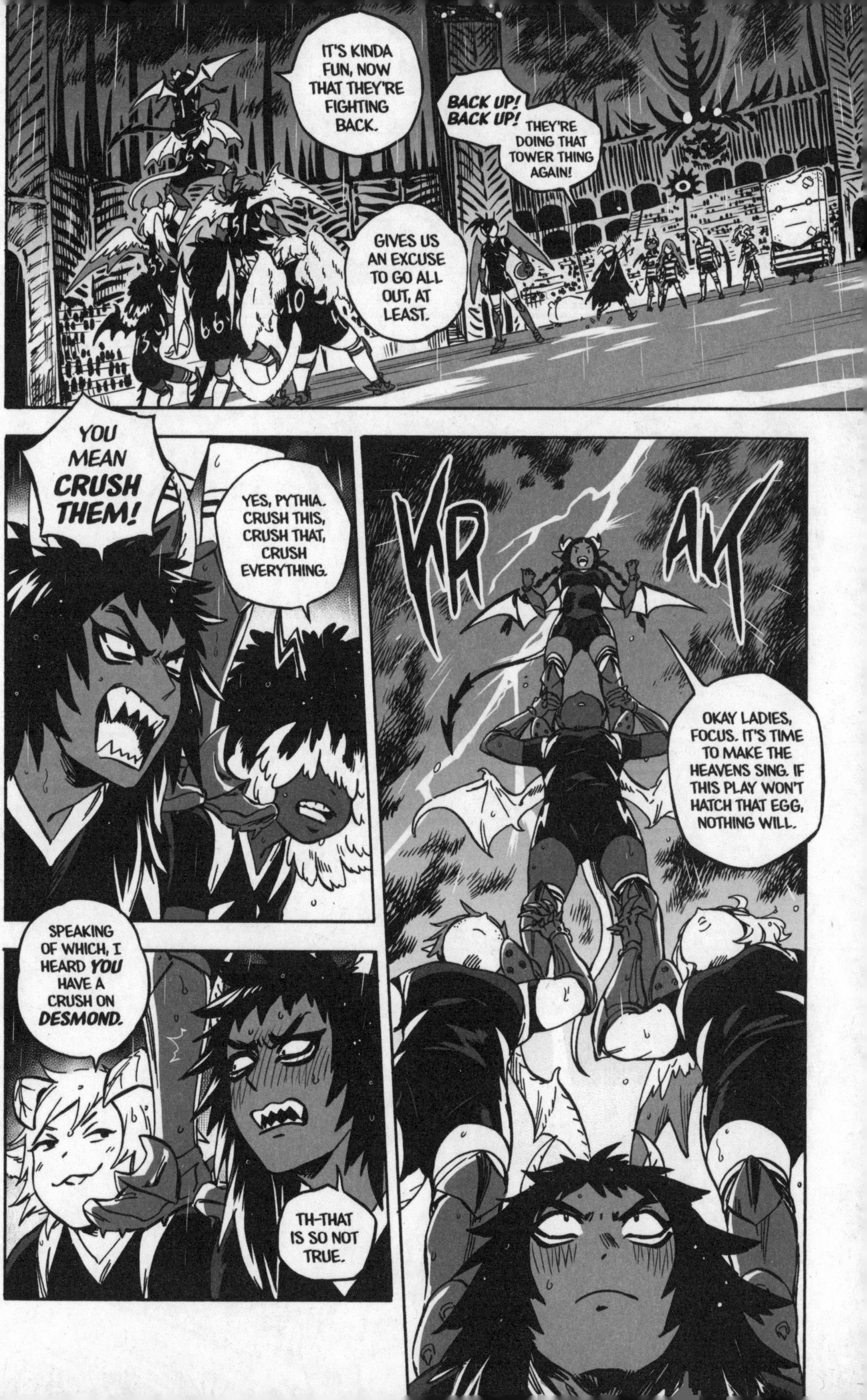
IT'S KINDA FUN, NOW THAT THEY'RE FIGHTING BACK.
BACK UP! BACK UP!
THEY'RE DOING THAT TOWER THING AGAIN!
GIVES US AN EXCUSE TO GO ALL OUT, AT LEAST.
YOU MEAN **CRUSH THEM!**
YES, PYTHIA. CRUSH THIS, CRUSH THAT, CRUSH EVERYTHING.
SPEAKING OF WHICH, I HEARD ***YOU*** HAVE A CRUSH ON ***DESMOND.***
TH-THAT IS SO NOT TRUE.
KRAK
OKAY LADIES, FOCUS. IT'S TIME TO MAKE THE HEAVENS SING. IF THIS PLAY WON'T HATCH THAT EGG, NOTHING WILL.

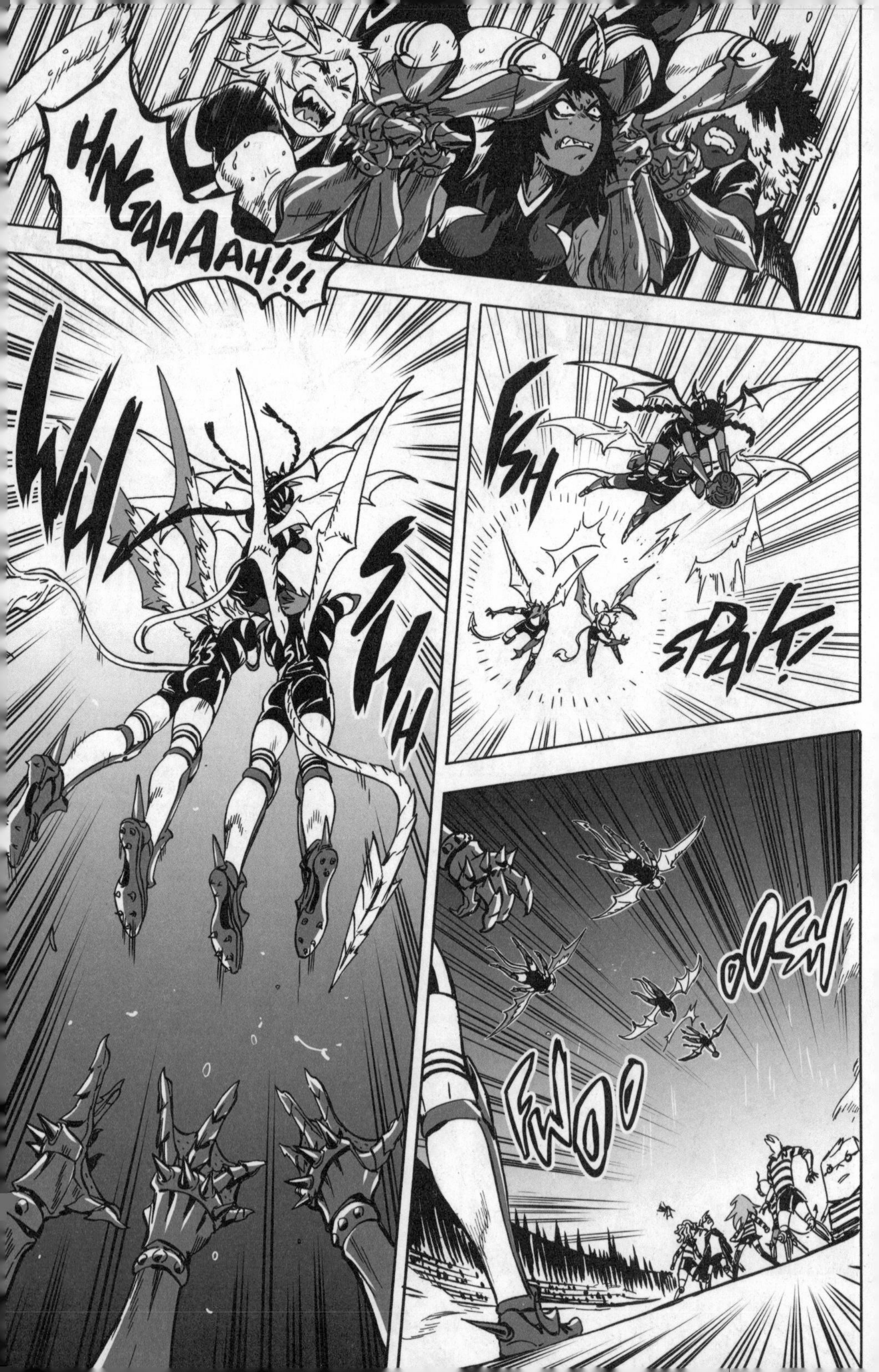
HNGAAAAAH!!!
WU
SHH
FSH
SPAK!
FWOO
OOSH

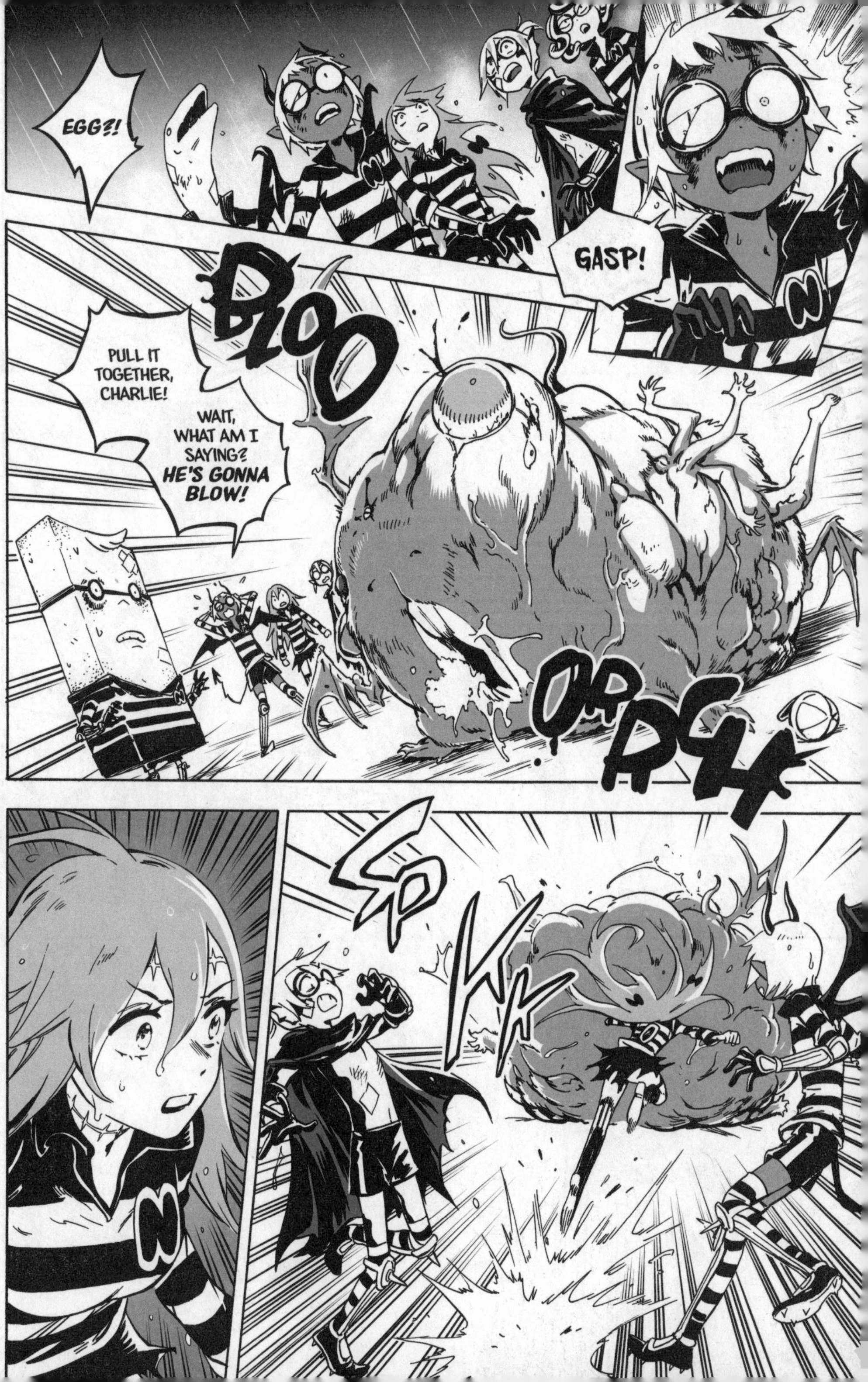
EGG?!
GASP!
PULL IT TOGETHER, CHARLIE!
WAIT, WHAT AM I SAYING? HE'S GONNA BLOW!

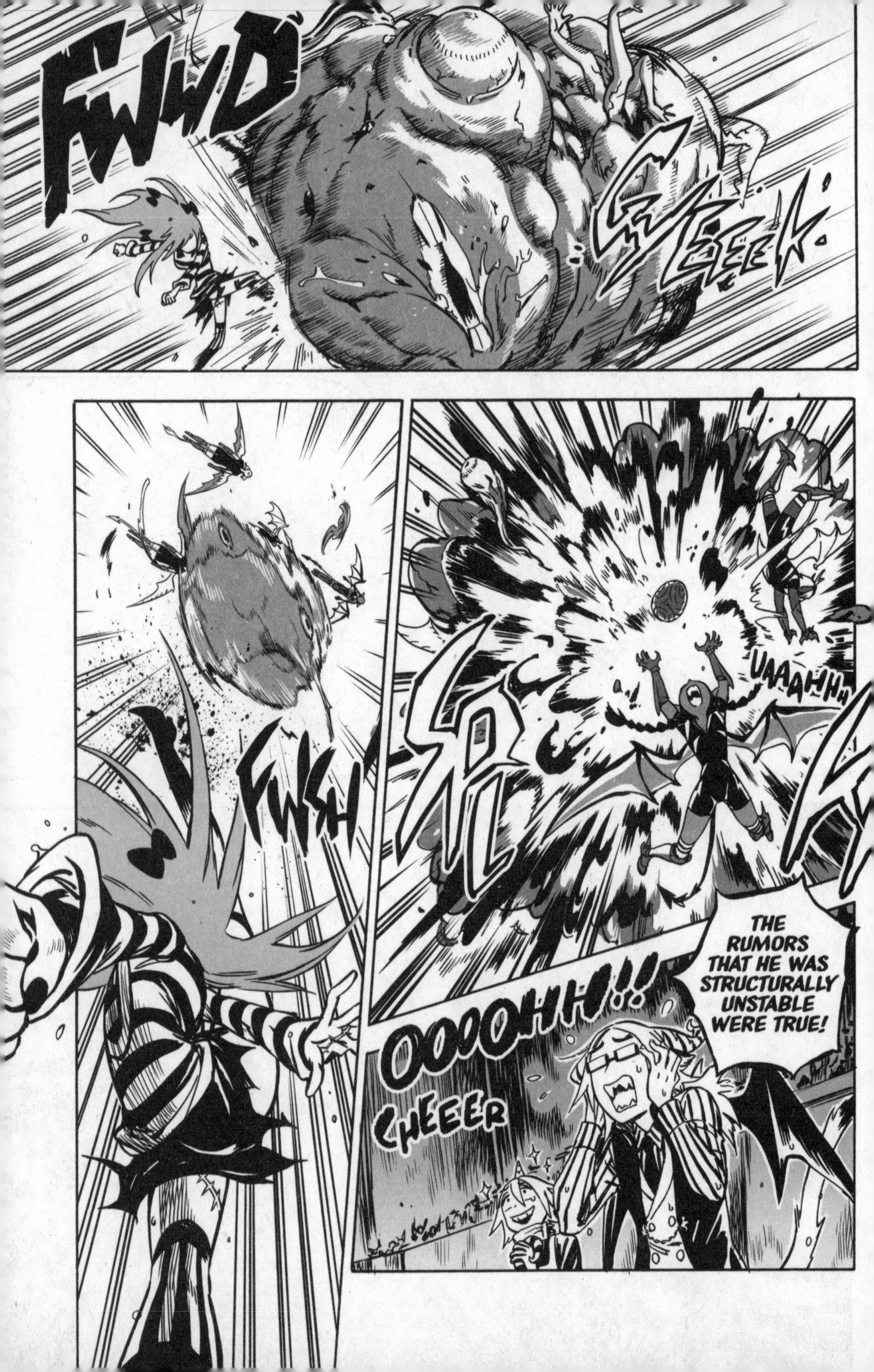
FWUD
GYEEEK
FWSH
UAAAHHH
OOOOHHH!!
CHEEER
THE RUMORS THAT HE WAS STRUCTURALLY UNSTABLE WERE TRUE!

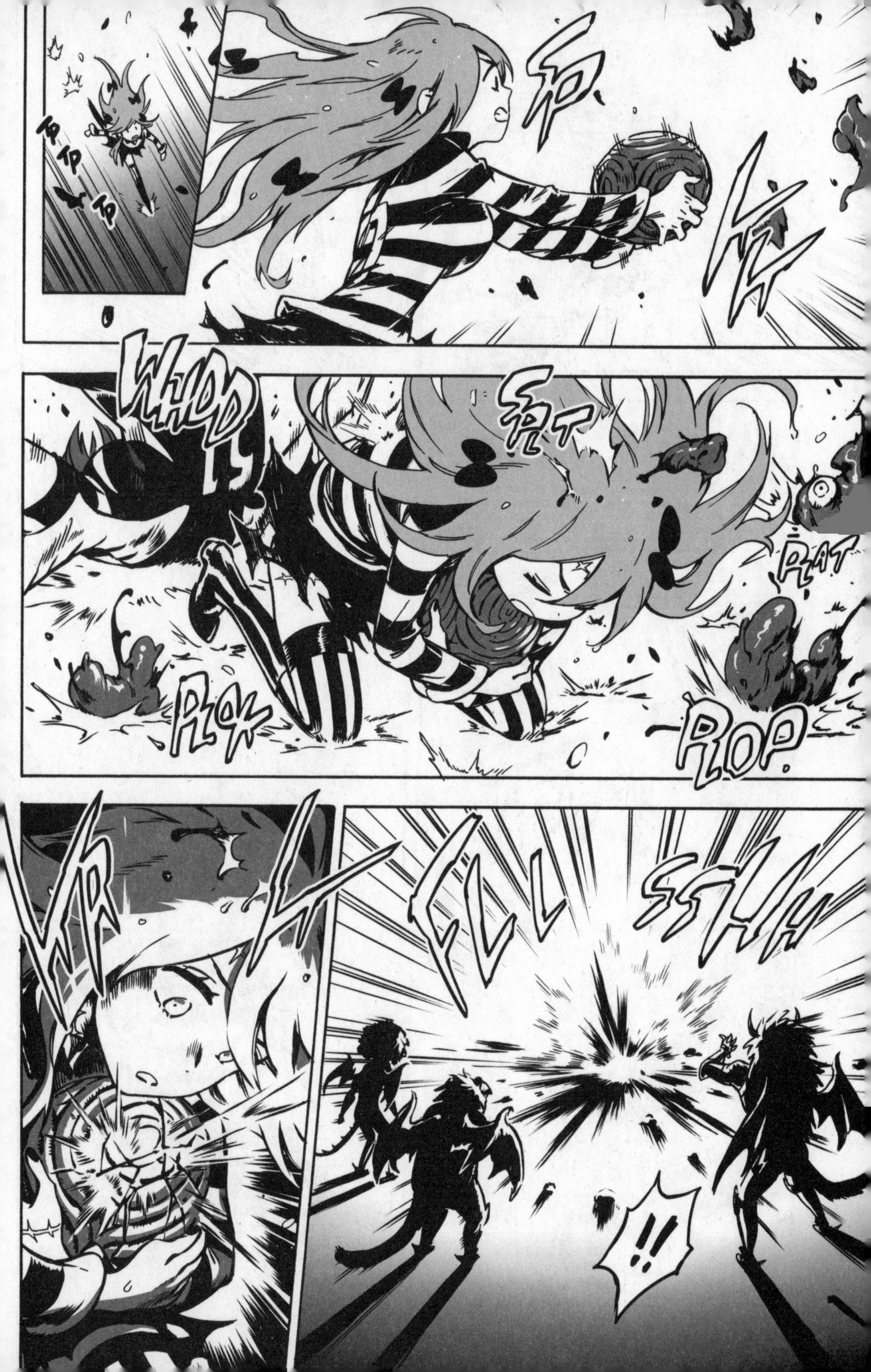
TP
TP
TP
TP
FP.
WHOO
PLAT
PLOP.
!!

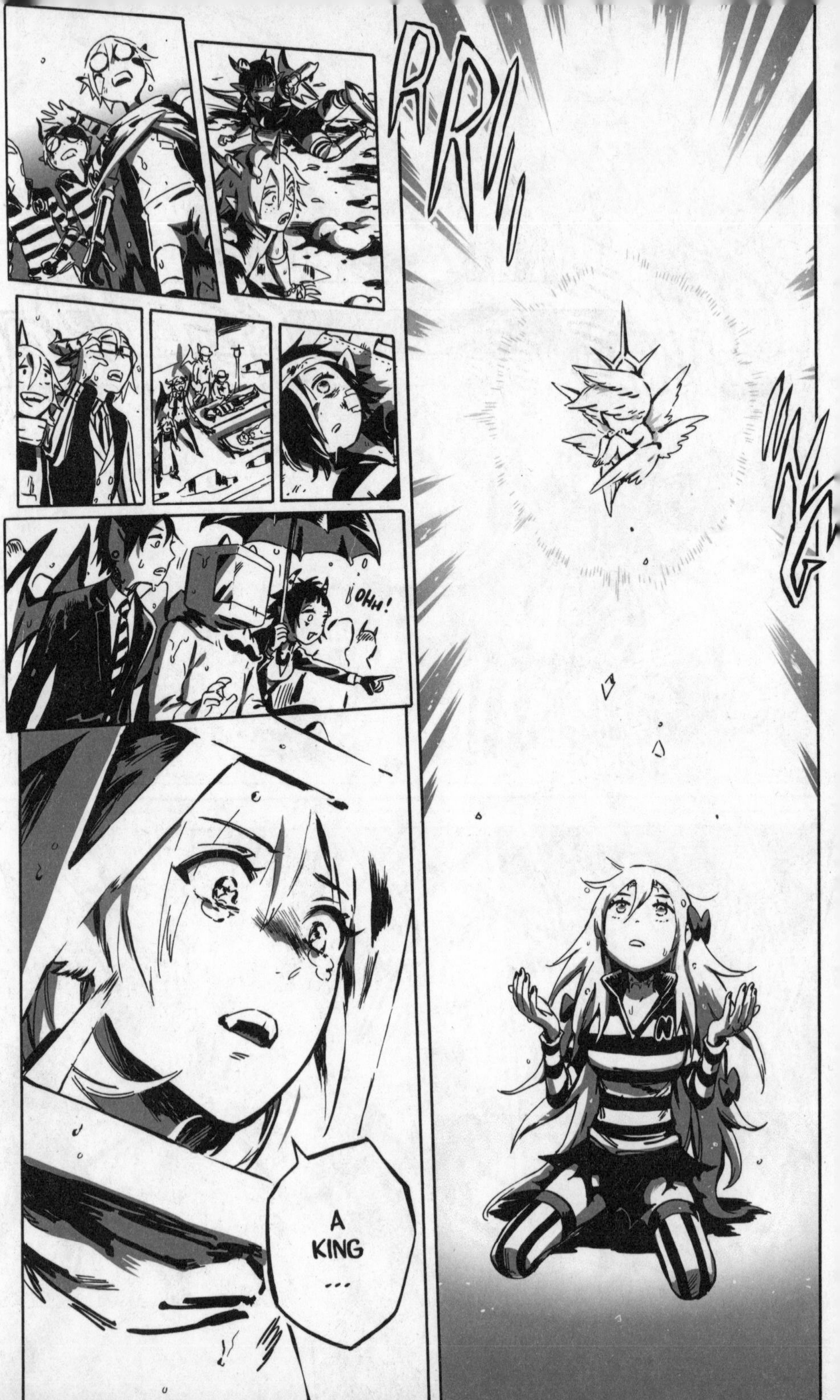

¡OHH!
A KING ...
RRI
NG

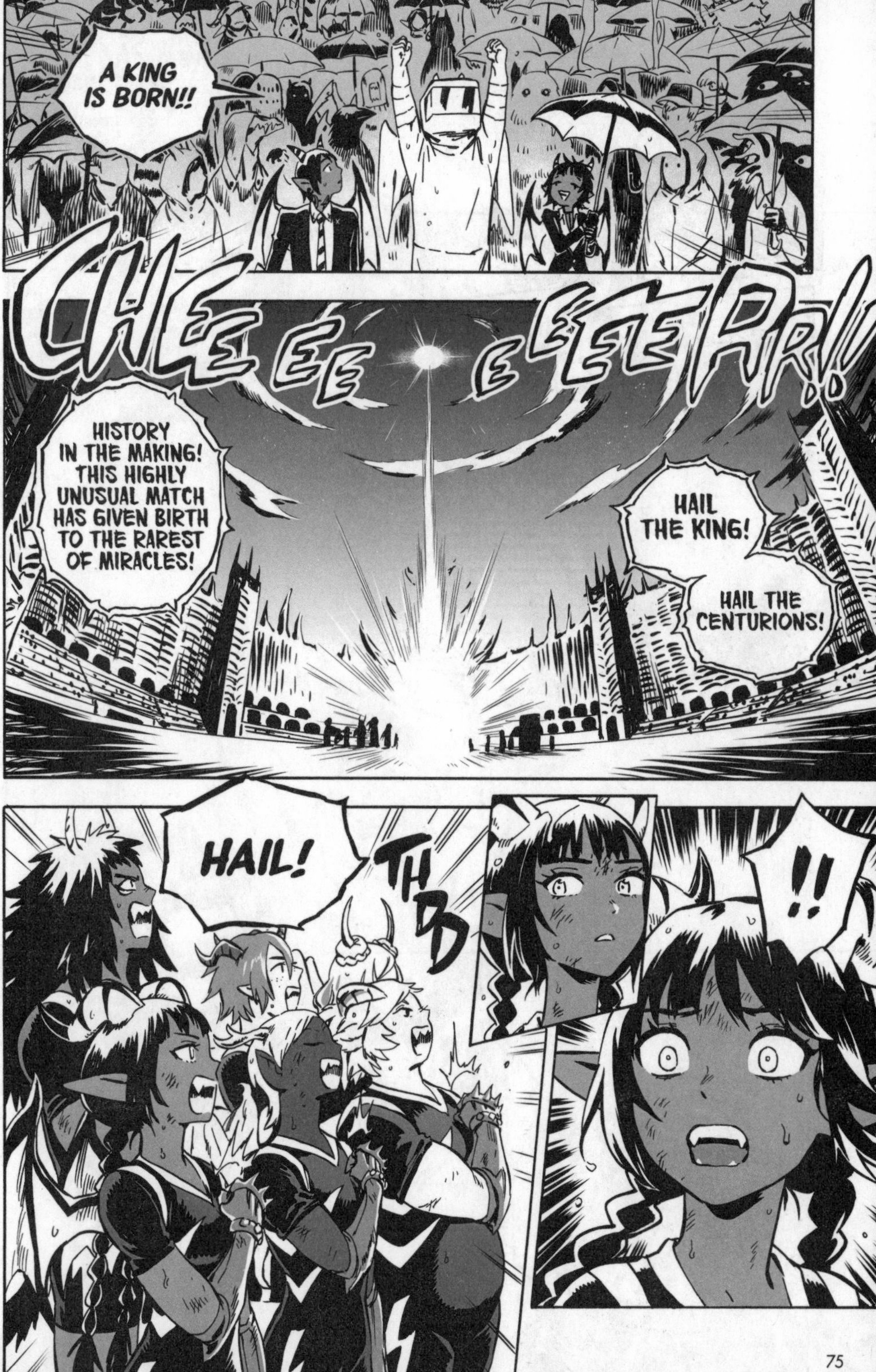
A KING IS BORN!!
CHEEEEEEEEERR!!
HISTORY IN THE MAKING! THIS HIGHLY UNUSUAL MATCH HAS GIVEN BIRTH TO THE RAREST OF MIRACLES!
HAIL THE KING!
HAIL THE CENTURIONS!
HAIL!
THBD
!!

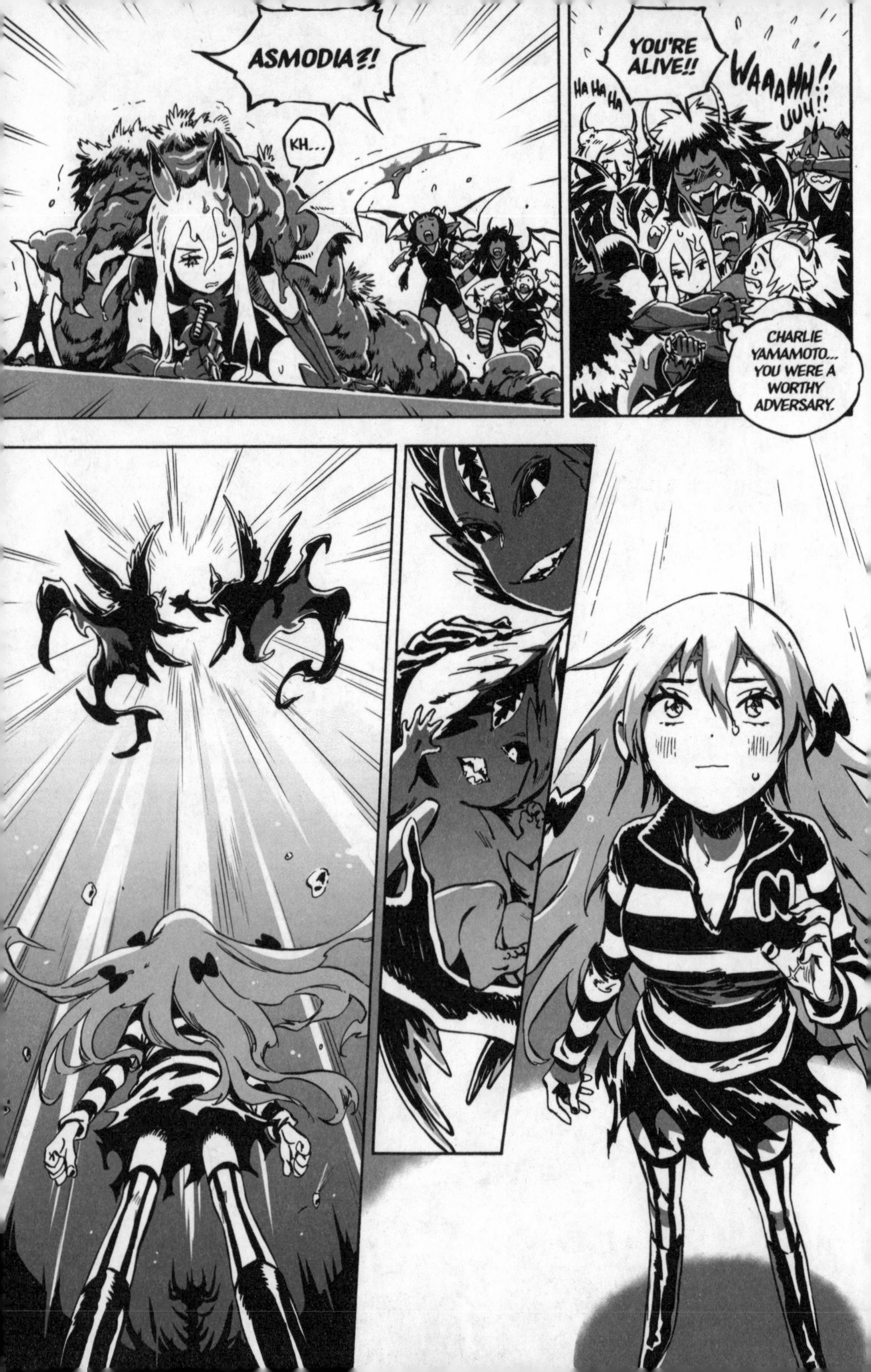
ASMODIA?!
KH...
YOU'RE ALIVE!!
HA HA HA
WAAAHH!!
UUH!!
CHARLIE YAMAMOTO... YOU WERE A WORTHY ADVERSARY.

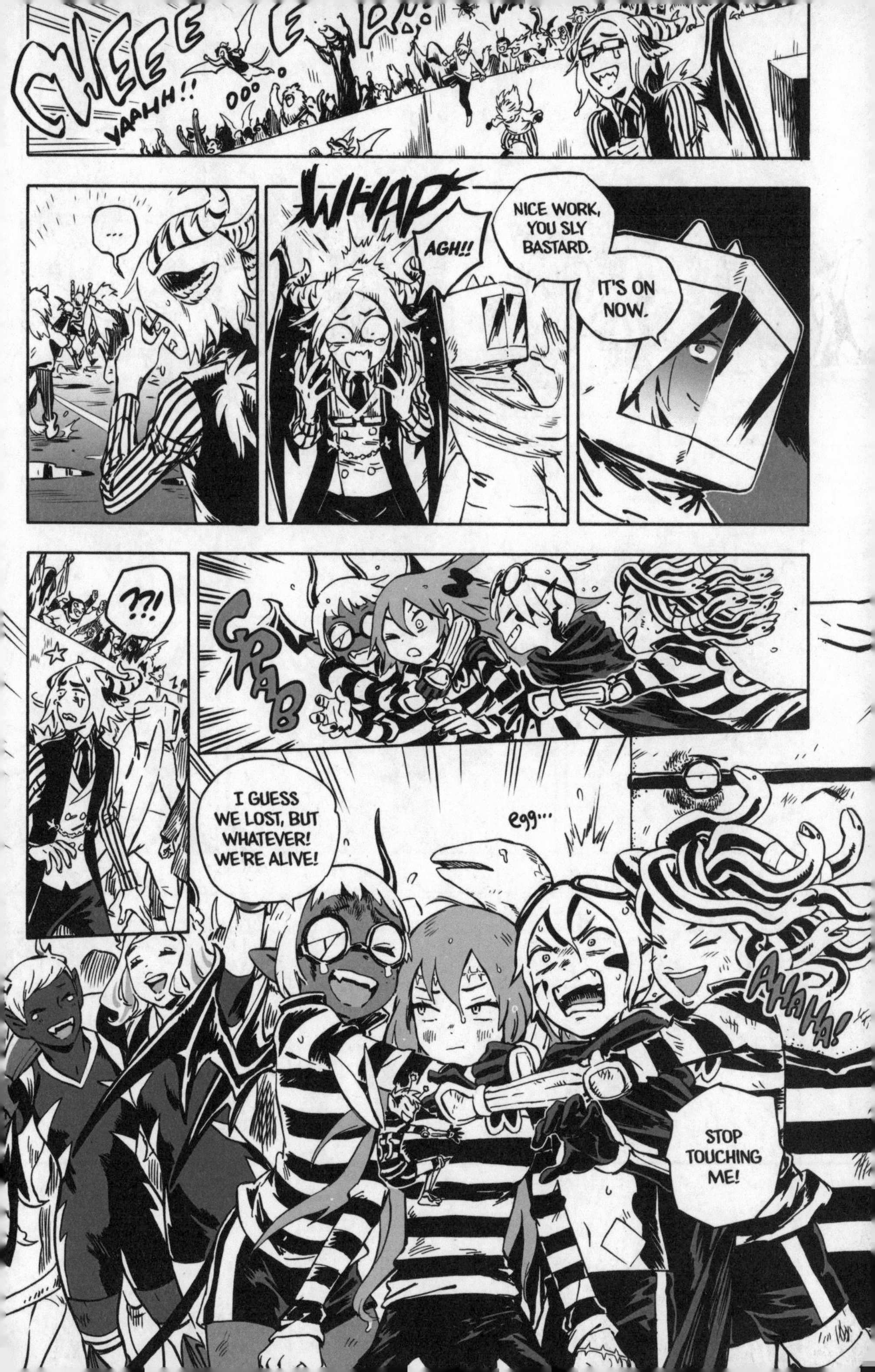

YAAHH!!
OOO
...
WHAP
AGH!!
NICE WORK, YOU SLY BASTARD.
IT'S ON NOW.
??!
GRAB
I GUESS WE LOST, BUT WHATEVER! WE'RE ALIVE!
egg...
AHAHA!
STOP TOUCHING ME!

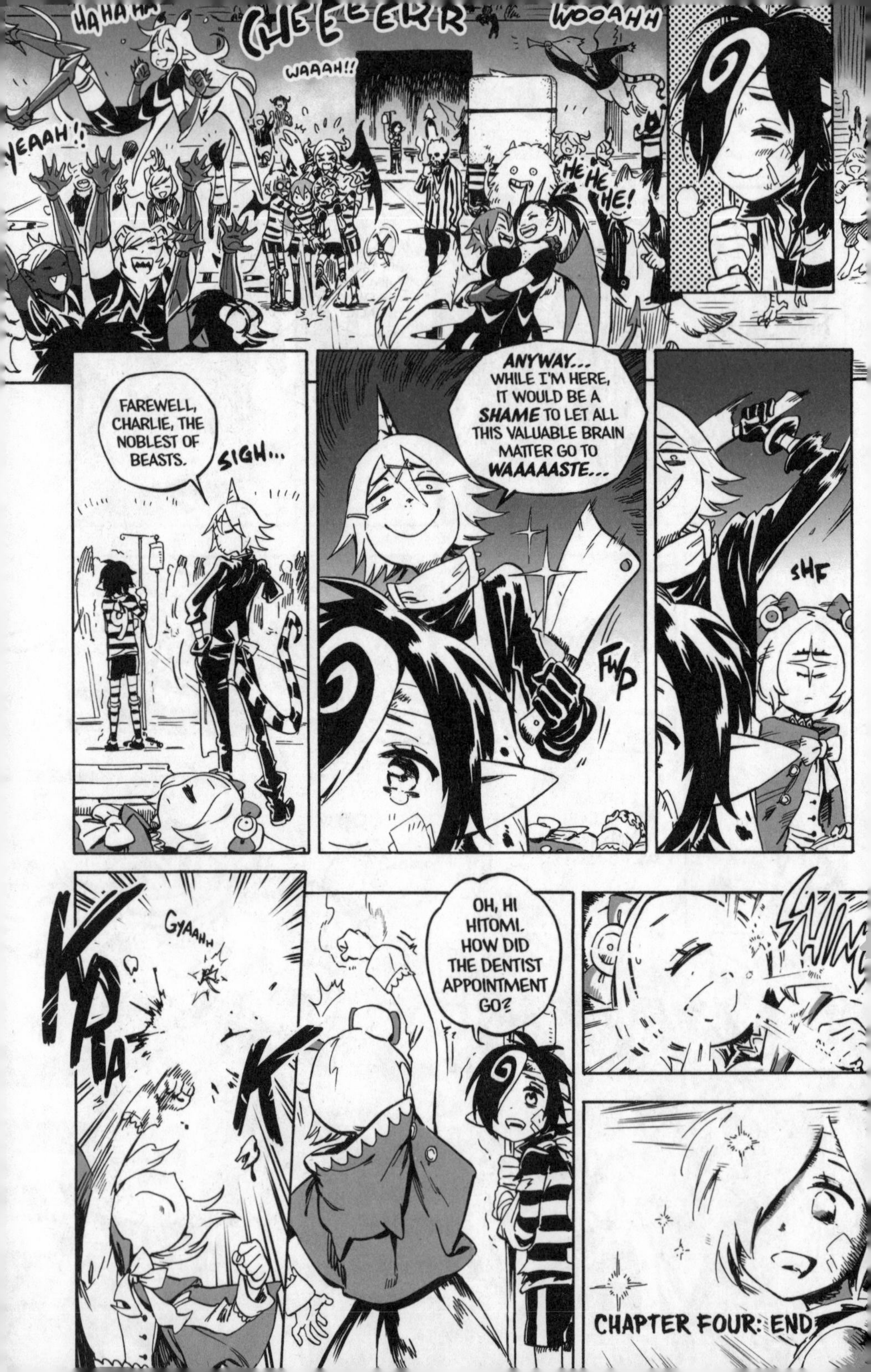
HAHAHA
CHEEEERR
WAAAH!!
WOOAHH
YEAAH!!
HE HE HE!
FAREWELL, CHARLIE, THE NOBLEST OF BEASTS.
SIGH...
ANYWAY... WHILE I'M HERE, IT WOULD BE A SHAME TO LET ALL THIS VALUABLE BRAIN MATTER GO TO WAAAAASTE...
FWP
SHF
KRAK
GYAAHH
OH, HI HITOMI. HOW DID THE DENTIST APPOINTMENT GO?
SHING
CHAPTER FOUR: END

HOME LIFE

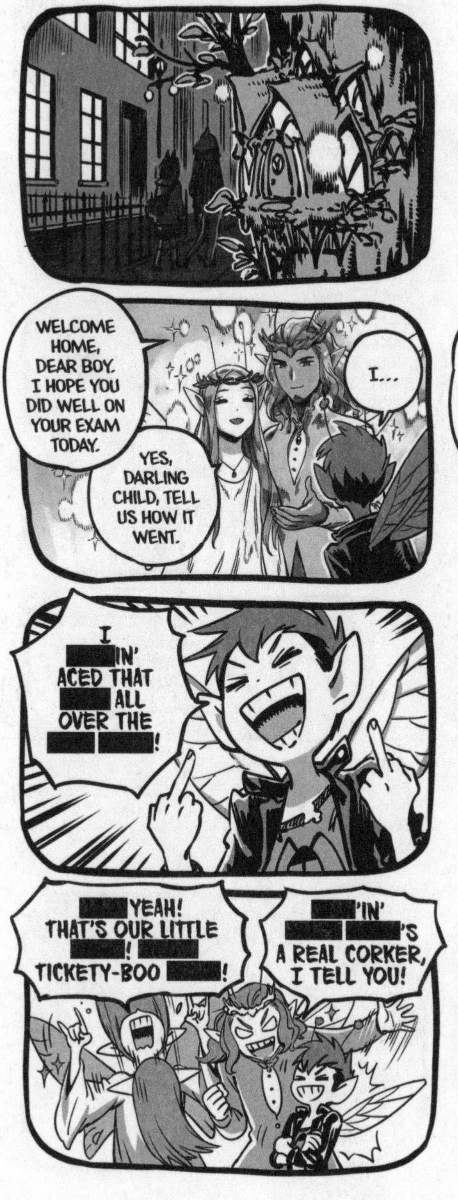
WELCOME HOME, DEAR BOY. I HOPE YOU DID WELL ON YOUR EXAM TODAY.
I...
YES, DARLING CHILD, TELL US HOW IT WENT.
I [redacted]IN' ACED THAT [redacted] ALL OVER THE [redacted] [redacted]!
[redacted] YEAH! THAT'S OUR LITTLE [redacted]! [redacted] TICKETY-BOO [redacted]!
[redacted]'IN' [redacted] [redacted]'S A REAL CORKER, I TELL YOU!

LOVE LIFE

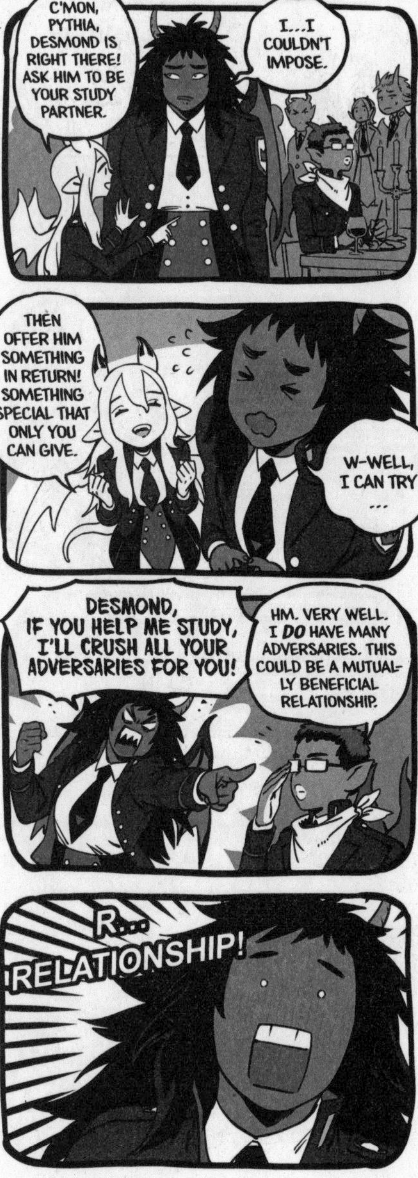
C'MON, PYTHIA, DESMOND IS RIGHT THERE! ASK HIM TO BE YOUR STUDY PARTNER.
I...I COULDN'T IMPOSE.
THEN OFFER HIM SOMETHING IN RETURN! SOMETHING SPECIAL THAT ONLY YOU CAN GIVE.
W-WELL, I CAN TRY ...
DESMOND, IF YOU HELP ME STUDY, I'LL CRUSH ALL YOUR ADVERSARIES FOR YOU!
HM. VERY WELL. I *DO* HAVE MANY ADVERSARIES. THIS COULD BE A MUTUALLY BENEFICIAL RELATIONSHIP.
R... RELATIONSHIP!

NIGHT LIFE

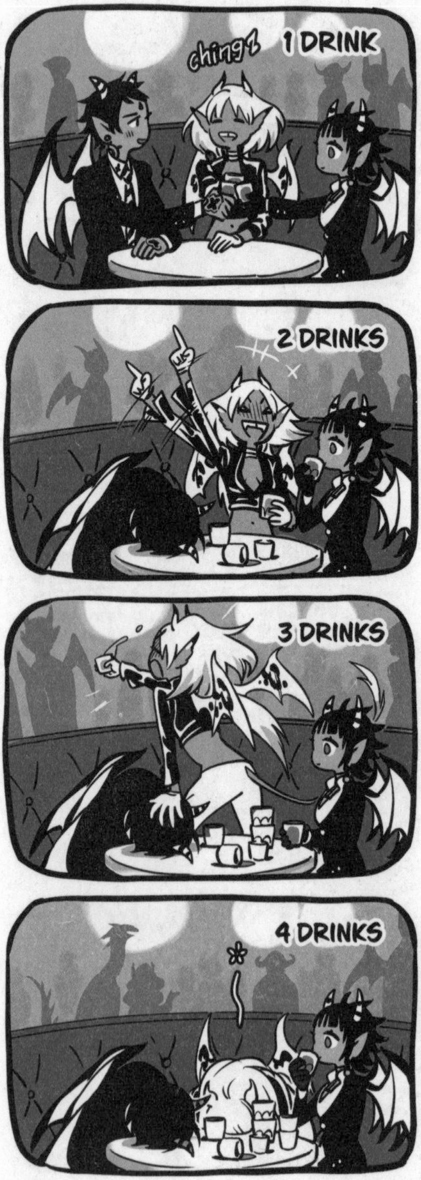
ching!
1 DRINK
2 DRINKS
3 DRINKS
4 DRINKS

SPACE LIFE

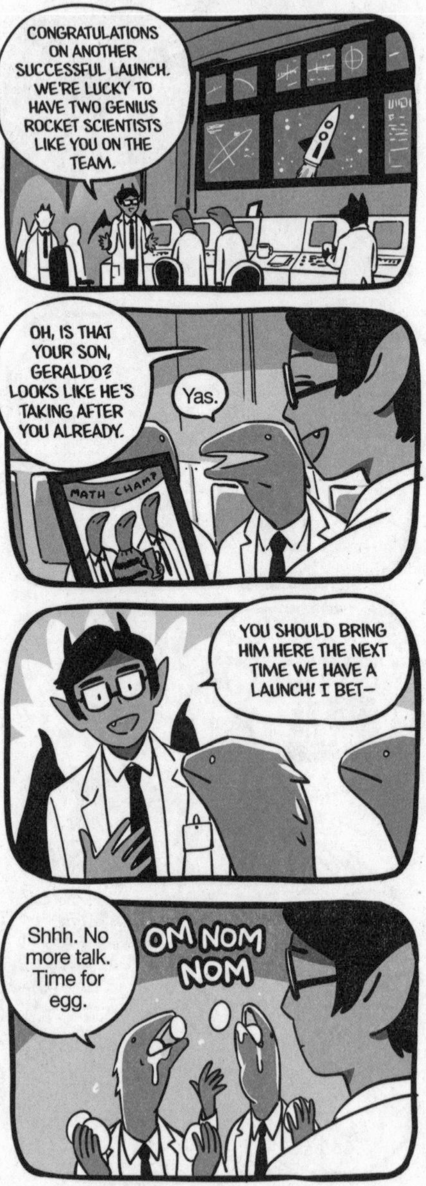
CONGRATULATIONS ON ANOTHER SUCCESSFUL LAUNCH. WE'RE LUCKY TO HAVE TWO GENIUS ROCKET SCIENTISTS LIKE YOU ON THE TEAM.
OH, IS THAT YOUR SON, GERALDO? LOOKS LIKE HE'S TAKING AFTER YOU ALREADY.
Yas.
MATH CHAMP
YOU SHOULD BRING HIM HERE THE NEXT TIME WE HAVE A LAUNCH! I BET—
Shhh. No more talk. Time for egg.
OM NOM NOM

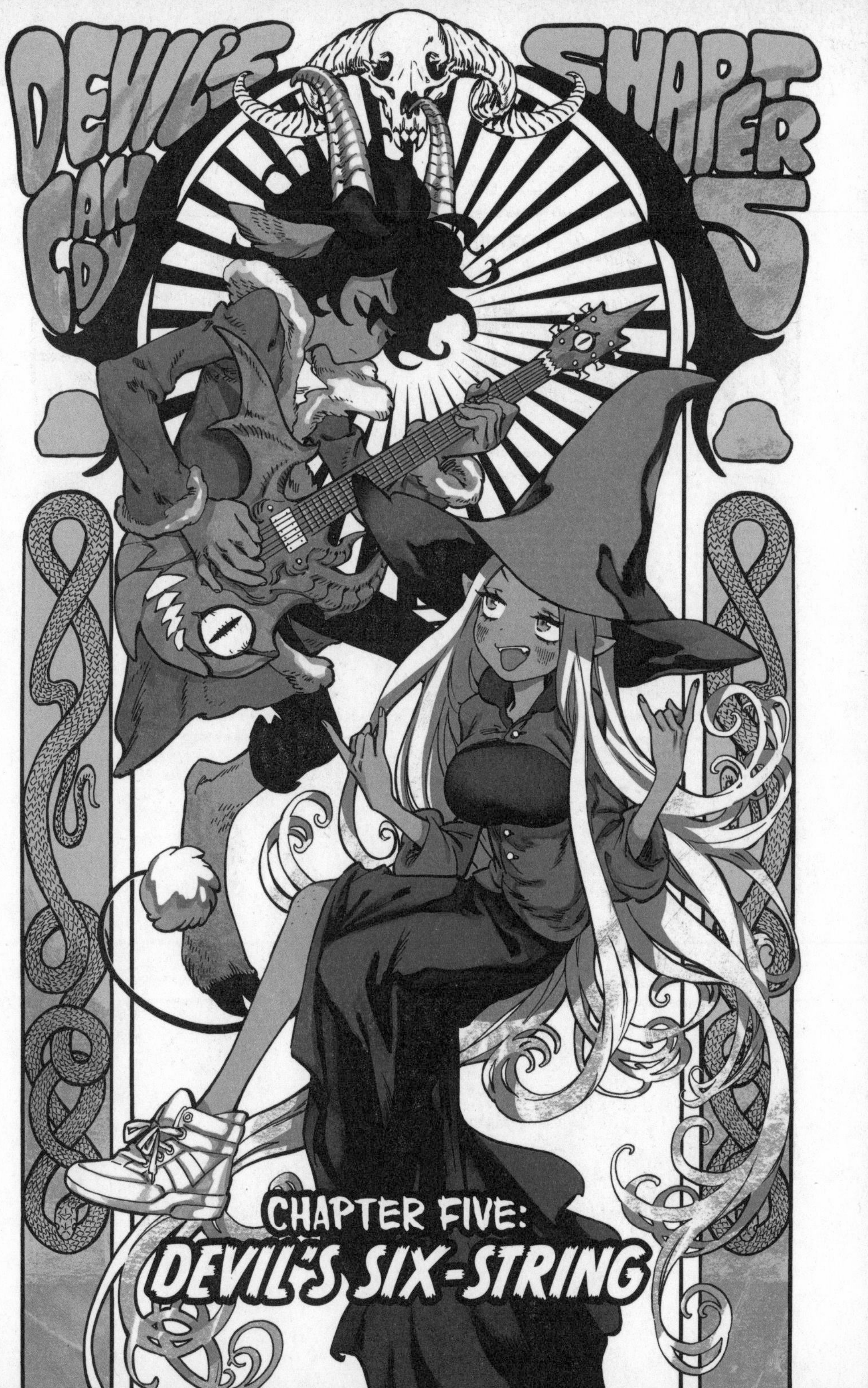
DEVIL'S CANDY
CHAPTER 5
CHAPTER FIVE:
DEVIL'S SIX-STRING

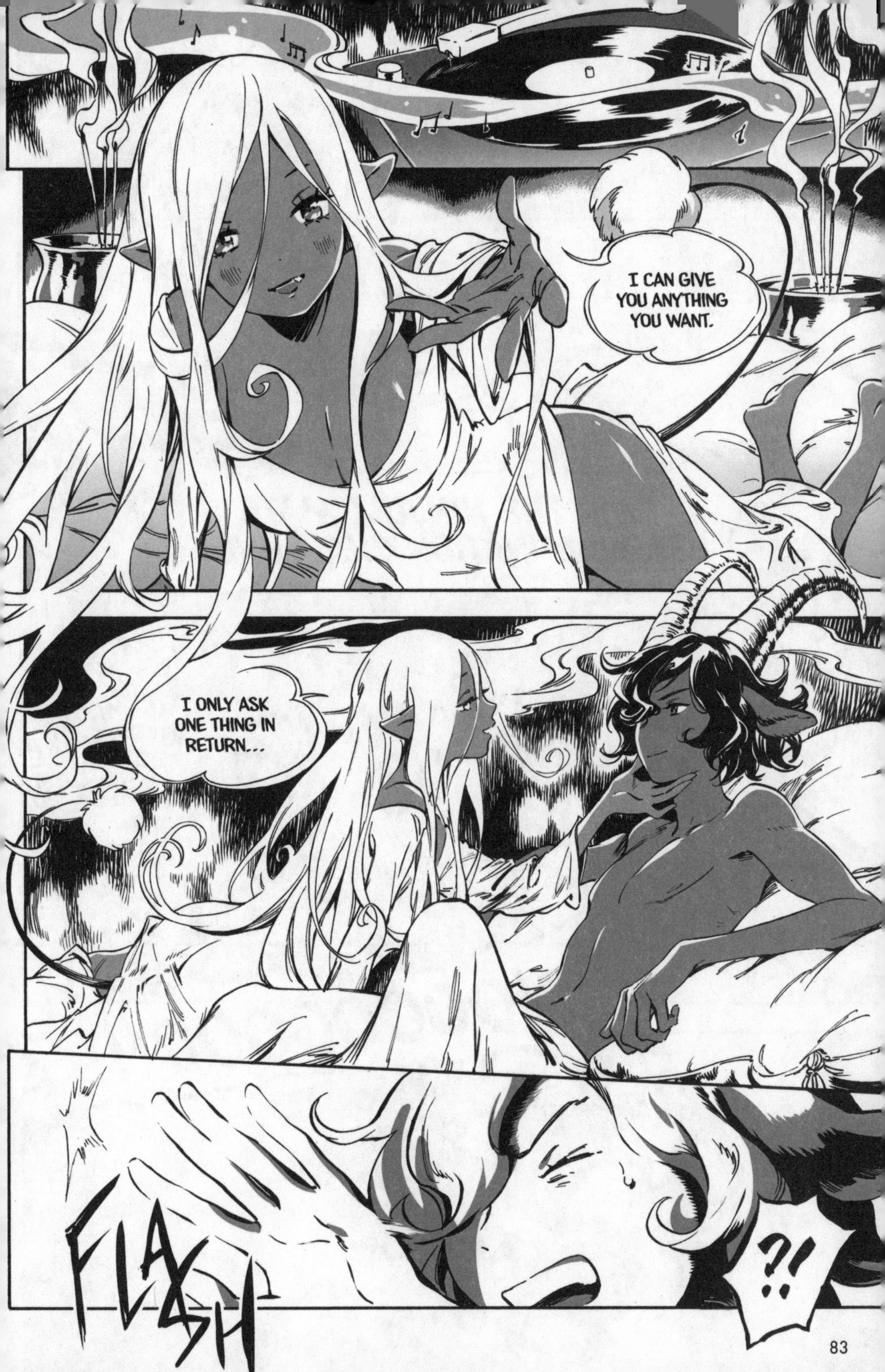
I CAN GIVE YOU ANYTHING YOU WANT.
I ONLY ASK ONE THING IN RETURN...
FLASH
?!

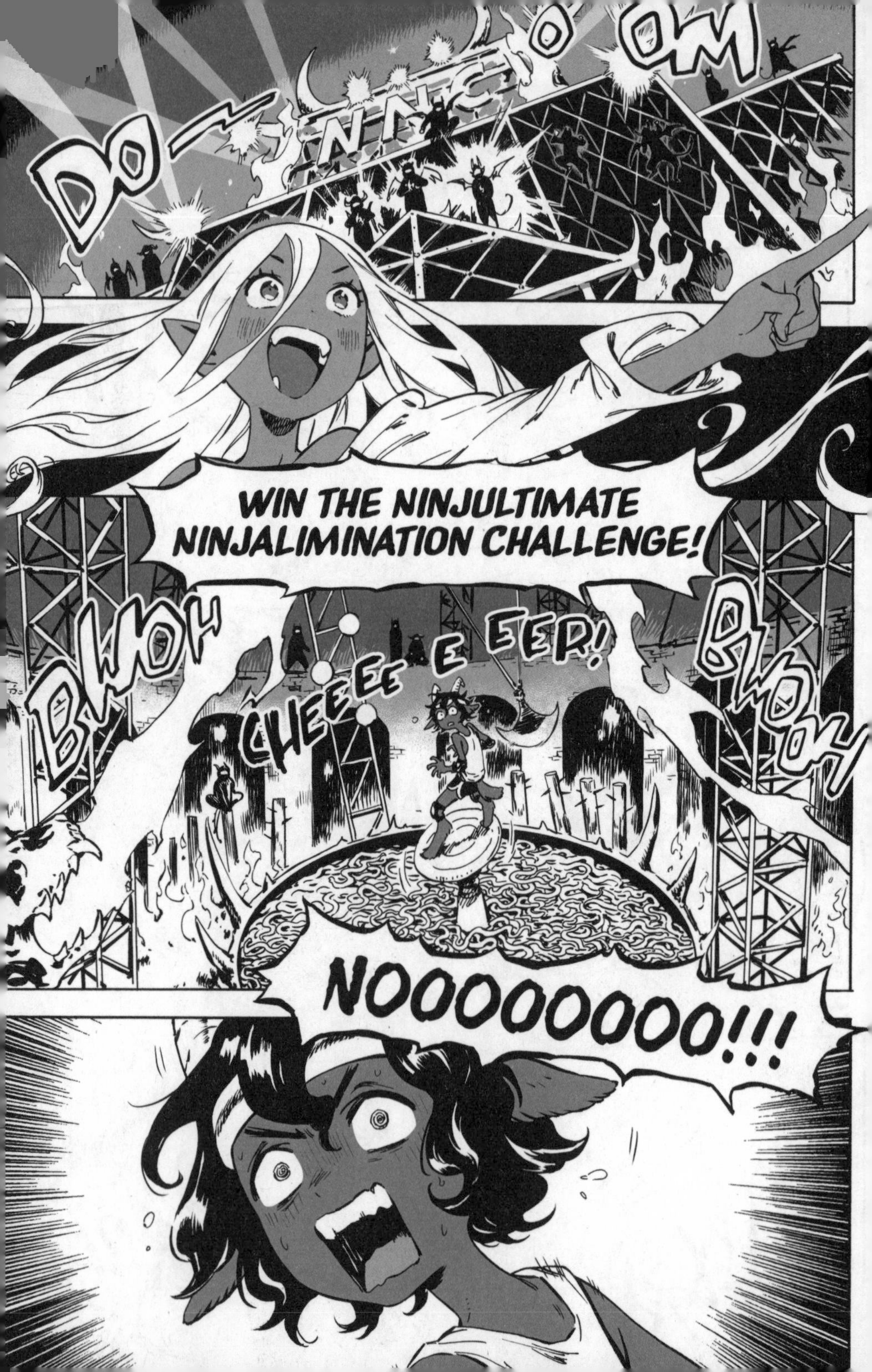
DO—NNGO OM
WIN THE NINJULTIMATE NINJALIMINATION CHALLENGE!
BWOH
CHEEEEE E EER!
BWOH
NOOOOOOOOO!!!

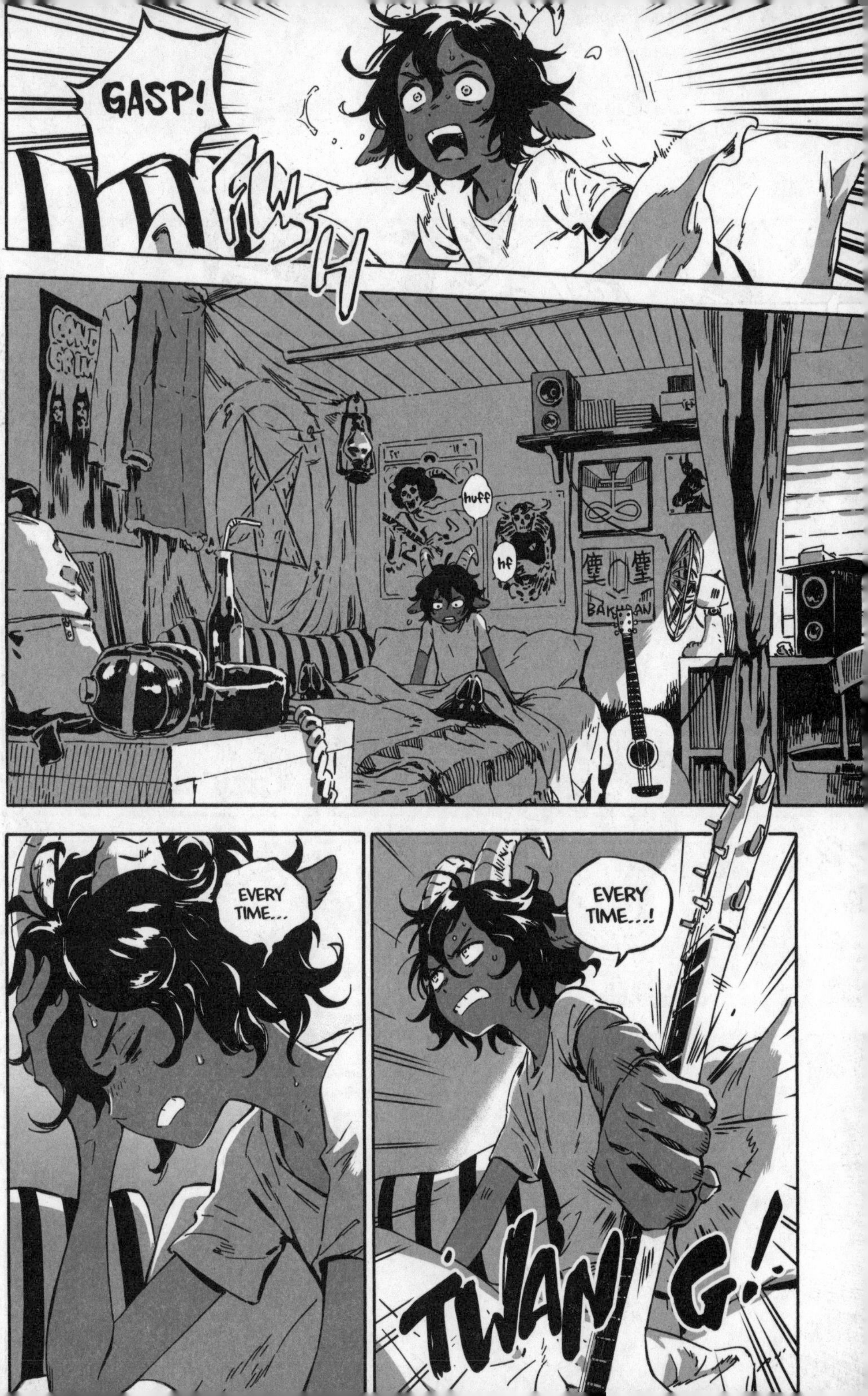
GASP!
FWSH
huff
hf
EVERY TIME...
EVERY TIME...!
TWANG!

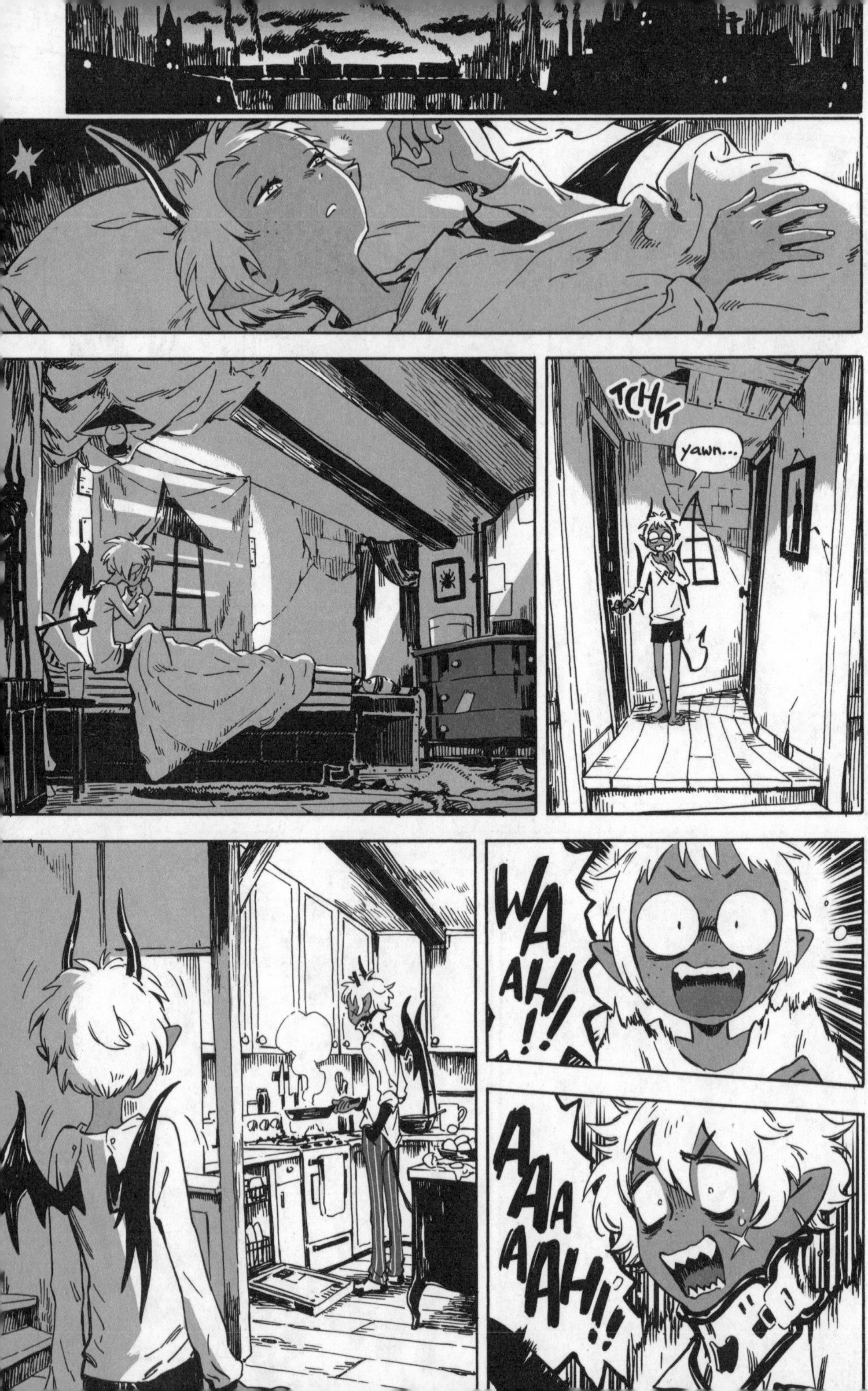
TCHK
yawn...
WAAAH!!
AAAAAH!!

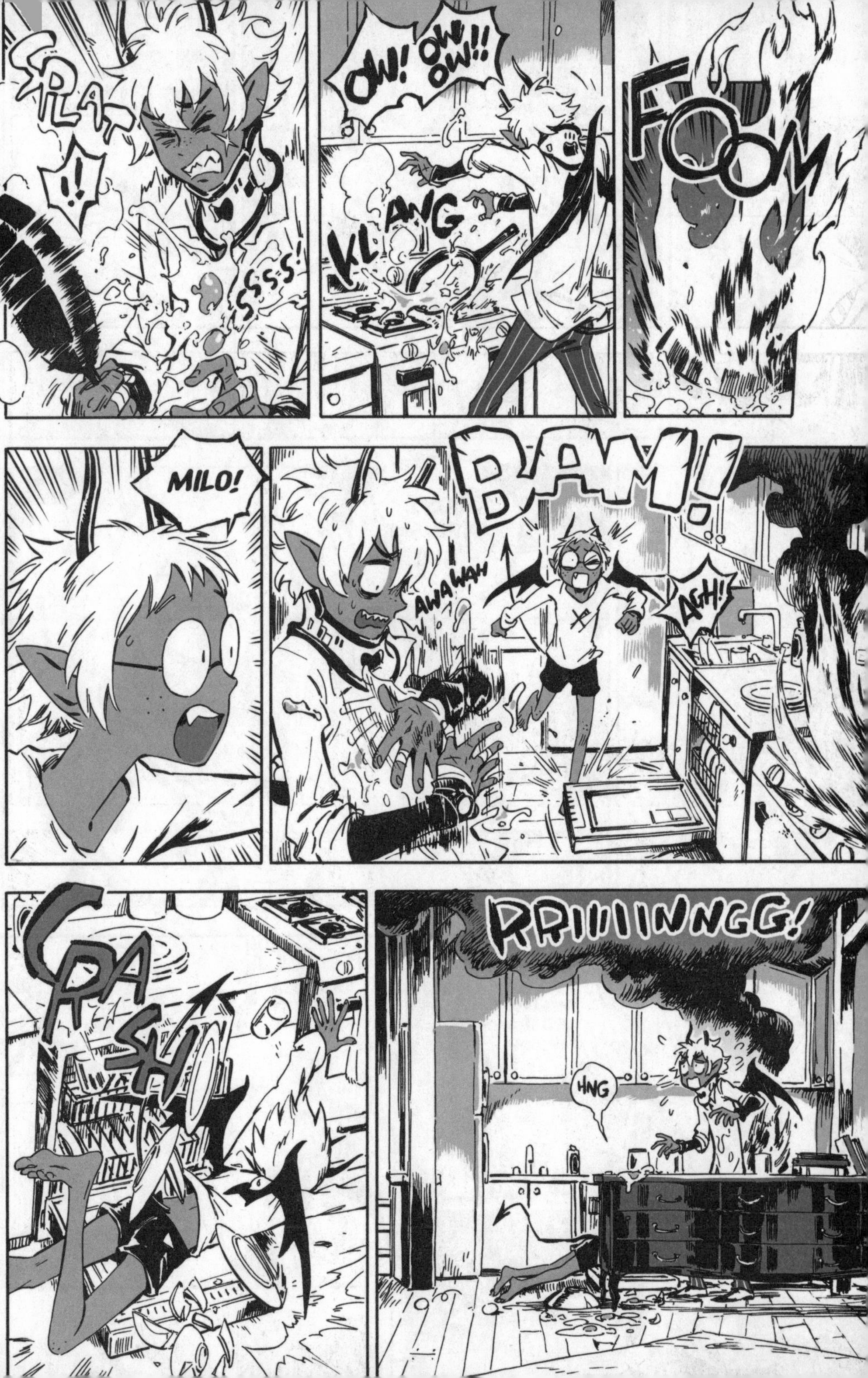
SPLAT
!!
SSSSS!
OW! OW! OW!!
KLANG
FOOM
MILO!
BAM!
AWAWAH
AGH!
CRASH
RRIIIIINNGG!
HNG

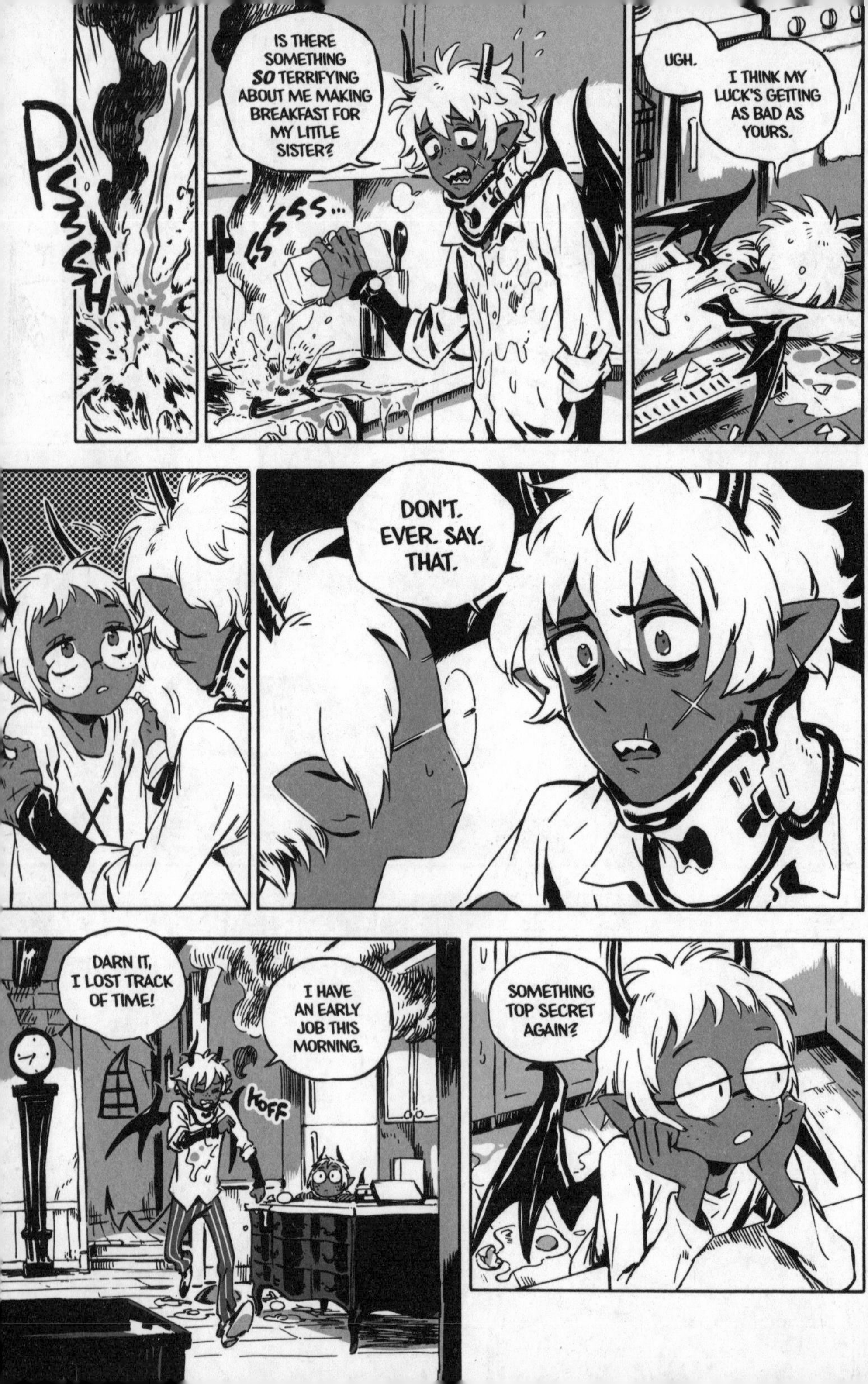
PSSSSH
IS THERE SOMETHING SO TERRIFYING ABOUT ME MAKING BREAKFAST FOR MY LITTLE SISTER?
SSSS...
UGH.
I THINK MY LUCK'S GETTING AS BAD AS YOURS.
DON'T. EVER. SAY. THAT.
DARN IT, I LOST TRACK OF TIME!
I HAVE AN EARLY JOB THIS MORNING.
KOFF
SOMETHING TOP SECRET AGAIN?

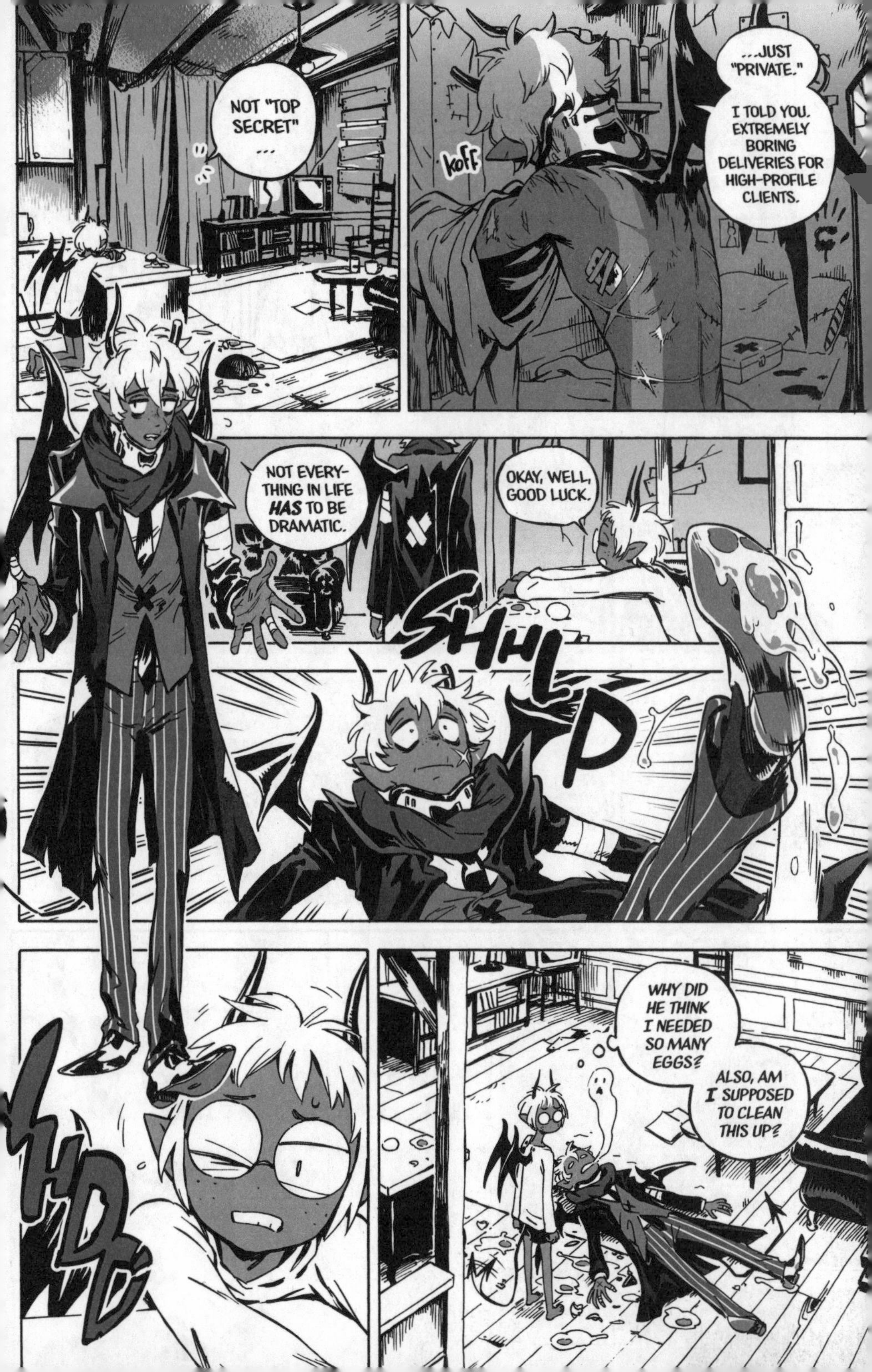
NOT "TOP SECRET"
...
...JUST "PRIVATE."
KOFF
I TOLD YOU. EXTREMELY BORING DELIVERIES FOR HIGH-PROFILE CLIENTS.
NOT EVERYTHING IN LIFE HAS TO BE DRAMATIC.
OKAY, WELL, GOOD LUCK.
SHHLLP
WHY DID HE THINK I NEEDED SO MANY EGGS?
ALSO, AM I SUPPOSED TO CLEAN THIS UP?

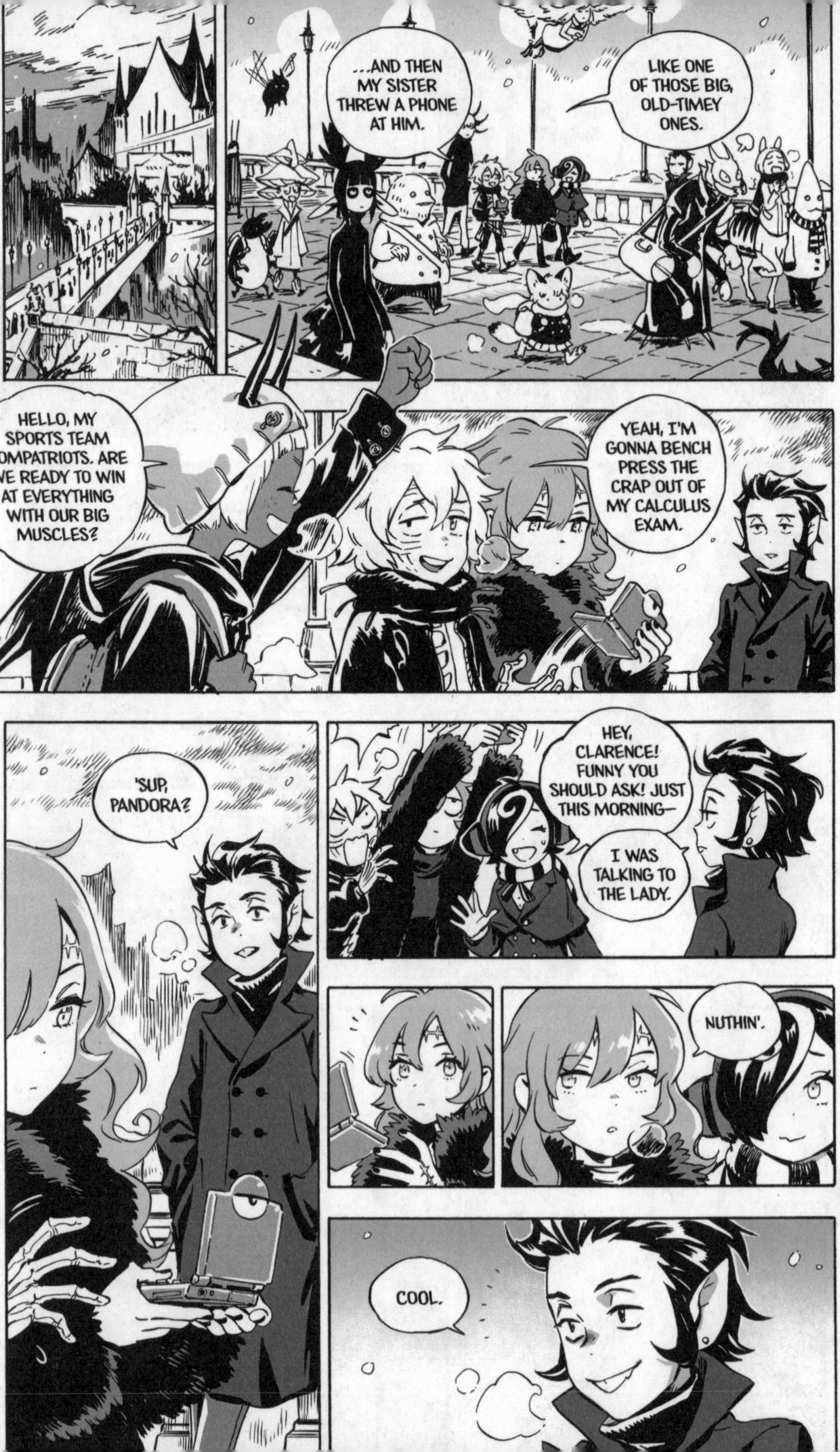
...AND THEN MY SISTER THREW A PHONE AT HIM.
LIKE ONE OF THOSE BIG, OLD-TIMEY ONES.
HELLO, MY SPORTS TEAM COMPATRIOTS. ARE WE READY TO WIN AT EVERYTHING WITH OUR BIG MUSCLES?
YEAH, I'M GONNA BENCH PRESS THE CRAP OUT OF MY CALCULUS EXAM.
'SUP, PANDORA?
HEY, CLARENCE! FUNNY YOU SHOULD ASK! JUST THIS MORNING—
I WAS TALKING TO THE LADY.
NUTHIN'.
COOL.

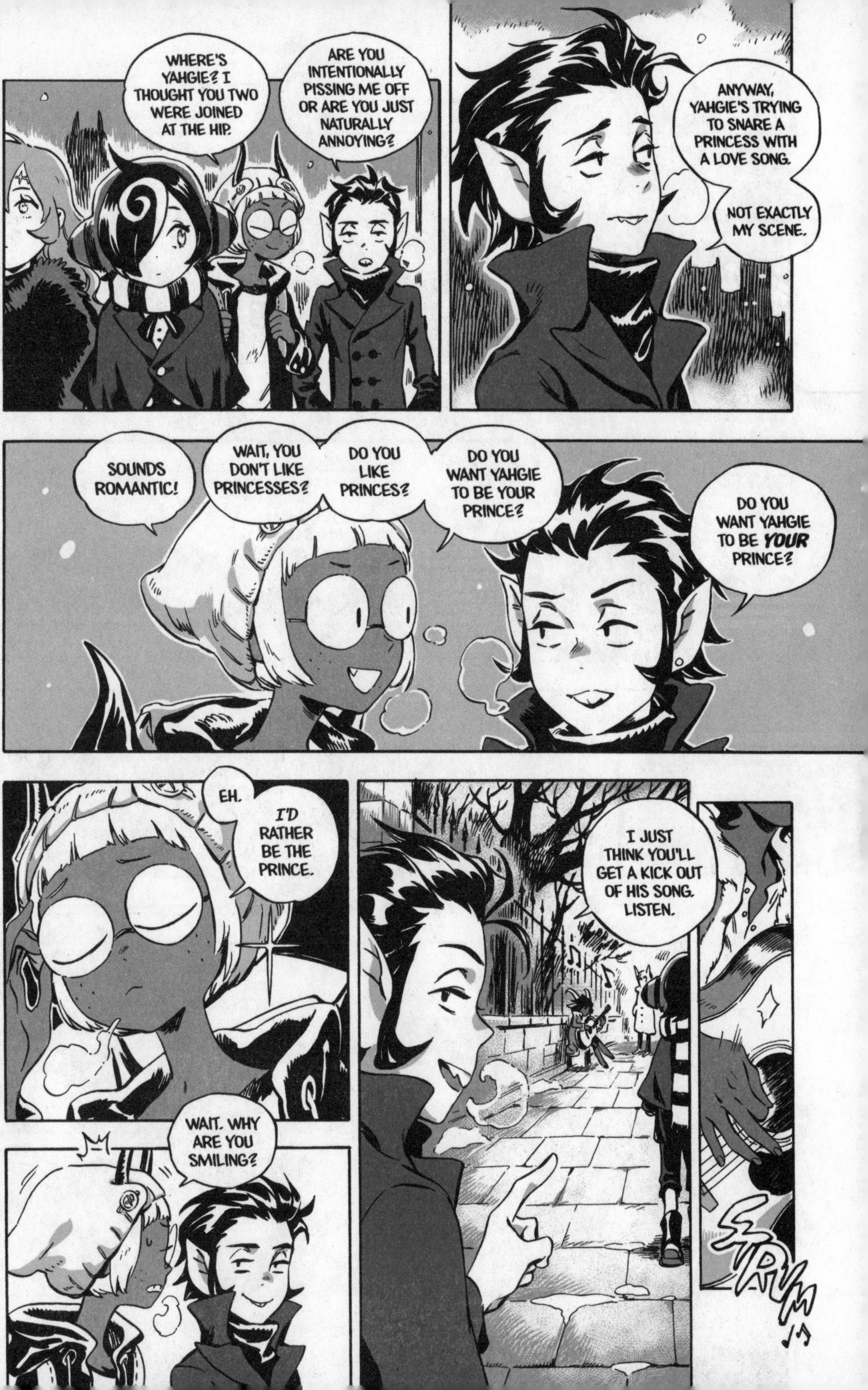
WHERE'S YAHGIE? I THOUGHT YOU TWO WERE JOINED AT THE HIP.
ARE YOU INTENTIONALLY PISSING ME OFF OR ARE YOU JUST NATURALLY ANNOYING?
ANYWAY, YAHGIE'S TRYING TO SNARE A PRINCESS WITH A LOVE SONG.
NOT EXACTLY MY SCENE.
SOUNDS ROMANTIC!
WAIT, YOU DON'T LIKE PRINCESSES?
DO YOU LIKE PRINCES?
DO YOU WANT YAHGIE TO BE YOUR PRINCE?
DO YOU WANT YAHGIE TO BE *YOUR* PRINCE?
EH.
I'D RATHER BE THE PRINCE.
WAIT. WHY ARE YOU SMILING?
I JUST THINK YOU'LL GET A KICK OUT OF HIS SONG. LISTEN.
STRUM

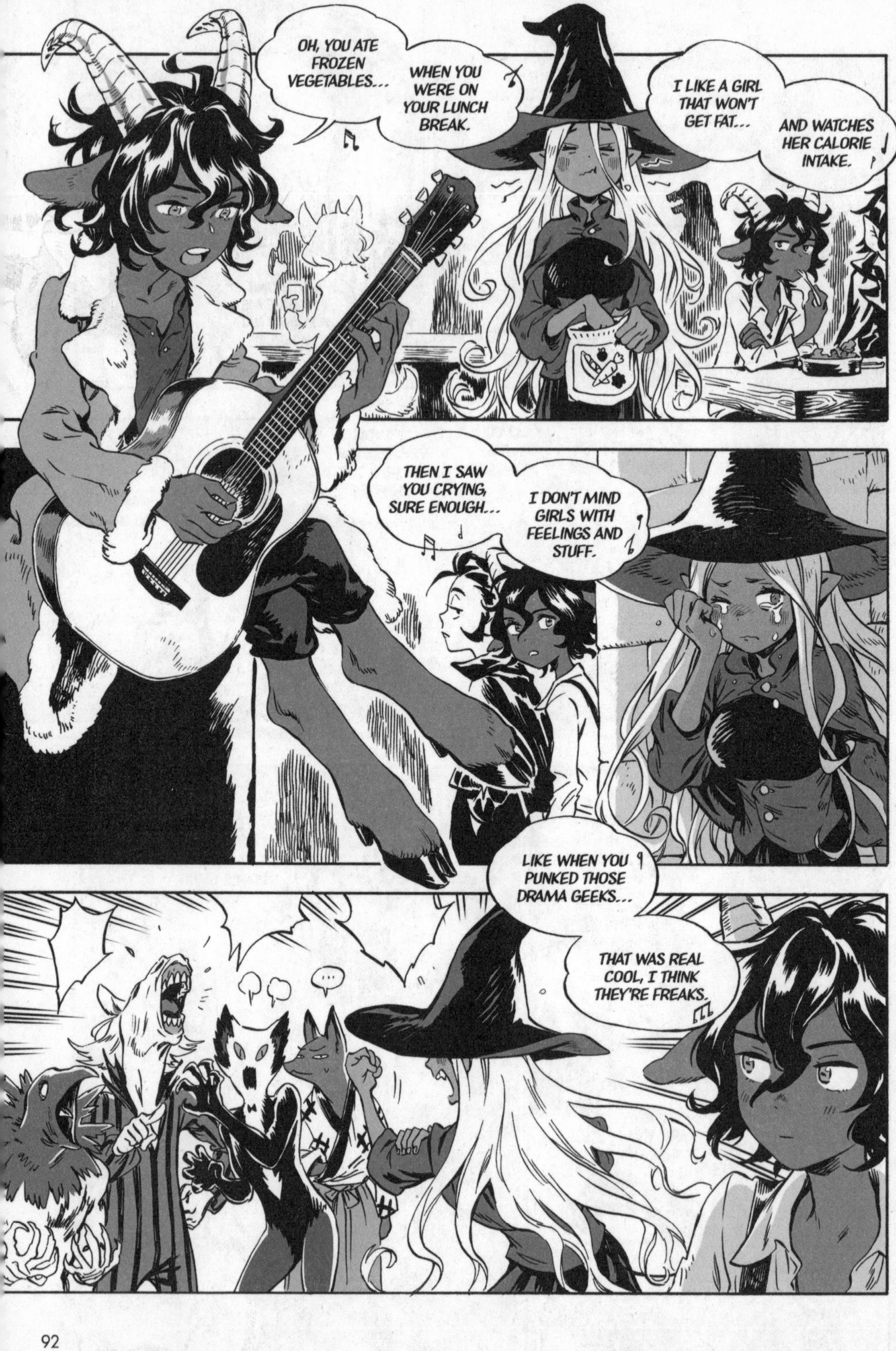
OH, YOU ATE FROZEN VEGETABLES...
WHEN YOU WERE ON YOUR LUNCH BREAK.
I LIKE A GIRL THAT WON'T GET FAT...
AND WATCHES HER CALORIE INTAKE.
THEN I SAW YOU CRYING, SURE ENOUGH...
I DON'T MIND GIRLS WITH FEELINGS AND STUFF.
LIKE WHEN YOU PUNKED THOSE DRAMA GEEKS...
...
THAT WAS REAL COOL, I THINK THEY'RE FREAKS.

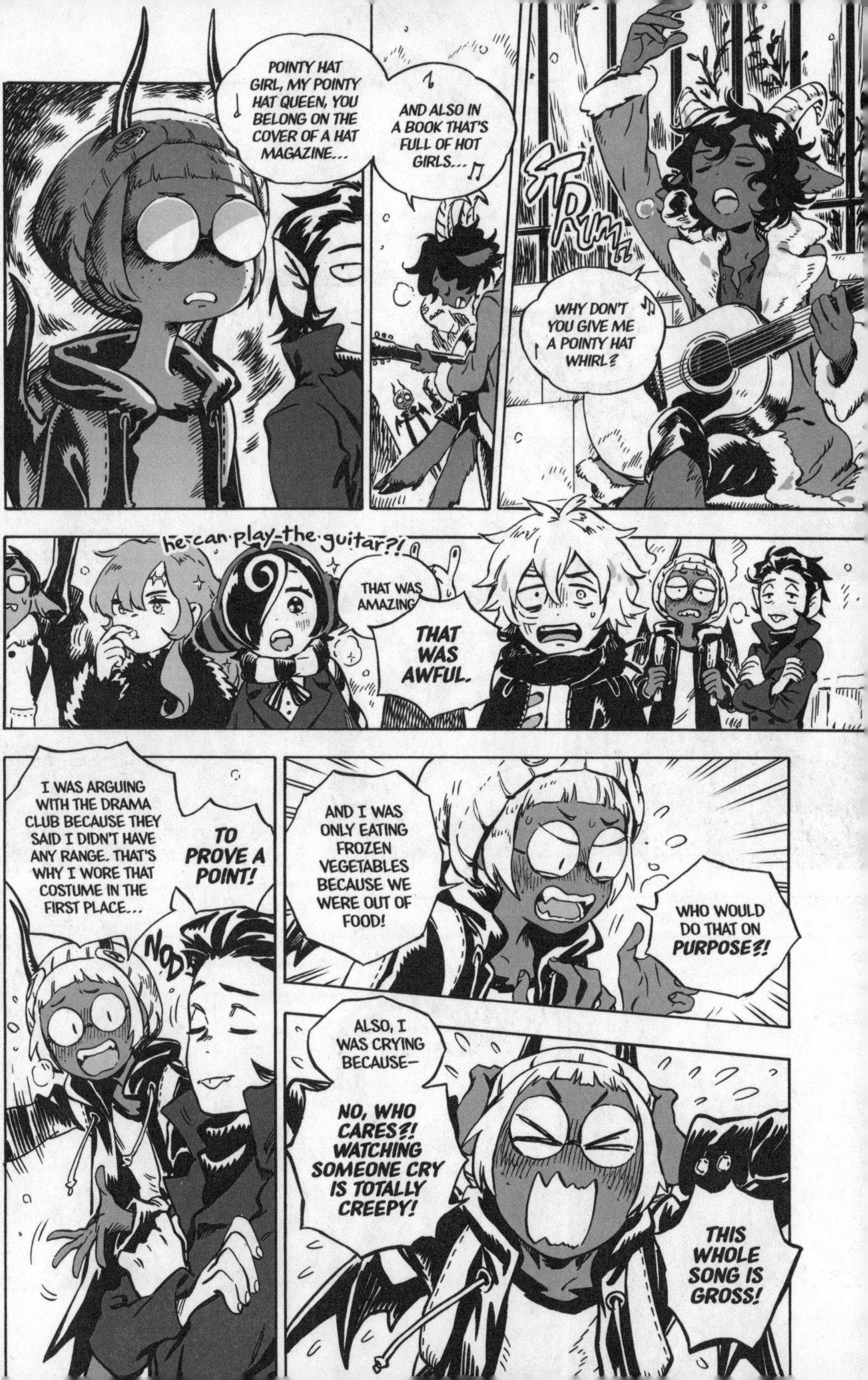
POINTY HAT GIRL, MY POINTY HAT QUEEN, YOU BELONG ON THE COVER OF A HAT MAGAZINE...
AND ALSO IN A BOOK THAT'S FULL OF HOT GIRLS...
STRUM
WHY DON'T YOU GIVE ME A POINTY HAT WHIRL?
he can play the guitar?!
THAT WAS AMAZING
THAT WAS AWFUL.
I WAS ARGUING WITH THE DRAMA CLUB BECAUSE THEY SAID I DIDN'T HAVE ANY RANGE. THAT'S WHY I WORE THAT COSTUME IN THE FIRST PLACE...
TO PROVE A POINT!
NOD
AND I WAS ONLY EATING FROZEN VEGETABLES BECAUSE WE WERE OUT OF FOOD!
WHO WOULD DO THAT ON PURPOSE?!
ALSO, I WAS CRYING BECAUSE—
NO, WHO CARES?! WATCHING SOMEONE CRY IS TOTALLY CREEPY!
THIS WHOLE SONG IS GROSS!

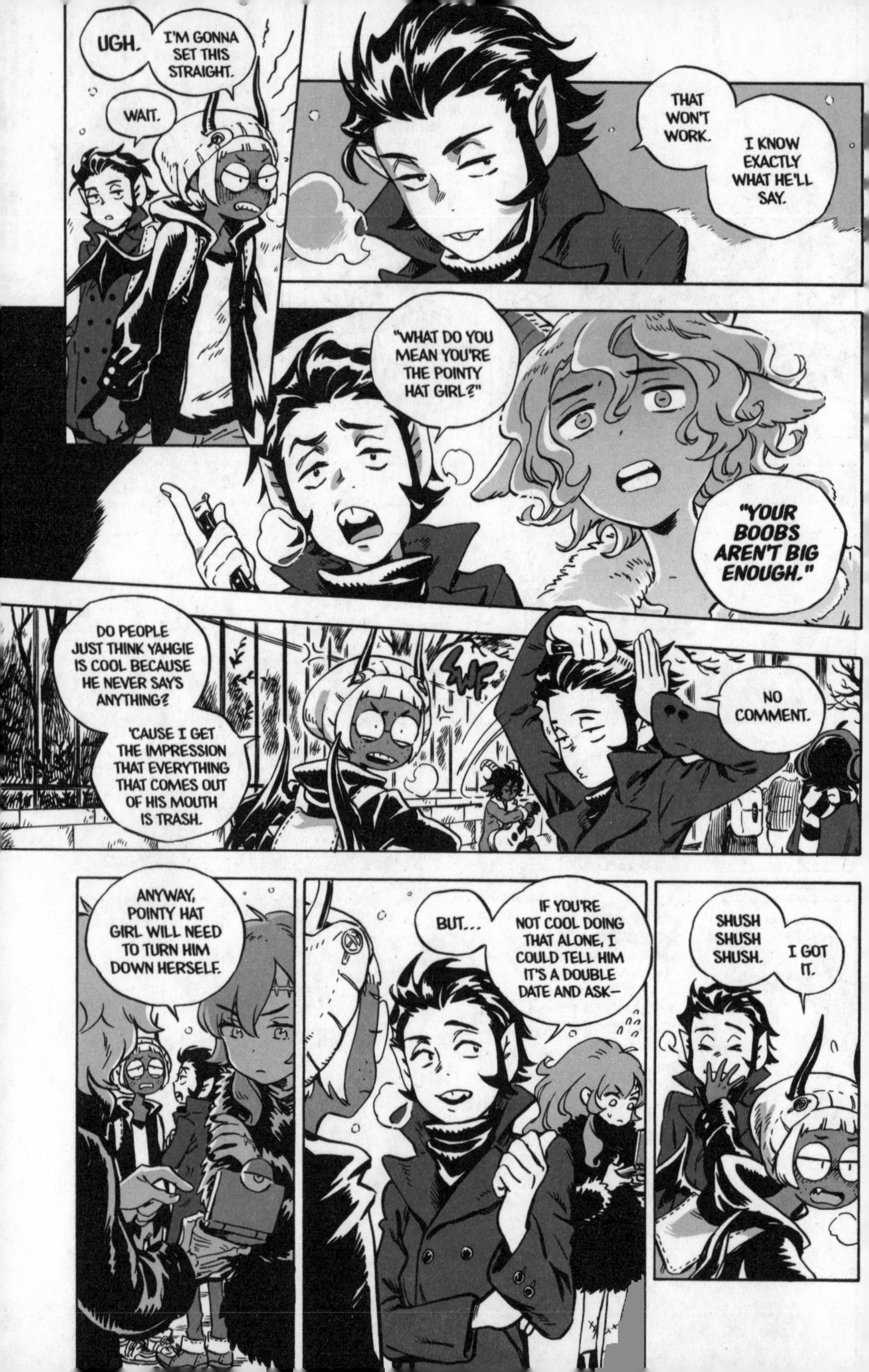
UGH.
I'M GONNA SET THIS STRAIGHT.
WAIT.
THAT WON'T WORK.
I KNOW EXACTLY WHAT HE'LL SAY.
"WHAT DO YOU MEAN YOU'RE THE POINTY HAT GIRL?"
"YOUR BOOBS AREN'T BIG ENOUGH."
DO PEOPLE JUST THINK YAHGIE IS COOL BECAUSE HE NEVER SAYS ANYTHING?
'CAUSE I GET THE IMPRESSION THAT EVERYTHING THAT COMES OUT OF HIS MOUTH IS TRASH.
SWF
NO COMMENT.
ANYWAY, POINTY HAT GIRL WILL NEED TO TURN HIM DOWN HERSELF.
BUT...
IF YOU'RE NOT COOL DOING THAT ALONE, I COULD TELL HIM IT'S A DOUBLE DATE AND ASK–
SHUSH SHUSH SHUSH.
I GOT IT.

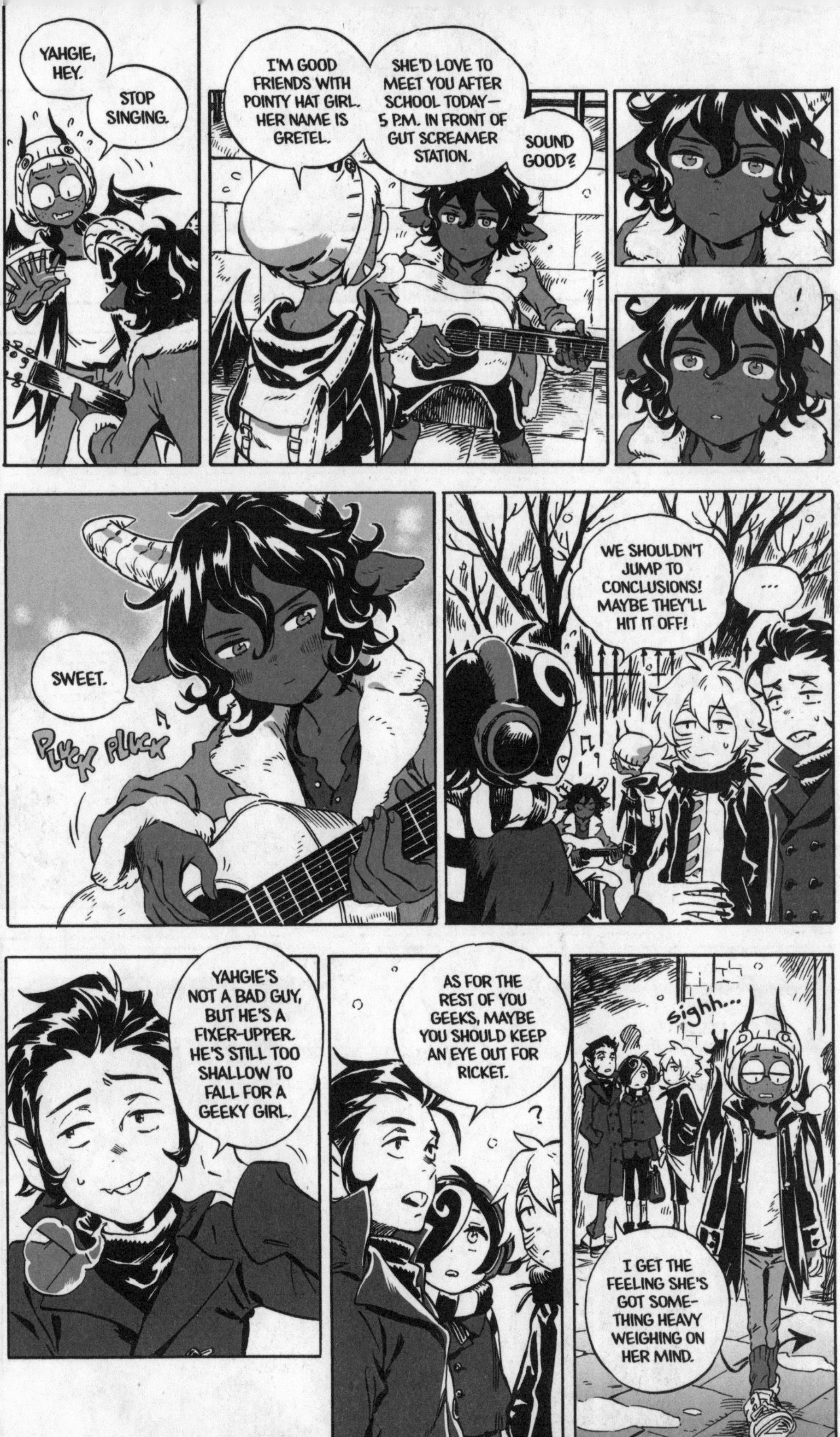
YAHGIE, HEY.
STOP SINGING.
I'M GOOD FRIENDS WITH POINTY HAT GIRL. HER NAME IS GRETEL.
SHE'D LOVE TO MEET YOU AFTER SCHOOL TODAY— 5 P.M. IN FRONT OF GUT SCREAMER STATION.
SOUND GOOD?
!
SWEET.
PLUCK PLUCK
WE SHOULDN'T JUMP TO CONCLUSIONS! MAYBE THEY'LL HIT IT OFF!
...
YAHGIE'S NOT A BAD GUY, BUT HE'S A FIXER-UPPER. HE'S STILL TOO SHALLOW TO FALL FOR A GEEKY GIRL.
AS FOR THE REST OF YOU GEEKS, MAYBE YOU SHOULD KEEP AN EYE OUT FOR RICKET.
?
sighh...
I GET THE FEELING SHE'S GOT SOME-THING HEAVY WEIGHING ON HER MIND.

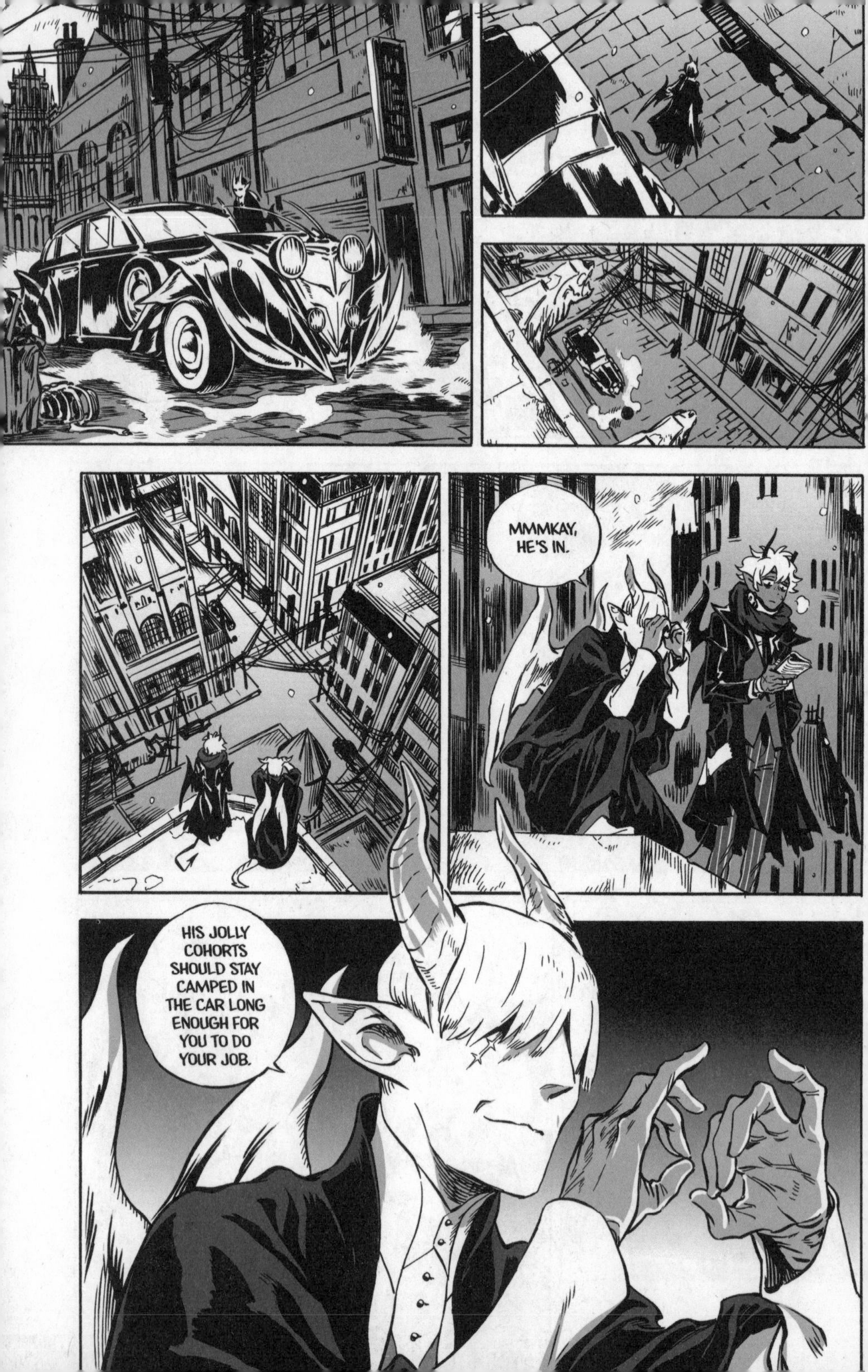
MMMKAY, HE'S IN.
HIS JOLLY COHORTS SHOULD STAY CAMPED IN THE CAR LONG ENOUGH FOR YOU TO DO YOUR JOB.

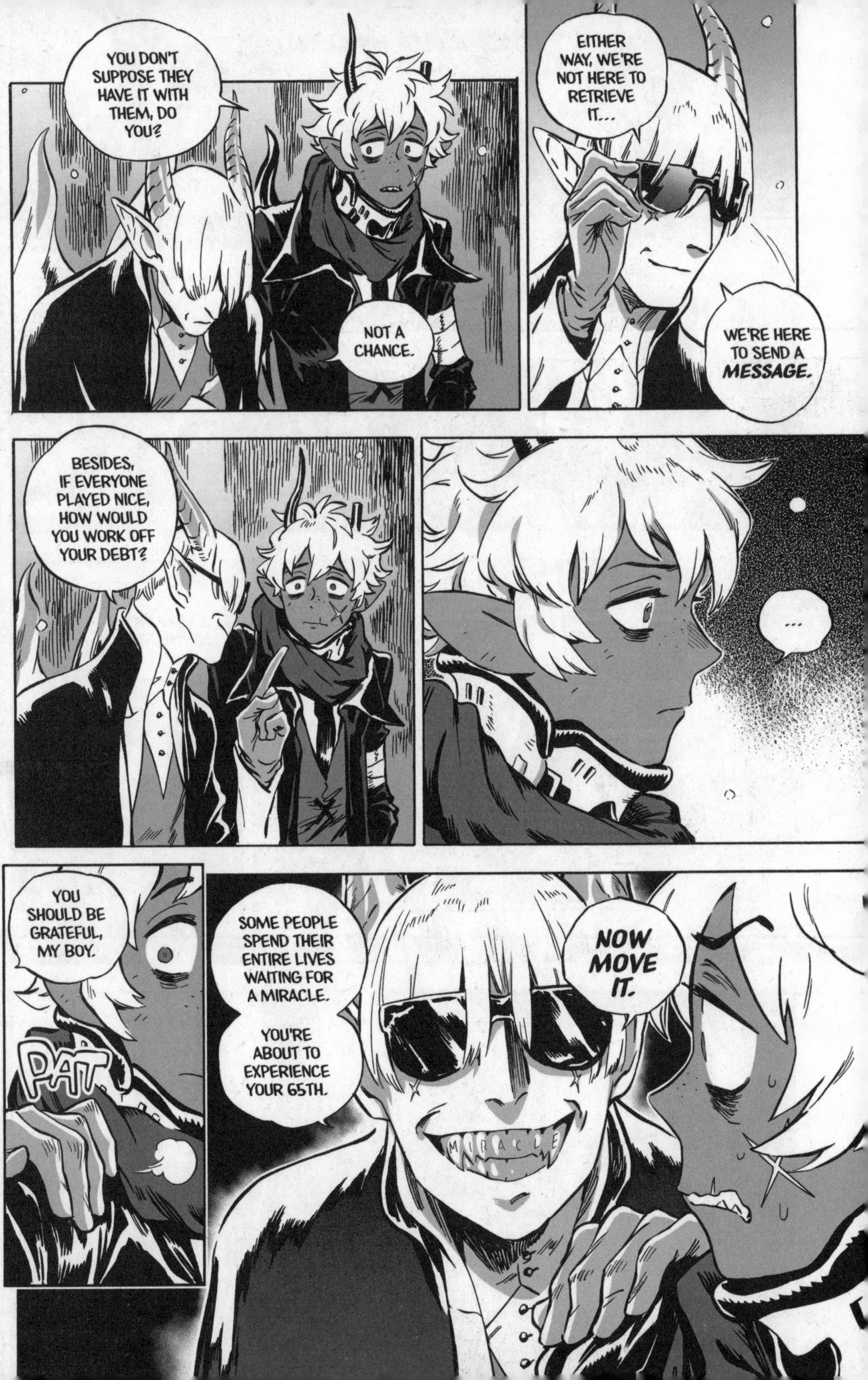
YOU DON'T SUPPOSE THEY HAVE IT WITH THEM, DO YOU?
NOT A CHANCE.
EITHER WAY, WE'RE NOT HERE TO RETRIEVE IT...
WE'RE HERE TO SEND A *MESSAGE.*
BESIDES, IF EVERYONE PLAYED NICE, HOW WOULD YOU WORK OFF YOUR DEBT?
...
YOU SHOULD BE GRATEFUL, MY BOY.
PAT
SOME PEOPLE SPEND THEIR ENTIRE LIVES WAITING FOR A MIRACLE.
YOU'RE ABOUT TO EXPERIENCE YOUR 65TH.
MIRACLE
NOW MOVE IT.

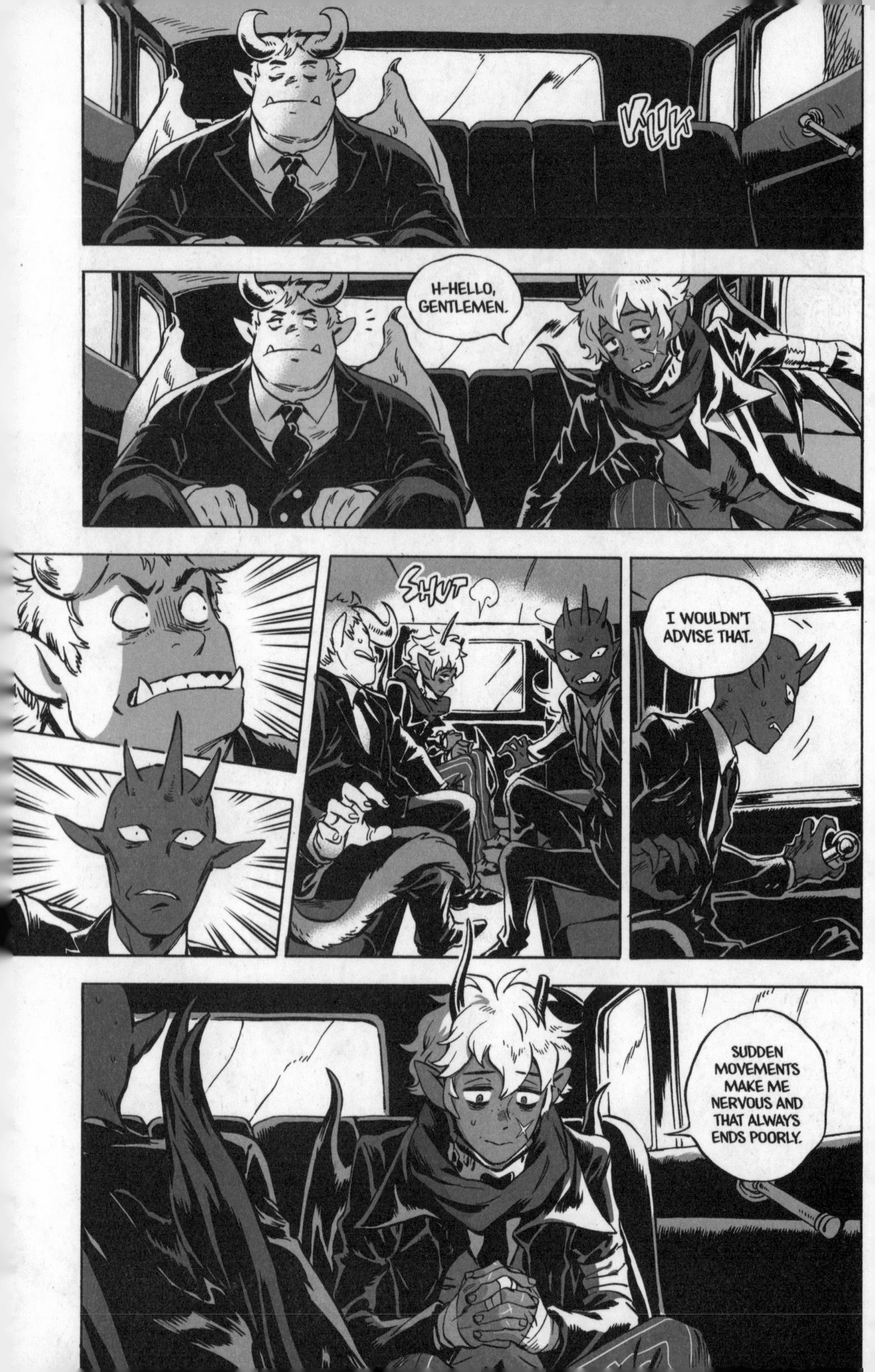
VKLIK
H-HELLO, GENTLEMEN.
SHUT
I WOULDN'T ADVISE THAT.
SUDDEN MOVEMENTS MAKE ME NERVOUS AND THAT ALWAYS ENDS POORLY.

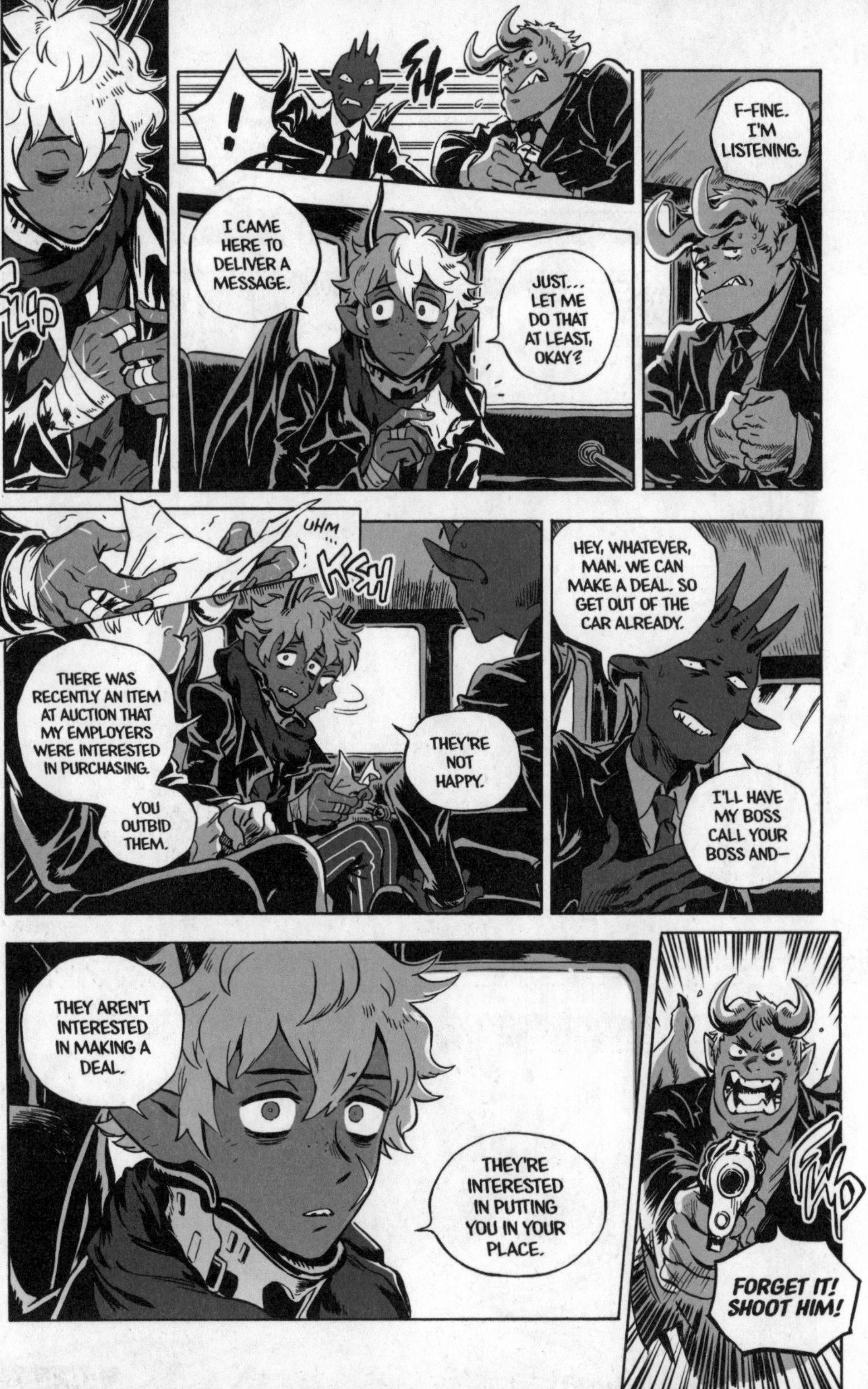
SLIP
!
SHF
I CAME HERE TO DELIVER A MESSAGE.
JUST... LET ME DO THAT AT LEAST, OKAY?
F-FINE. I'M LISTENING.
UHM
KSH
THERE WAS RECENTLY AN ITEM AT AUCTION THAT MY EMPLOYERS WERE INTERESTED IN PURCHASING.
YOU OUTBID THEM.
THEY'RE NOT HAPPY.
HEY, WHATEVER, MAN. WE CAN MAKE A DEAL. SO GET OUT OF THE CAR ALREADY.
I'LL HAVE MY BOSS CALL YOUR BOSS AND—
THEY AREN'T INTERESTED IN MAKING A DEAL.
THEY'RE INTERESTED IN PUTTING YOU IN YOUR PLACE.
FWP
FORGET IT! SHOOT HIM!

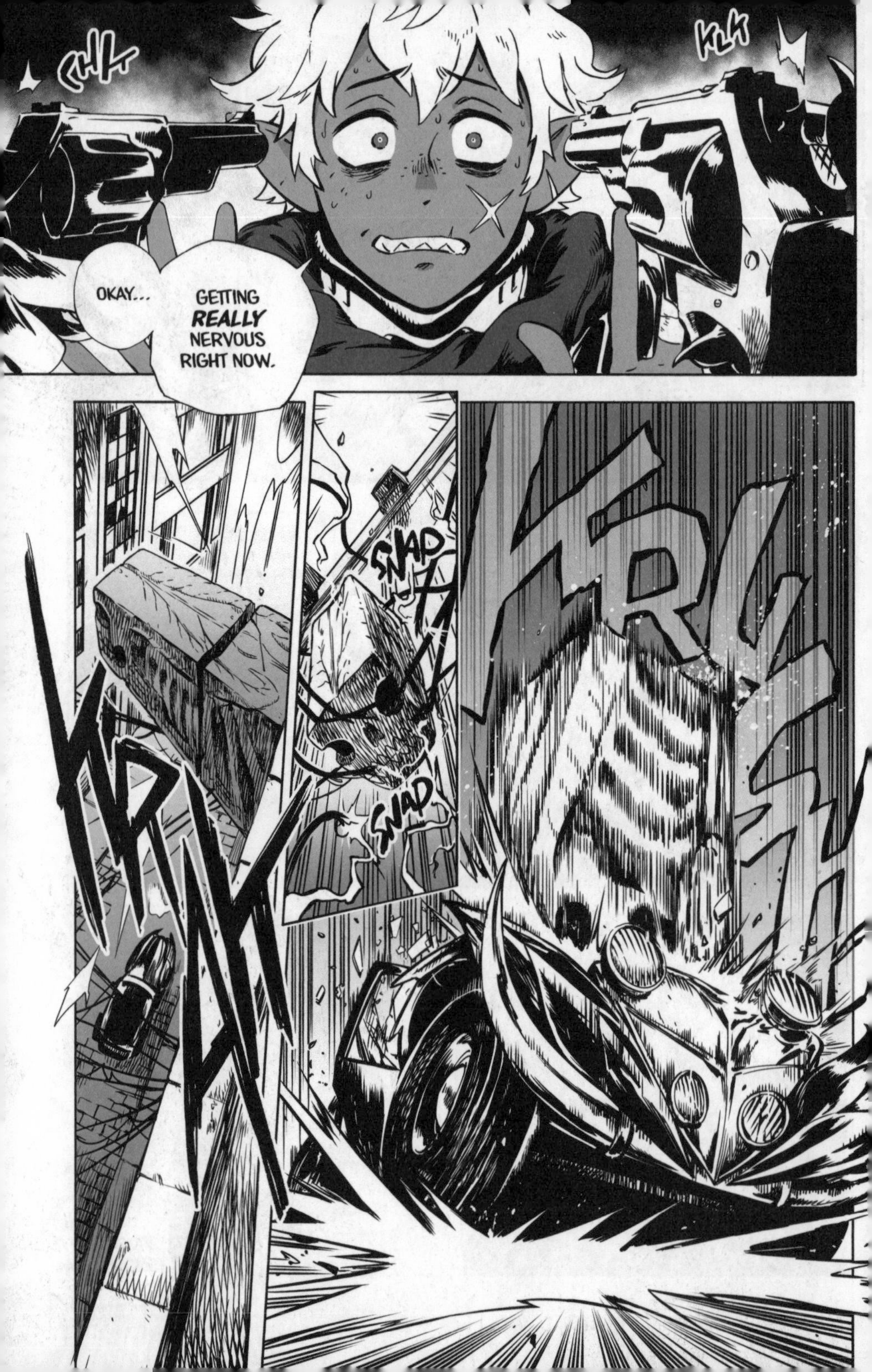
CHK
KLK
OKAY... GETTING REALLY NERVOUS RIGHT NOW.
SNAP
SNAP

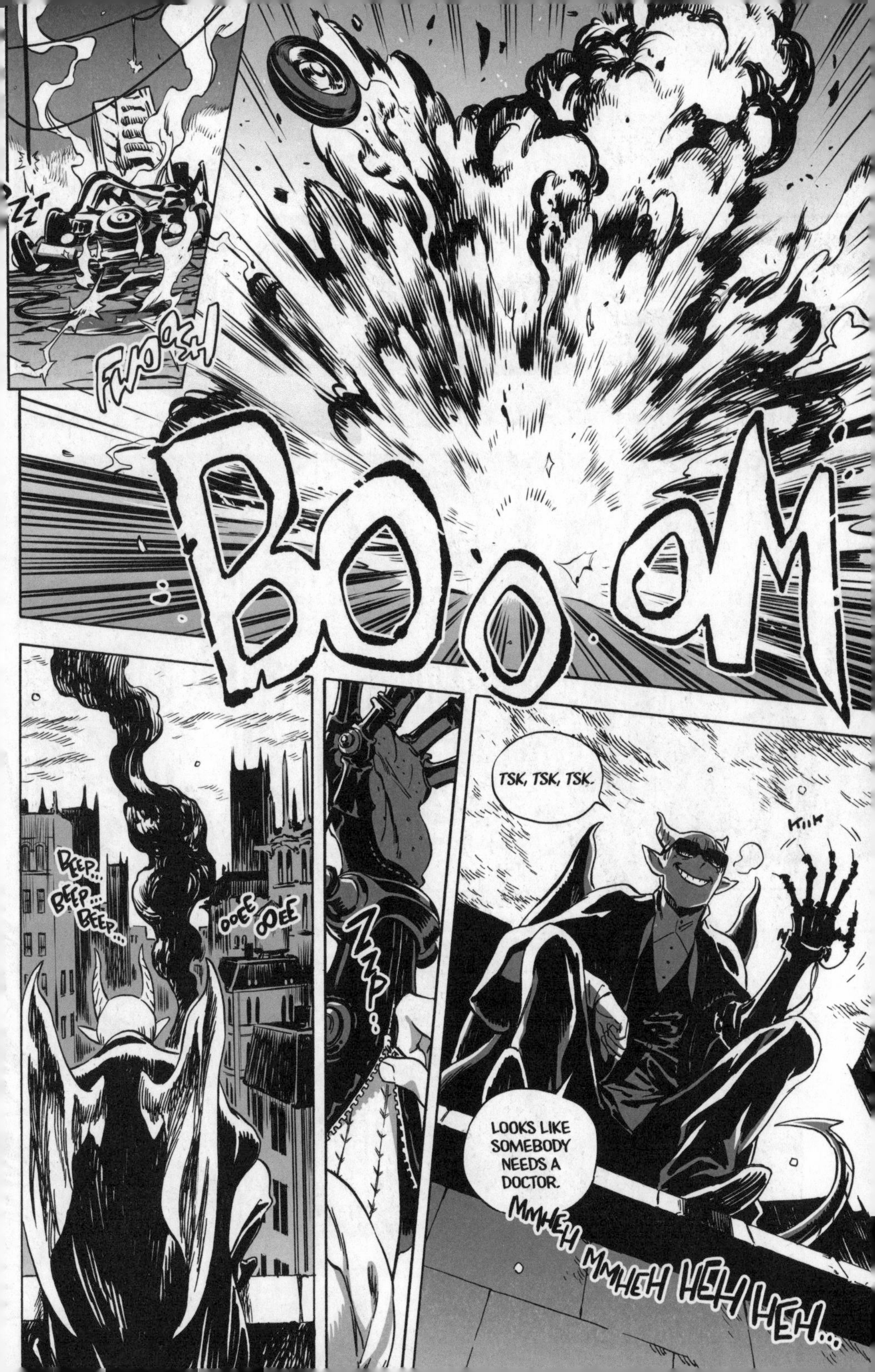
ZZZT
FWOOSH
BOOOM
BEEP... BEEP... BEEP...
OOEE OOEE
NNP..
TSK, TSK, TSK.
KLIK
LOOKS LIKE SOMEBODY NEEDS A DOCTOR.
MMHEH MMHEH HEH HEH HEH...

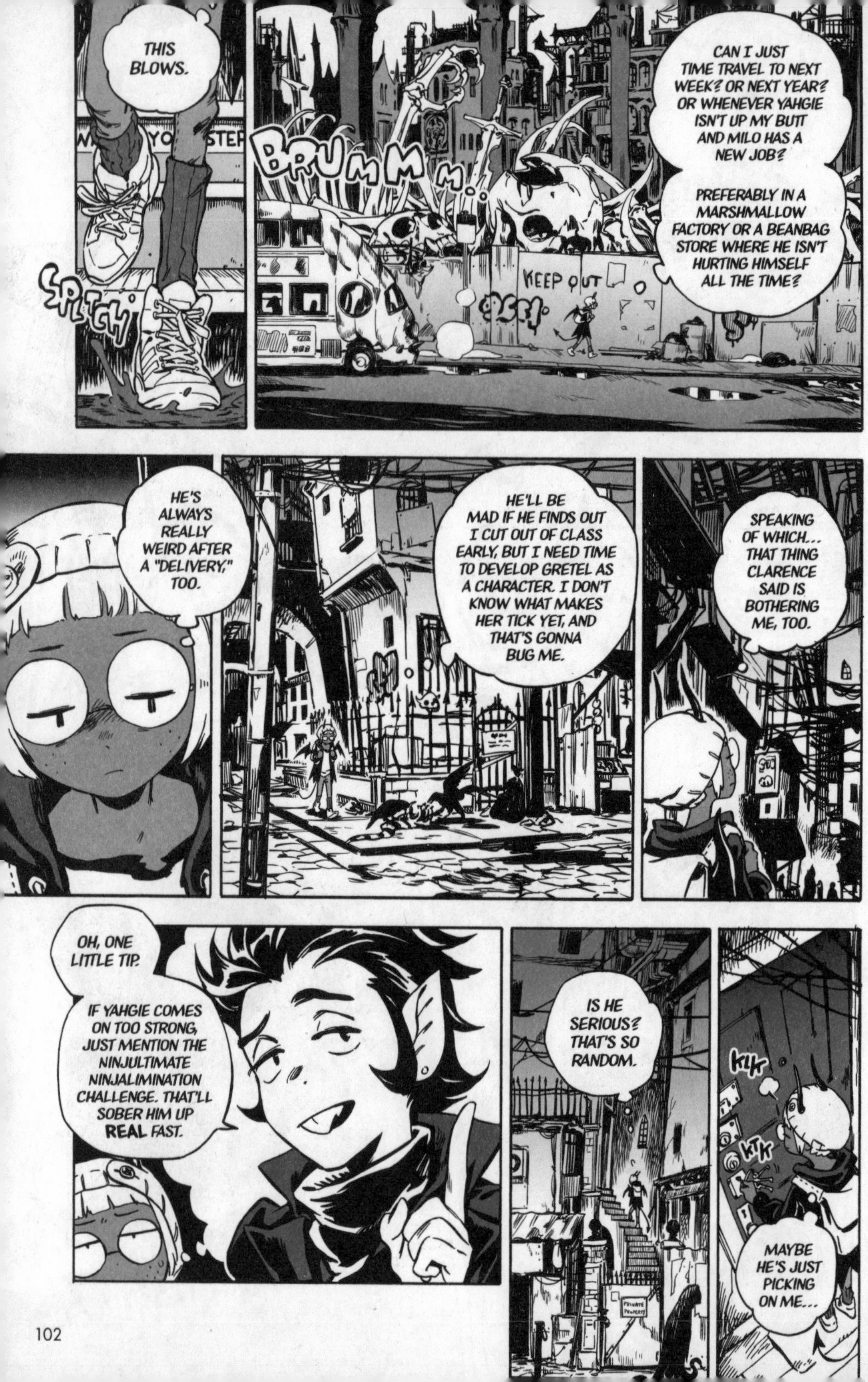
THIS BLOWS.
BRUMMM..
CAN I JUST TIME TRAVEL TO NEXT WEEK? OR NEXT YEAR? OR WHENEVER YAHGIE ISN'T UP MY BUTT AND MILO HAS A NEW JOB?
PREFERABLY IN A MARSHMALLOW FACTORY OR A BEANBAG STORE WHERE HE ISN'T HURTING HIMSELF ALL THE TIME?
KEEP OUT
HE'S ALWAYS REALLY WEIRD AFTER A "DELIVERY," TOO.
HE'LL BE MAD IF HE FINDS OUT I CUT OUT OF CLASS EARLY, BUT I NEED TIME TO DEVELOP GRETEL AS A CHARACTER. I DON'T KNOW WHAT MAKES HER TICK YET, AND THAT'S GONNA BUG ME.
SPEAKING OF WHICH... THAT THING CLARENCE SAID IS BOTHERING ME, TOO.
OH, ONE LITTLE TIP.
IF YAHGIE COMES ON TOO STRONG, JUST MENTION THE NINJULTIMATE NINJALIMINATION CHALLENGE. THAT'LL SOBER HIM UP **REAL** FAST.
IS HE SERIOUS? THAT'S SO RANDOM.
MAYBE HE'S JUST PICKING ON ME...

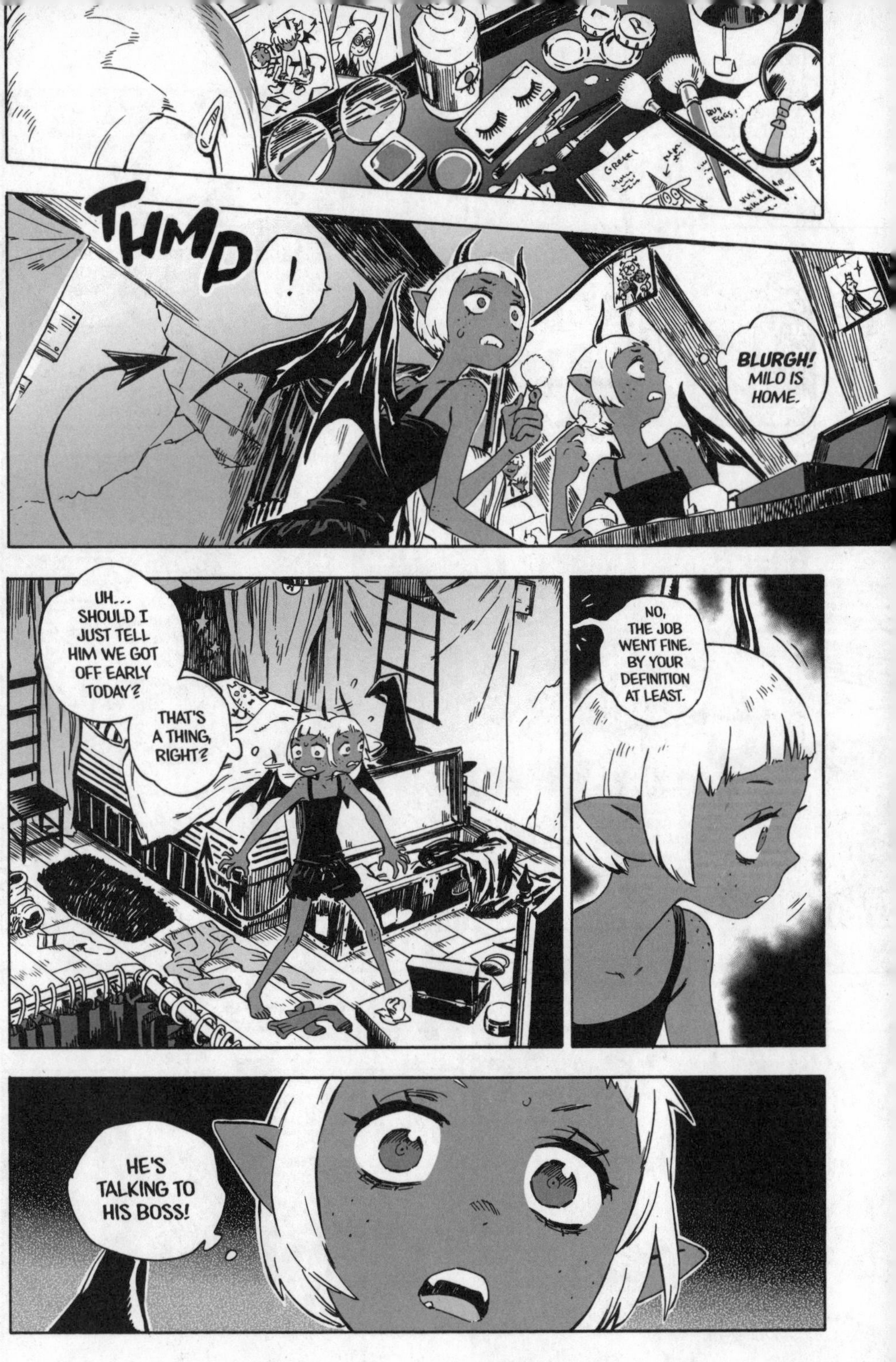
THMP
!
BLURGH! MILO IS HOME.
UH... SHOULD I JUST TELL HIM WE GOT OFF EARLY TODAY?
THAT'S A THING, RIGHT?
NO, THE JOB WENT FINE. BY YOUR DEFINITION AT LEAST.
HE'S TALKING TO HIS BOSS!

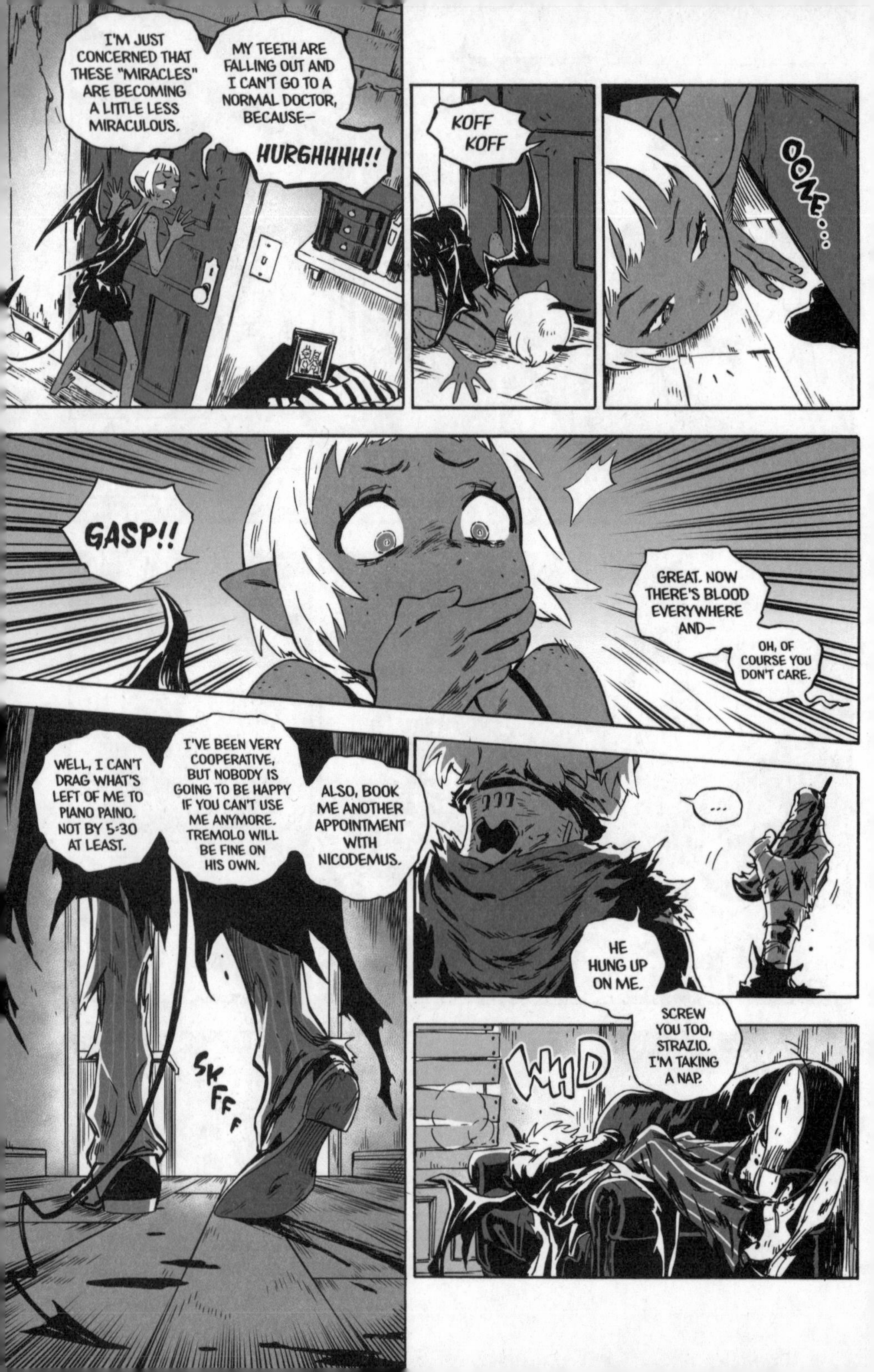

I'M JUST CONCERNED THAT THESE "MIRACLES" ARE BECOMING A LITTLE LESS MIRACULOUS.
MY TEETH ARE FALLING OUT AND I CAN'T GO TO A NORMAL DOCTOR, BECAUSE—
HURGHHHH!!
KOFF KOFF
OOZE...
GASP!!
GREAT. NOW THERE'S BLOOD EVERYWHERE AND—
OH, OF COURSE YOU DON'T CARE.
WELL, I CAN'T DRAG WHAT'S LEFT OF ME TO PIANO PAINO. NOT BY 5:30 AT LEAST.
I'VE BEEN VERY COOPERATIVE, BUT NOBODY IS GOING TO BE HAPPY IF YOU CAN'T USE ME ANYMORE. TREMOLO WILL BE FINE ON HIS OWN.
ALSO, BOOK ME ANOTHER APPOINTMENT WITH NICODEMUS.
SKFFF
...
HE HUNG UP ON ME.
SCREW YOU TOO, STRAZIO. I'M TAKING A NAP.
WHD

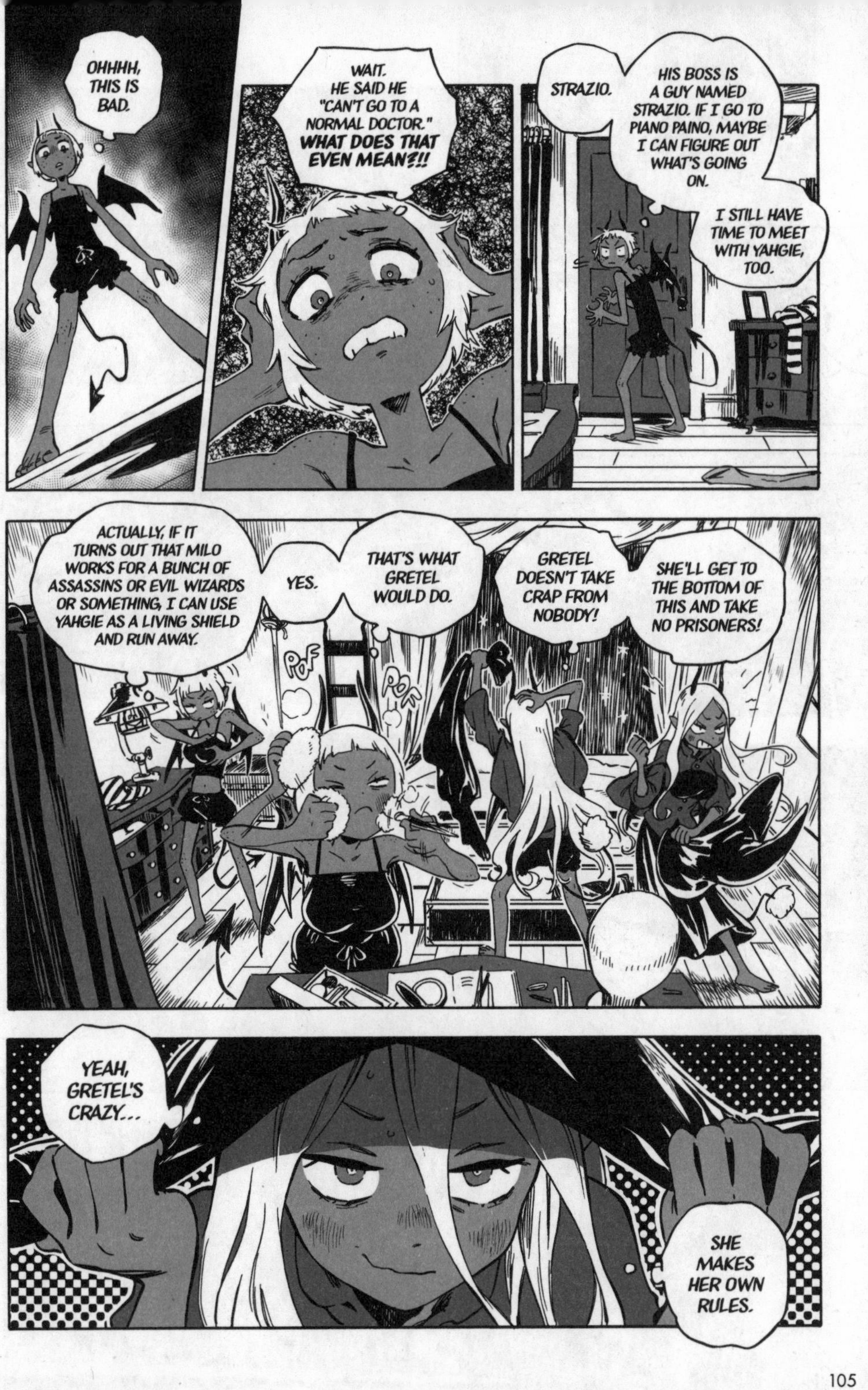

OHHHH, THIS IS BAD.
WAIT. HE SAID HE "CAN'T GO TO A NORMAL DOCTOR." WHAT DOES THAT EVEN MEAN?!!
STRAZIO.
HIS BOSS IS A GUY NAMED STRAZIO. IF I GO TO PIANO PAINO, MAYBE I CAN FIGURE OUT WHAT'S GOING ON.
I STILL HAVE TIME TO MEET WITH YAHGIE, TOO.
ACTUALLY, IF IT TURNS OUT THAT MILO WORKS FOR A BUNCH OF ASSASSINS OR EVIL WIZARDS OR SOMETHING, I CAN USE YAHGIE AS A LIVING SHIELD AND RUN AWAY.
YES.
THAT'S WHAT GRETEL WOULD DO.
POF
POF
GRETEL DOESN'T TAKE CRAP FROM NOBODY!
SHE'LL GET TO THE BOTTOM OF THIS AND TAKE NO PRISONERS!
YEAH, GRETEL'S CRAZY...
SHE MAKES HER OWN RULES.

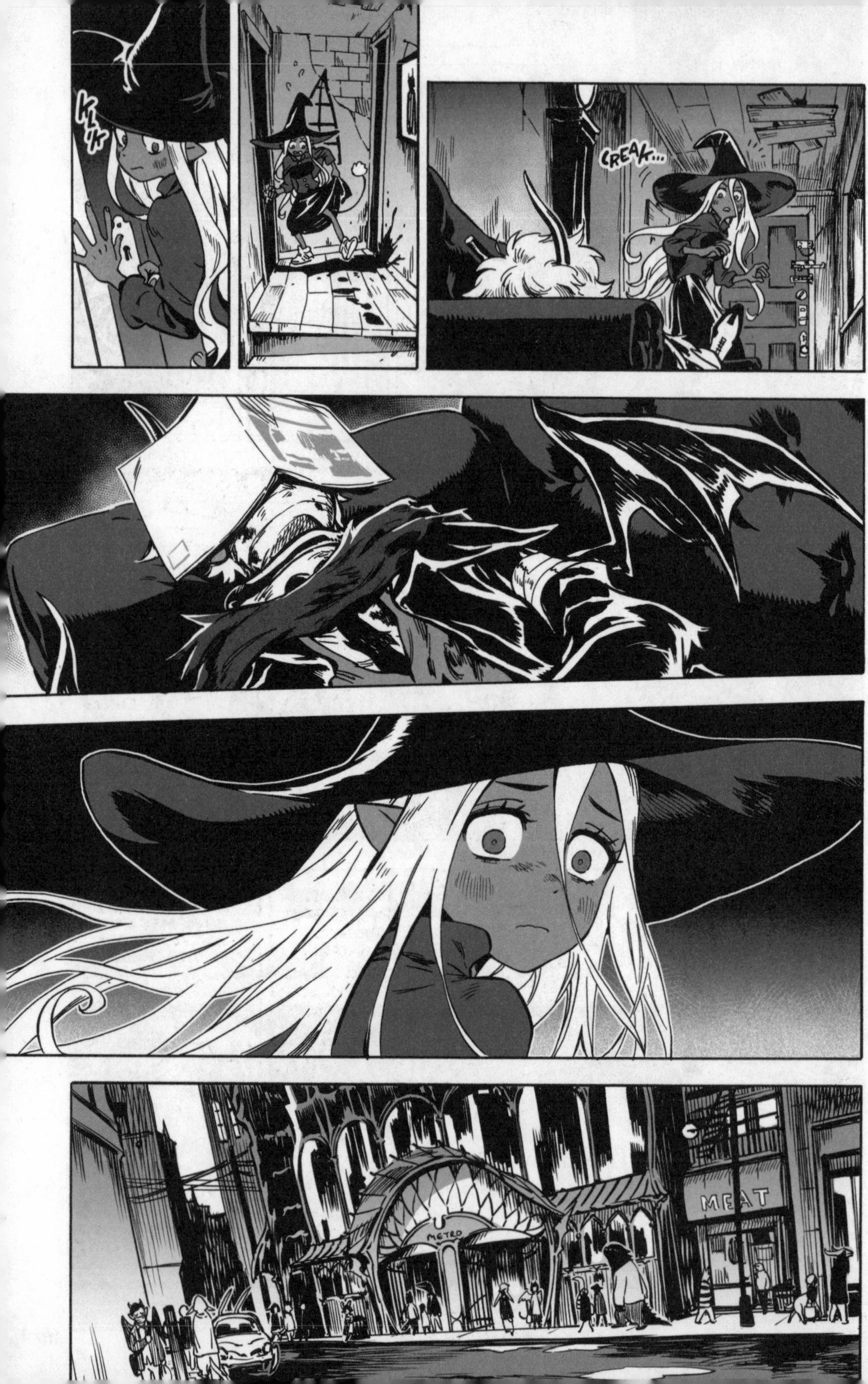
KLIK
CREAK...
MEAT
METRO

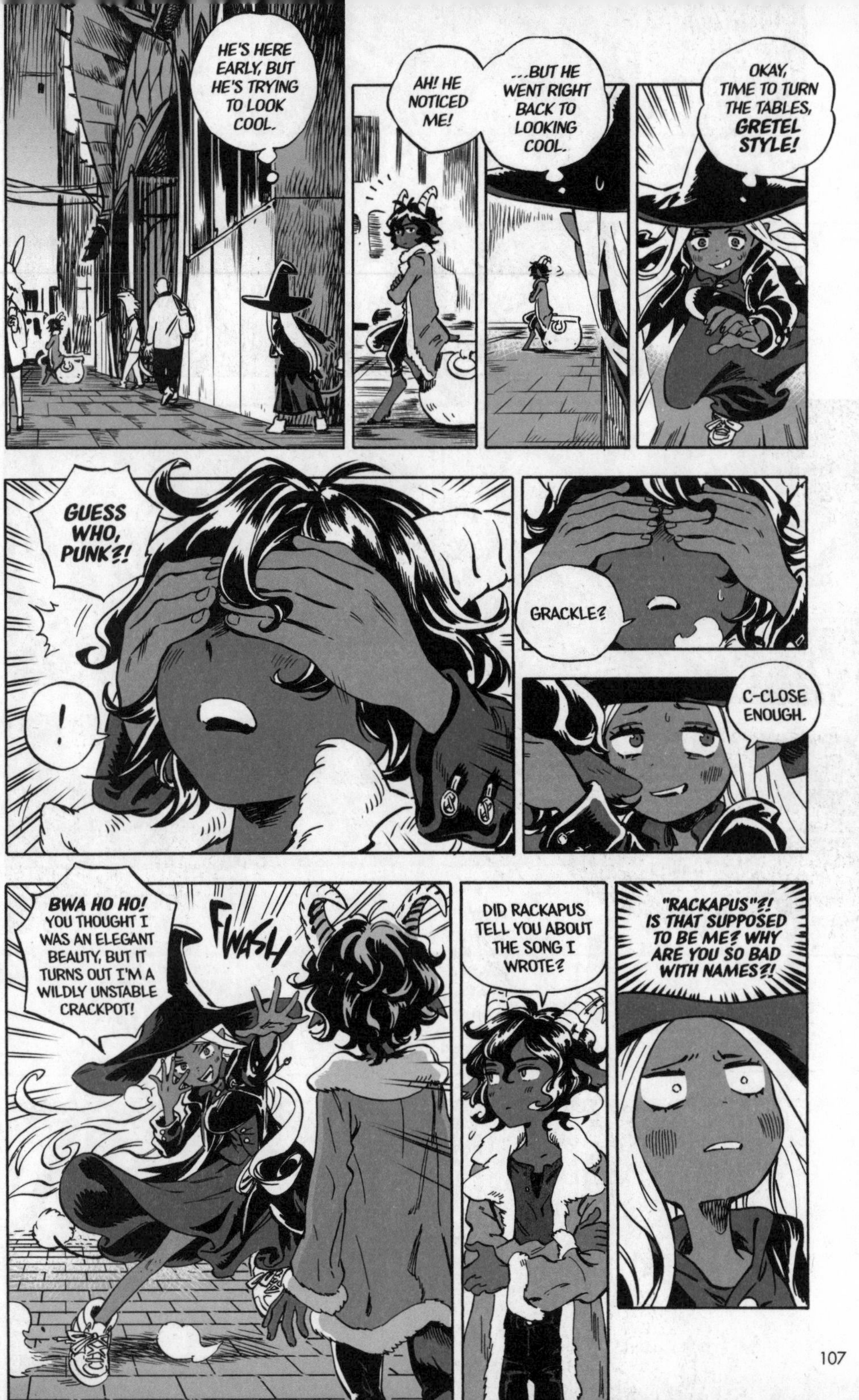
HE'S HERE EARLY, BUT HE'S TRYING TO LOOK COOL.
AH! HE NOTICED ME!
...BUT HE WENT RIGHT BACK TO LOOKING COOL.
OKAY, TIME TO TURN THE TABLES, GRETEL STYLE!
GUESS WHO, PUNK?!
!
GRACKLE?
C-CLOSE ENOUGH.
BWA HO HO! YOU THOUGHT I WAS AN ELEGANT BEAUTY, BUT IT TURNS OUT I'M A WILDLY UNSTABLE CRACKPOT!
FWASH
DID RACKAPUS TELL YOU ABOUT THE SONG I WROTE?
"RACKAPUS"?! IS THAT SUPPOSED TO BE ME? WHY ARE YOU SO BAD WITH NAMES?!

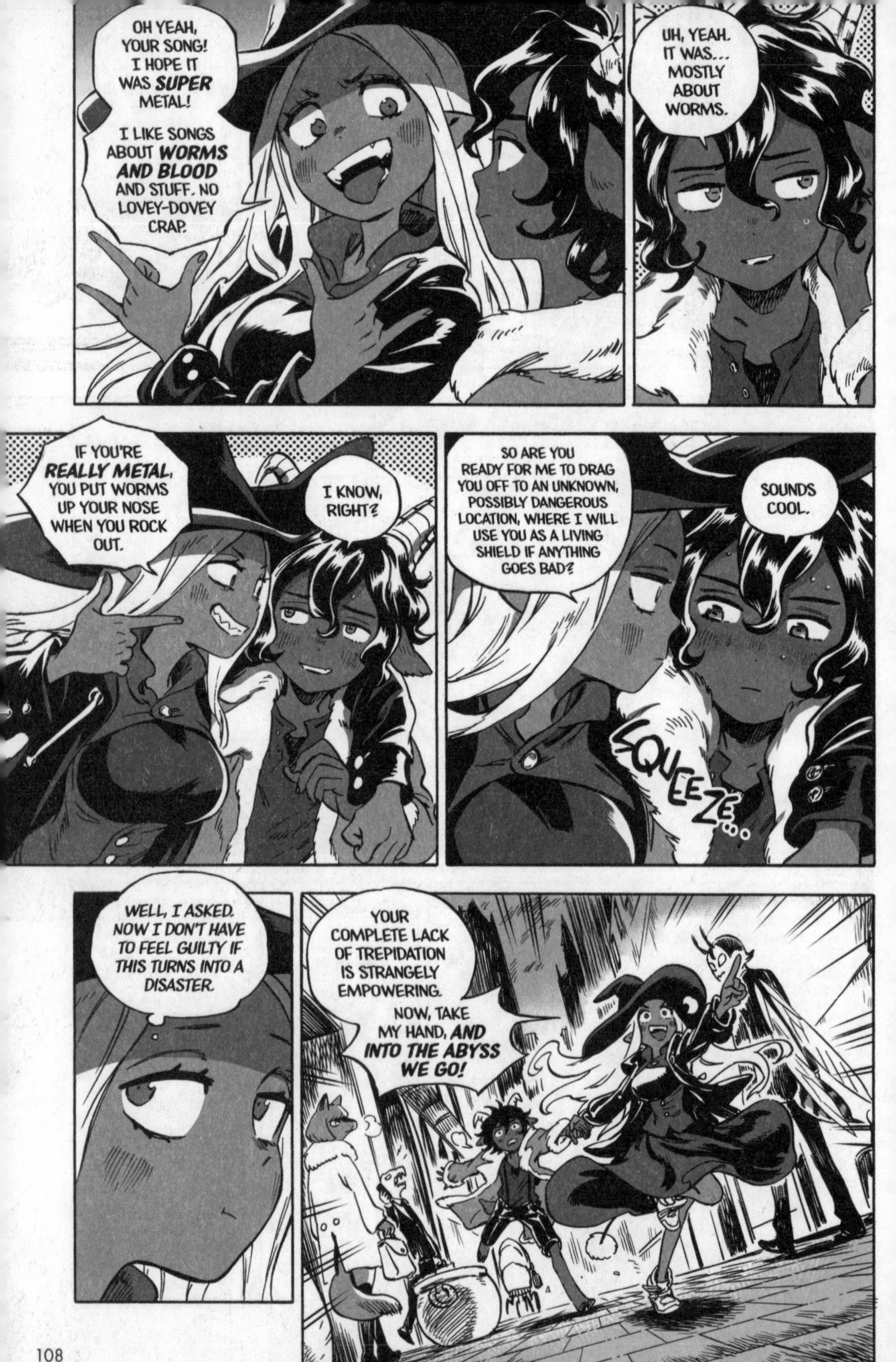
OH YEAH, YOUR SONG! I HOPE IT WAS SUPER METAL!
I LIKE SONGS ABOUT WORMS AND BLOOD AND STUFF. NO LOVEY-DOVEY CRAP.
UH, YEAH. IT WAS... MOSTLY ABOUT WORMS.
IF YOU'RE REALLY METAL, YOU PUT WORMS UP YOUR NOSE WHEN YOU ROCK OUT.
I KNOW, RIGHT?
SO ARE YOU READY FOR ME TO DRAG YOU OFF TO AN UNKNOWN, POSSIBLY DANGEROUS LOCATION, WHERE I WILL USE YOU AS A LIVING SHIELD IF ANYTHING GOES BAD?
SOUNDS COOL.
SQUEEZE...
WELL, I ASKED. NOW I DON'T HAVE TO FEEL GUILTY IF THIS TURNS INTO A DISASTER.
YOUR COMPLETE LACK OF TREPIDATION IS STRANGELY EMPOWERING.
NOW, TAKE MY HAND, AND INTO THE ABYSS WE GO!

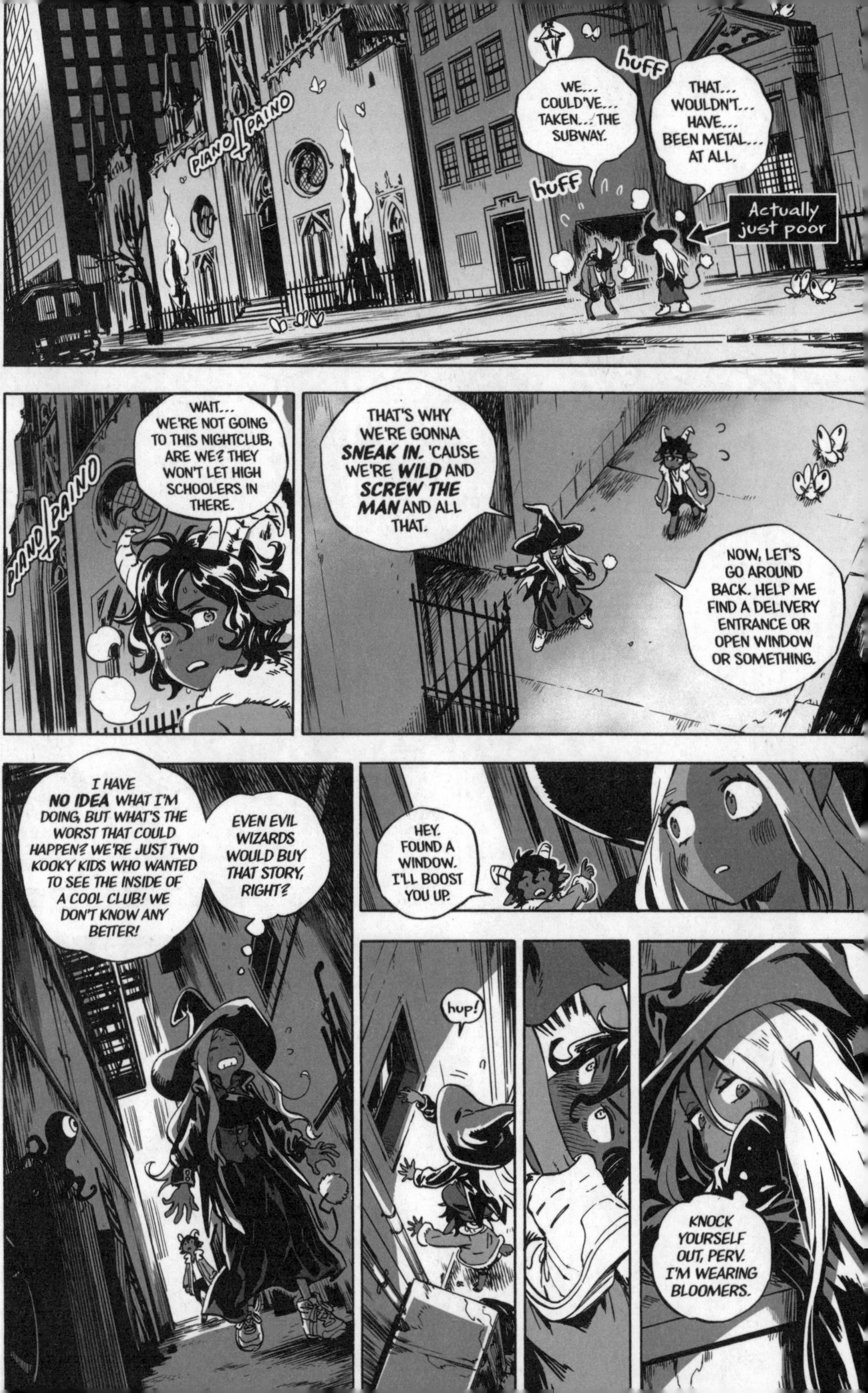
PIANO PAINO
huff
WE... COULD'VE... TAKEN... THE SUBWAY.
huff
THAT... WOULDN'T... HAVE... BEEN METAL... AT ALL.
Actually just poor
PIANO PAINO
WAIT... WE'RE NOT GOING TO THIS NIGHTCLUB, ARE WE? THEY WON'T LET HIGH SCHOOLERS IN THERE.
THAT'S WHY WE'RE GONNA **SNEAK IN.** 'CAUSE WE'RE **WILD** AND **SCREW THE MAN** AND ALL THAT.
NOW, LET'S GO AROUND BACK. HELP ME FIND A DELIVERY ENTRANCE OR OPEN WINDOW OR SOMETHING.
I HAVE **NO IDEA** WHAT I'M DOING, BUT WHAT'S THE WORST THAT COULD HAPPEN? WE'RE JUST TWO KOOKY KIDS WHO WANTED TO SEE THE INSIDE OF A COOL CLUB! WE DON'T KNOW ANY BETTER!
EVEN EVIL WIZARDS WOULD BUY THAT STORY, RIGHT?
HEY. FOUND A WINDOW. I'LL BOOST YOU UP.
hup!
KNOCK YOURSELF OUT, PERV. I'M WEARING BLOOMERS.

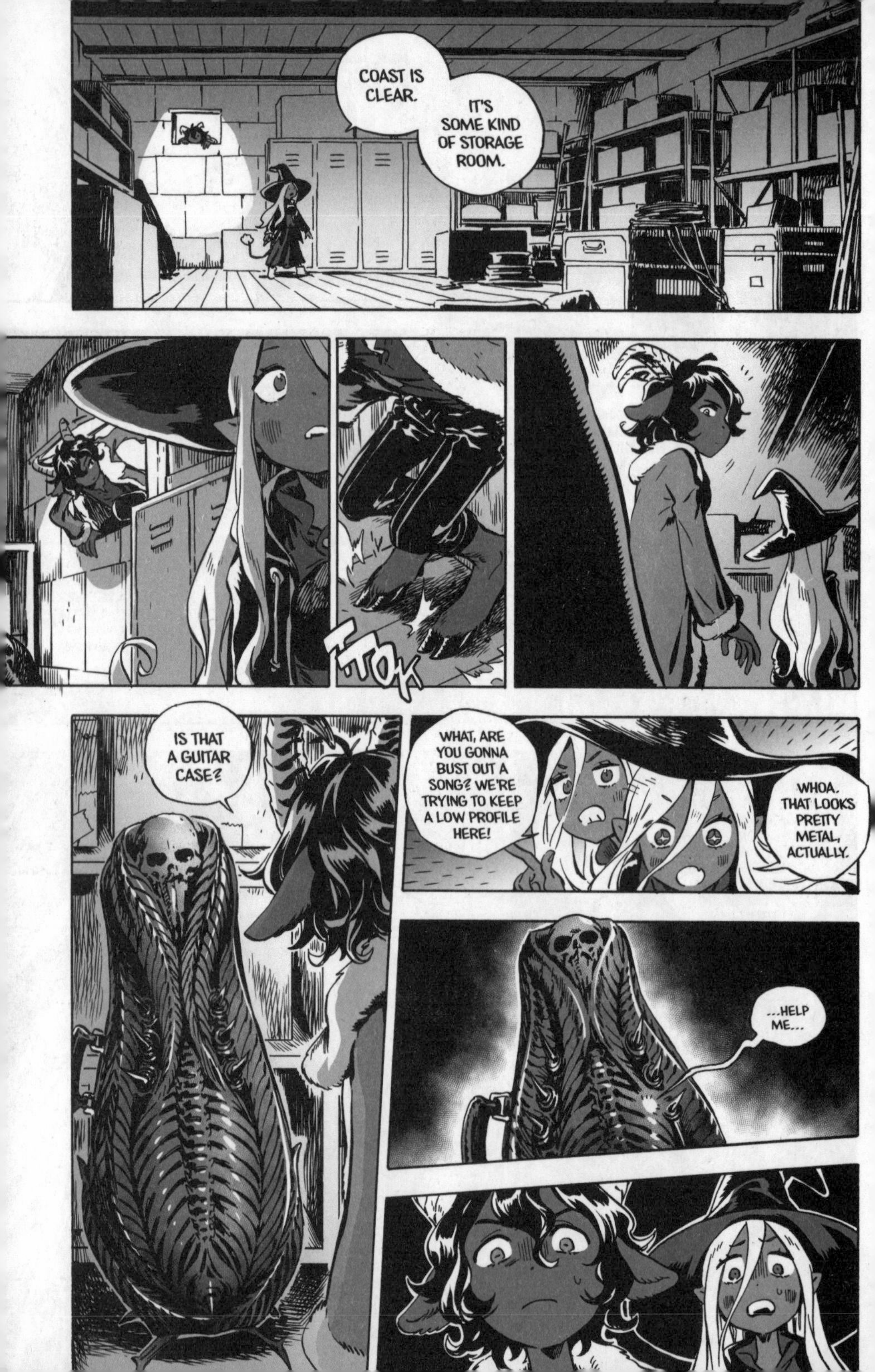
COAST IS CLEAR.
IT'S SOME KIND OF STORAGE ROOM.
TTOK
IS THAT A GUITAR CASE?
WHAT, ARE YOU GONNA BUST OUT A SONG? WE'RE TRYING TO KEEP A LOW PROFILE HERE!
WHOA. THAT LOOKS PRETTY METAL, ACTUALLY.
...HELP ME...

I-IS SOMEBODY IN THERE?

...LET ME OUT...

DEFINITELY GHOSTS.

SO CONFIDENT! SO STUPID!

NAH, BRO. YOUUUU ARE *THE CHOSEN ONEEE!*

OPEN THE CASE *AND EMBRACE YOUR DESTINY!* It'll be totally sick, I promise!

KREAK

OH, IT'S A GUITAR.

COOL.

blink

blink

WHEW, THANKS MAN. SOME JERKS ARE TRYING TO PAWN ME OFF.

YOU GOTTA GET ME OUTTA HERE. LIKE, PRONTO!

JERKS? WHAT JERKS? WAS ONE OF THEM NAMED STRAZIO?

HUH? YEAH. THAT'S HIM. HE'S WORKING WITH A DUDE NAMED TREMOLO, WHO WANTS ME REAL BAD.

ANYWAY, I'M OBVIOUSLY JUST A PLAIN OLD GUITAR-SHAPED DEVIL AND NOT AN ACTUAL GUITAR, SO SELLING ME IS LIKE SLAVERY, RIGHT?

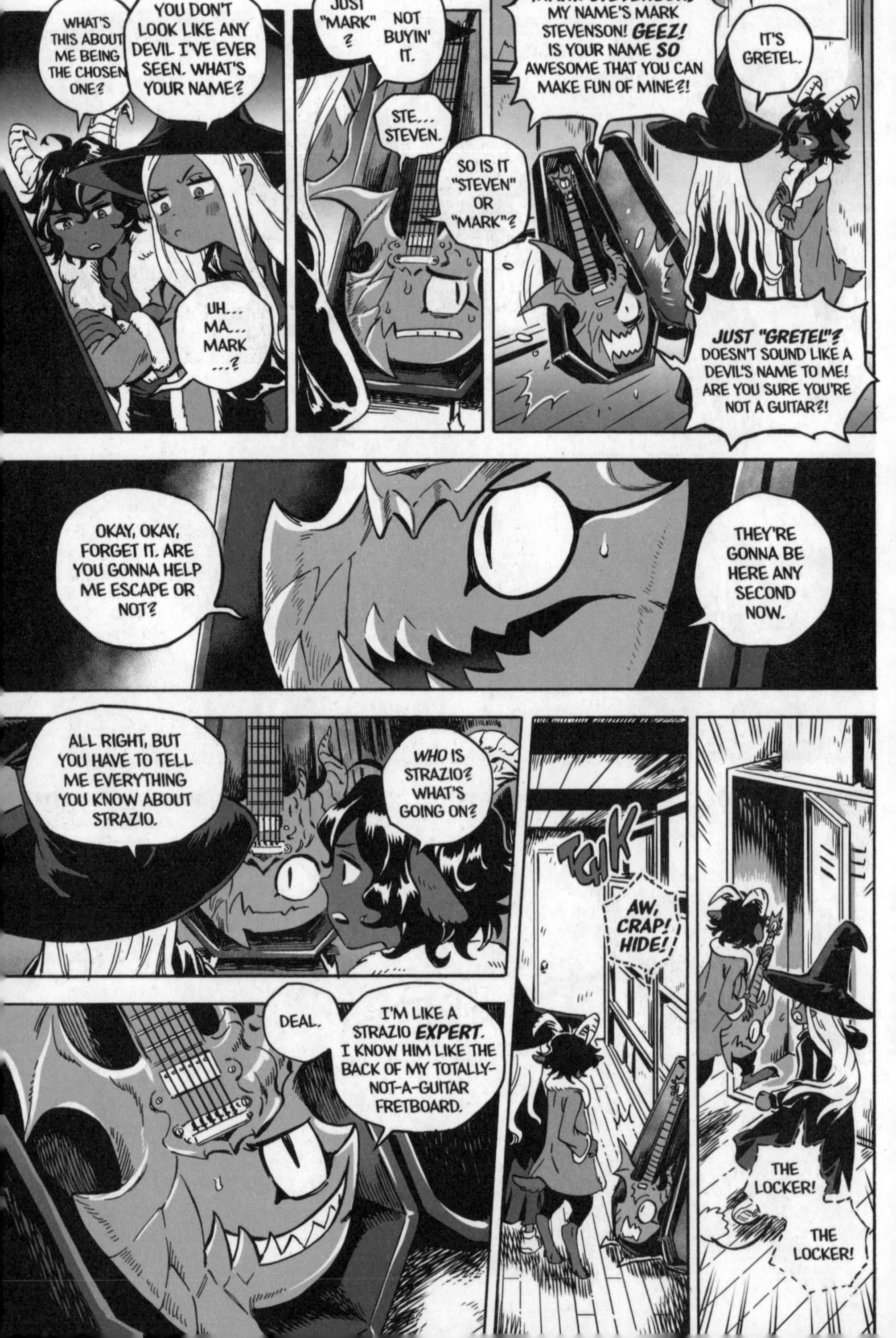
WHAT'S THIS ABOUT ME BEING THE CHOSEN ONE?
YOU DON'T LOOK LIKE ANY DEVIL I'VE EVER SEEN. WHAT'S YOUR NAME?
UH... MA... MARK ...?
JUST "MARK"?
NOT BUYIN' IT.
STE... STEVEN.
SO IS IT "STEVEN" OR "MARK"?
MARK STEVENSON! MY NAME'S MARK STEVENSON! GEEZ! IS YOUR NAME SO AWESOME THAT YOU CAN MAKE FUN OF MINE?!
IT'S GRETEL.
JUST "GRETEL"? DOESN'T SOUND LIKE A DEVIL'S NAME TO ME! ARE YOU SURE YOU'RE NOT A GUITAR?!
OKAY, OKAY, FORGET IT. ARE YOU GONNA HELP ME ESCAPE OR NOT?
THEY'RE GONNA BE HERE ANY SECOND NOW.
ALL RIGHT, BUT YOU HAVE TO TELL ME EVERYTHING YOU KNOW ABOUT STRAZIO.
WHO IS STRAZIO? WHAT'S GOING ON?
DEAL.
I'M LIKE A STRAZIO EXPERT. I KNOW HIM LIKE THE BACK OF MY TOTALLY-NOT-A-GUITAR FRETBOARD.
TCHK
AW, CRAP! HIDE!
THE LOCKER!
THE LOCKER!

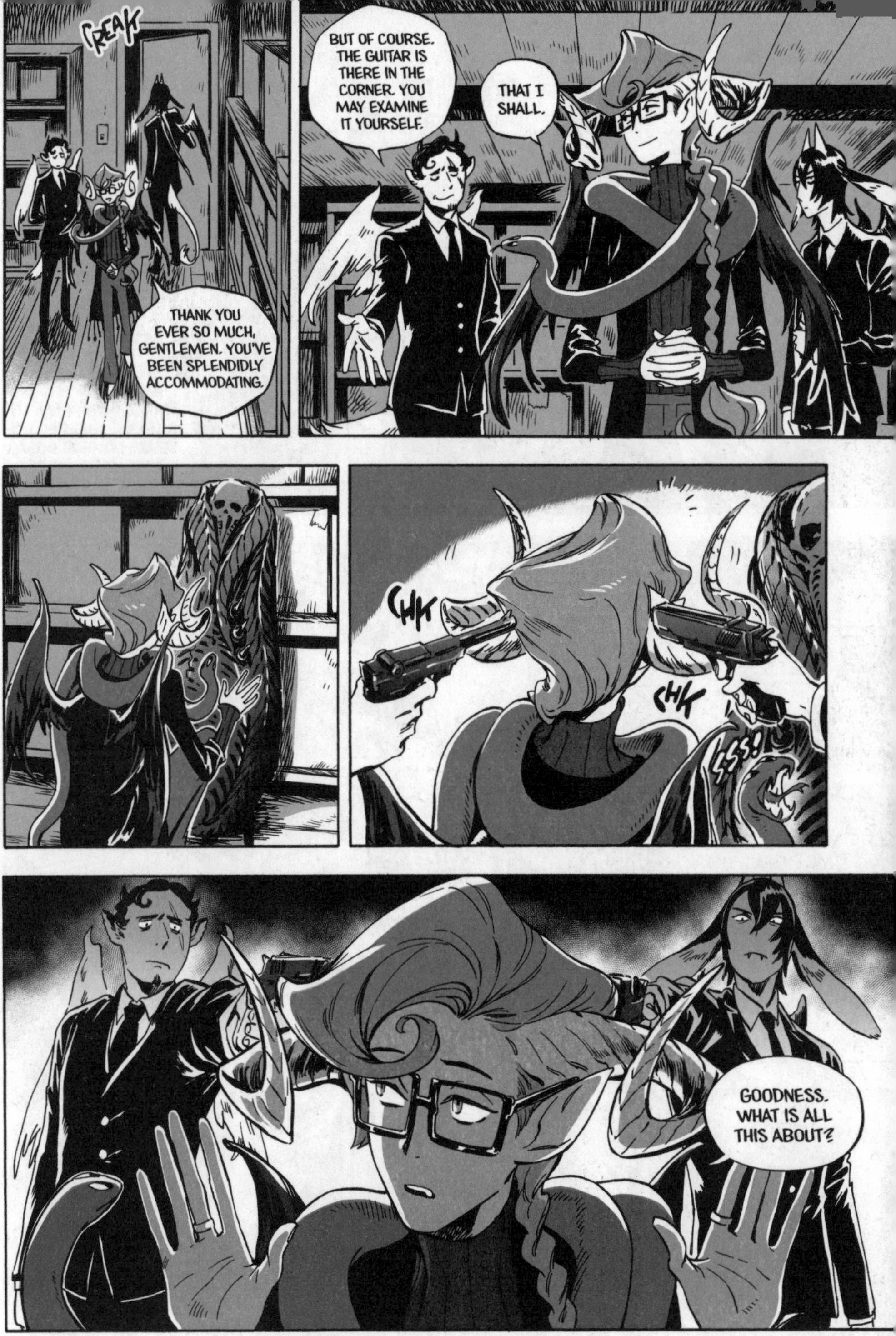
CREAK
THANK YOU EVER SO MUCH, GENTLEMEN. YOU'VE BEEN SPLENDIDLY ACCOMMODATING.
BUT OF COURSE. THE GUITAR IS THERE IN THE CORNER. YOU MAY EXAMINE IT YOURSELF.
THAT I SHALL.
CHK
CHK
SSS!
GOODNESS. WHAT IS ALL THIS ABOUT?

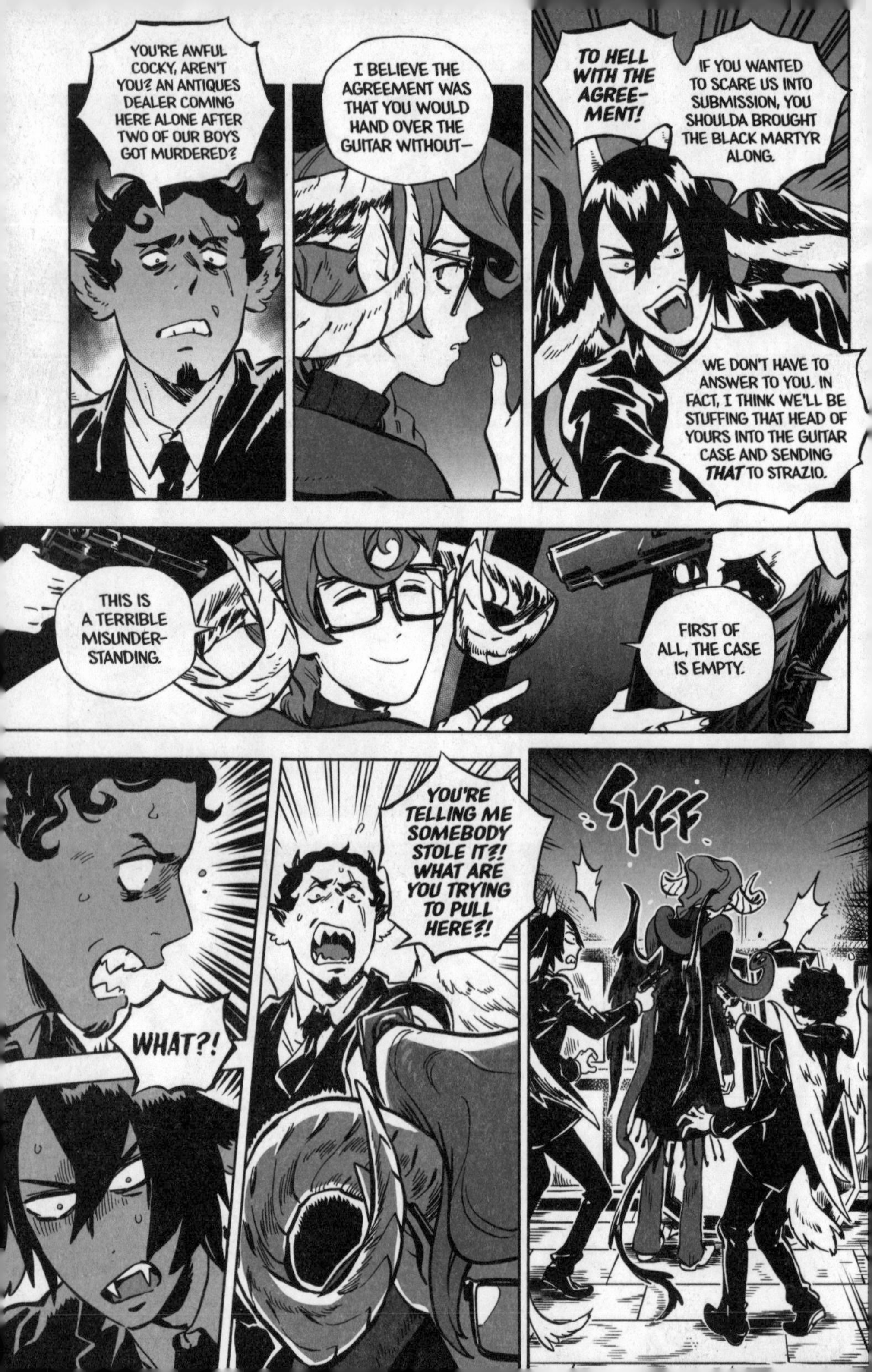
YOU'RE AWFUL COCKY, AREN'T YOU? AN ANTIQUES DEALER COMING HERE ALONE AFTER TWO OF OUR BOYS GOT MURDERED?
I BELIEVE THE AGREEMENT WAS THAT YOU WOULD HAND OVER THE GUITAR WITHOUT—
TO HELL WITH THE AGREE-MENT!
IF YOU WANTED TO SCARE US INTO SUBMISSION, YOU SHOULDA BROUGHT THE BLACK MARTYR ALONG.
WE DON'T HAVE TO ANSWER TO YOU. IN FACT, I THINK WE'LL BE STUFFING THAT HEAD OF YOURS INTO THE GUITAR CASE AND SENDING THAT TO STRAZIO.
THIS IS A TERRIBLE MISUNDER-STANDING.
FIRST OF ALL, THE CASE IS EMPTY.
WHAT?!
YOU'RE TELLING ME SOMEBODY STOLE IT?! WHAT ARE YOU TRYING TO PULL HERE?!
SKFF

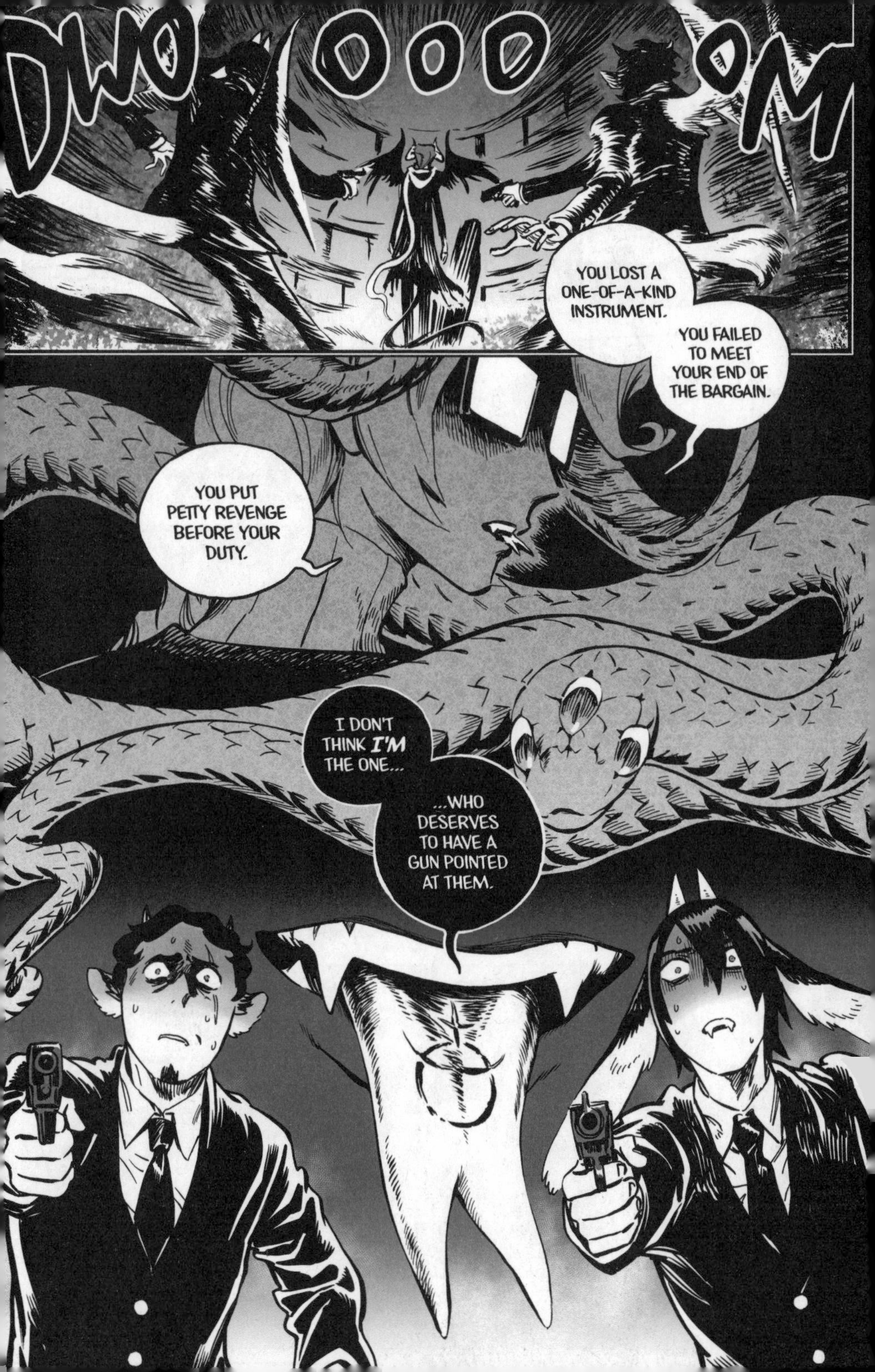
DWOOOOOOM
YOU LOST A ONE-OF-A-KIND INSTRUMENT.
YOU FAILED TO MEET YOUR END OF THE BARGAIN.
YOU PUT PETTY REVENGE BEFORE YOUR DUTY.
I DON'T THINK *I'M* THE ONE...
...WHO DESERVES TO HAVE A GUN POINTED AT THEM.

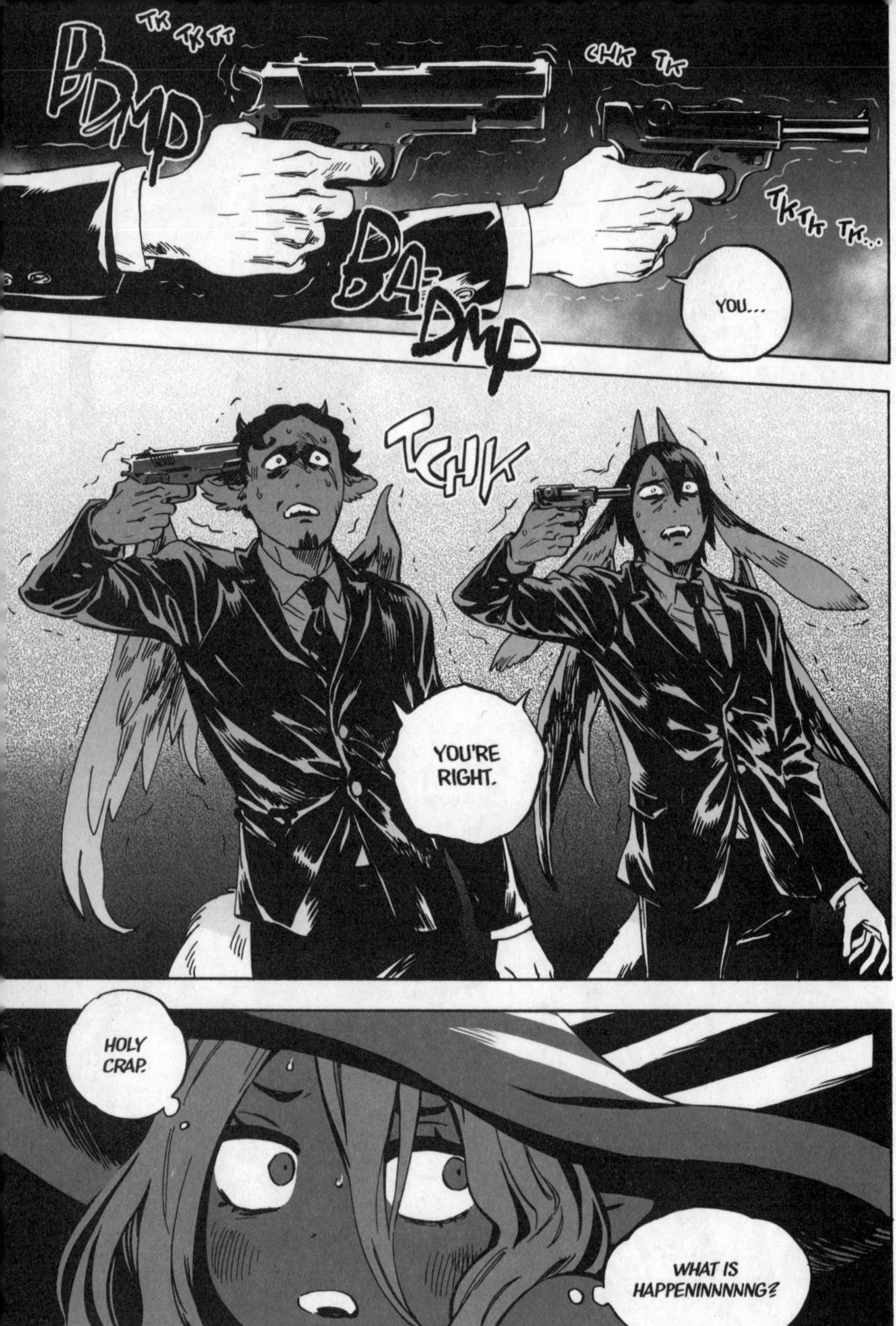
BDMP
TK TK TT
CHK TK
TKTK TK...
BA-DMP
YOU...
TCHK
YOU'RE RIGHT.
HOLY CRAP.
WHAT IS HAPPENINNNNNG?

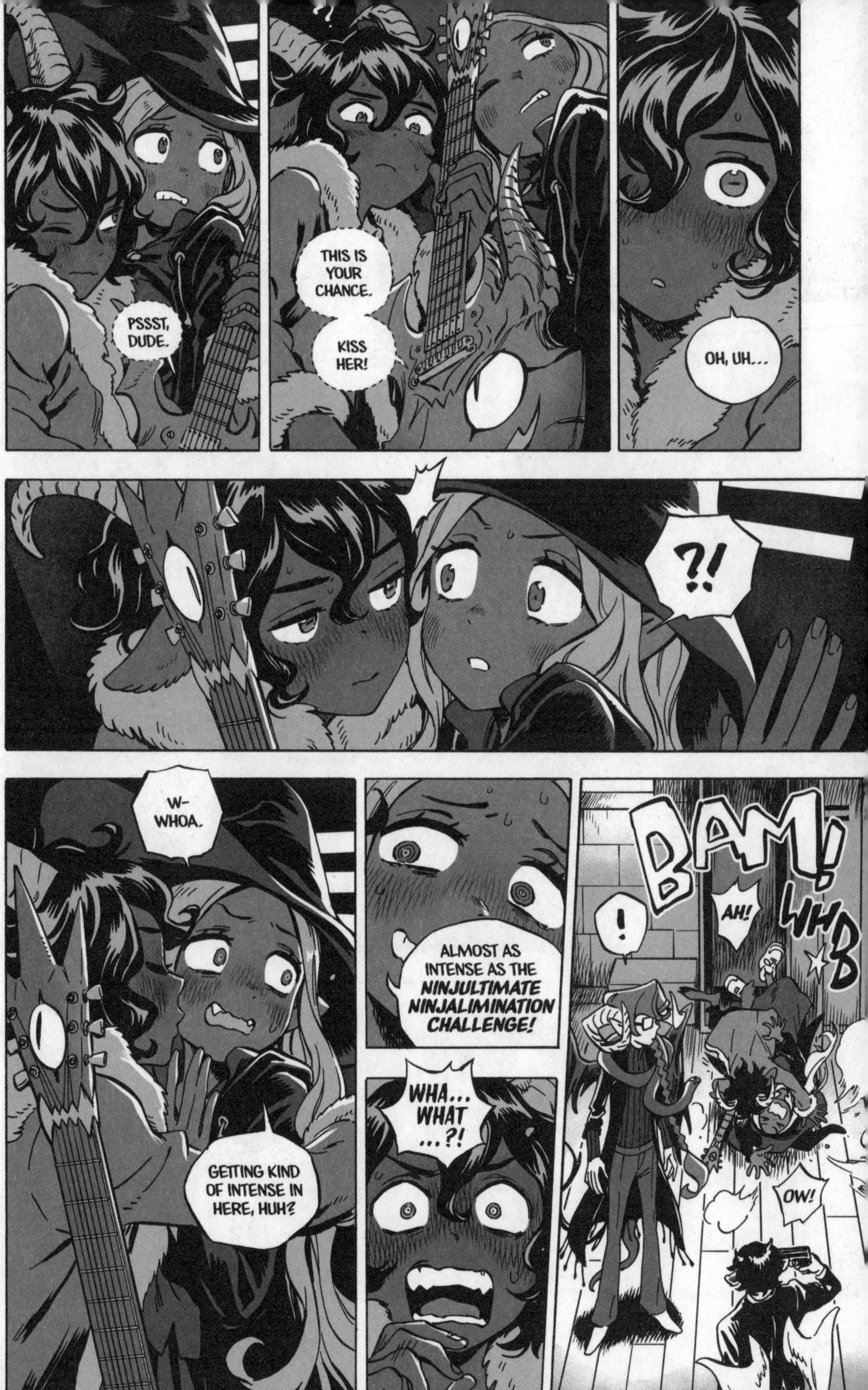
PSSST, DUDE.
THIS IS YOUR CHANCE.
KISS HER!
OH, UH...
?!
W-WHOA.
GETTING KIND OF INTENSE IN HERE, HUH?
ALMOST AS INTENSE AS THE ***NINJULTIMATE NINJALIMINATION CHALLENGE!***
WHA... WHAT ...?!
BAM!
!
AH!
OW!

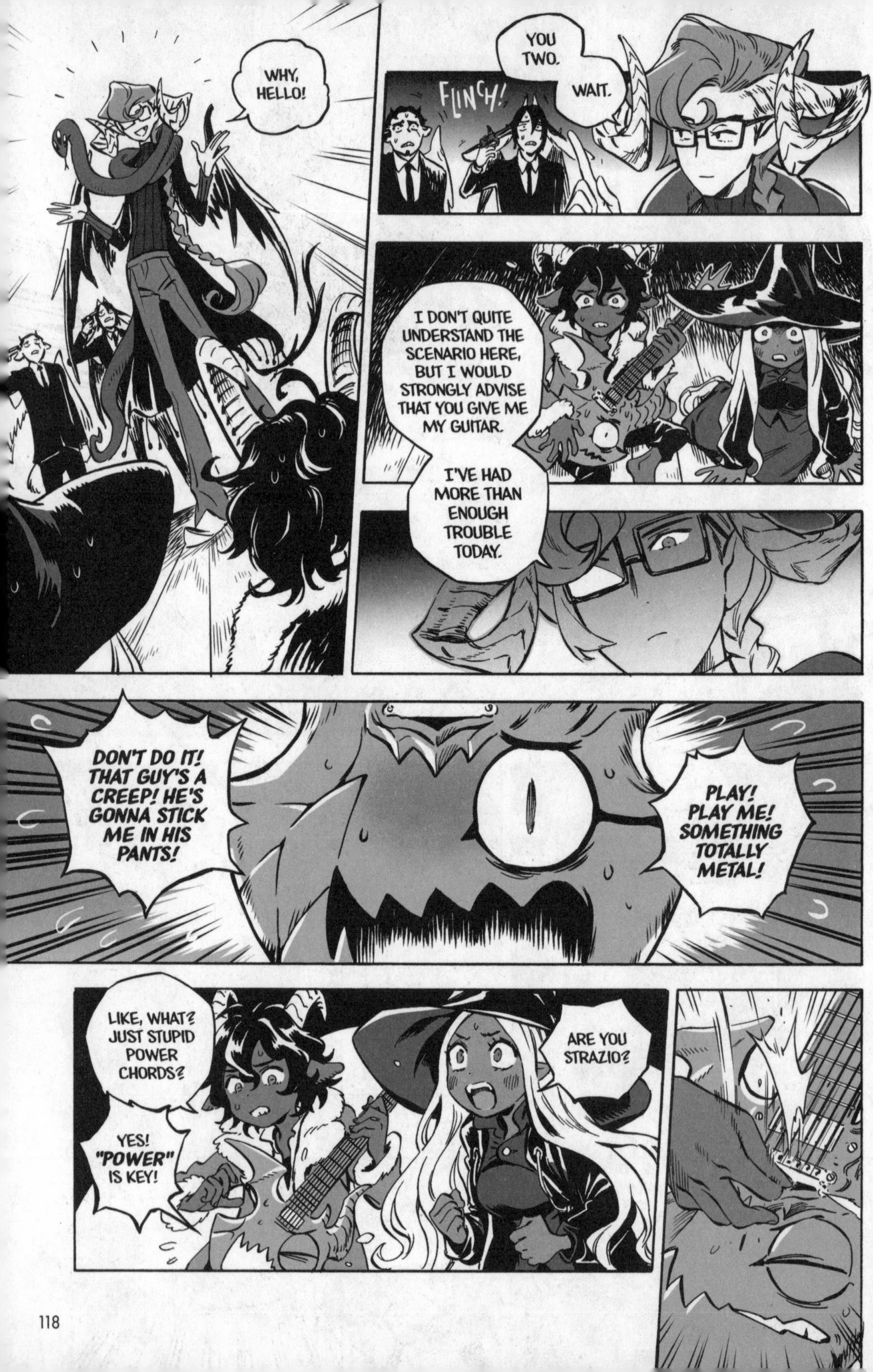
WHY, HELLO!
YOU TWO.
FLINCH!
WAIT.
I DON'T QUITE UNDERSTAND THE SCENARIO HERE, BUT I WOULD STRONGLY ADVISE THAT YOU GIVE ME MY GUITAR.
I'VE HAD MORE THAN ENOUGH TROUBLE TODAY.
DON'T DO IT! THAT GUY'S A CREEP! HE'S GONNA STICK ME IN HIS PANTS!
PLAY! PLAY ME! SOMETHING TOTALLY METAL!
LIKE, WHAT? JUST STUPID POWER CHORDS?
YES! "POWER" IS KEY!
ARE YOU STRAZIO?

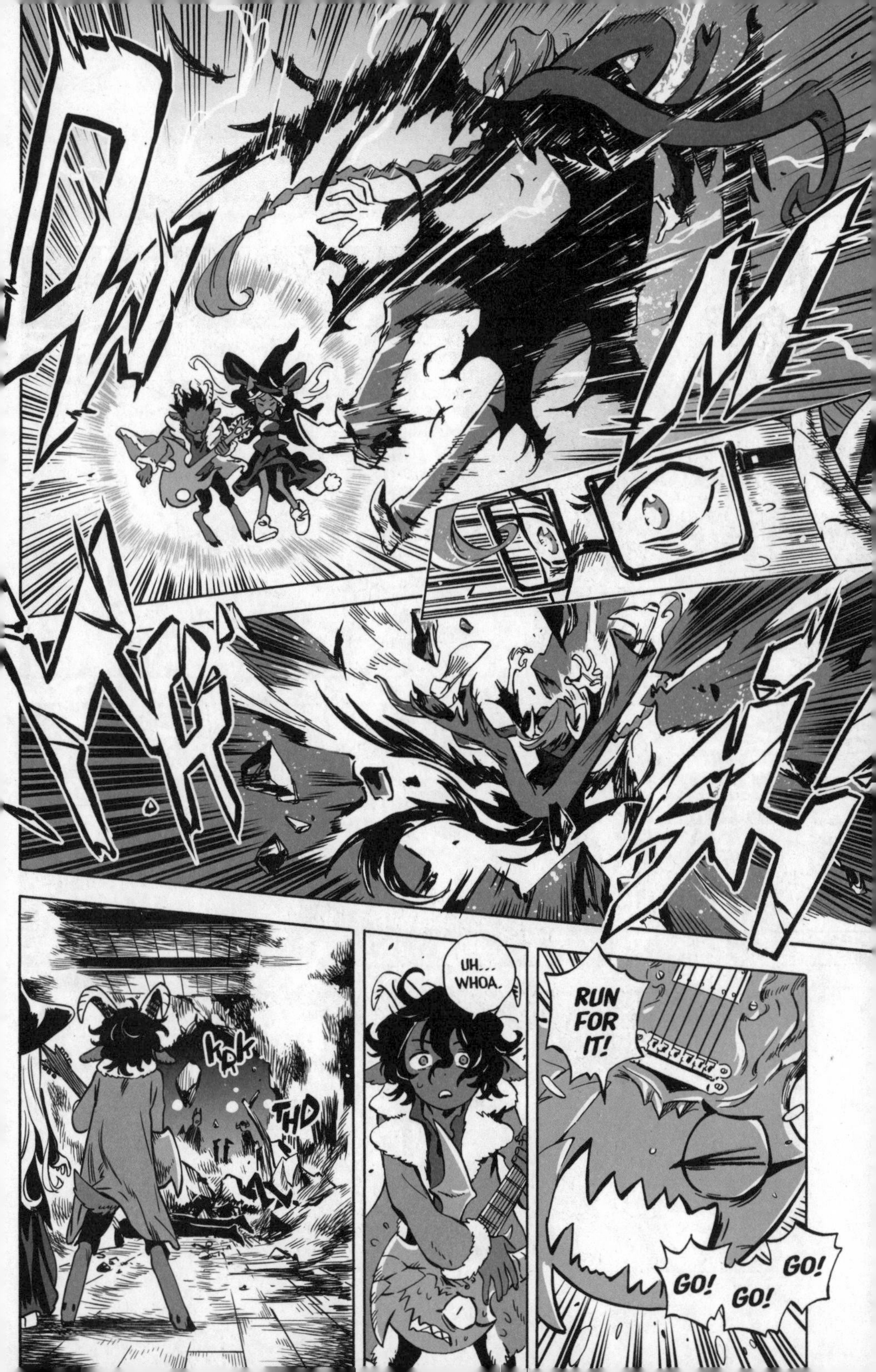
KRK
THD
UH... WHOA.
RUN FOR IT!
GO!
GO!
GO!

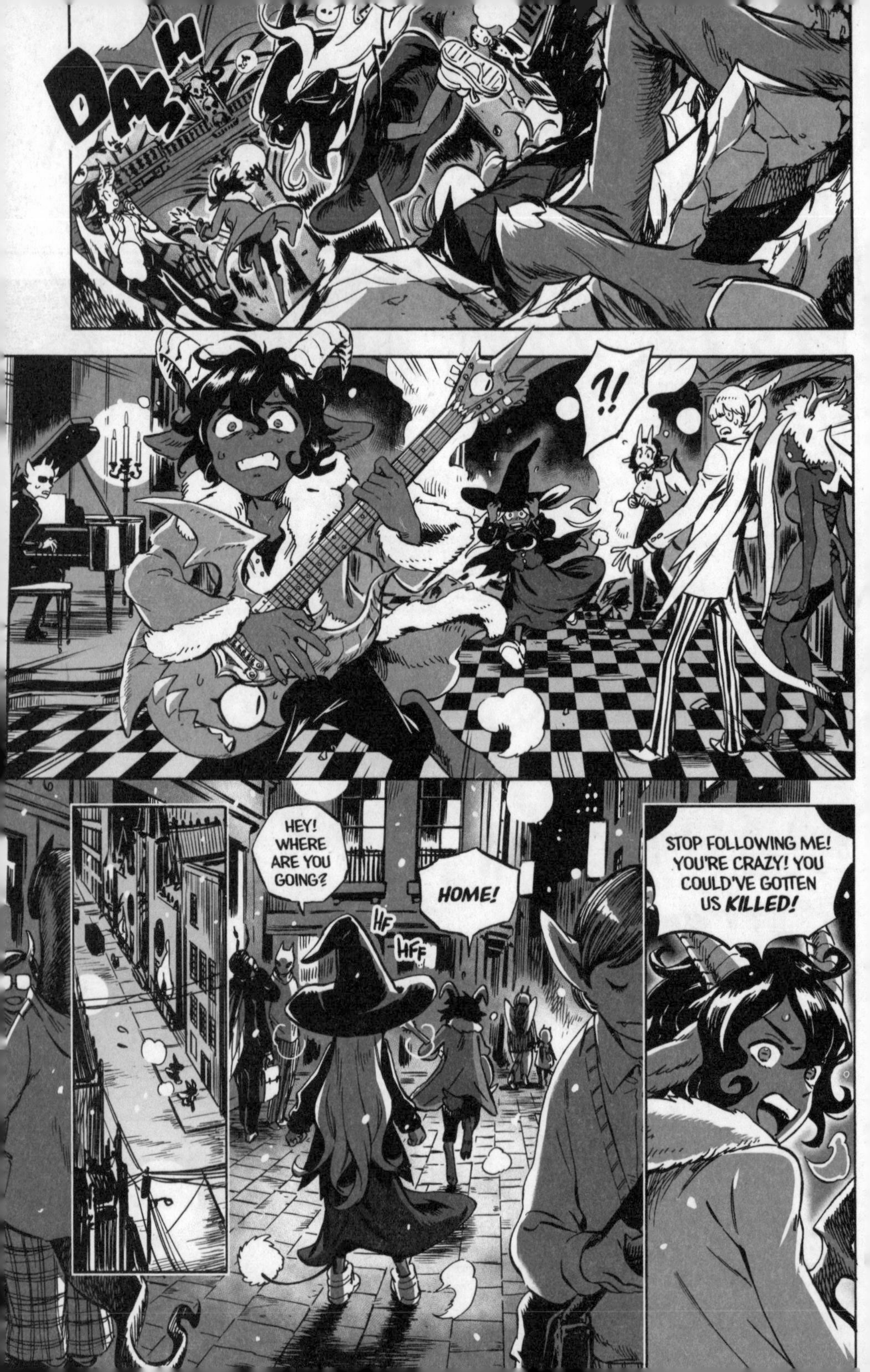
DASH
?!!
HEY! WHERE ARE YOU GOING?
HF HFF
HOME!
STOP FOLLOWING ME! YOU'RE CRAZY! YOU COULD'VE GOTTEN US KILLED!

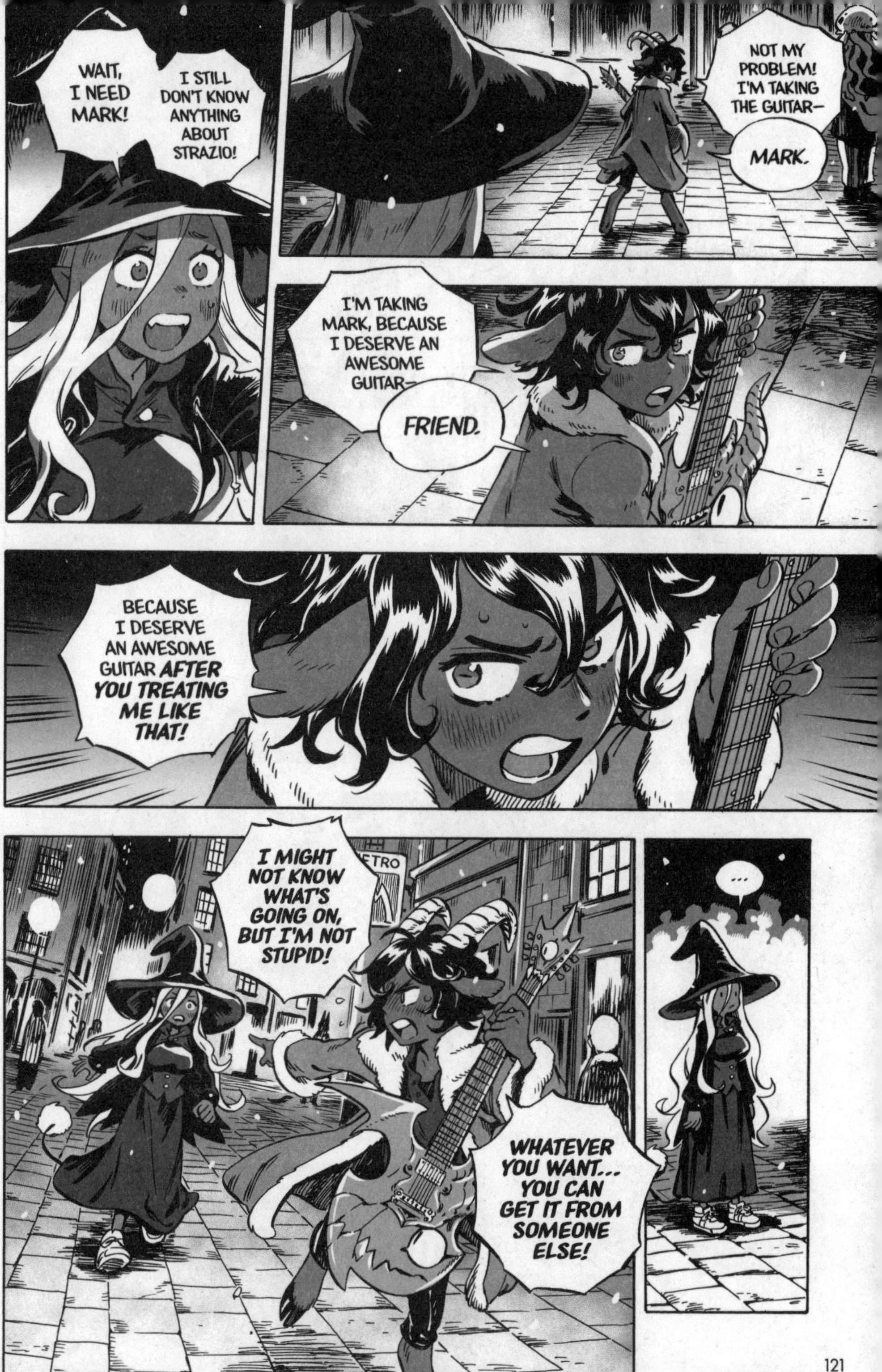
WAIT, I NEED MARK!
I STILL DON'T KNOW ANYTHING ABOUT STRAZIO!
NOT MY PROBLEM! I'M TAKING THE GUITAR—
MARK.
I'M TAKING MARK, BECAUSE I DESERVE AN AWESOME GUITAR—
FRIEND.
BECAUSE I DESERVE AN AWESOME GUITAR AFTER YOU TREATING ME LIKE THAT!
I MIGHT NOT KNOW WHAT'S GOING ON, BUT I'M NOT STUPID!
WHATEVER YOU WANT... YOU CAN GET IT FROM SOMEONE ELSE!
...

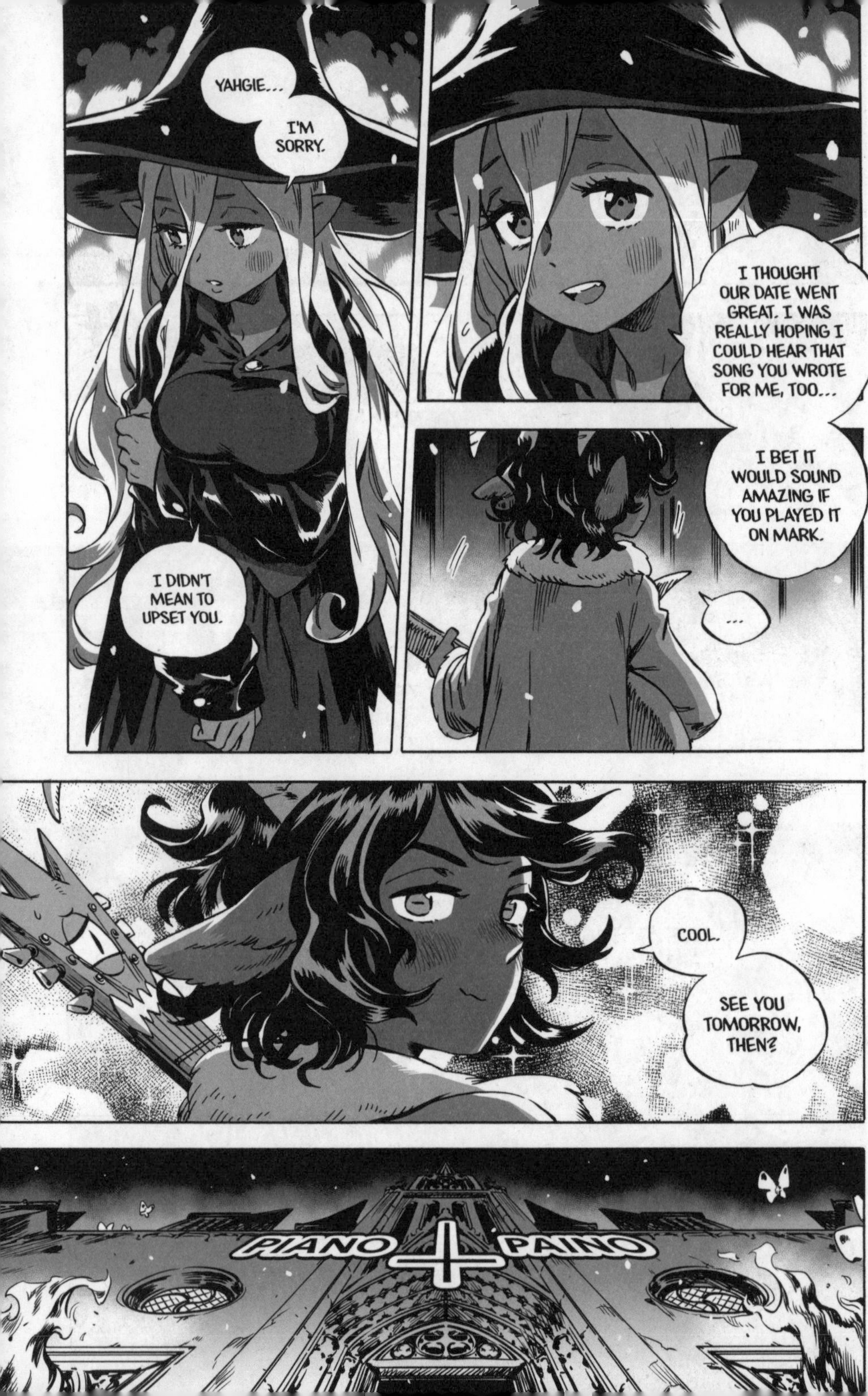
YAHGIE...
I'M SORRY.
I DIDN'T MEAN TO UPSET YOU.
I THOUGHT OUR DATE WENT GREAT. I WAS REALLY HOPING I COULD HEAR THAT SONG YOU WROTE FOR ME, TOO...
I BET IT WOULD SOUND AMAZING IF YOU PLAYED IT ON MARK.
...
COOL.
SEE YOU TOMORROW, THEN?
PIANO PAINO

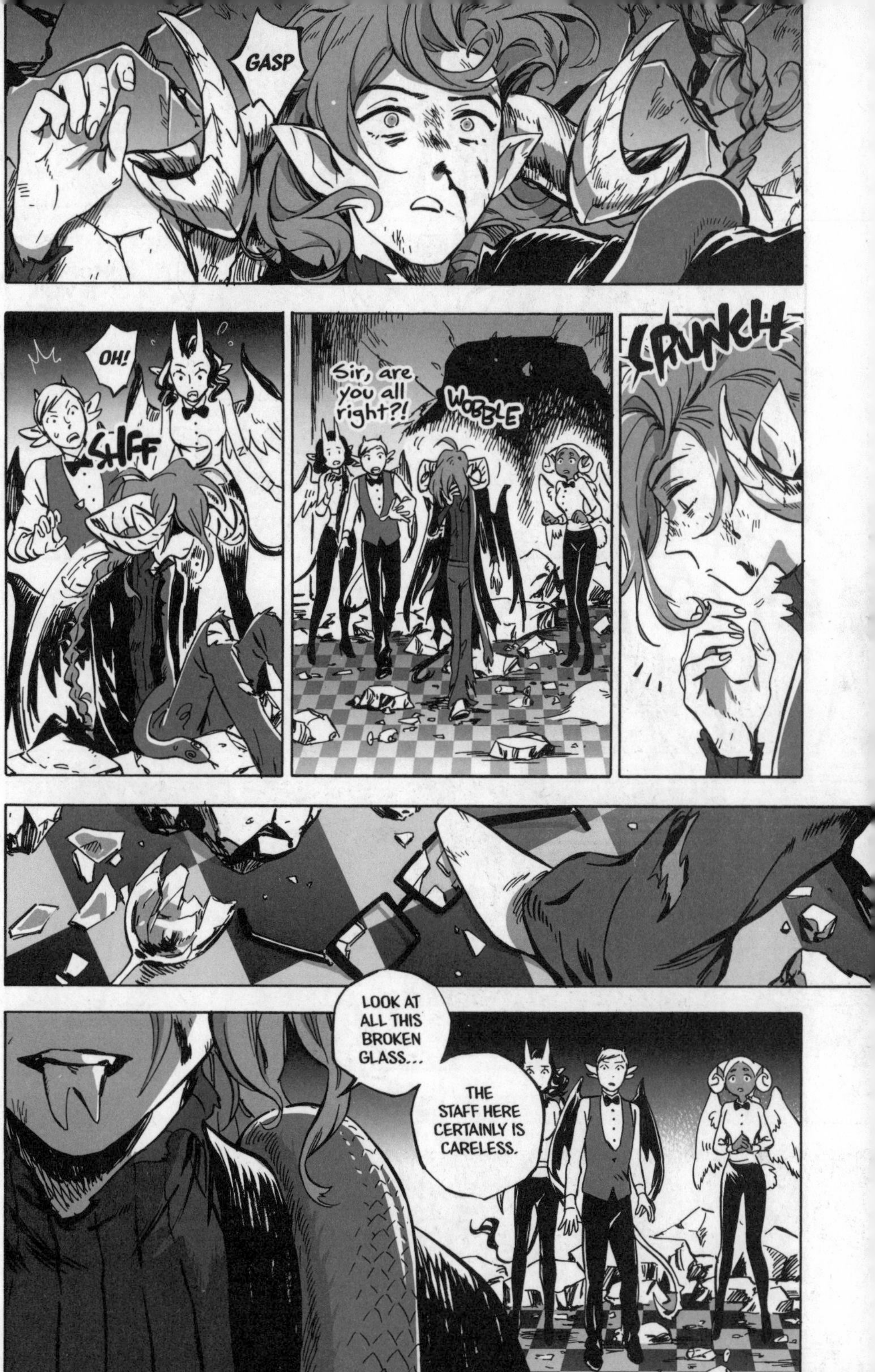
GASP
OH!
SHFF
Sir, are you all right?!
WOBBLE
CRUNCH
LOOK AT ALL THIS BROKEN GLASS...
THE STAFF HERE CERTAINLY IS CARELESS.

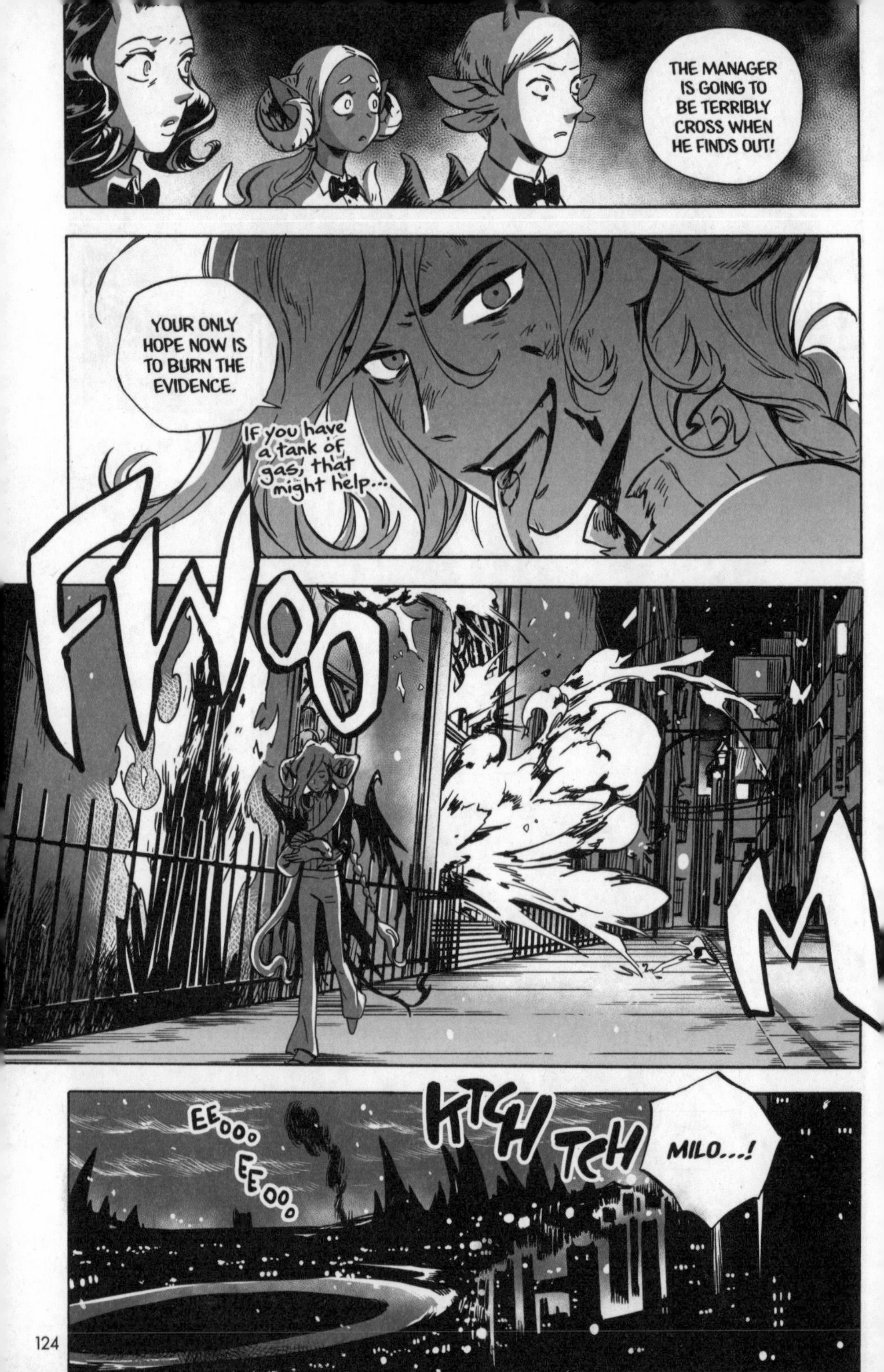
THE MANAGER IS GOING TO BE TERRIBLY CROSS WHEN HE FINDS OUT!
YOUR ONLY HOPE NOW IS TO BURN THE EVIDENCE.
If you have a tank of gas, that might help...
FWOOM
EEooo EEoo
KTCH TCH
MILO...!

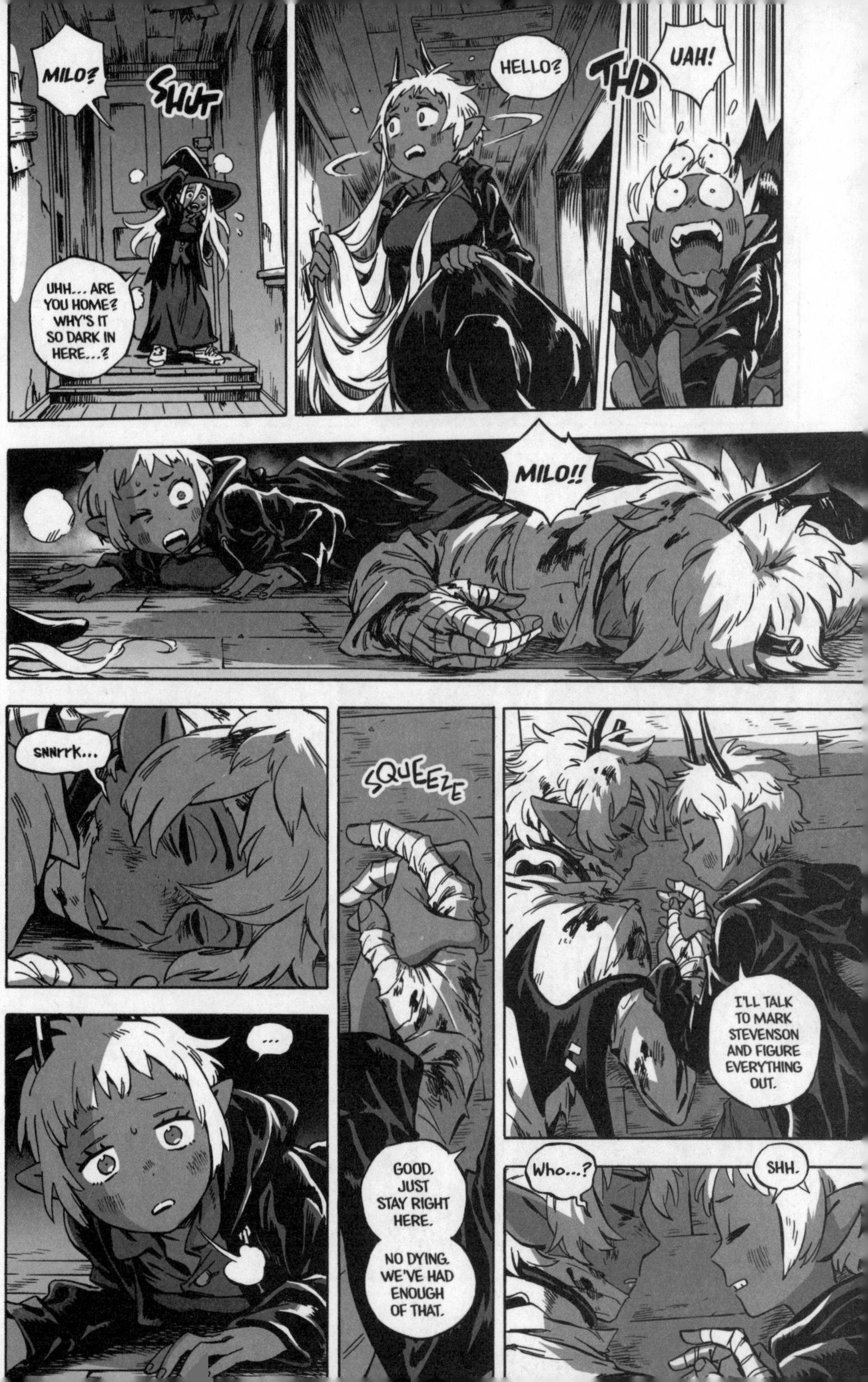
MILO?
SHUT
UHH... ARE YOU HOME? WHY'S IT SO DARK IN HERE...?
HELLO?
THD
UAH!
MILO!!
snnrrk...
SQUEEZE
I'LL TALK TO MARK STEVENSON AND FIGURE EVERYTHING OUT.
...
GOOD. JUST STAY RIGHT HERE.
NO DYING. WE'VE HAD ENOUGH OF THAT.
Who...?
SHH.

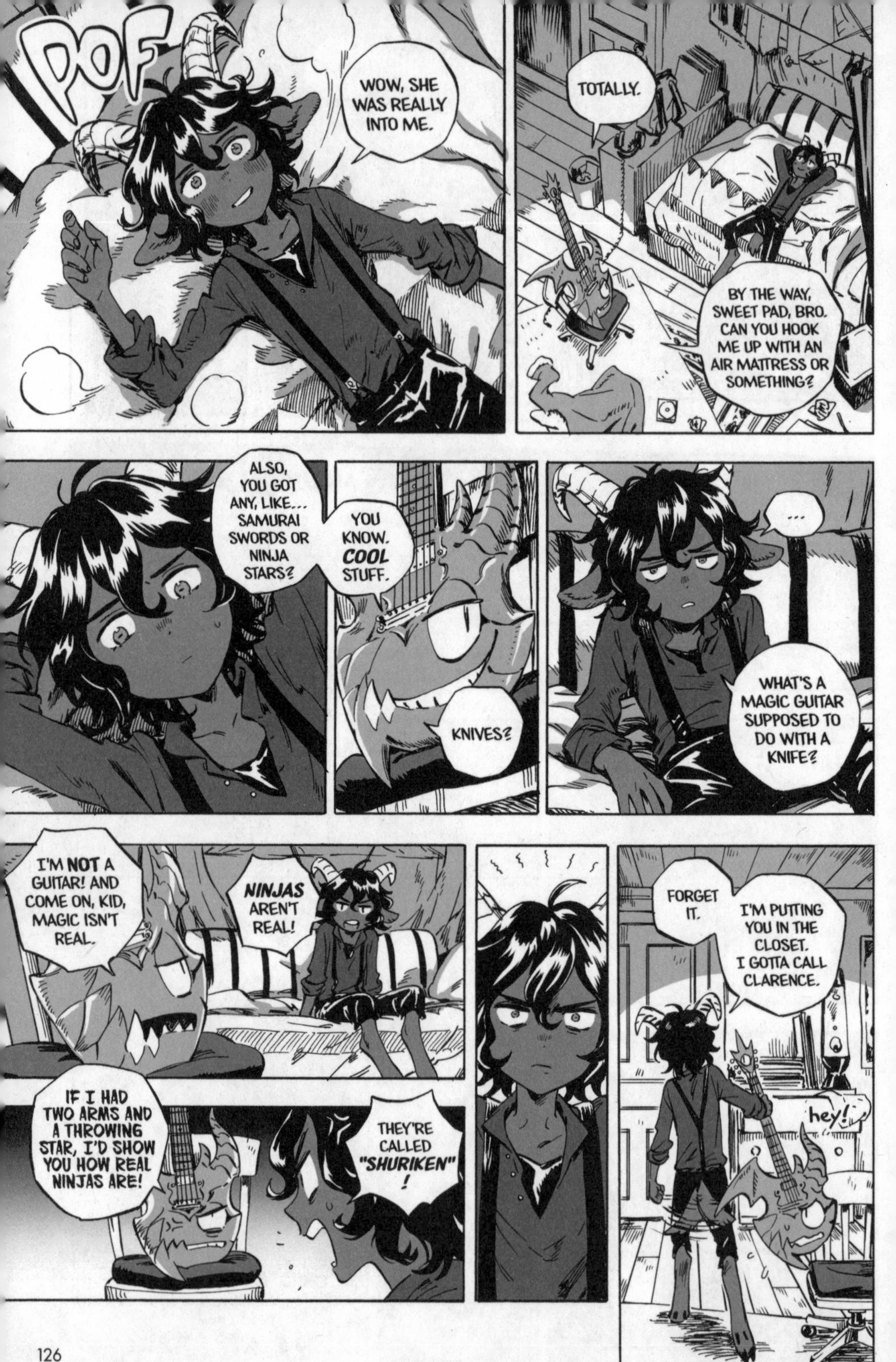
POF
WOW, SHE WAS REALLY INTO ME.
TOTALLY.
BY THE WAY, SWEET PAD, BRO. CAN YOU HOOK ME UP WITH AN AIR MATTRESS OR SOMETHING?
ALSO, YOU GOT ANY, LIKE... SAMURAI SWORDS OR NINJA STARS?
YOU KNOW. **COOL** STUFF.
KNIVES?
...
WHAT'S A MAGIC GUITAR SUPPOSED TO DO WITH A KNIFE?
I'M **NOT** A GUITAR! AND COME ON, KID, MAGIC ISN'T REAL.
NINJAS AREN'T REAL!
IF I HAD TWO ARMS AND A THROWING STAR, I'D SHOW YOU HOW REAL NINJAS ARE!
THEY'RE CALLED ***"SHURIKEN"*** !
FORGET IT.
I'M PUTTING YOU IN THE CLOSET. I GOTTA CALL CLARENCE.
hey!

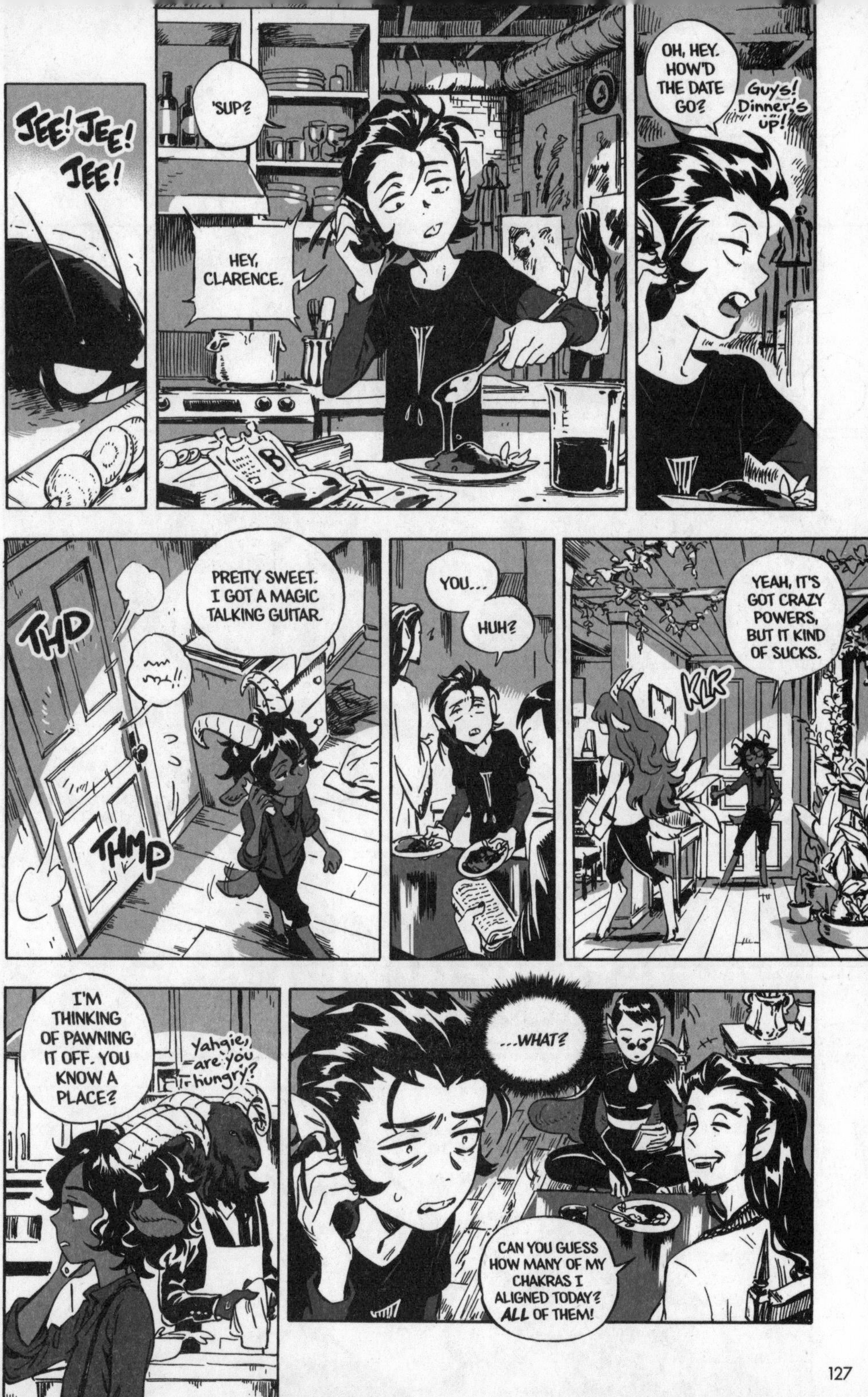
JEE! JEE! JEE!
'SUP?
HEY, CLARENCE.
OH, HEY. HOW'D THE DATE GO?
Guys! Dinner's up!
THD
PRETTY SWEET. I GOT A MAGIC TALKING GUITAR.
THMP
YOU...
HUH?
YEAH, IT'S GOT CRAZY POWERS, BUT IT KIND OF SUCKS.
KLK
I'M THINKING OF PAWNING IT OFF. YOU KNOW A PLACE?
Yahgie, are you hungry?
...WHAT?
CAN YOU GUESS HOW MANY OF MY CHAKRAS I ALIGNED TODAY? ALL OF THEM!

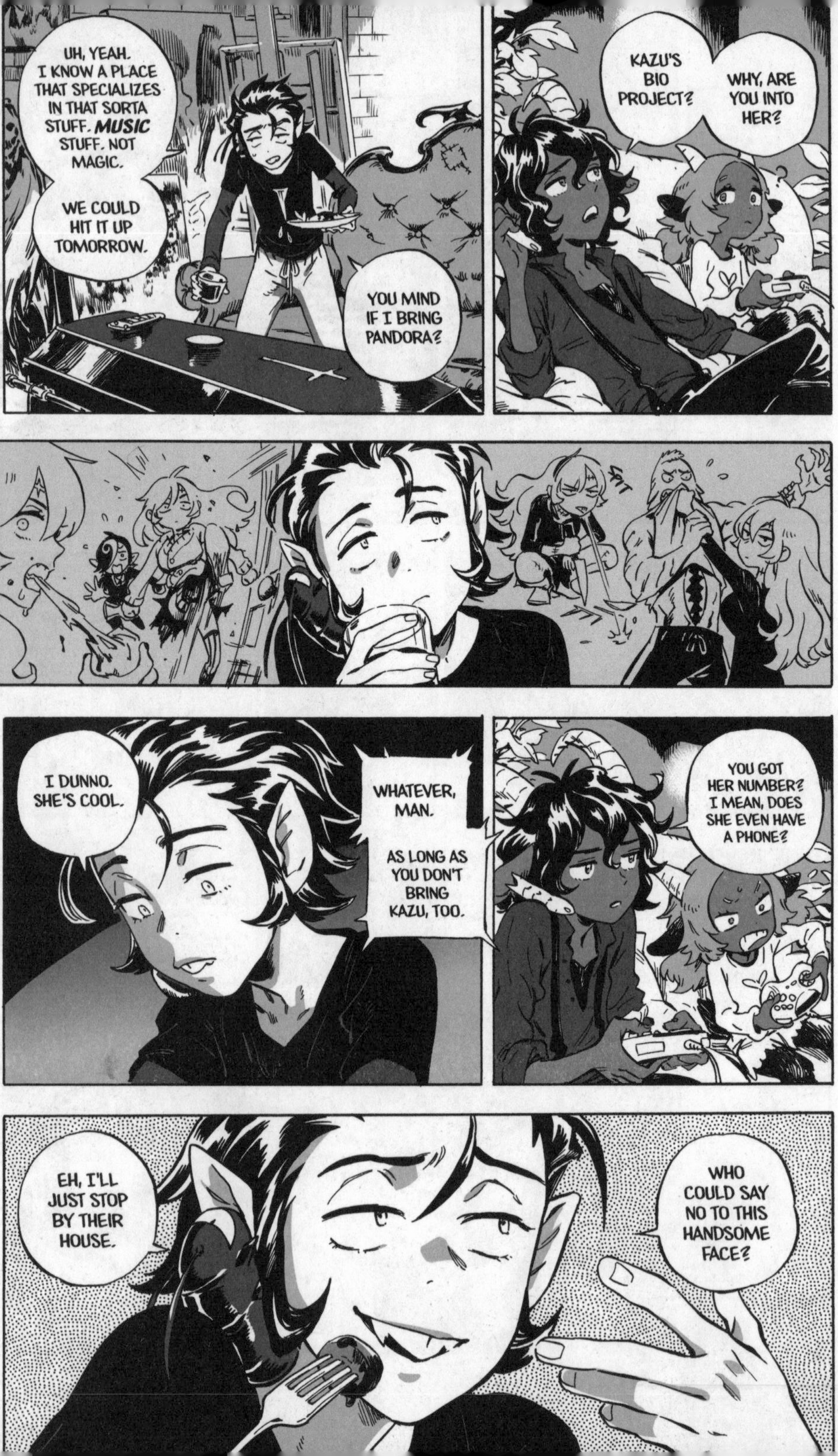
UH, YEAH. I KNOW A PLACE THAT SPECIALIZES IN THAT SORTA STUFF. *MUSIC* STUFF. NOT MAGIC.
WE COULD HIT IT UP TOMORROW.
YOU MIND IF I BRING PANDORA?
KAZU'S BIO PROJECT?
WHY, ARE YOU INTO HER?
I DUNNO. SHE'S COOL.
WHATEVER, MAN.
AS LONG AS YOU DON'T BRING KAZU, TOO.
YOU GOT HER NUMBER? I MEAN, DOES SHE EVEN HAVE A PHONE?
EH, I'LL JUST STOP BY THEIR HOUSE.
WHO COULD SAY NO TO THIS HANDSOME FACE?

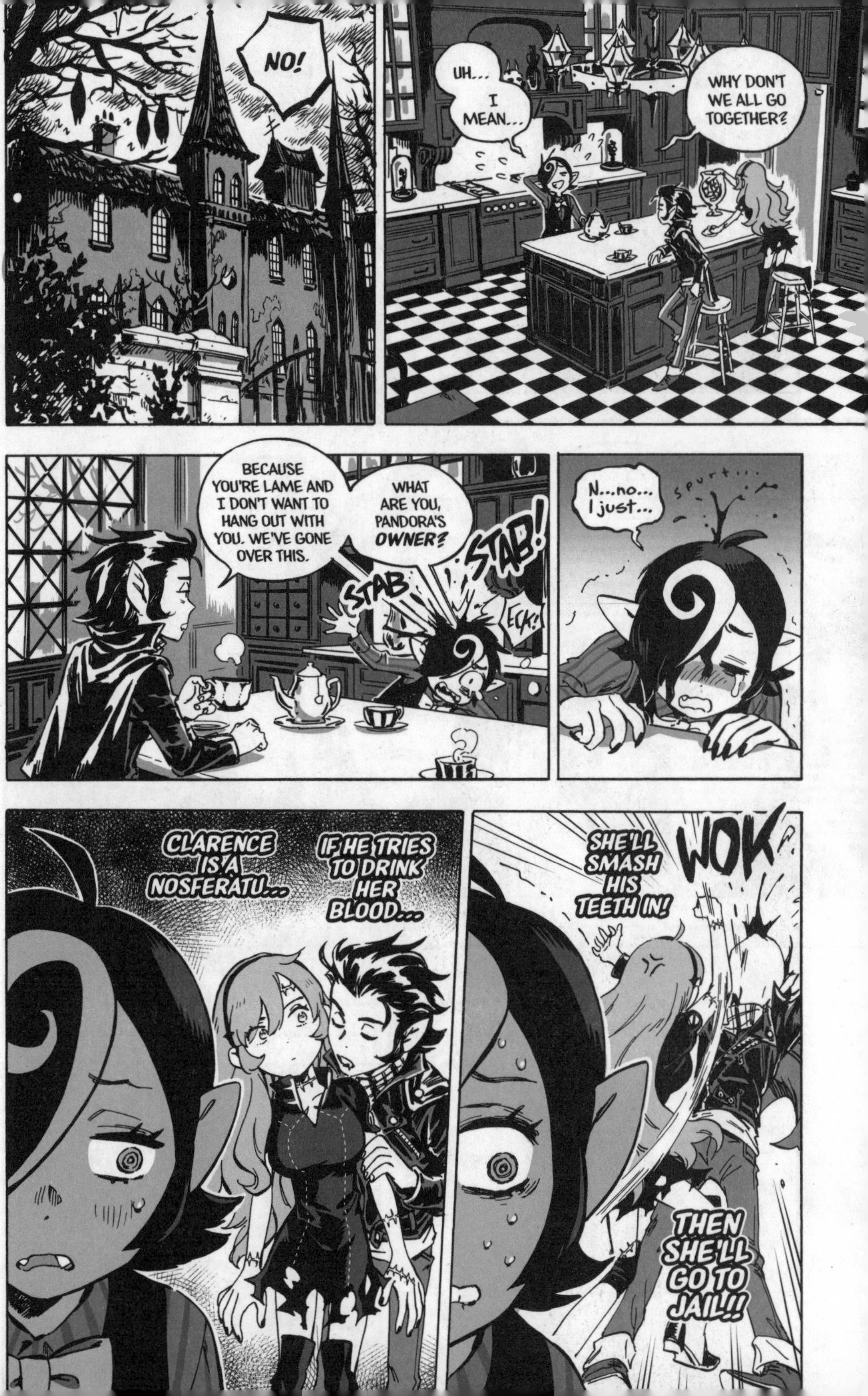
NO!
UH... I MEAN...
WHY DON'T WE ALL GO TOGETHER?
BECAUSE YOU'RE LAME AND I DON'T WANT TO HANG OUT WITH YOU. WE'VE GONE OVER THIS.
WHAT ARE YOU, PANDORA'S OWNER?
STAB
STAB!
ECK!
N...no... I just...
spurt...
CLARENCE IS A NOSFERATU...
IF HE TRIES TO DRINK HER BLOOD...
SHE'LL SMASH HIS TEETH IN!
WOK
THEN SHE'LL GO TO JAIL!!

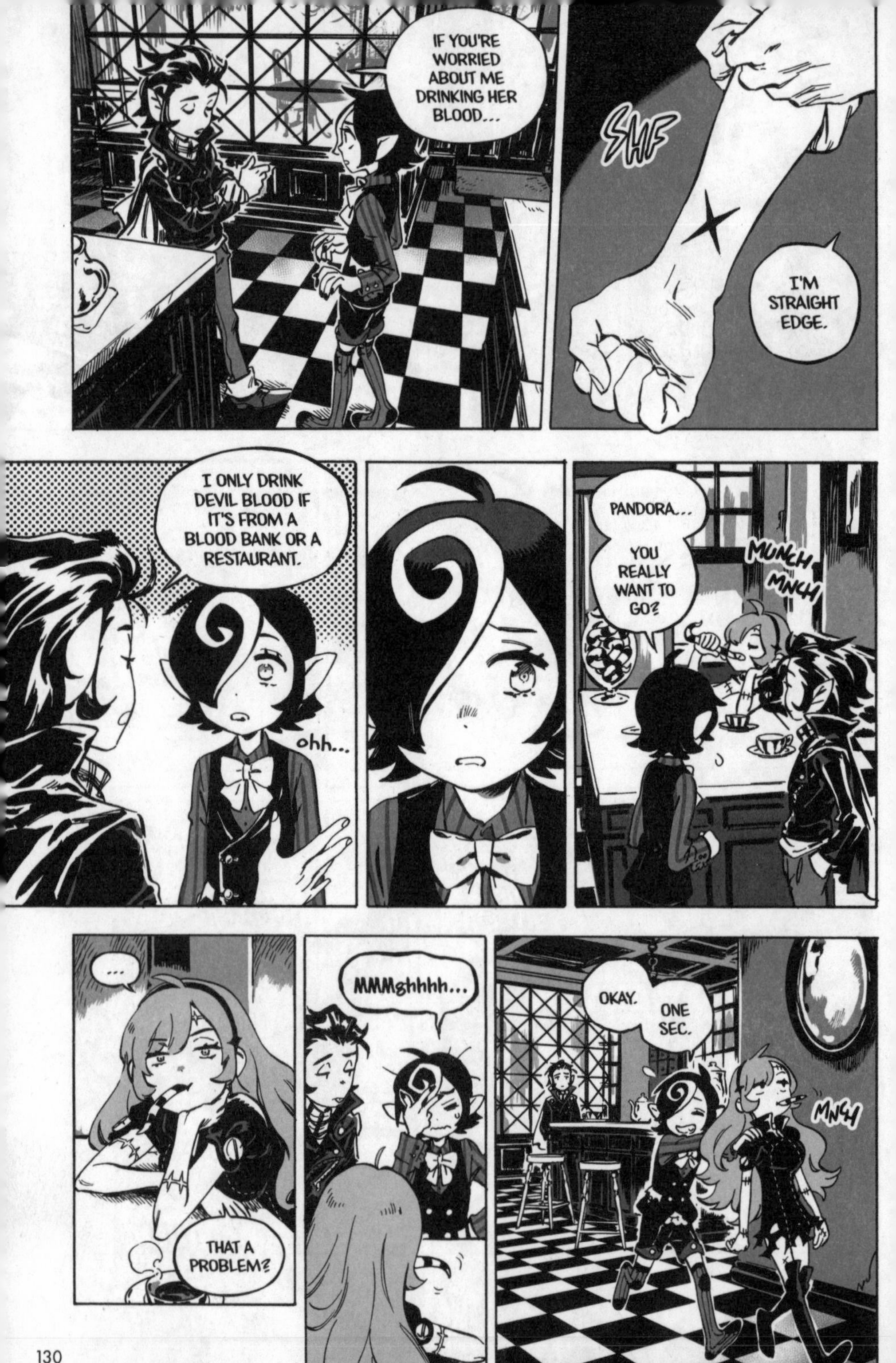
IF YOU'RE WORRIED ABOUT ME DRINKING HER BLOOD...
SHF
I'M STRAIGHT EDGE.
I ONLY DRINK DEVIL BLOOD IF IT'S FROM A BLOOD BANK OR A RESTAURANT.
ohh...
PANDORA...
YOU REALLY WANT TO GO?
MUNCH
MNCH
...
THAT A PROBLEM?
MMMghhhh...
OKAY.
ONE SEC.
MNCH

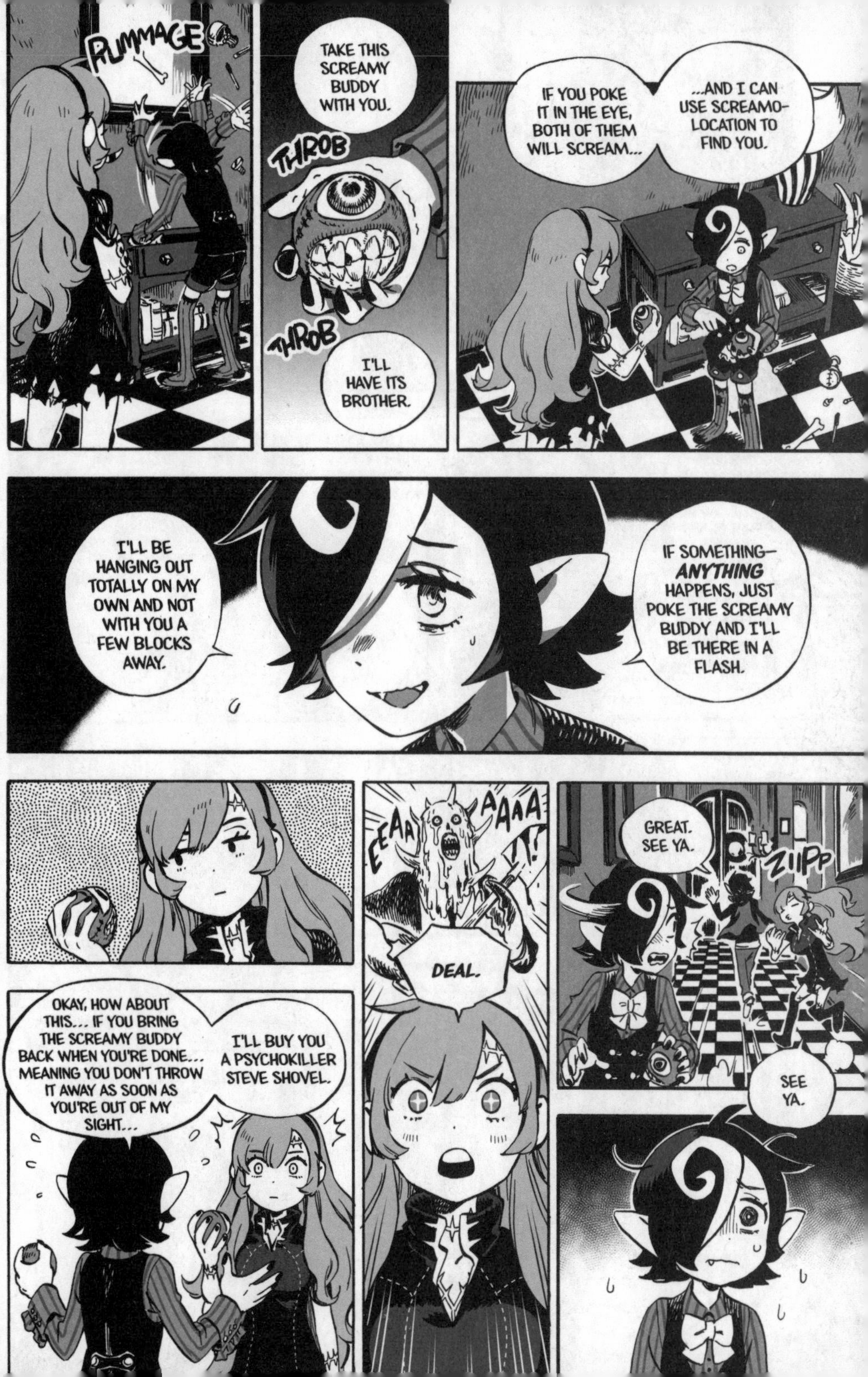
RUMMAGE
TAKE THIS SCREAMY BUDDY WITH YOU.
THROB
THROB
I'LL HAVE ITS BROTHER.
IF YOU POKE IT IN THE EYE, BOTH OF THEM WILL SCREAM...
...AND I CAN USE SCREAMO-LOCATION TO FIND YOU.
I'LL BE HANGING OUT TOTALLY ON MY OWN AND NOT WITH YOU A FEW BLOCKS AWAY.
IF SOMETHING— ***ANYTHING*** HAPPENS, JUST POKE THE SCREAMY BUDDY AND I'LL BE THERE IN A FLASH.
OKAY, HOW ABOUT THIS... IF YOU BRING THE SCREAMY BUDDY BACK WHEN YOU'RE DONE... MEANING YOU DON'T THROW IT AWAY AS SOON AS YOU'RE OUT OF MY SIGHT...
I'LL BUY YOU A PSYCHOKILLER STEVE SHOVEL.
EEAAAAAA
DEAL.
GREAT. SEE YA.
ZIIPP
SEE YA.

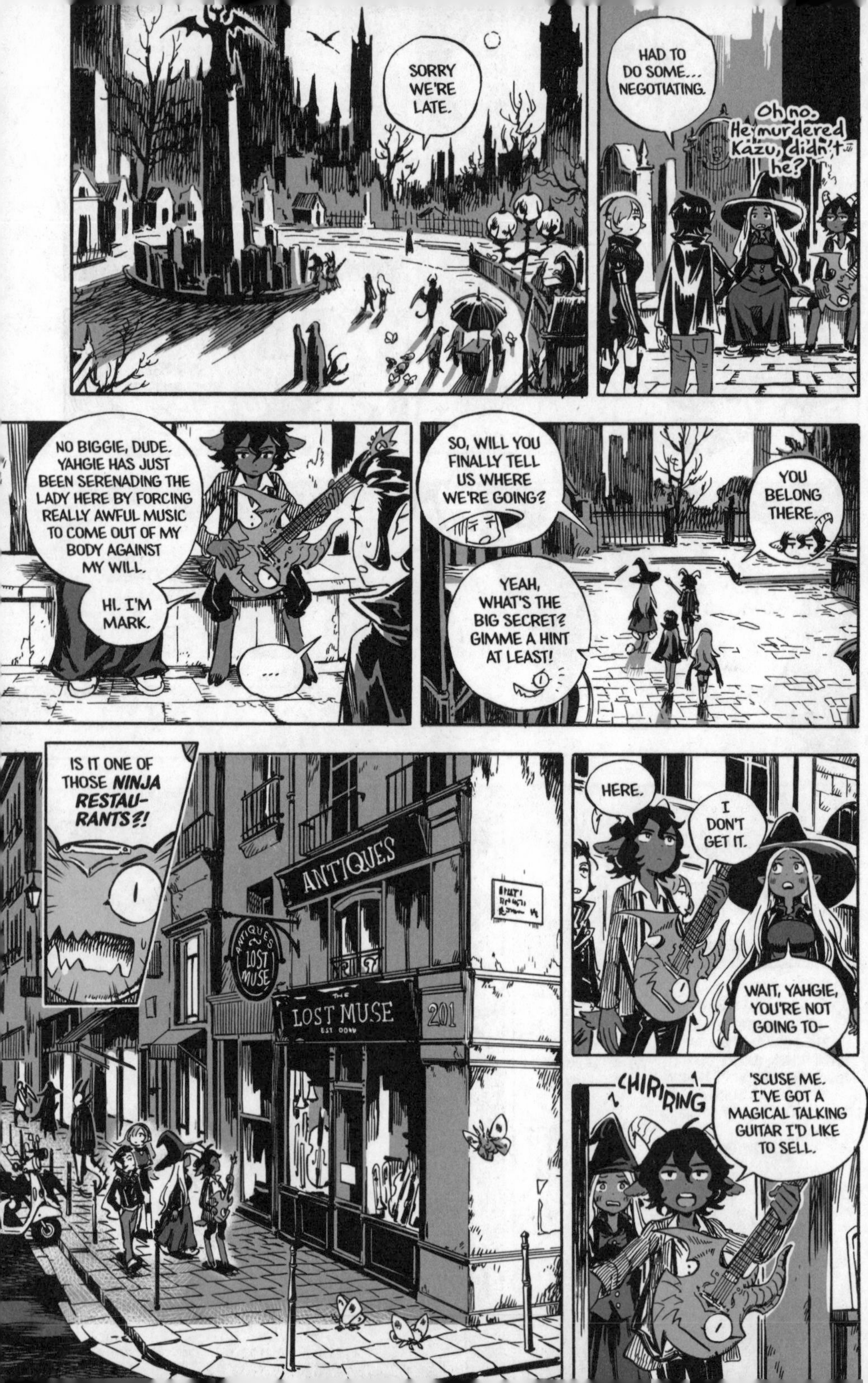
SORRY WE'RE LATE.
HAD TO DO SOME... NEGOTIATING.
Oh no. He murdered Kazu, didn't he?
NO BIGGIE, DUDE. YAHGIE HAS JUST BEEN SERENADING THE LADY HERE BY FORCING REALLY AWFUL MUSIC TO COME OUT OF MY BODY AGAINST MY WILL.
HI. I'M MARK.
...
SO, WILL YOU FINALLY TELL US WHERE WE'RE GOING?
YOU BELONG THERE.
YEAH, WHAT'S THE BIG SECRET? GIMME A HINT AT LEAST!
IS IT ONE OF THOSE NINJA RESTAU-RANTS?!
ANTIQUES
ANTIQUES LOST MUSE
THE LOST MUSE
201
HERE.
I DON'T GET IT.
WAIT, YAHGIE, YOU'RE NOT GOING TO—
CHIRIRING
'SCUSE ME. I'VE GOT A MAGICAL TALKING GUITAR I'D LIKE TO SELL.

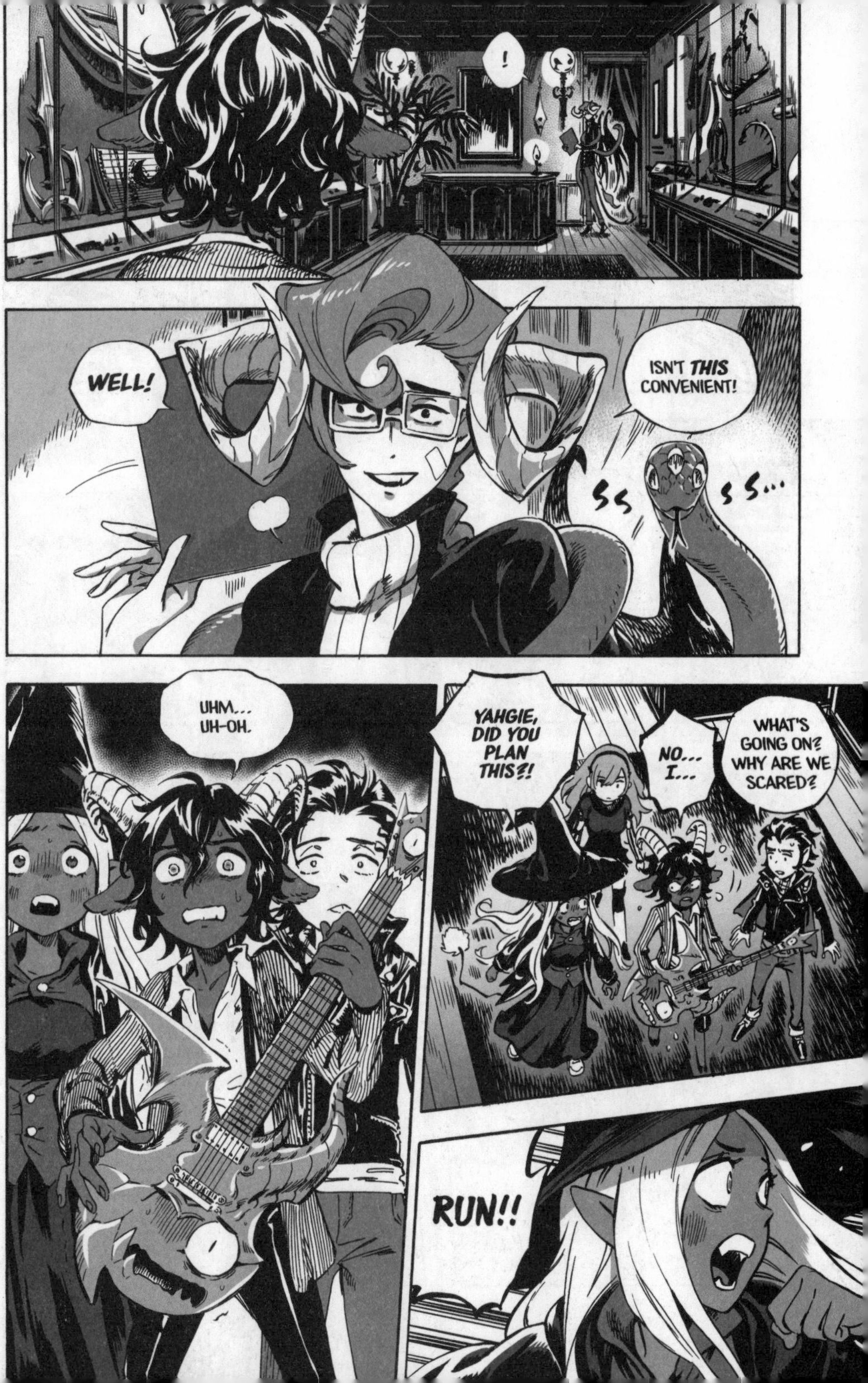
!
WELL!
ISN'T THIS CONVENIENT!
SS
SS...
UHM... UH-OH.
YAHGIE, DID YOU PLAN THIS?!
NO... I...
WHAT'S GOING ON? WHY ARE WE SCARED?
RUN!!

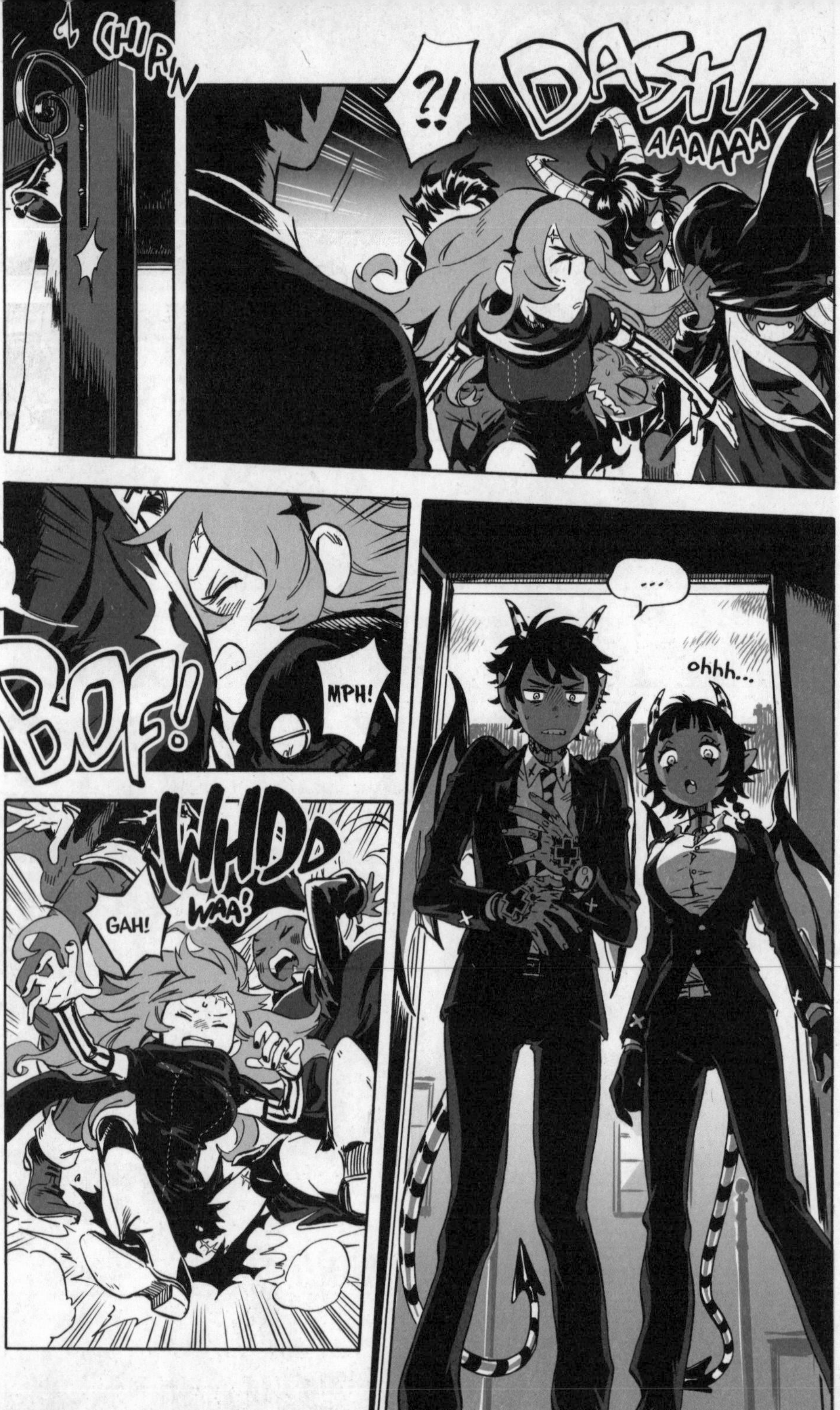
CHIRIN
?!
DASH
AAAAAA
BOF!
MPH!
WHDD
WAA!
GAH!
...
ohhh...

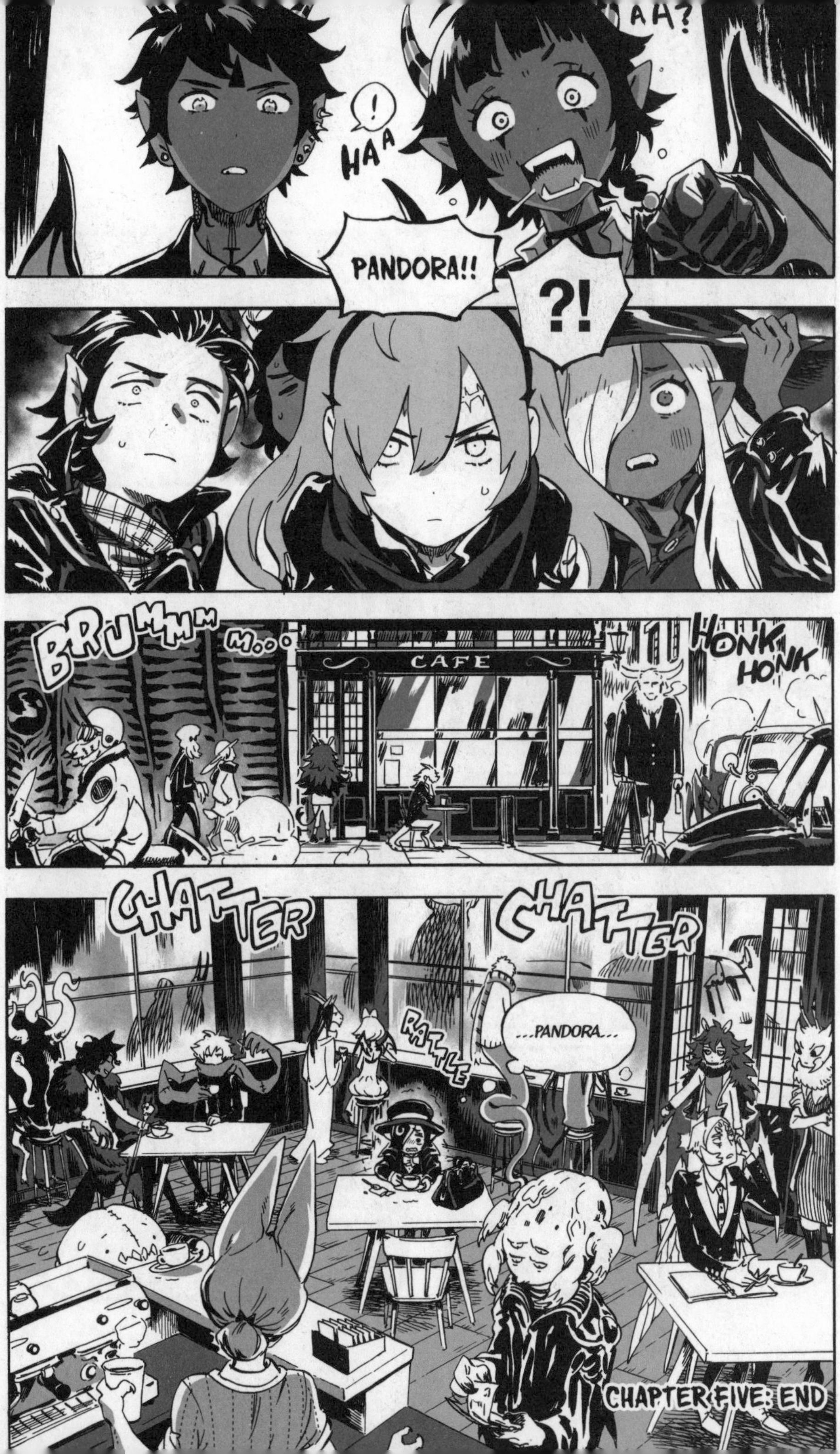
!
HAA
AH?
PANDORA!!
?!
BRUMMMM M...
CAFE
HONK HONK
CHATTER
CHATTER
RATTLE
...PANDORA...
CHAPTER FIVE: END

FIREFIGHTER

FOOM
PIANO PAINO
I DON'T THINK EVERYONE MADE IT OUT OF THERE!!
KOFF
NEVER FEAR!
I SHALL SAVE THEM!
FIRE DPT
WSH
ZOOM
KRASH
SMASH!
WHD
CHAKKA CHAKKA WHOOP
WHDD
AH!
OOF

PKS

HFF—
HFF
This is Psycho-killer Steve.
HFF—
HFF—
SALE
He never goes anywhere without his trusty shovel.
He gets into all sorts of trouble.
LUNCHTIIIME!!
His catch-phrase is a real hit with the kids.

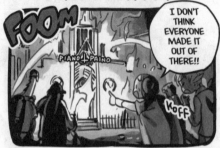

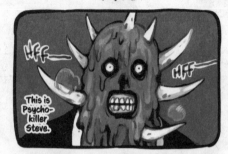

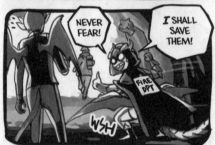

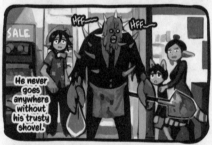

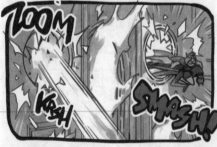

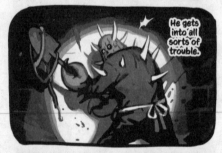

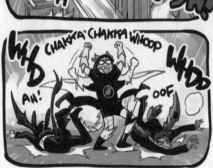

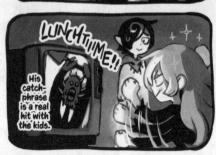

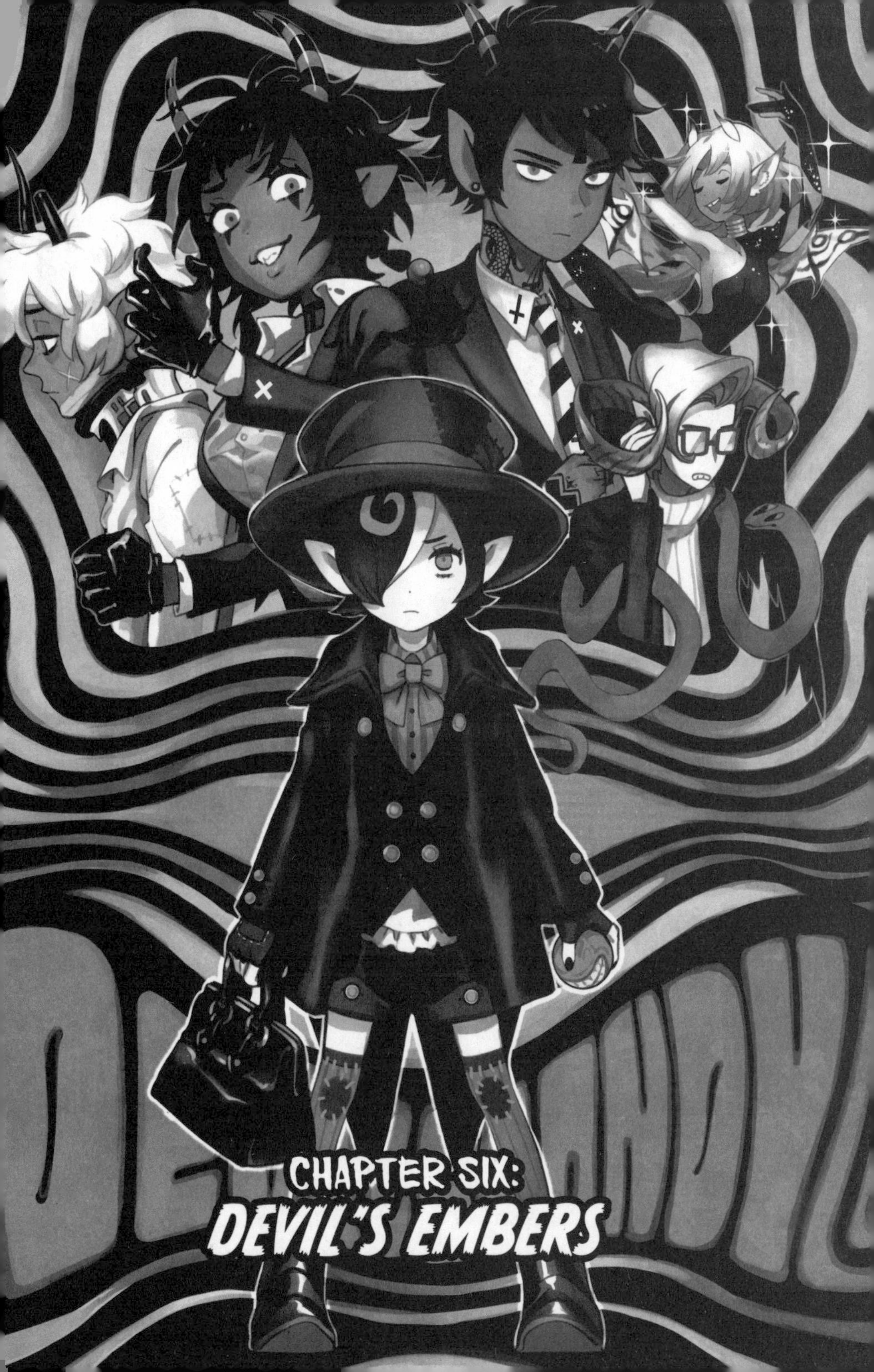
CHAPTER SIX:
DEVIL'S EMBERS

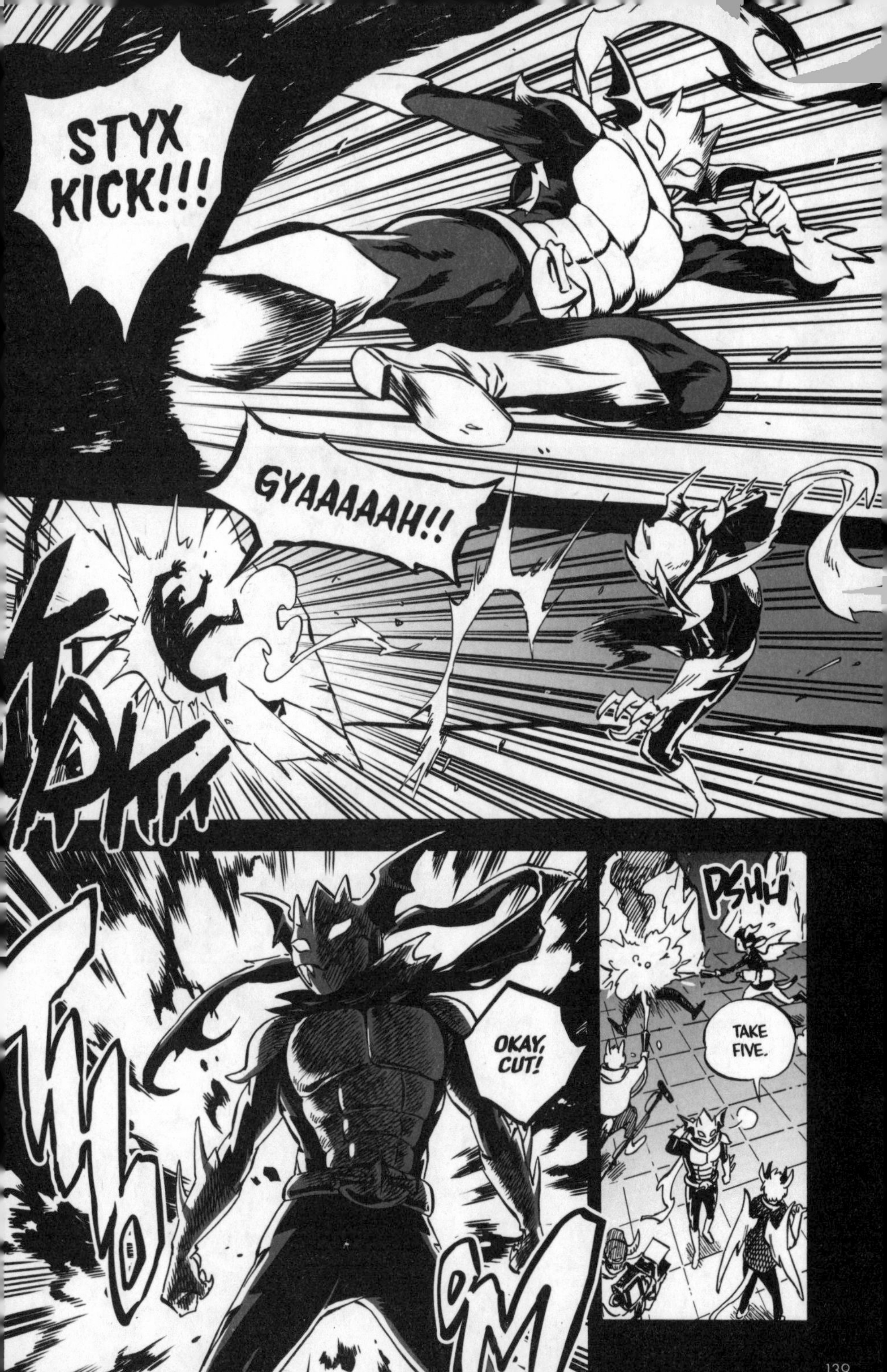
STYX KICK!!!
GYAAAAAH!!
KRAKK
OKAY, CUT!
WOM
PSHH
TAKE FIVE.

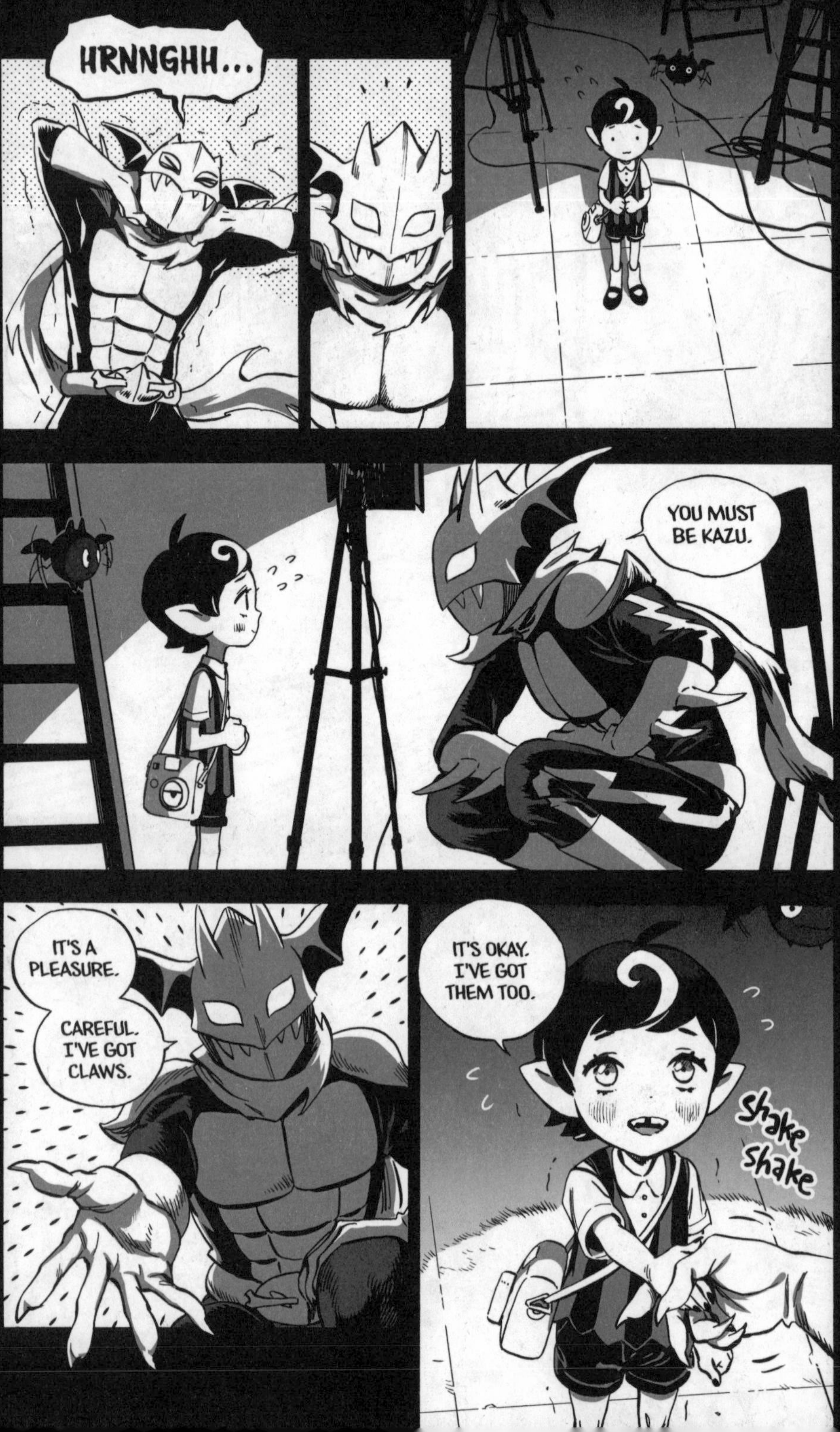
HRNNGHH...
YOU MUST BE KAZU.
IT'S A PLEASURE.
CAREFUL. I'VE GOT CLAWS.
IT'S OKAY. I'VE GOT THEM TOO.
Shake shake

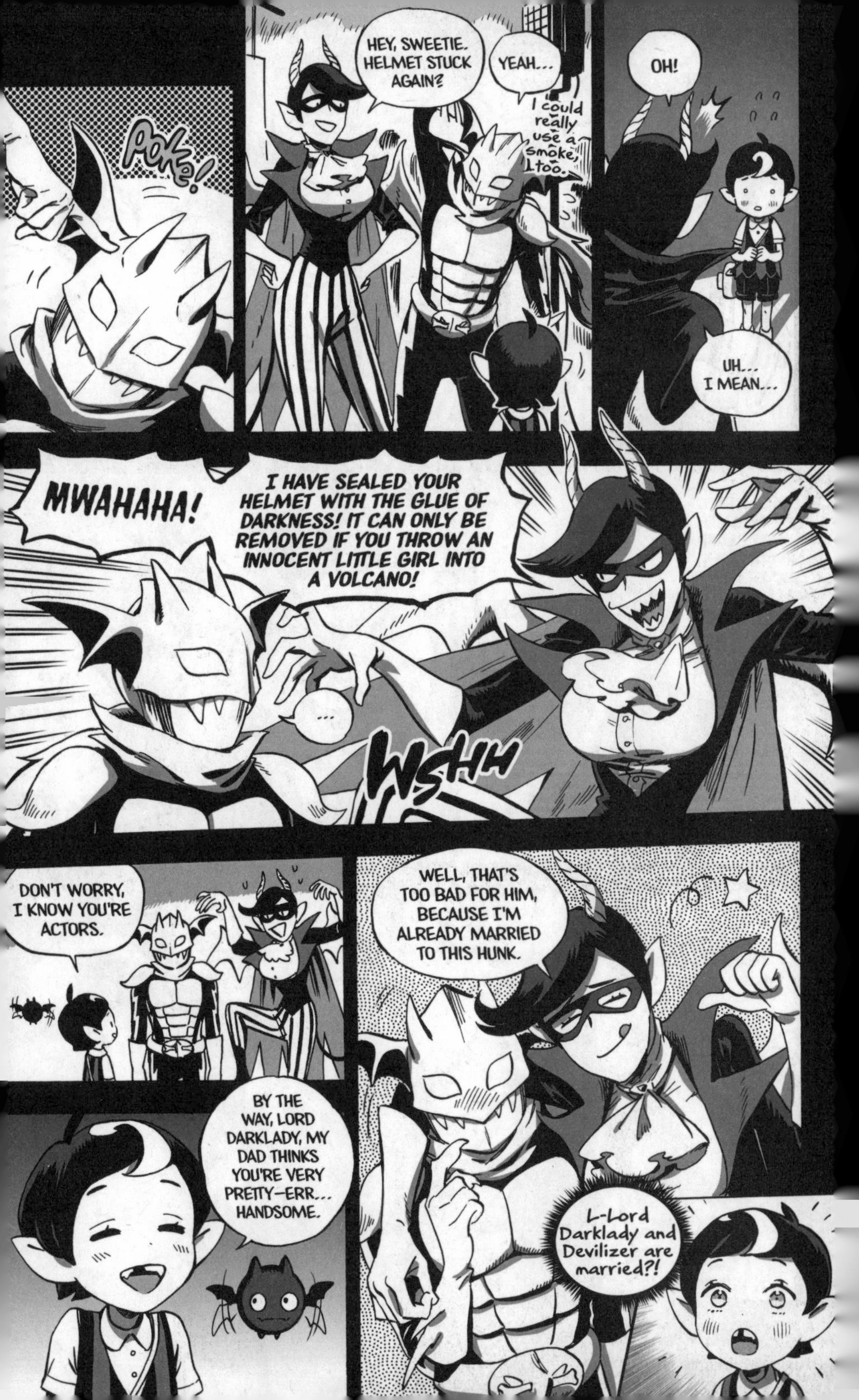
POKE!
HEY, SWEETIE. HELMET STUCK AGAIN?
YEAH...
I could really use a smoke, too.
OH!
UH... I MEAN...
MWAHAHA!
I HAVE SEALED YOUR HELMET WITH THE GLUE OF DARKNESS! IT CAN ONLY BE REMOVED IF YOU THROW AN INNOCENT LITTLE GIRL INTO A VOLCANO!
...
WSHH
DON'T WORRY, I KNOW YOU'RE ACTORS.
WELL, THAT'S TOO BAD FOR HIM, BECAUSE I'M ALREADY MARRIED TO THIS HUNK.
BY THE WAY, LORD DARKLADY, MY DAD THINKS YOU'RE VERY PRETTY—ERR... HANDSOME.
L-Lord Darklady and Devilizer are married?!

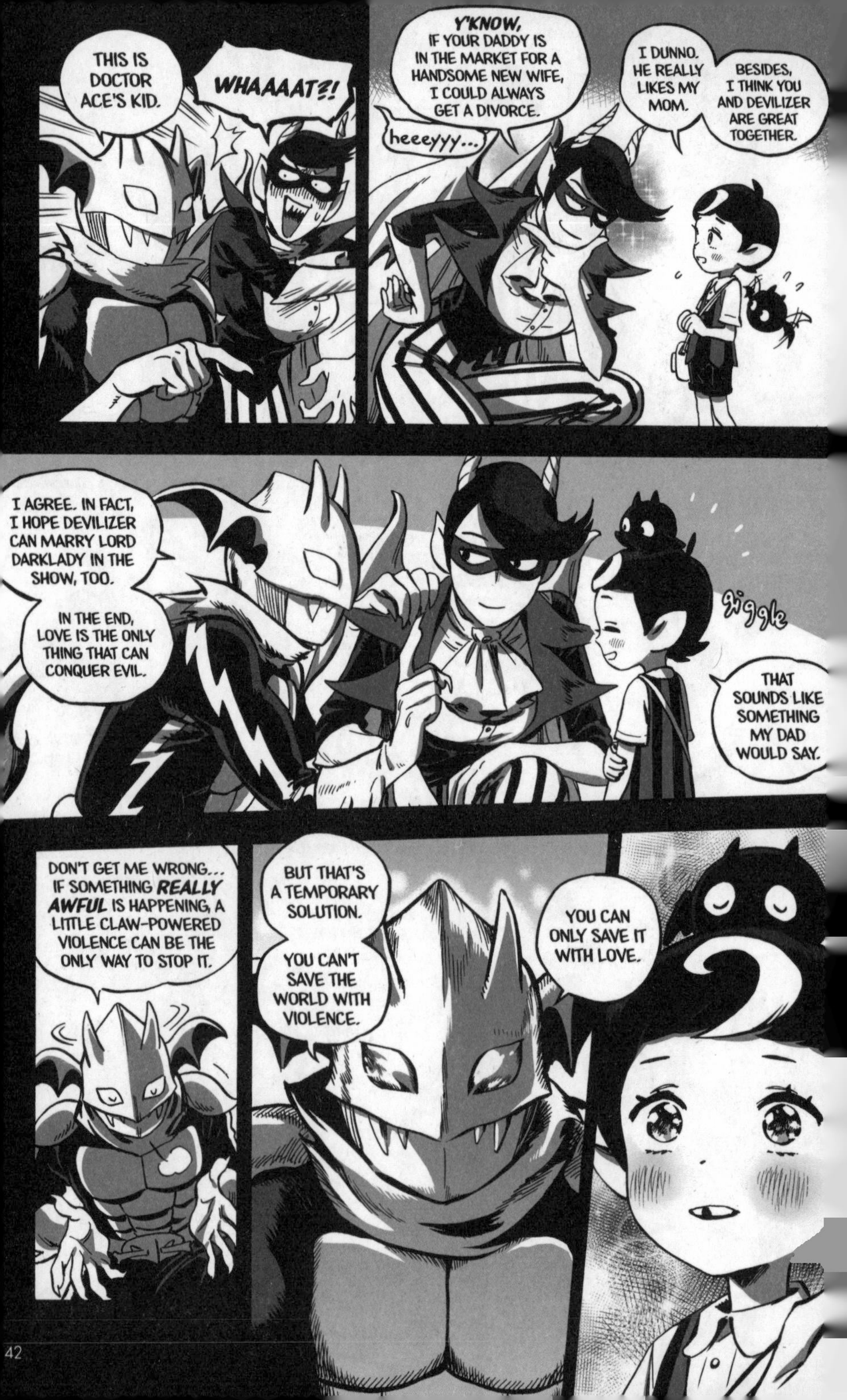
THIS IS DOCTOR ACE'S KID.
WHAAAAT?!
Y'KNOW, IF YOUR DADDY IS IN THE MARKET FOR A HANDSOME NEW WIFE, I COULD ALWAYS GET A DIVORCE.
heeeyyy...
I DUNNO. HE REALLY LIKES MY MOM.
BESIDES, I THINK YOU AND DEVILIZER ARE GREAT TOGETHER.
I AGREE. IN FACT, I HOPE DEVILIZER CAN MARRY LORD DARKLADY IN THE SHOW, TOO.
IN THE END, LOVE IS THE ONLY THING THAT CAN CONQUER EVIL.
giggle
THAT SOUNDS LIKE SOMETHING MY DAD WOULD SAY.
DON'T GET ME WRONG... IF SOMETHING REALLY AWFUL IS HAPPENING, A LITTLE CLAW-POWERED VIOLENCE CAN BE THE ONLY WAY TO STOP IT.
BUT THAT'S A TEMPORARY SOLUTION.
YOU CAN'T SAVE THE WORLD WITH VIOLENCE.
YOU CAN ONLY SAVE IT WITH LOVE.

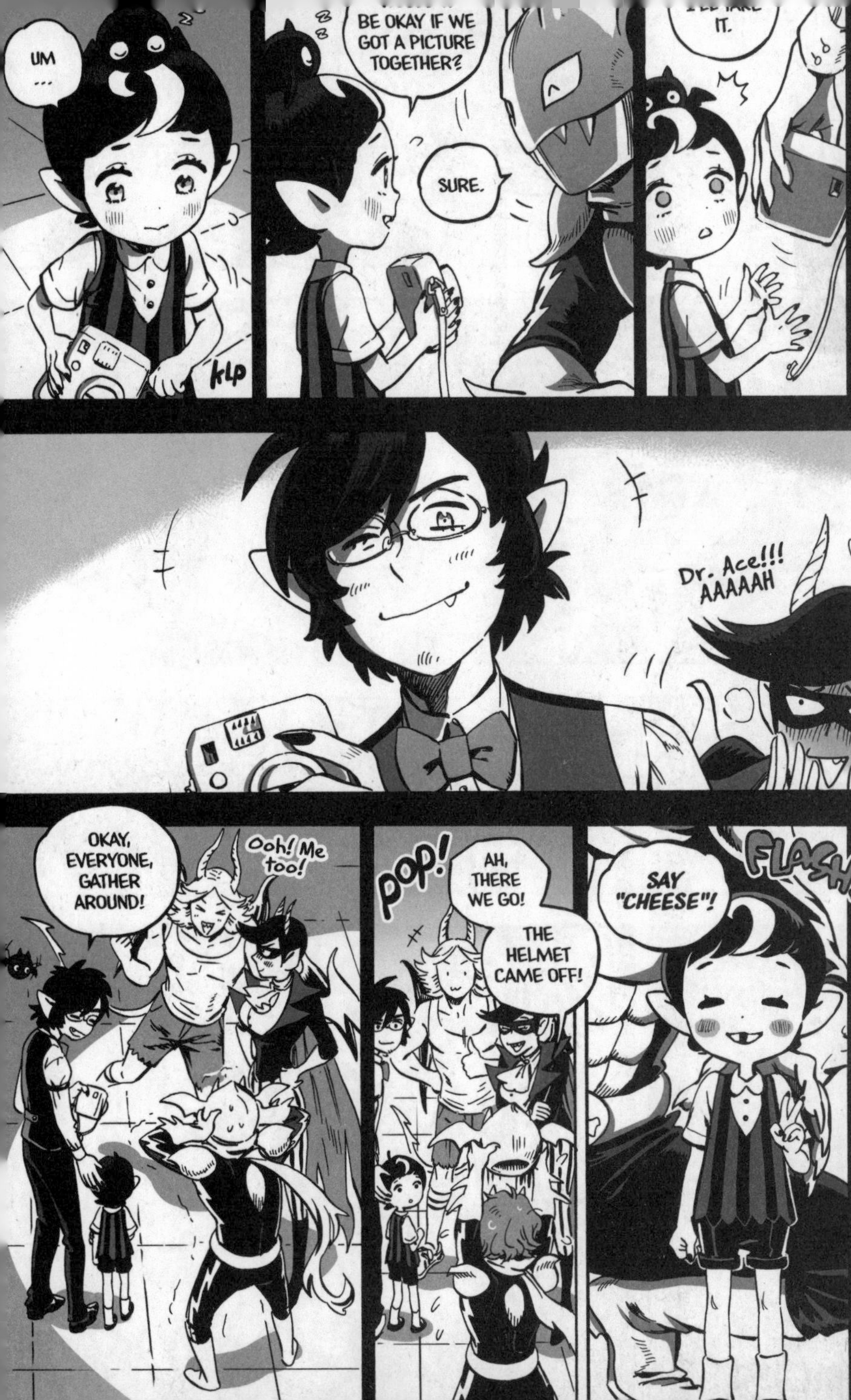
UM ...
klp
BE OKAY IF WE GOT A PICTURE TOGETHER?
SURE.
IT.
Dr. Ace!!! AAAAAH
OKAY, EVERYONE, GATHER AROUND!
Ooh! Me too!
POP!
AH, THERE WE GO!
THE HELMET CAME OFF!
FLASH!
SAY "CHEESE"!

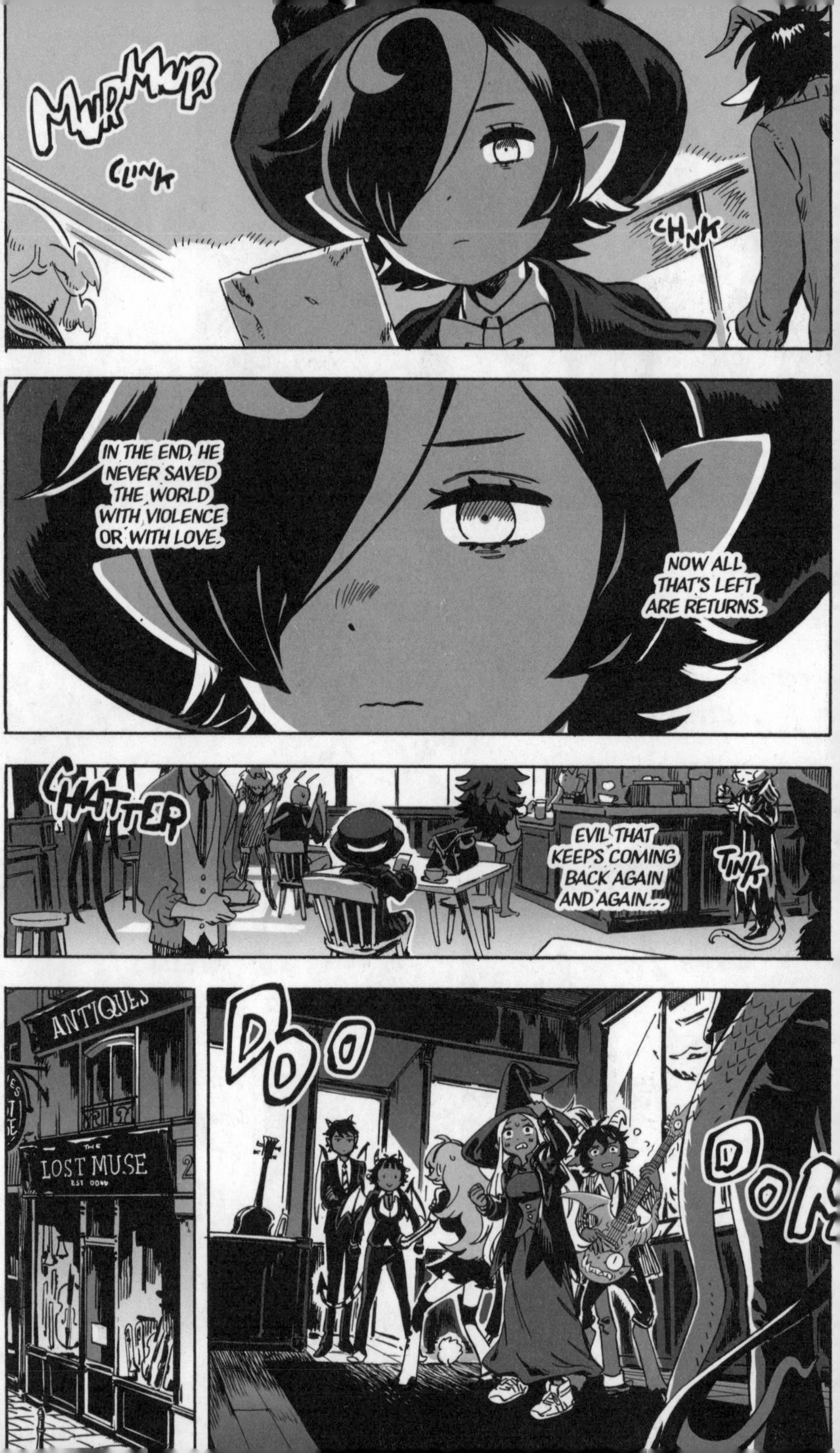
MURMUR
CLINK
CHNK
IN THE END, HE NEVER SAVED THE WORLD WITH VIOLENCE OR WITH LOVE.
NOW ALL THAT'S LEFT ARE RETURNS.
CHATTER
EVIL THAT KEEPS COMING BACK AGAIN AND AGAIN...
TINK
ANTIQUES
THE LOST MUSE
DOO
DOM

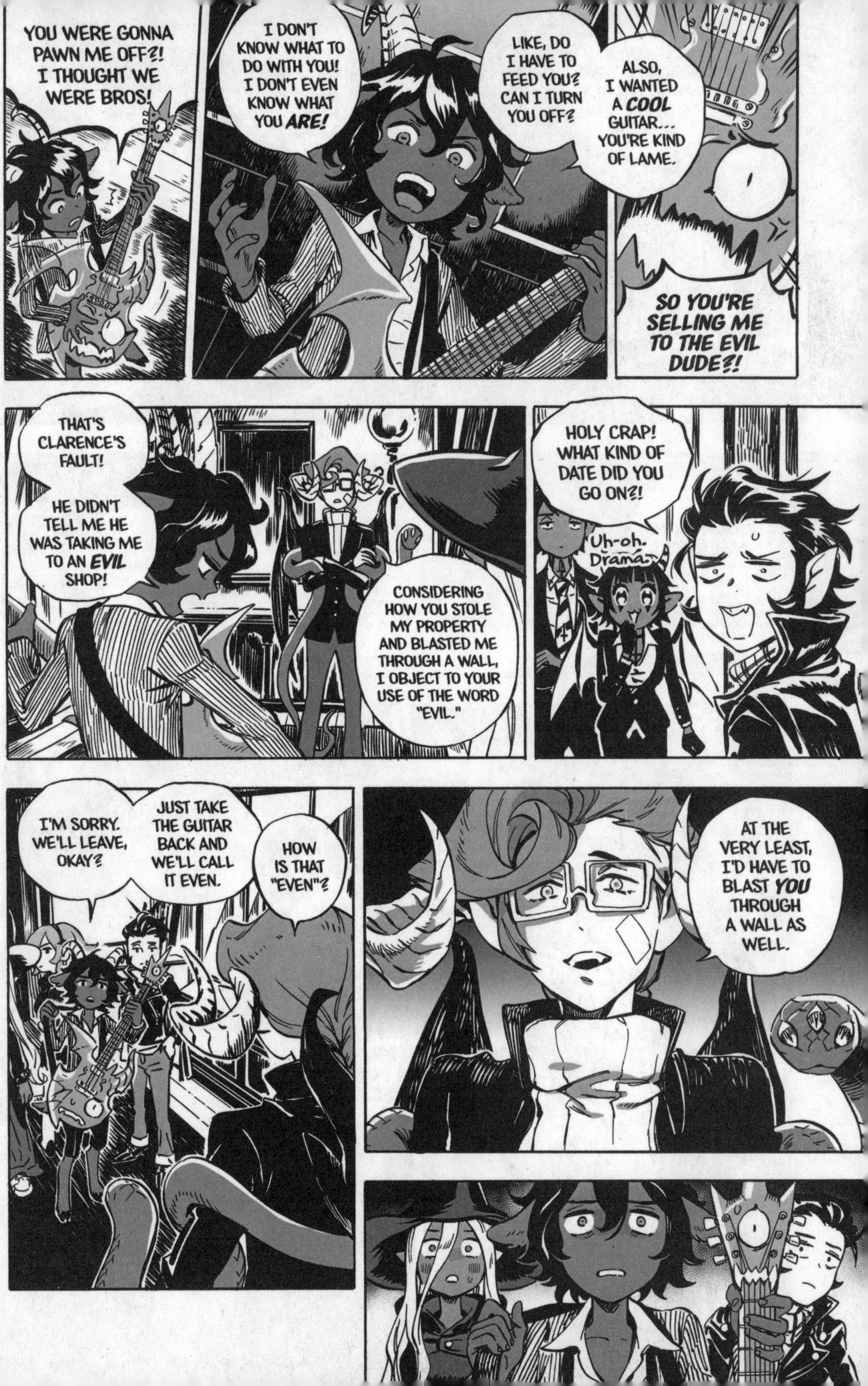
YOU WERE GONNA PAWN ME OFF?! I THOUGHT WE WERE BROS!
I DON'T KNOW WHAT TO DO WITH YOU! I DON'T EVEN KNOW WHAT YOU ARE!
LIKE, DO I HAVE TO FEED YOU? CAN I TURN YOU OFF?
ALSO, I WANTED A COOL GUITAR... YOU'RE KIND OF LAME.
SO YOU'RE SELLING ME TO THE EVIL DUDE?!
THAT'S CLARENCE'S FAULT!
HE DIDN'T TELL ME HE WAS TAKING ME TO AN EVIL SHOP!
CONSIDERING HOW YOU STOLE MY PROPERTY AND BLASTED ME THROUGH A WALL, I OBJECT TO YOUR USE OF THE WORD "EVIL."
HOLY CRAP! WHAT KIND OF DATE DID YOU GO ON?!
Uh-oh. Drama.
I'M SORRY. WE'LL LEAVE, OKAY?
JUST TAKE THE GUITAR BACK AND WE'LL CALL IT EVEN.
HOW IS THAT "EVEN"?
AT THE VERY LEAST, I'D HAVE TO BLAST YOU THROUGH A WALL AS WELL.

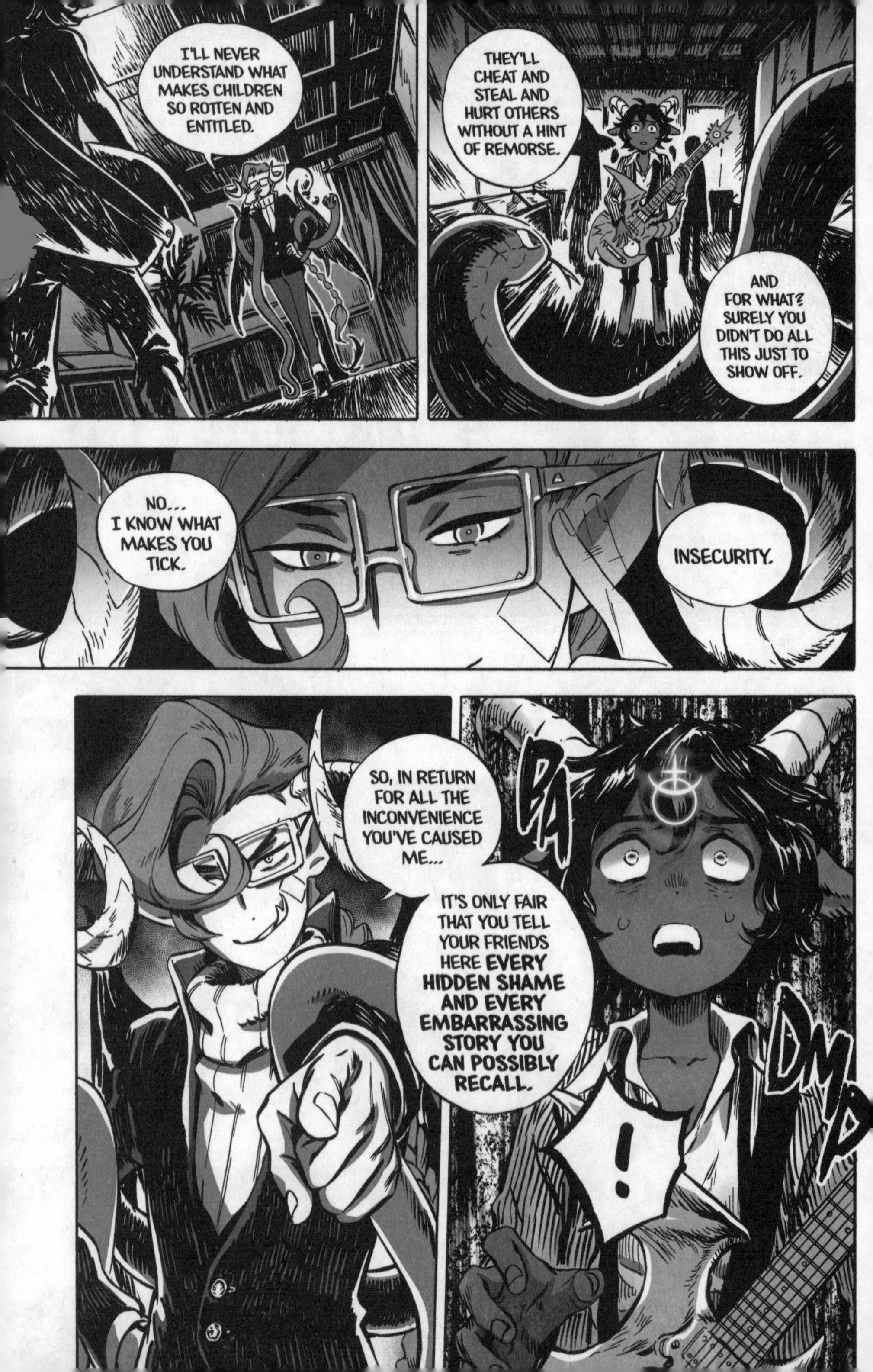
I'LL NEVER UNDERSTAND WHAT MAKES CHILDREN SO ROTTEN AND ENTITLED.
THEY'LL CHEAT AND STEAL AND HURT OTHERS WITHOUT A HINT OF REMORSE.
AND FOR WHAT? SURELY YOU DIDN'T DO ALL THIS JUST TO SHOW OFF.
NO... I KNOW WHAT MAKES YOU TICK.
INSECURITY.
SO, IN RETURN FOR ALL THE INCONVENIENCE YOU'VE CAUSED ME...
IT'S ONLY FAIR THAT YOU TELL YOUR FRIENDS HERE **EVERY HIDDEN SHAME AND EVERY EMBARRASSING STORY YOU CAN POSSIBLY RECALL.**
BA
DMP
!

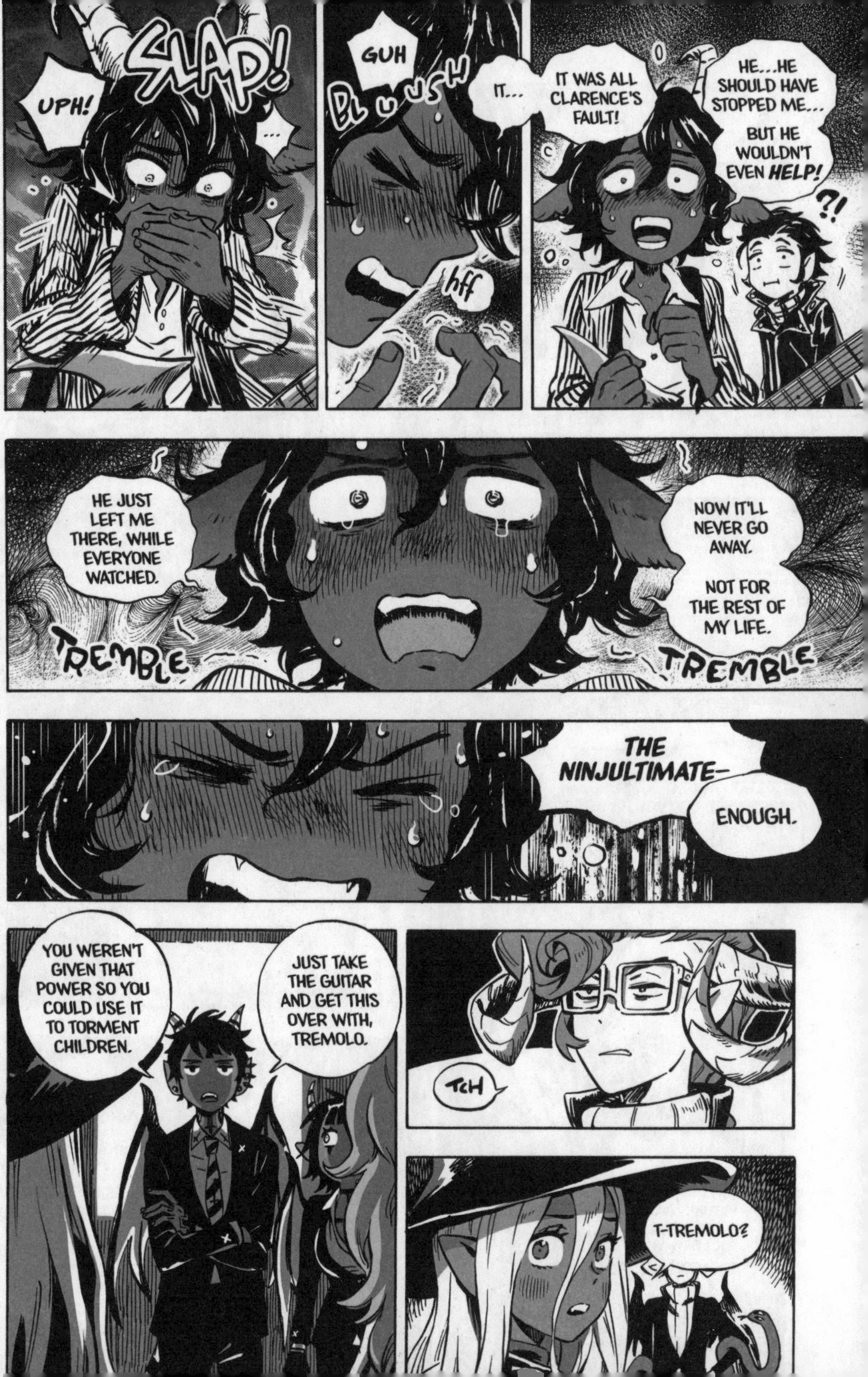
SLAP!
UPH!
...
GUH
BLUSH
hff
IT...
IT WAS ALL CLARENCE'S FAULT!
HE...HE SHOULD HAVE STOPPED ME...
BUT HE WOULDN'T EVEN HELP!
?!
HE JUST LEFT ME THERE, WHILE EVERYONE WATCHED.
NOW IT'LL NEVER GO AWAY.
NOT FOR THE REST OF MY LIFE.
TREMBLE
TREMBLE
THE NINJULTIMATE-
ENOUGH.
YOU WEREN'T GIVEN THAT POWER SO YOU COULD USE IT TO TORMENT CHILDREN.
JUST TAKE THE GUITAR AND GET THIS OVER WITH, TREMOLO.
TCH
T-TREMOLO?

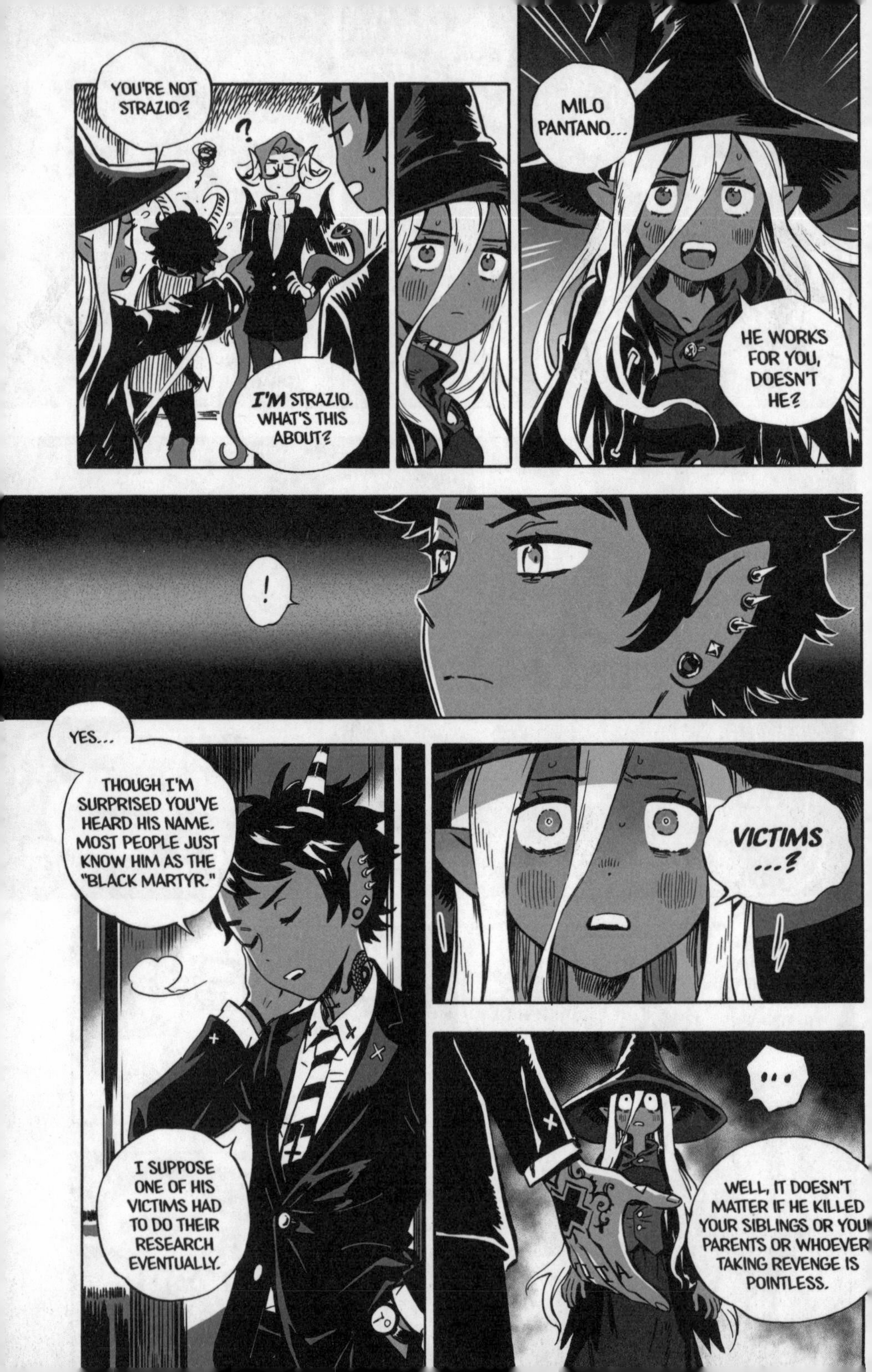
YOU'RE NOT STRAZIO?
?
I'M STRAZIO. WHAT'S THIS ABOUT?
MILO PANTANO...
HE WORKS FOR YOU, DOESN'T HE?
!
YES...
THOUGH I'M SURPRISED YOU'VE HEARD HIS NAME. MOST PEOPLE JUST KNOW HIM AS THE "BLACK MARTYR."
I SUPPOSE ONE OF HIS VICTIMS HAD TO DO THEIR RESEARCH EVENTUALLY.
VICTIMS ...?
...
WELL, IT DOESN'T MATTER IF HE KILLED YOUR SIBLINGS OR YOU PARENTS OR WHOEVER. TAKING REVENGE IS POINTLESS.

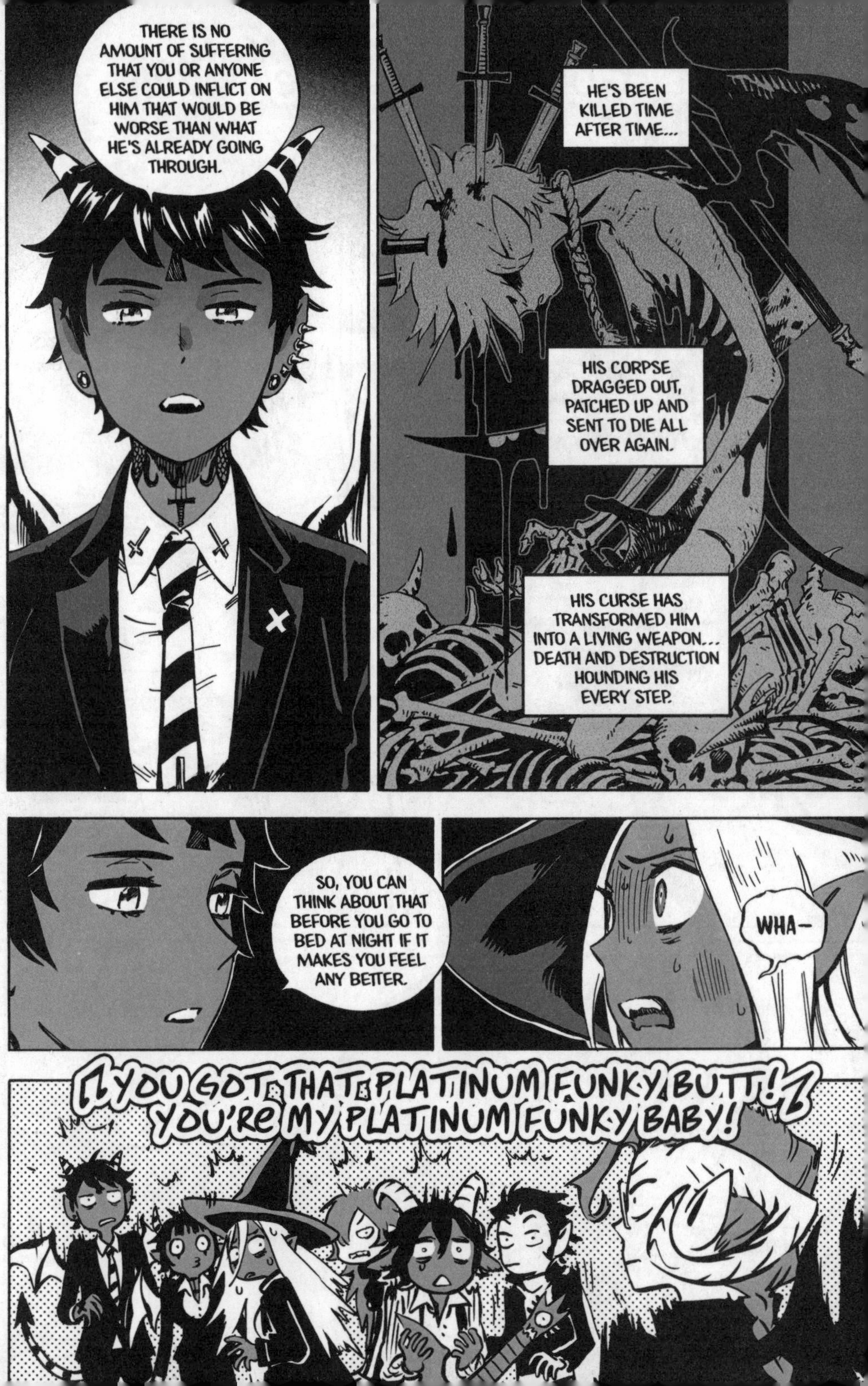
THERE IS NO AMOUNT OF SUFFERING THAT YOU OR ANYONE ELSE COULD INFLICT ON HIM THAT WOULD BE WORSE THAN WHAT HE'S ALREADY GOING THROUGH.
HE'S BEEN KILLED TIME AFTER TIME...
HIS CORPSE DRAGGED OUT, PATCHED UP AND SENT TO DIE ALL OVER AGAIN.
HIS CURSE HAS TRANSFORMED HIM INTO A LIVING WEAPON... DEATH AND DESTRUCTION HOUNDING HIS EVERY STEP.
SO, YOU CAN THINK ABOUT THAT BEFORE YOU GO TO BED AT NIGHT IF IT MAKES YOU FEEL ANY BETTER.
WHA-
YOU GOT THAT PLATINUM FUNKY BUTT! YOU'RE MY PLATINUM FUNKY BABY!

2 SHAKIN' SHAKIN' MAKIN' BACON, SERVE IT UP AND DRIVE ME CRAZY!

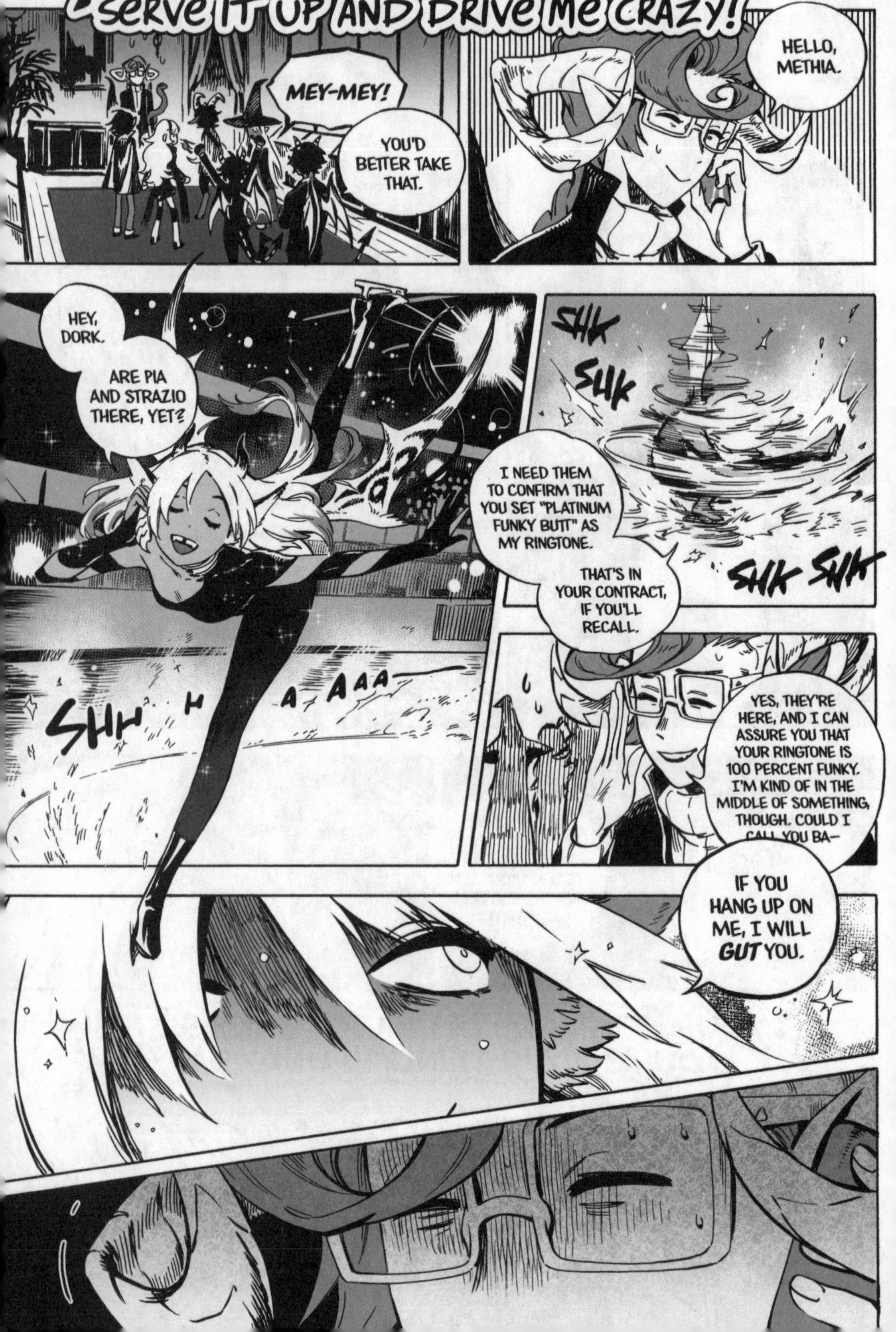
MEY-MEY!
YOU'D BETTER TAKE THAT.
HELLO, METHIA.
HEY, DORK.
ARE PIA AND STRAZIO THERE, YET?
I NEED THEM TO CONFIRM THAT YOU SET "PLATINUM FUNKY BUTT" AS MY RINGTONE.
THAT'S IN YOUR CONTRACT, IF YOU'LL RECALL.
SHH H
A A AAA
SHK
SUK
SHK SHK
YES, THEY'RE HERE, AND I CAN ASSURE YOU THAT YOUR RINGTONE IS 100 PERCENT FUNKY. I'M KIND OF IN THE MIDDLE OF SOMETHING, THOUGH. COULD I CALL YOU BA–
IF YOU HANG UP ON ME, I WILL *GUT* YOU.

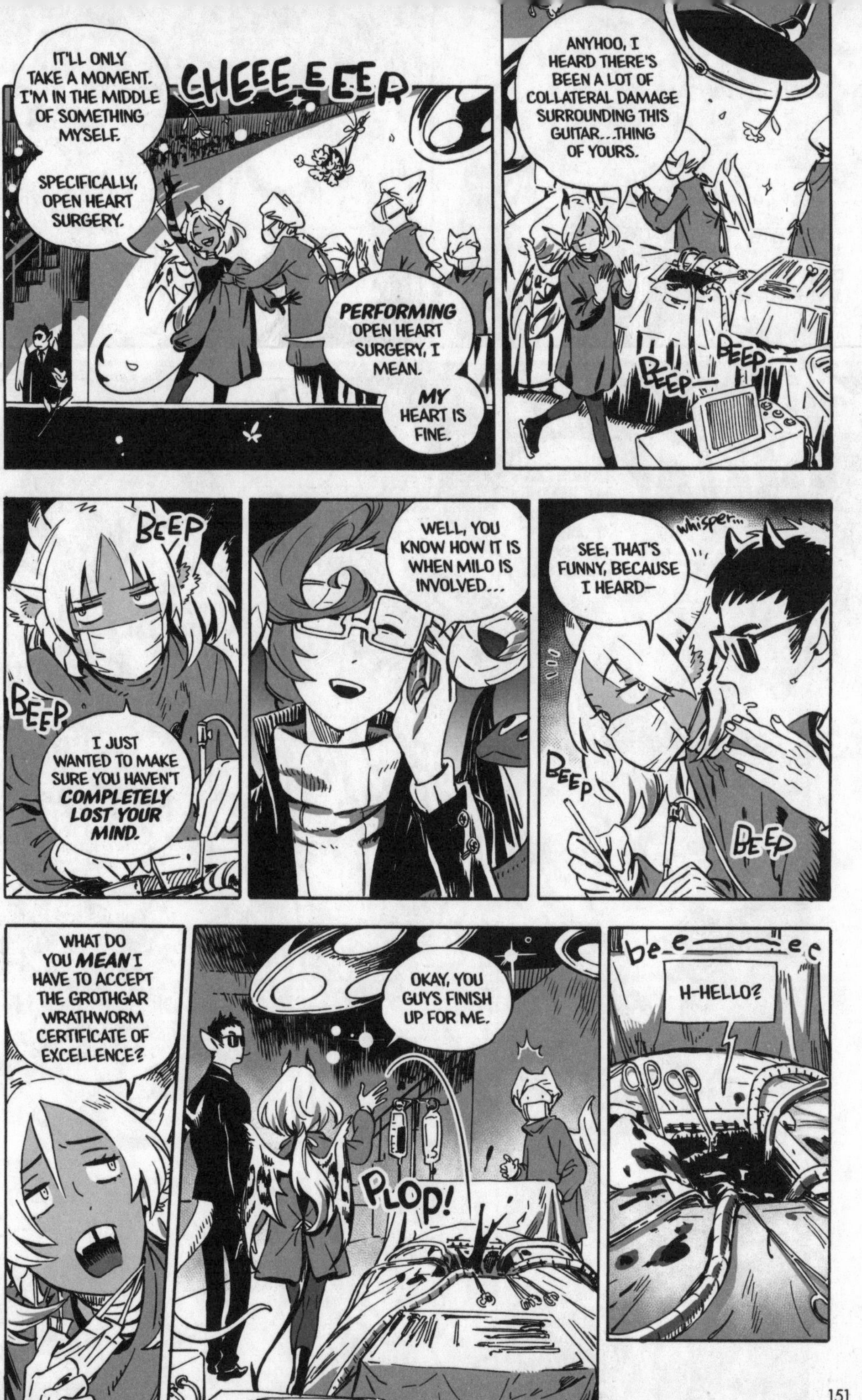
IT'LL ONLY TAKE A MOMENT. I'M IN THE MIDDLE OF SOMETHING MYSELF.
CHEEE EEER
SPECIFICALLY, OPEN HEART SURGERY.
PERFORMING OPEN HEART SURGERY, I MEAN.
MY HEART IS FINE.
ANYHOO, I HEARD THERE'S BEEN A LOT OF COLLATERAL DAMAGE SURROUNDING THIS GUITAR...THING OF YOURS.
BEEP
BEEP
BEEP
BEEP
I JUST WANTED TO MAKE SURE YOU HAVEN'T COMPLETELY LOST YOUR MIND.
WELL, YOU KNOW HOW IT IS WHEN MILO IS INVOLVED...
whisper...
SEE, THAT'S FUNNY, BECAUSE I HEARD—
BEEP
BEEP
WHAT DO YOU MEAN I HAVE TO ACCEPT THE GROTHGAR WRATHWORM CERTIFICATE OF EXCELLENCE?
OKAY, YOU GUYS FINISH UP FOR ME.
PLOP!
be e e e
H-HELLO?

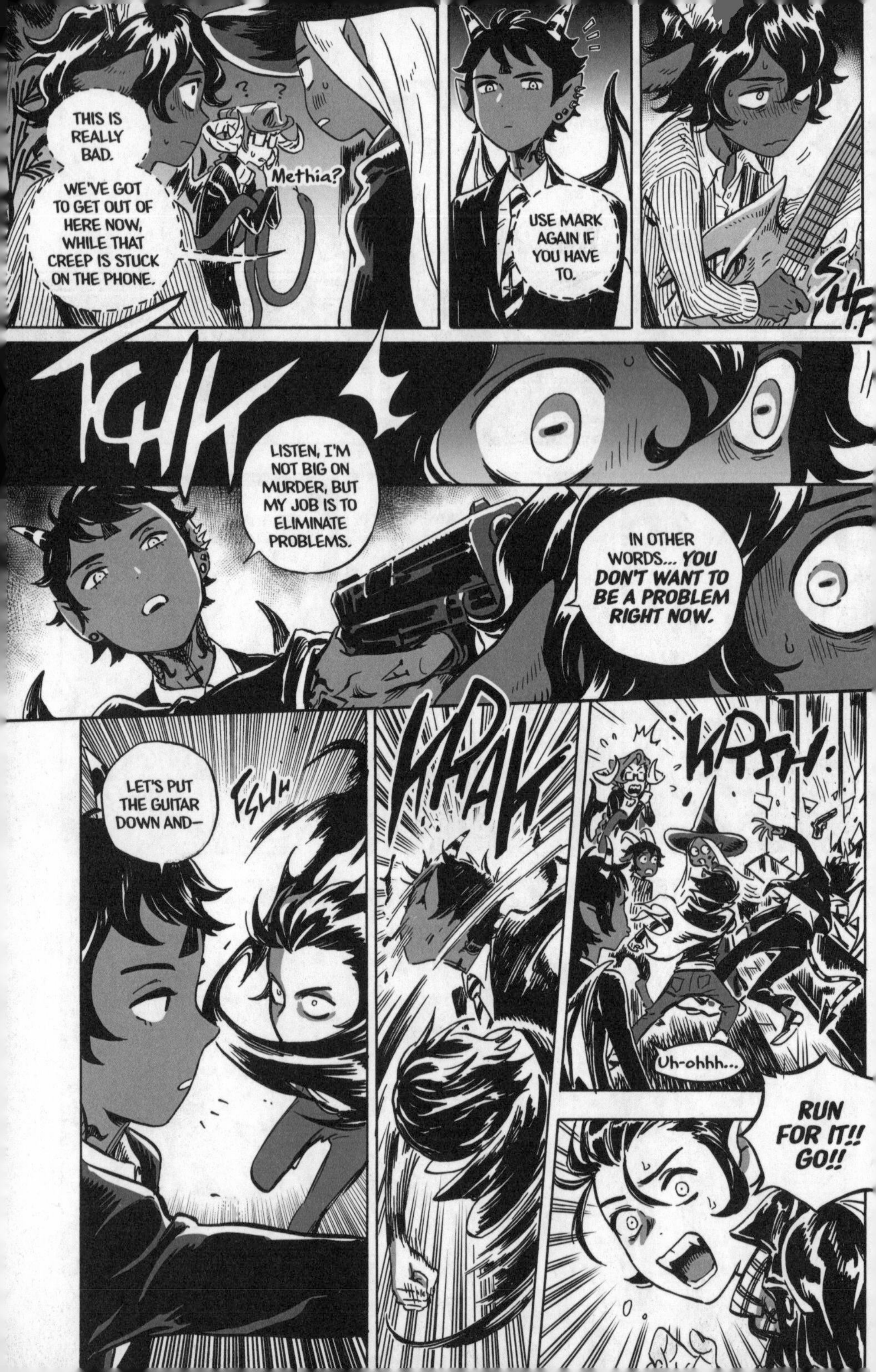

THIS IS REALLY BAD.
WE'VE GOT TO GET OUT OF HERE NOW, WHILE THAT CREEP IS STUCK ON THE PHONE.
Methia?
USE MARK AGAIN IF YOU HAVE TO.
LISTEN, I'M NOT BIG ON MURDER, BUT MY JOB IS TO ELIMINATE PROBLEMS.
IN OTHER WORDS... YOU DON'T WANT TO BE A PROBLEM RIGHT NOW.
LET'S PUT THE GUITAR DOWN AND—
KRAK
KRSH
Uh-ohhh...
RUN FOR IT!! GO!!

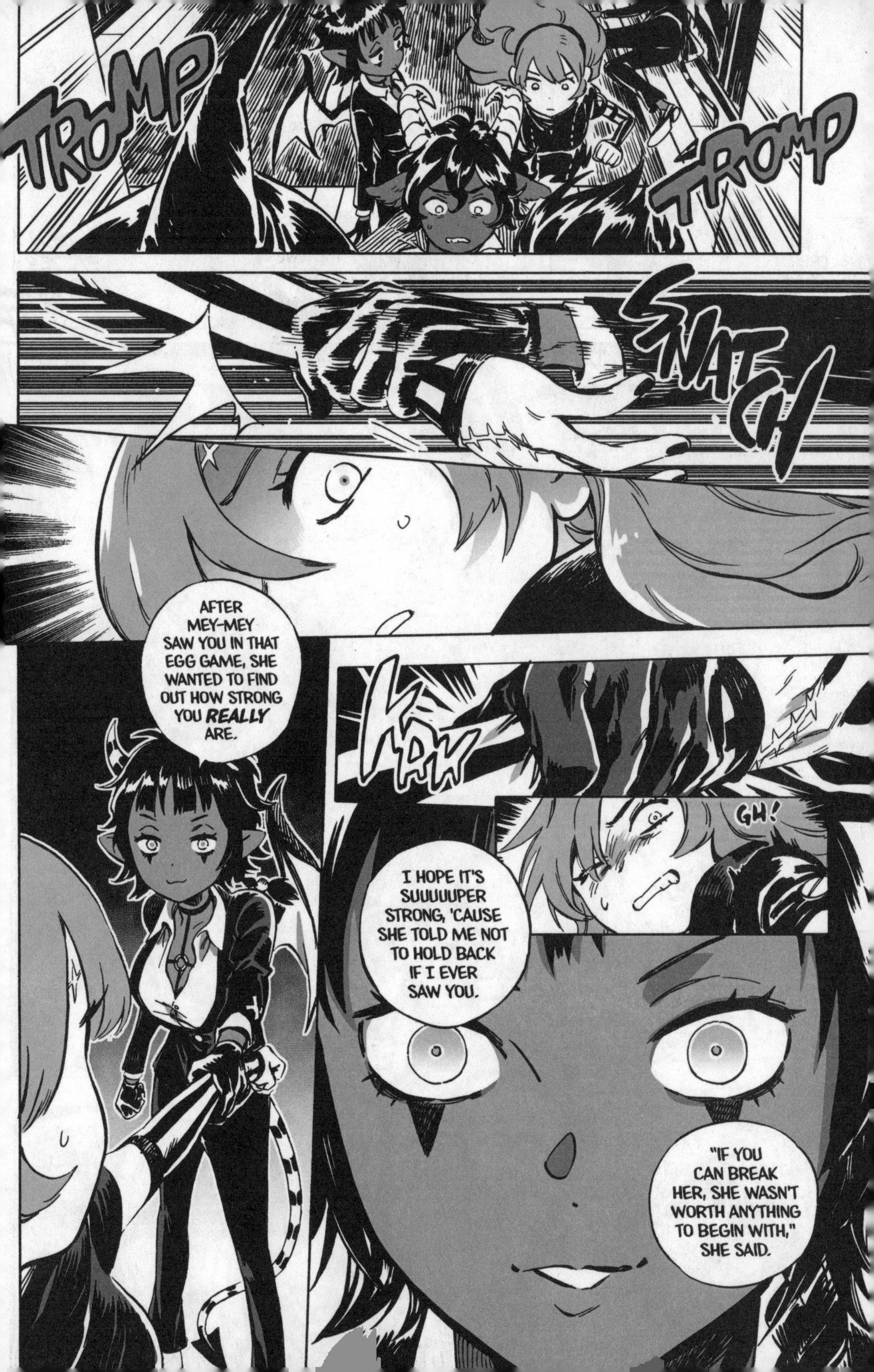
TROMP
TROMP
SNATCH
AFTER MEY-MEY SAW YOU IN THAT EGG GAME, SHE WANTED TO FIND OUT HOW STRONG YOU *REALLY* ARE.
KAW
GH!
I HOPE IT'S SUUUUUPER STRONG, 'CAUSE SHE TOLD ME NOT TO HOLD BACK IF I EVER SAW YOU.
"IF YOU CAN BREAK HER, SHE WASN'T WORTH ANYTHING TO BEGIN WITH," SHE SAID.

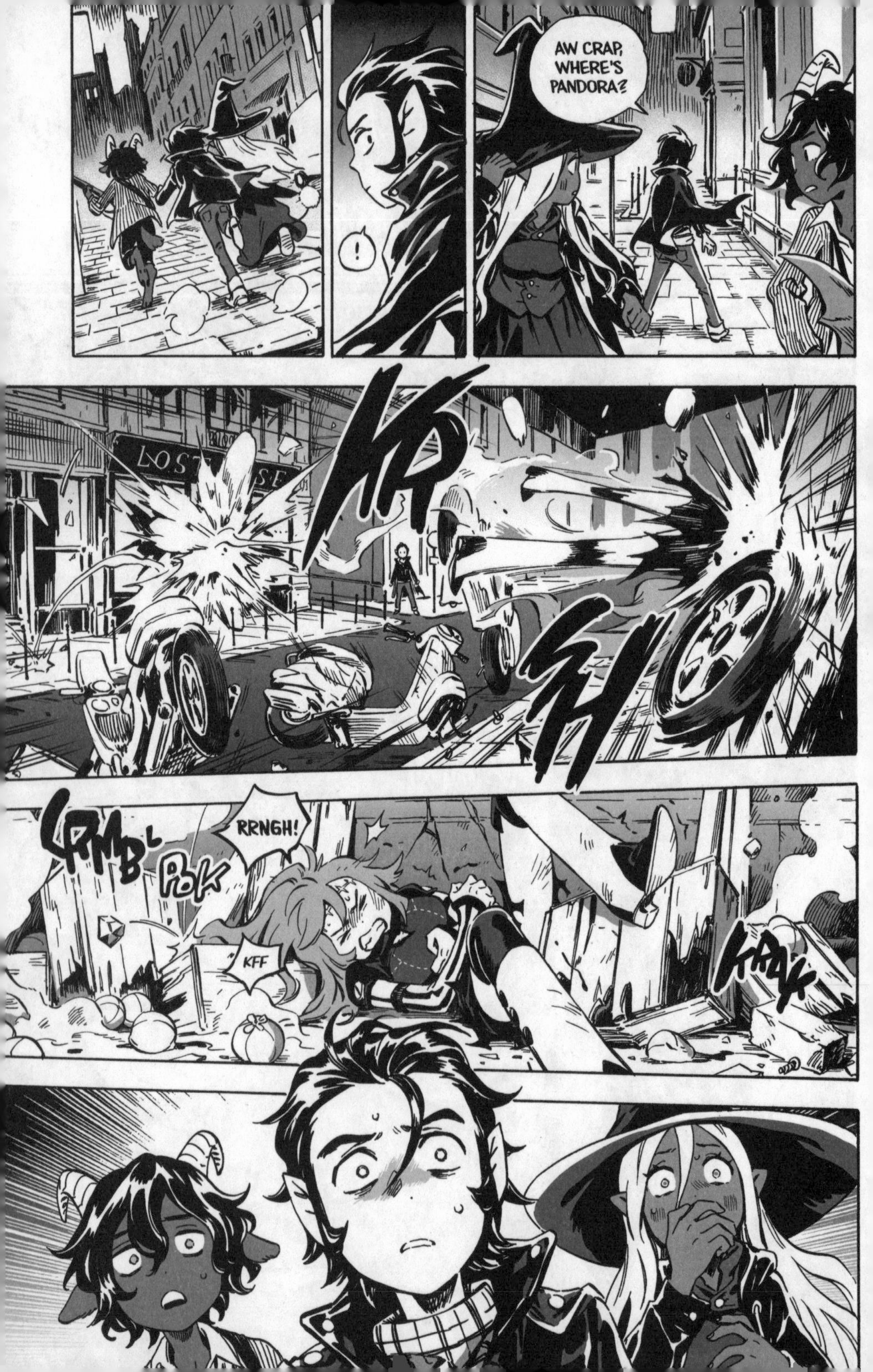
!
AW CRAP, WHERE'S PANDORA?
CRMBL
RRNGH!
POK
KFF
KRAK

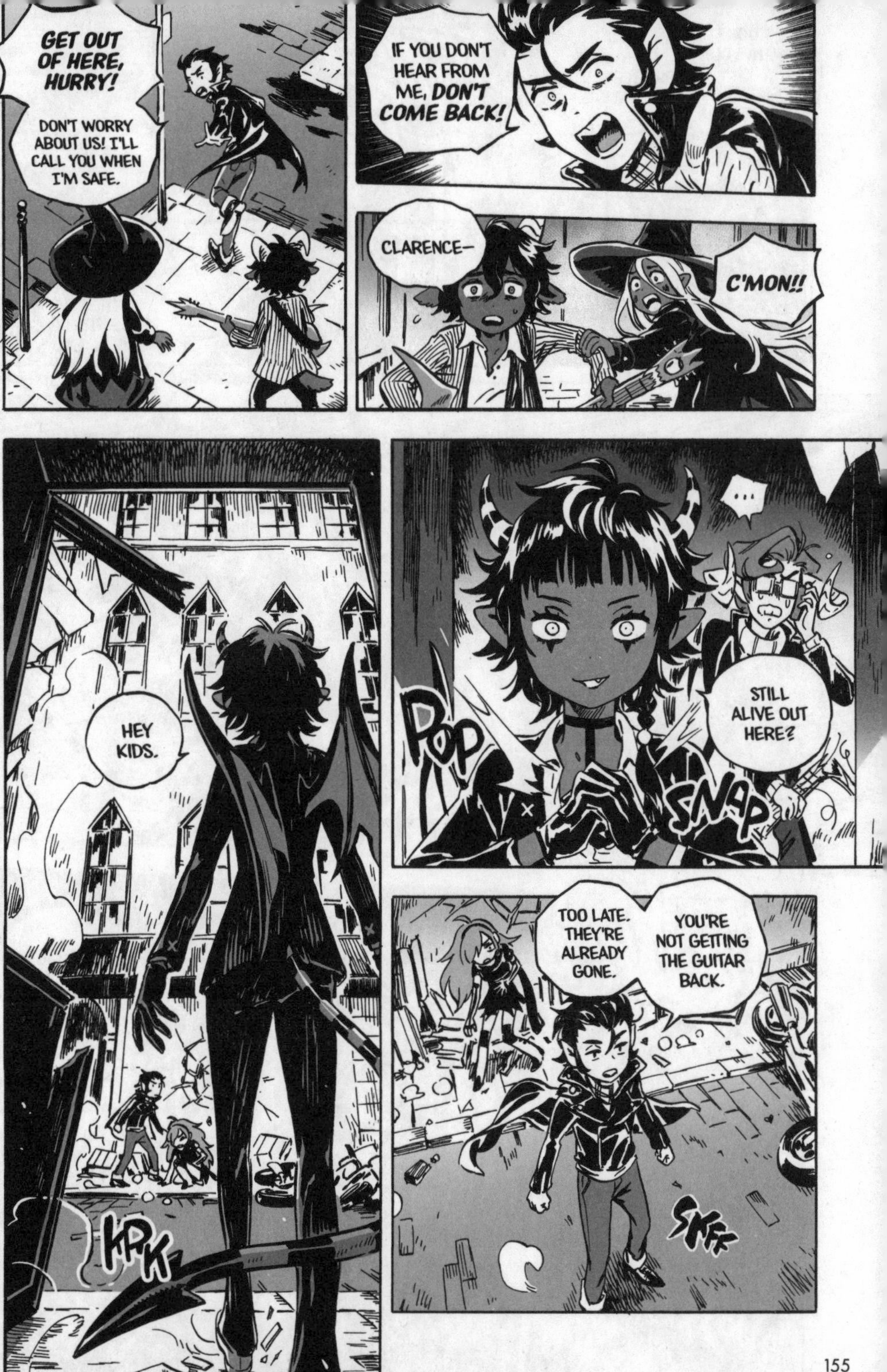
GET OUT OF HERE, HURRY!
DON'T WORRY ABOUT US! I'LL CALL YOU WHEN I'M SAFE.
IF YOU DON'T HEAR FROM ME, DON'T COME BACK!
CLARENCE—
C'MON!!
HEY KIDS.
KRK
...
POP
SNAP
STILL ALIVE OUT HERE?
TOO LATE. THEY'RE ALREADY GONE.
YOU'RE NOT GETTING THE GUITAR BACK.
SKFF

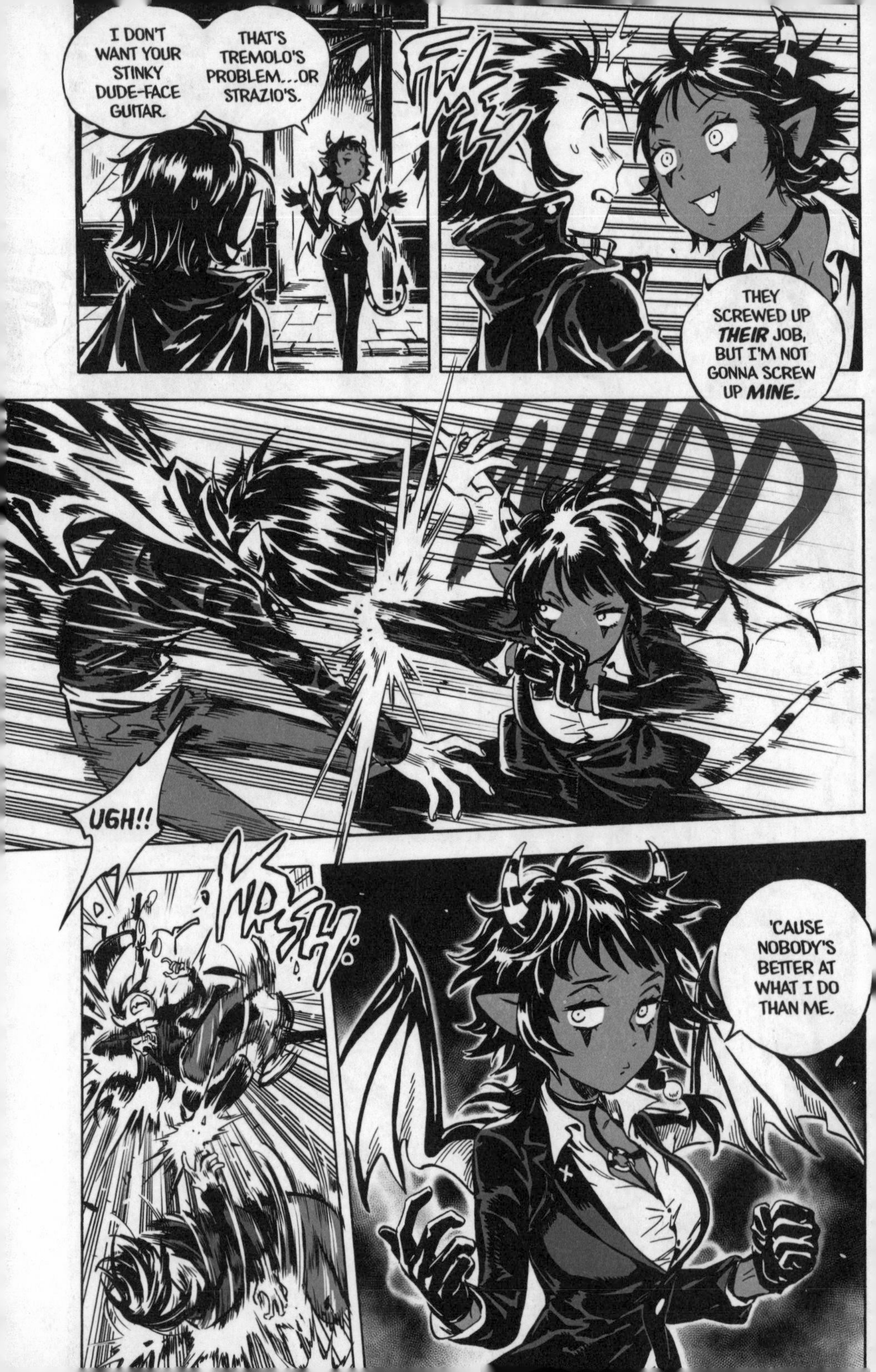
I DON'T WANT YOUR STINKY DUDE-FACE GUITAR.
THAT'S TREMOLO'S PROBLEM...OR STRAZIO'S.
FWLMMM
THEY SCREWED UP THEIR JOB, BUT I'M NOT GONNA SCREW UP MINE.
WHOOD
UGH!!
KRSSH
'CAUSE NOBODY'S BETTER AT WHAT I DO THAN ME.

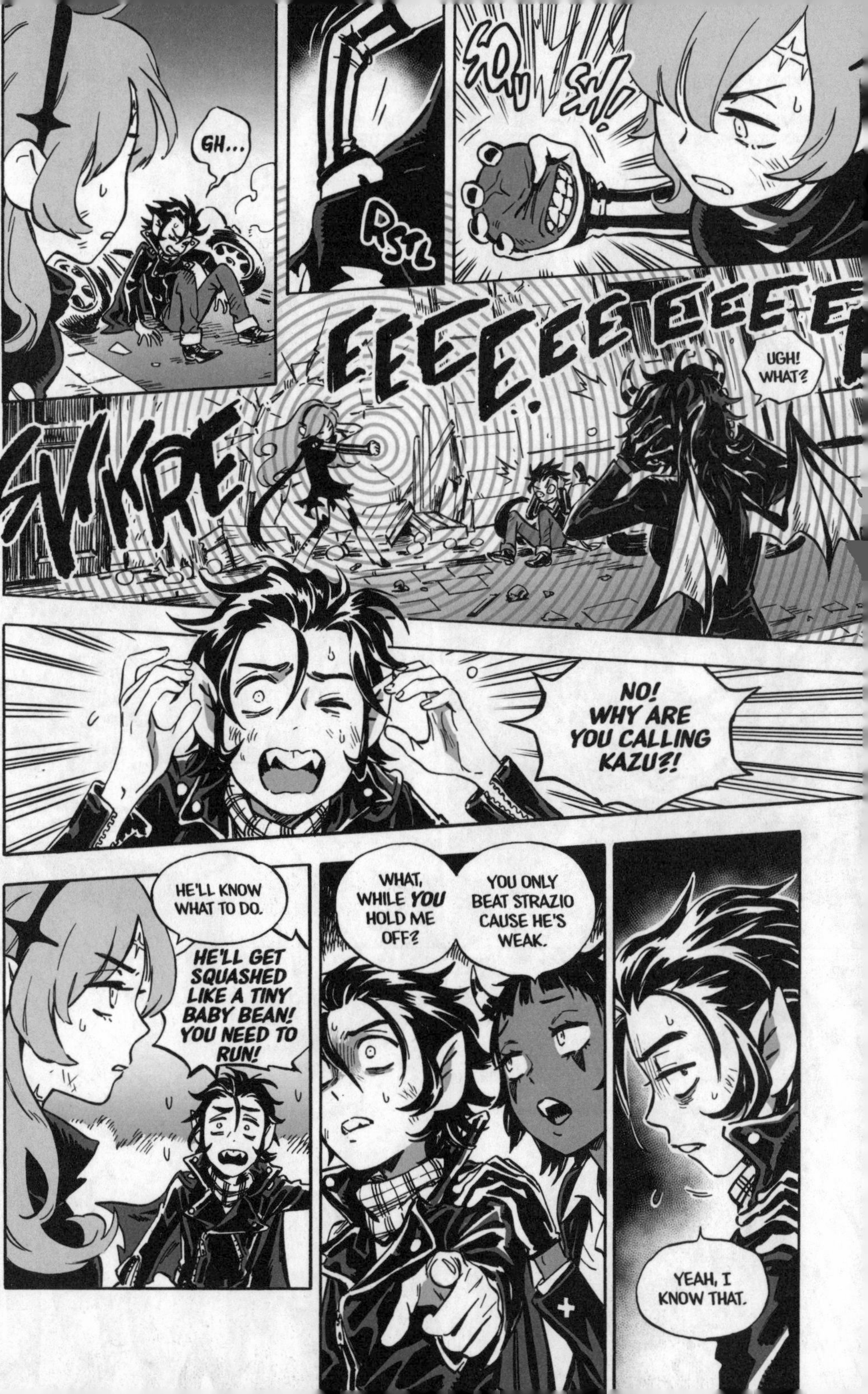
GH...
RSTL
SQUISH!
SKKRE
EEEEEEEEEE
UGH! WHAT?
NO! WHY ARE YOU CALLING KAZU?!
HE'LL KNOW WHAT TO DO.
HE'LL GET SQUASHED LIKE A TINY BABY BEAN! YOU NEED TO RUN!
WHAT, WHILE *YOU* HOLD ME OFF?
YOU ONLY BEAT STRAZIO CAUSE HE'S WEAK.
YEAH, I KNOW THAT.

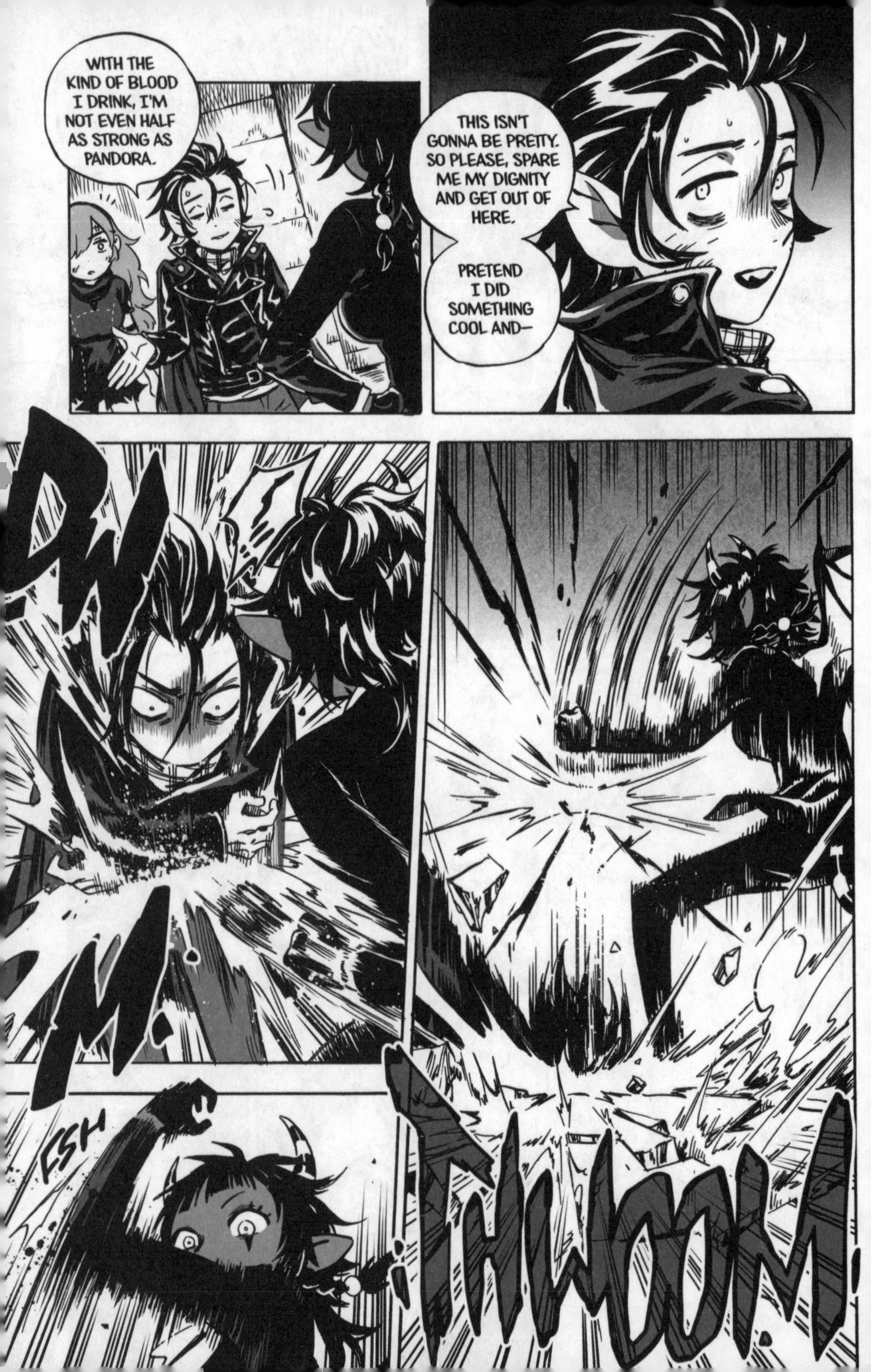
WITH THE KIND OF BLOOD I DRINK, I'M NOT EVEN HALF AS STRONG AS PANDORA.
THIS ISN'T GONNA BE PRETTY. SO PLEASE, SPARE ME MY DIGNITY AND GET OUT OF HERE.
PRETEND I DID SOMETHING COOL AND—
THWOOM!

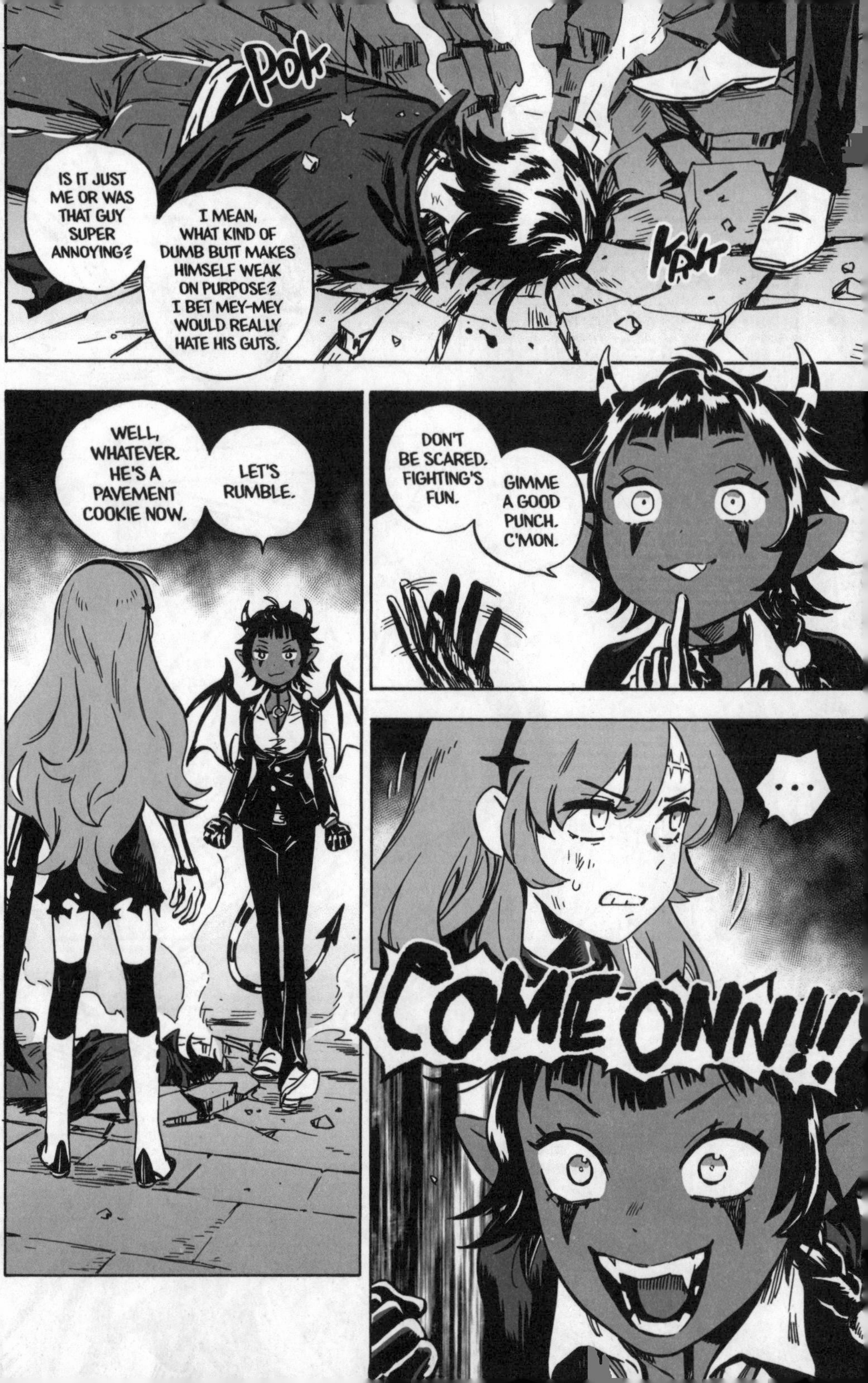
POK
IS IT JUST ME OR WAS THAT GUY SUPER ANNOYING?
I MEAN, WHAT KIND OF DUMB BUTT MAKES HIMSELF WEAK ON PURPOSE? I BET MEY-MEY WOULD REALLY HATE HIS GUTS.
KRAK
WELL, WHATEVER. HE'S A PAVEMENT COOKIE NOW.
LET'S RUMBLE.
DON'T BE SCARED. FIGHTING'S FUN.
GIMME A GOOD PUNCH. C'MON.
...
COME ONN!!

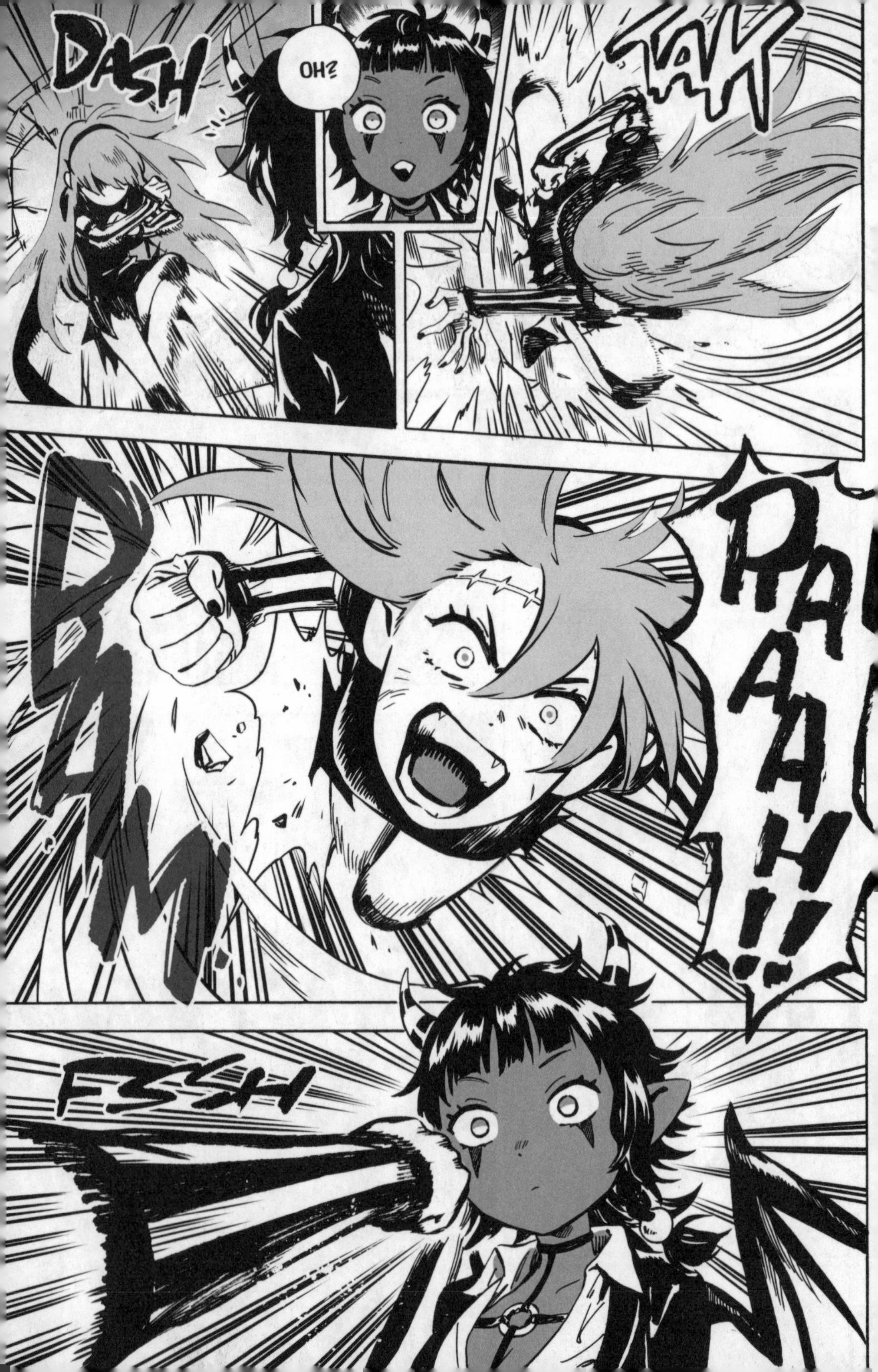
DASH
OH?
BAM
RAAAAH!!
FSSH

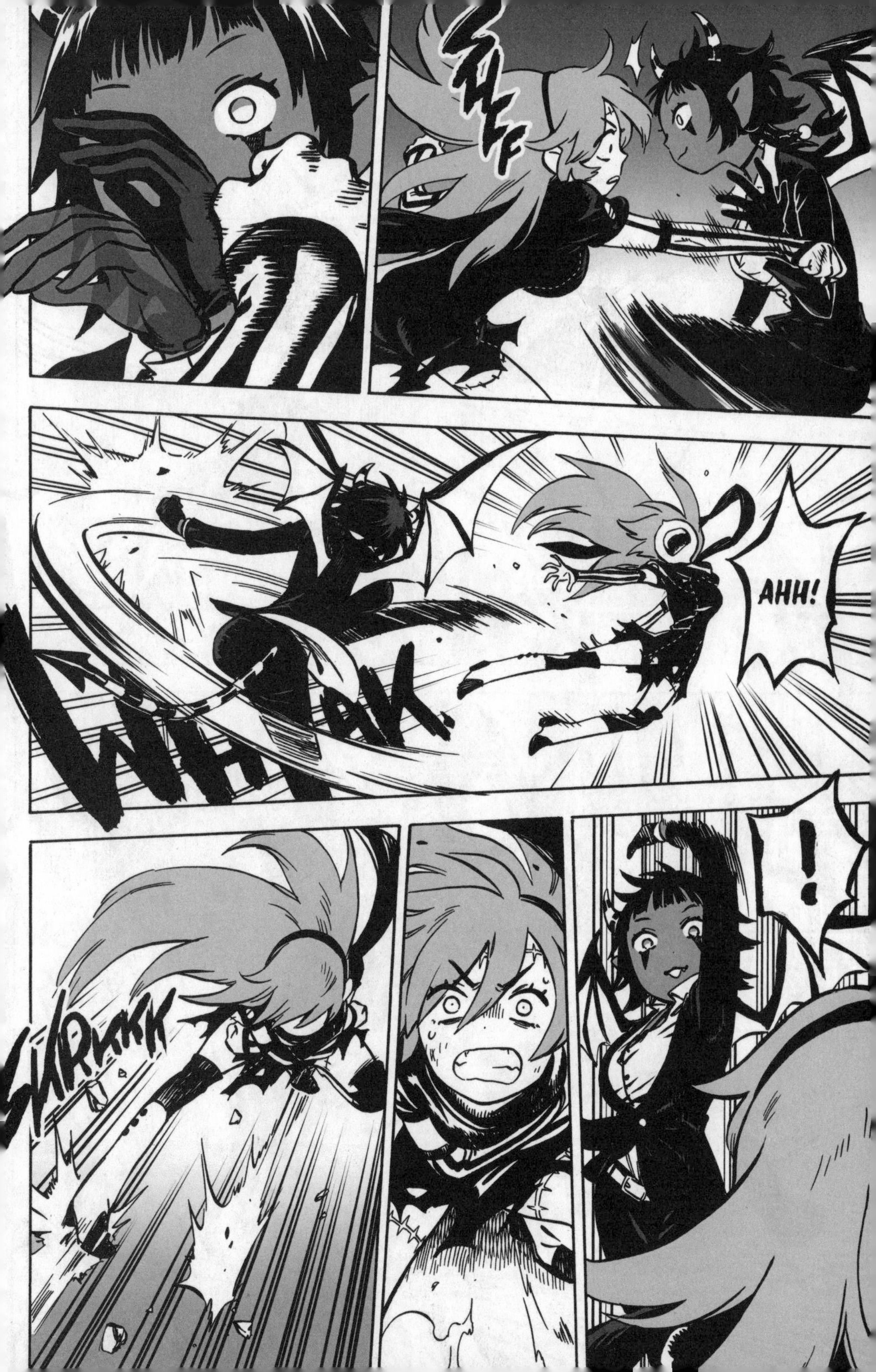
SHFF
WHACK
AHH!
SHRAKK
!

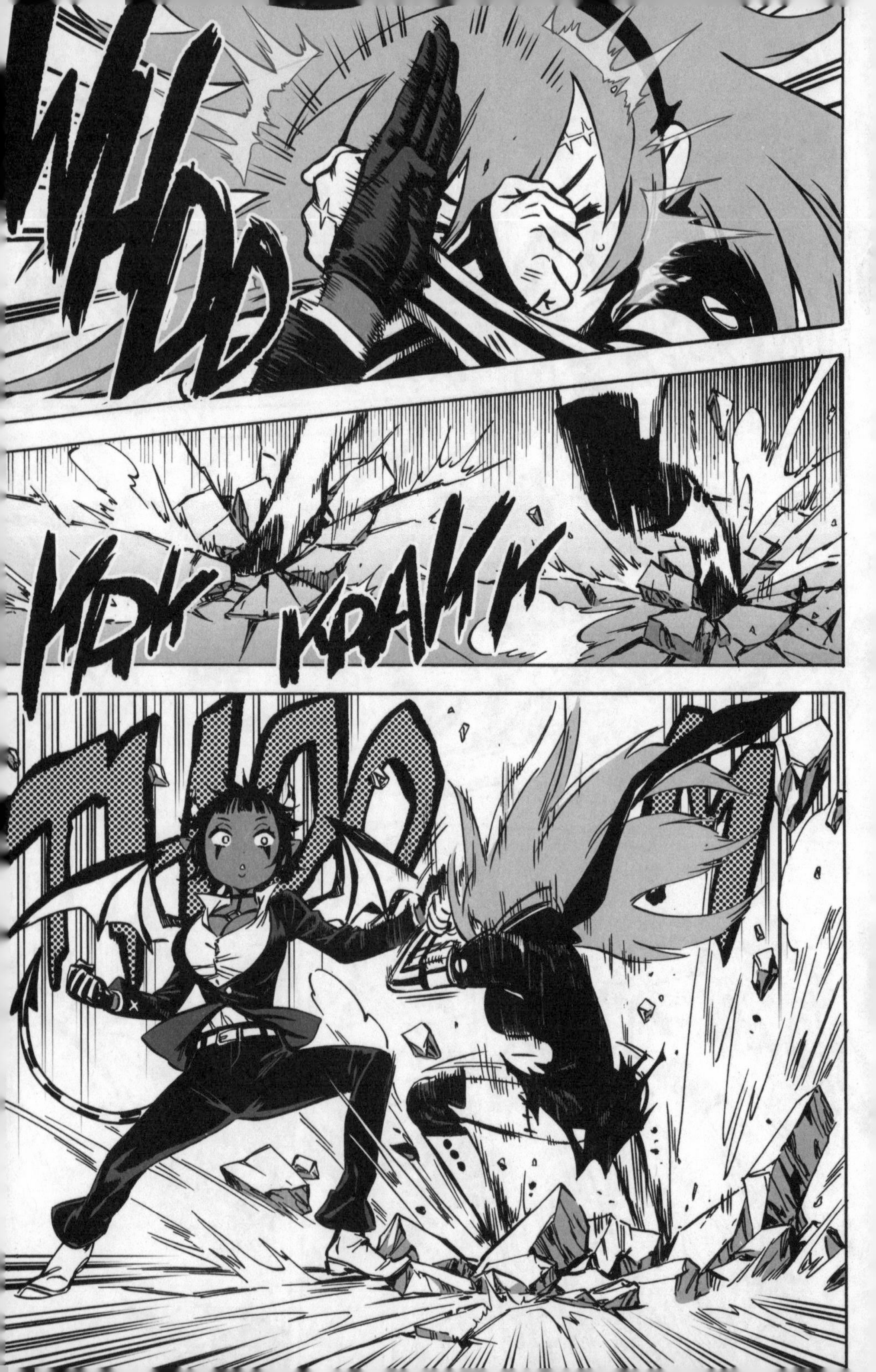
KRAK KRAKK
THOOM

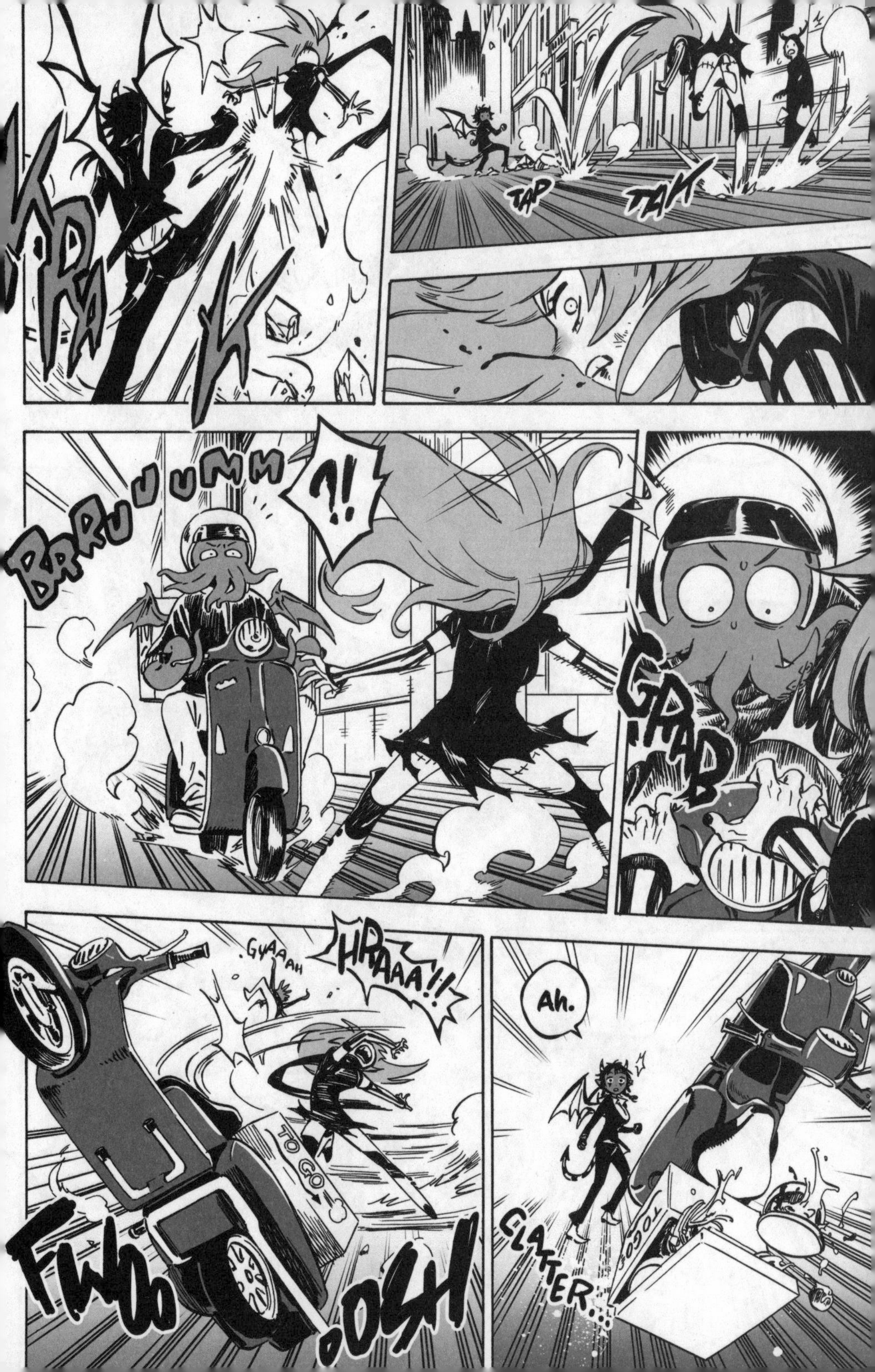
KRAAK
TAP
TAK
BRRUUUMM
?!
GRAB
GYAAAH
HRAAAA!!
FWOOOOSH
Ah.
TO GO
CLATTER...

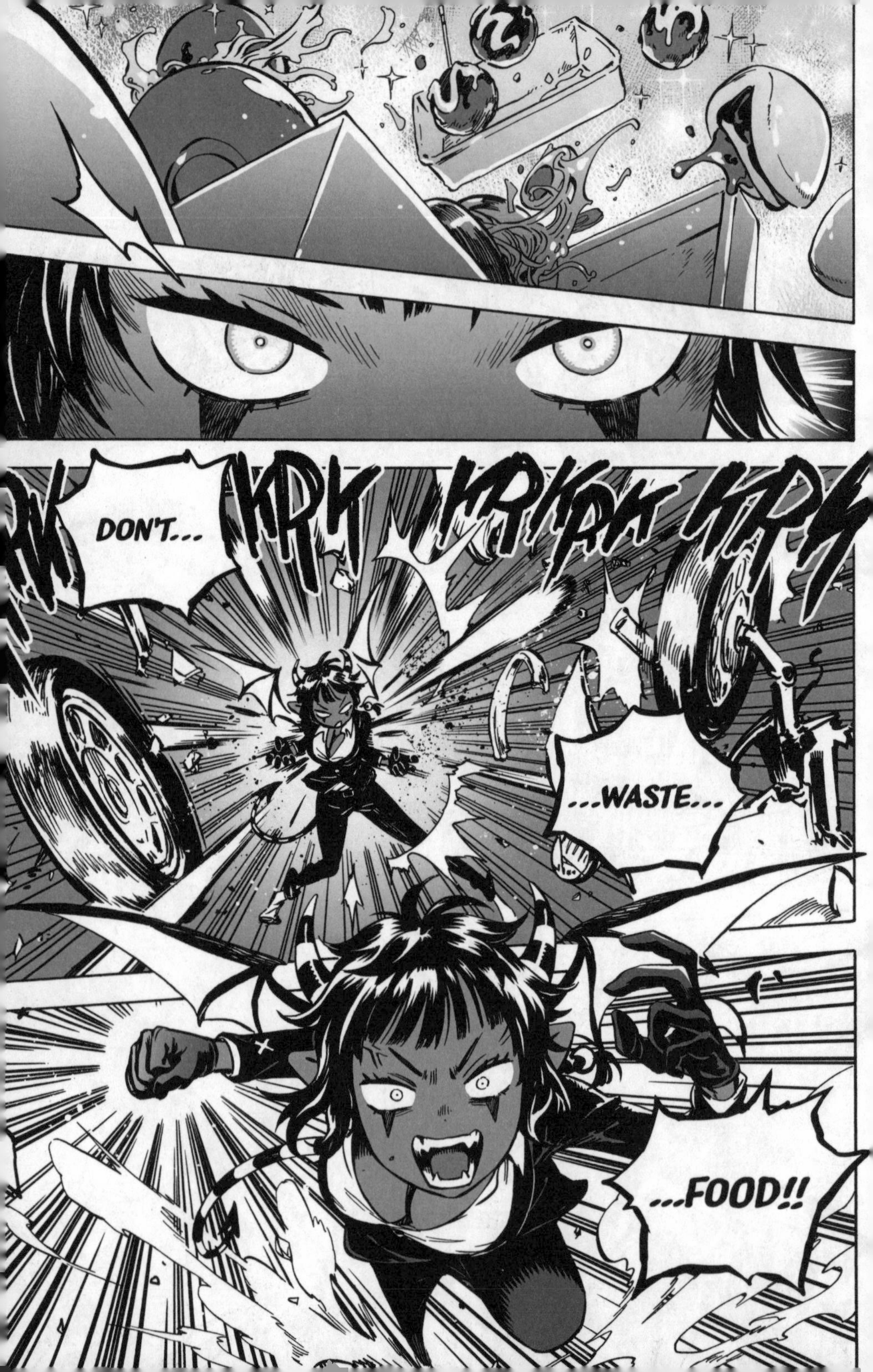
DON'T...
KRK
KRKRK
KRK
...WASTE...
...FOOD!!

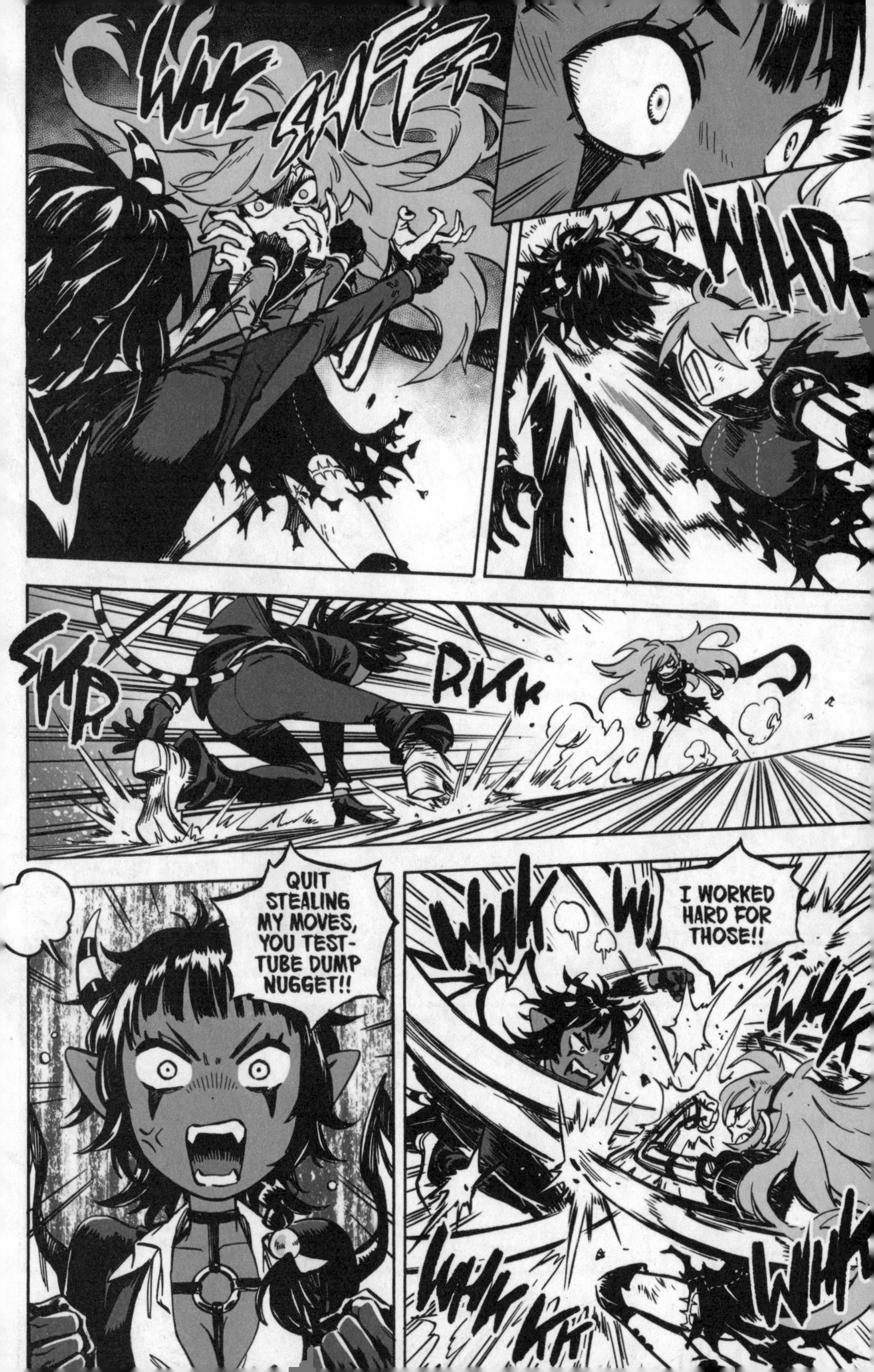

WHH
SWFF
WHR
SHP
RUKK
QUIT STEALING MY MOVES, YOU TEST-TUBE DUMP NUGGET!!
WHK
W
I WORKED HARD FOR THOSE!!
WHK
WHKKKK
WHK

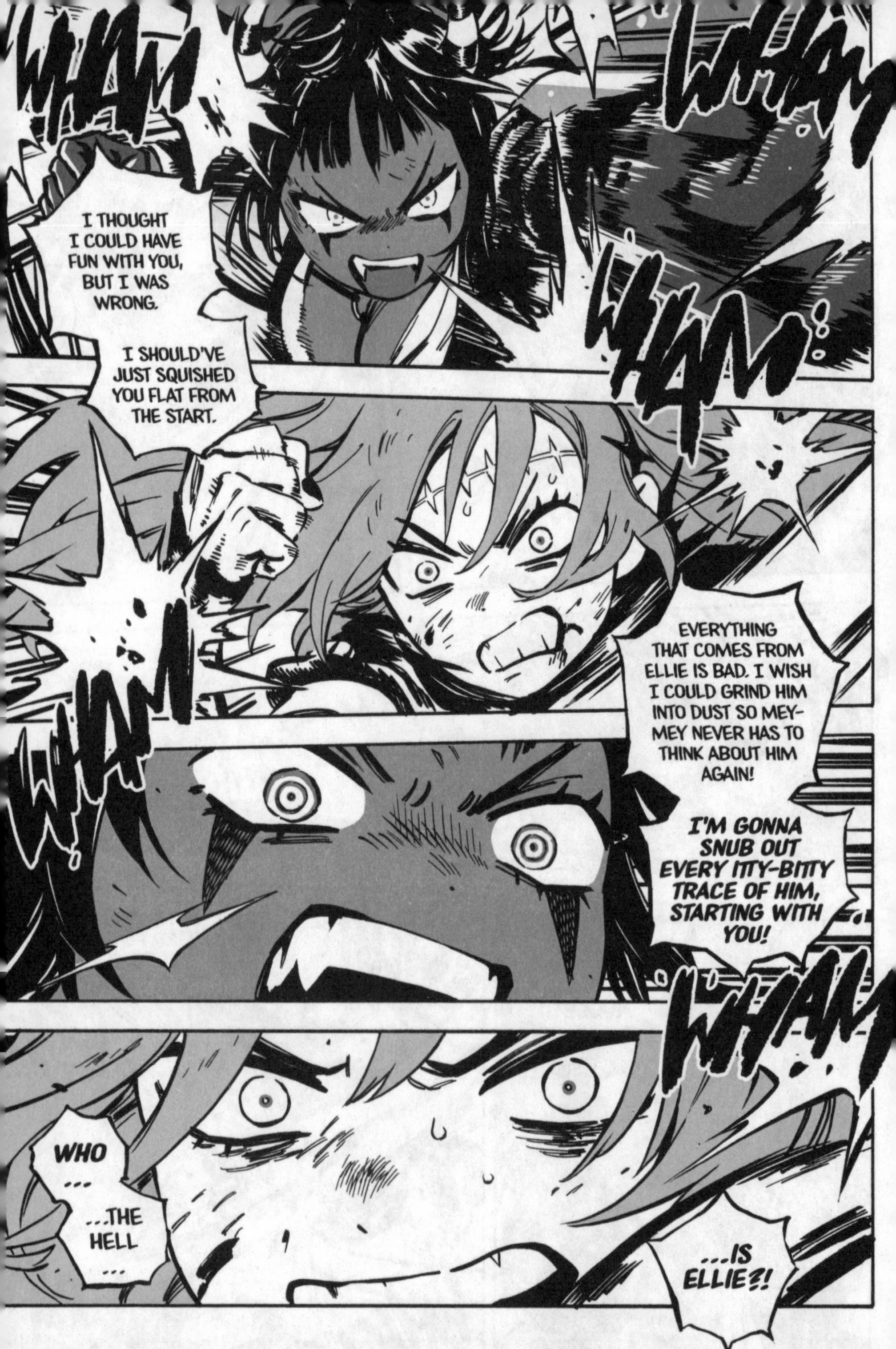
WHAM
WHAM
I THOUGHT I COULD HAVE FUN WITH YOU, BUT I WAS WRONG.
WHAM
I SHOULD'VE JUST SQUISHED YOU FLAT FROM THE START.
WHAM
EVERYTHING THAT COMES FROM ELLIE IS BAD. I WISH I COULD GRIND HIM INTO DUST SO MEY-MEY NEVER HAS TO THINK ABOUT HIM AGAIN!
WHAM
I'M GONNA SNUB OUT EVERY ITTY-BITTY TRACE OF HIM, STARTING WITH YOU!
WHAM
WHO ... ...THE HELL ...
...IS ELLIE?!

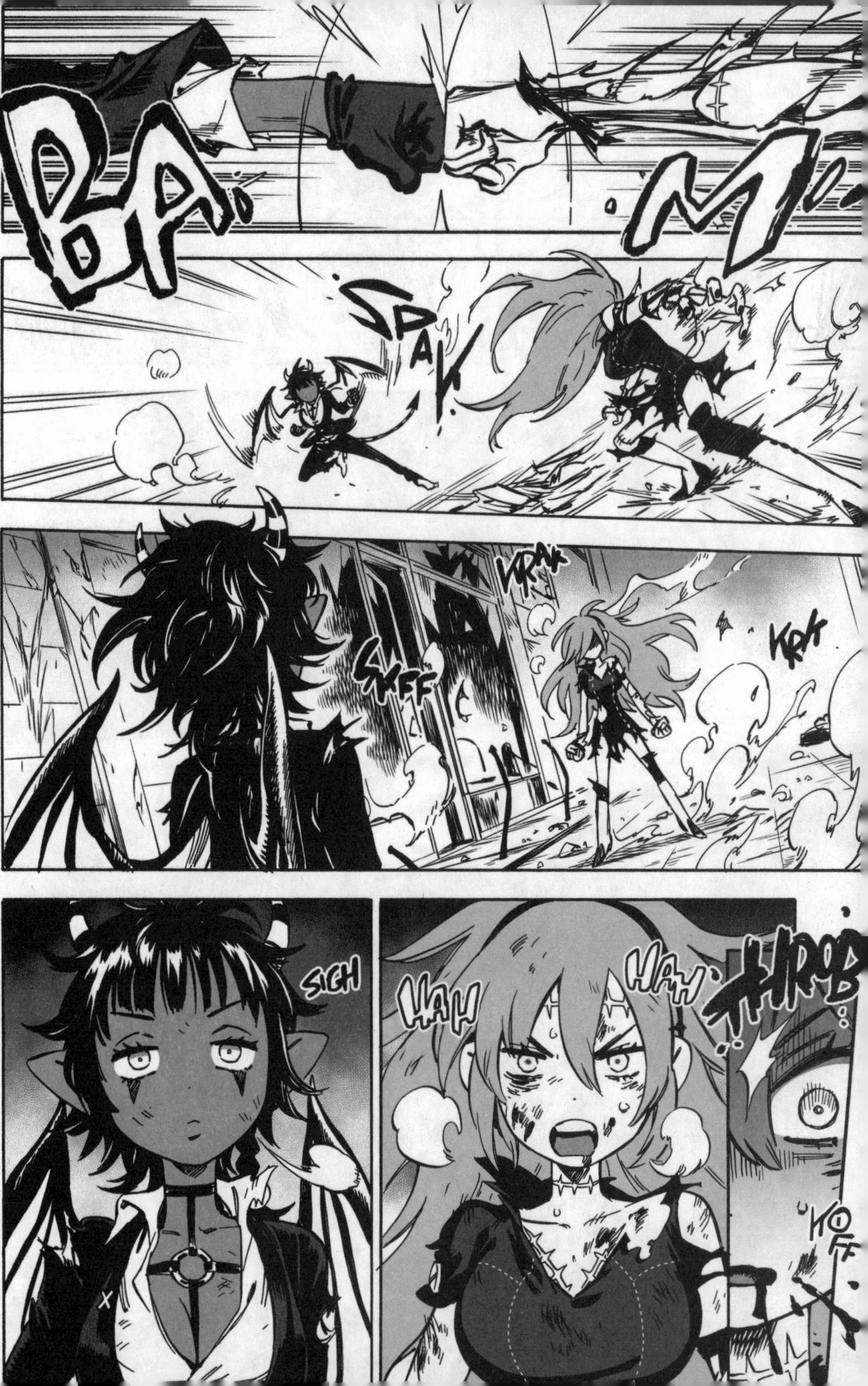
BAM
SPAK!
KRAK
SHFF
KRAK
SIGH
HAH
HAH
THROB
KOFF

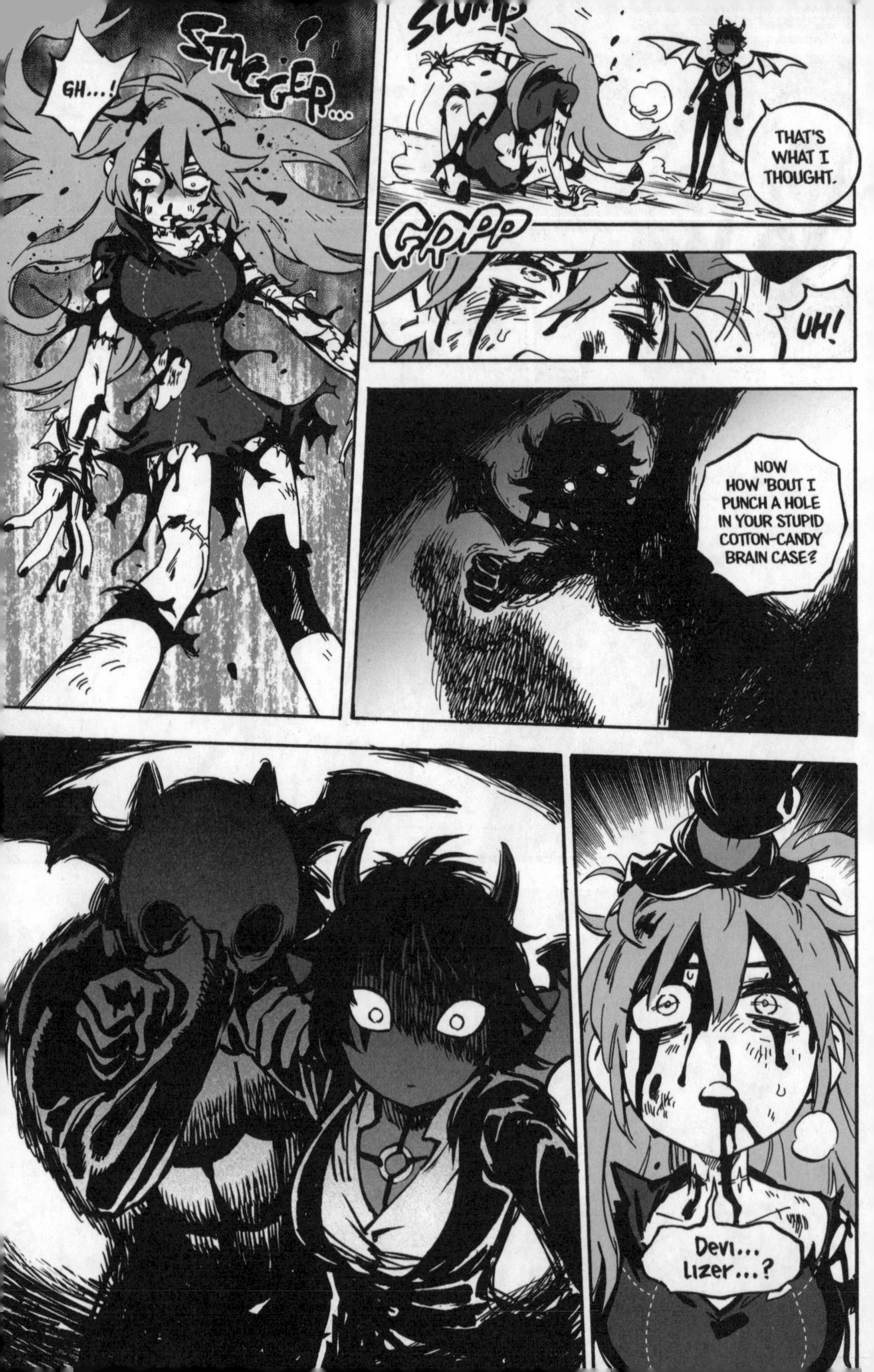
GH...!
STAGGER...
SLUMP
THAT'S WHAT I THOUGHT.
GRPP
UH!
NOW HOW 'BOUT I PUNCH A HOLE IN YOUR STUPID COTTON-CANDY BRAIN CASE?
Devi... lizer...?

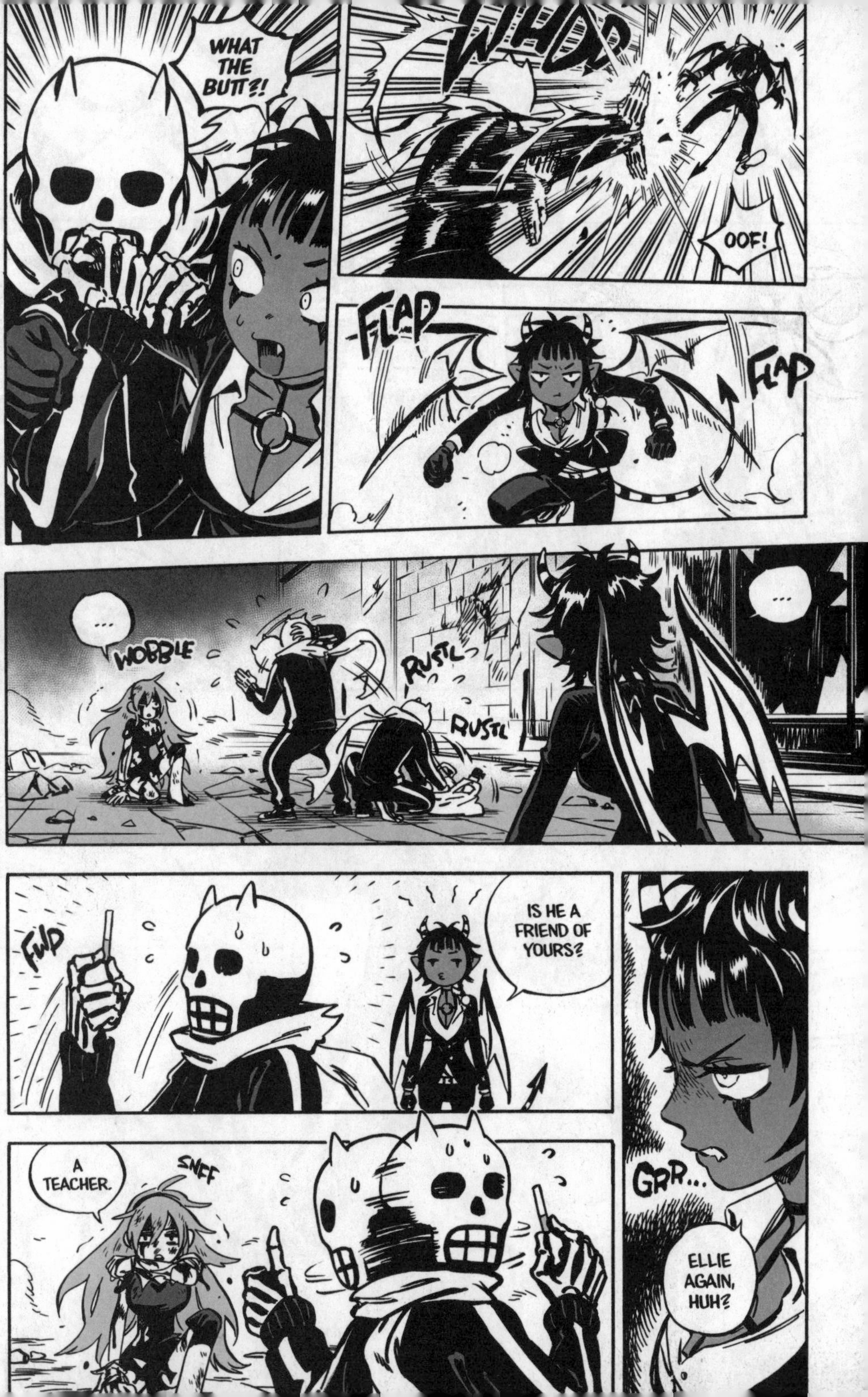
WHAT THE BUTT?!
WHOP
OOF!
FLAP
FLAP
...
WOBBLE
RUSTL
RUSTL
...
FWD
IS HE A FRIEND OF YOURS?
A TEACHER.
SNFF
GRR...
ELLIE AGAIN, HUH?

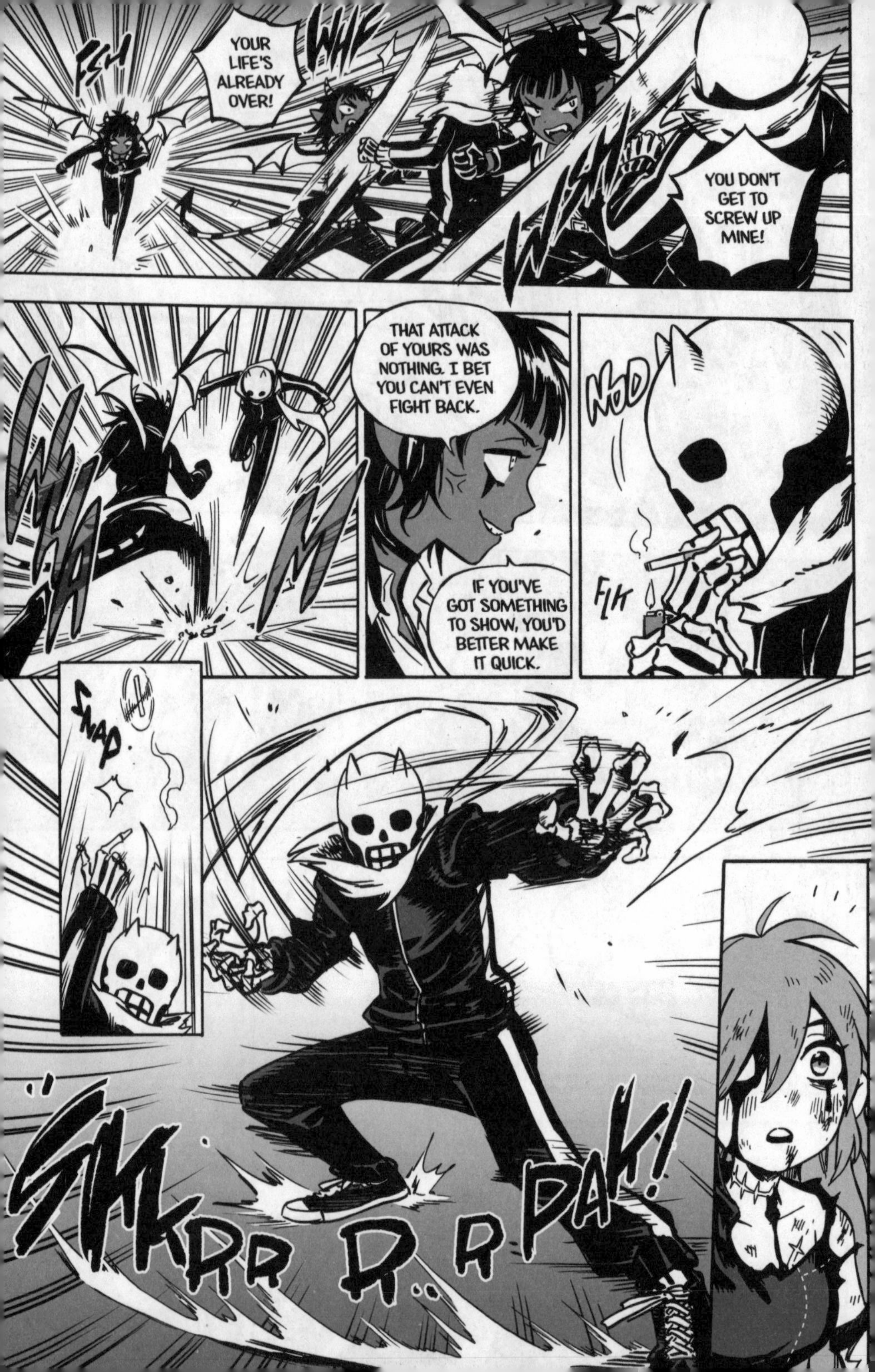
FSH
YOUR LIFE'S ALREADY OVER!
WHF
WHAM
YOU DON'T GET TO SCREW UP MINE!
THAT ATTACK OF YOURS WAS NOTHING. I BET YOU CAN'T EVEN FIGHT BACK.
IF YOU'VE GOT SOMETHING TO SHOW, YOU'D BETTER MAKE IT QUICK.
NOD
FLIK
SNAP
SHKRR D.. R DAK!

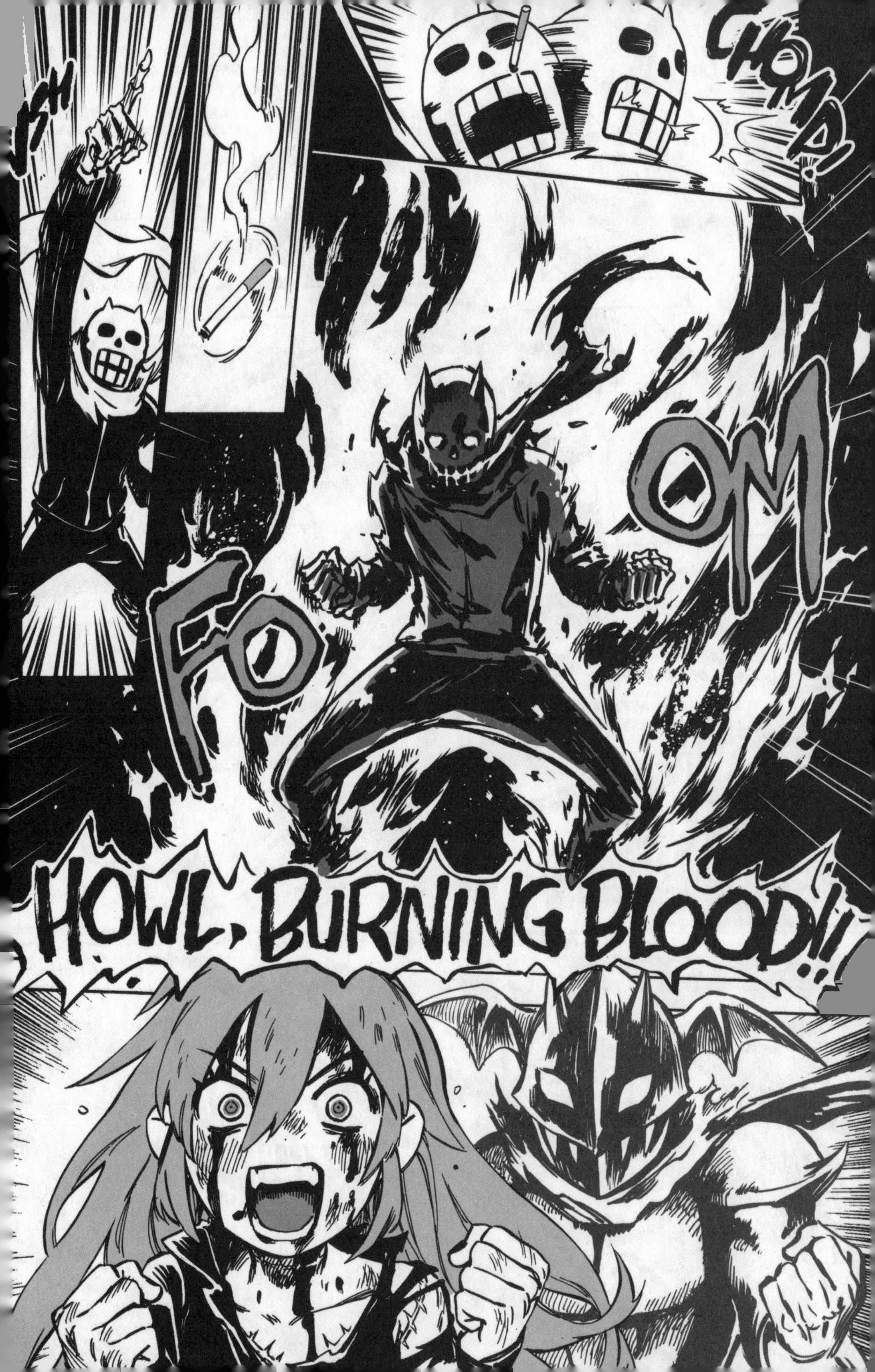
CHOMP!
FOOM
HOWL, BURNING BLOOD!!

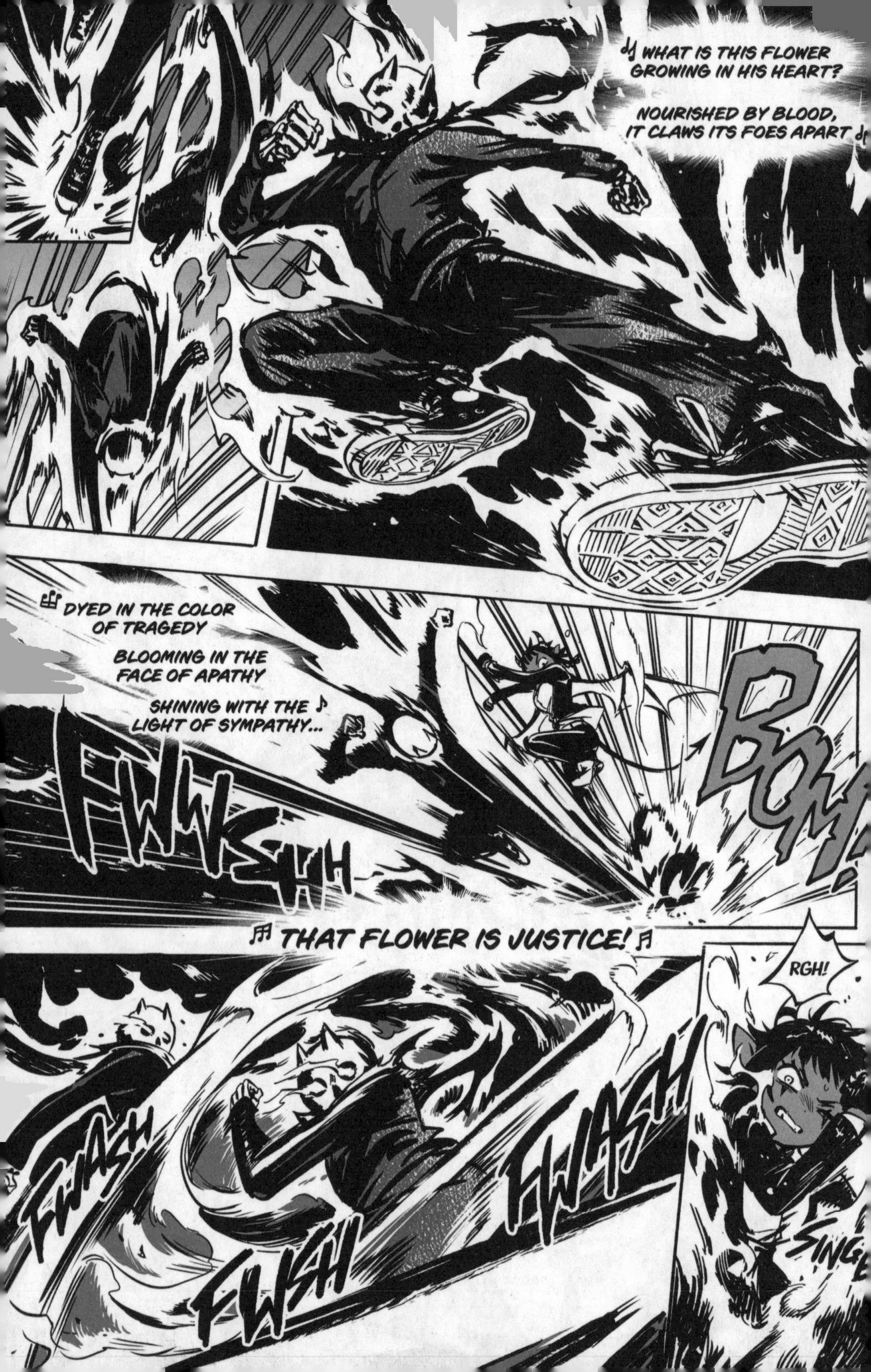
WHAT IS THIS FLOWER GROWING IN HIS HEART?
NOURISHED BY BLOOD, IT CLAWS ITS FOES APART
DYED IN THE COLOR OF TRAGEDY
BLOOMING IN THE FACE OF APATHY
SHINING WITH THE LIGHT OF SYMPATHY...
FWWKSHH
BOOM!
THAT FLOWER IS JUSTICE!
RGH!
FWASH
FWSH
FWASH
SING

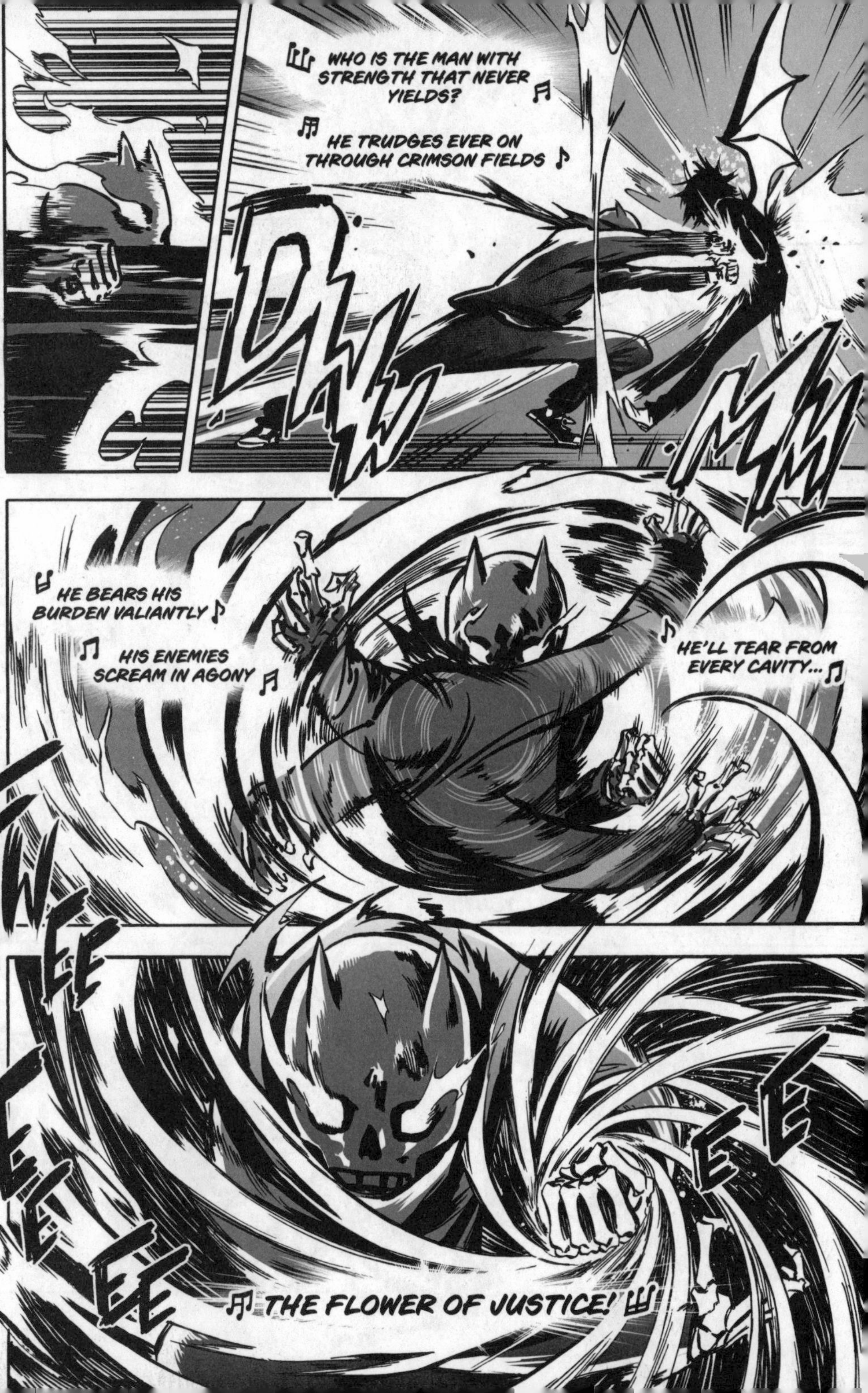
WHO IS THE MAN WITH STRENGTH THAT NEVER YIELDS?
HE TRUDGES EVER ON THROUGH CRIMSON FIELDS
HE BEARS HIS BURDEN VALIANTLY
HIS ENEMIES SCREAM IN AGONY
HE'LL TEAR FROM EVERY CAVITY...
THE FLOWER OF JUSTICE!

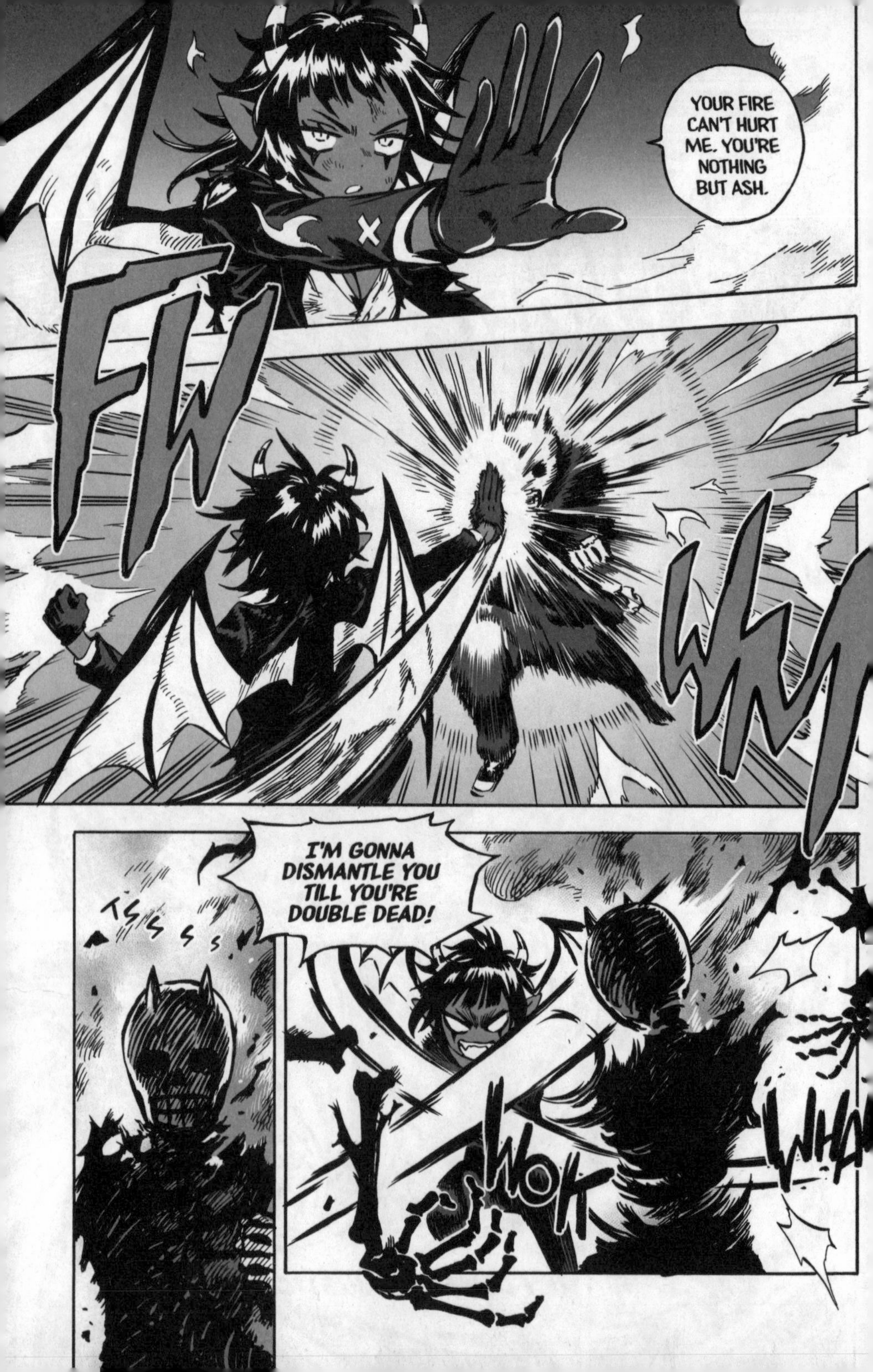
YOUR FIRE CAN'T HURT ME. YOU'RE NOTHING BUT ASH.
FW
WM
TSSSSS
I'M GONNA DISMANTLE YOU TILL YOU'RE DOUBLE DEAD!
WOK
WHA

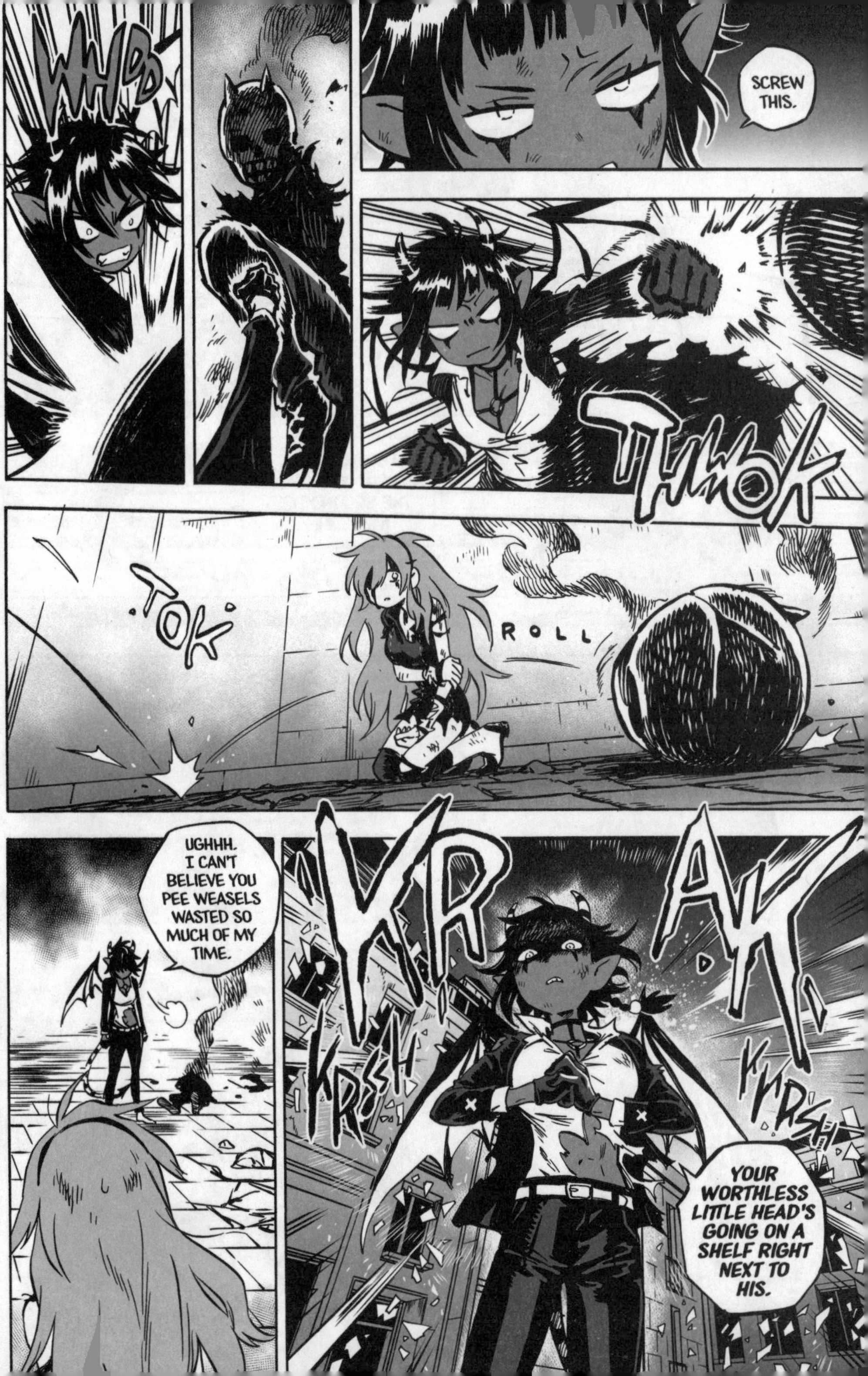
WHDD
SCREW THIS.
THWOK
TOK
ROLL
UGHHH. I CAN'T BELIEVE YOU PEE WEASELS WASTED SO MUCH OF MY TIME.
KRAK
KRSH
KRSH
YOUR WORTHLESS LITTLE HEAD'S GOING ON A SHELF RIGHT NEXT TO HIS.

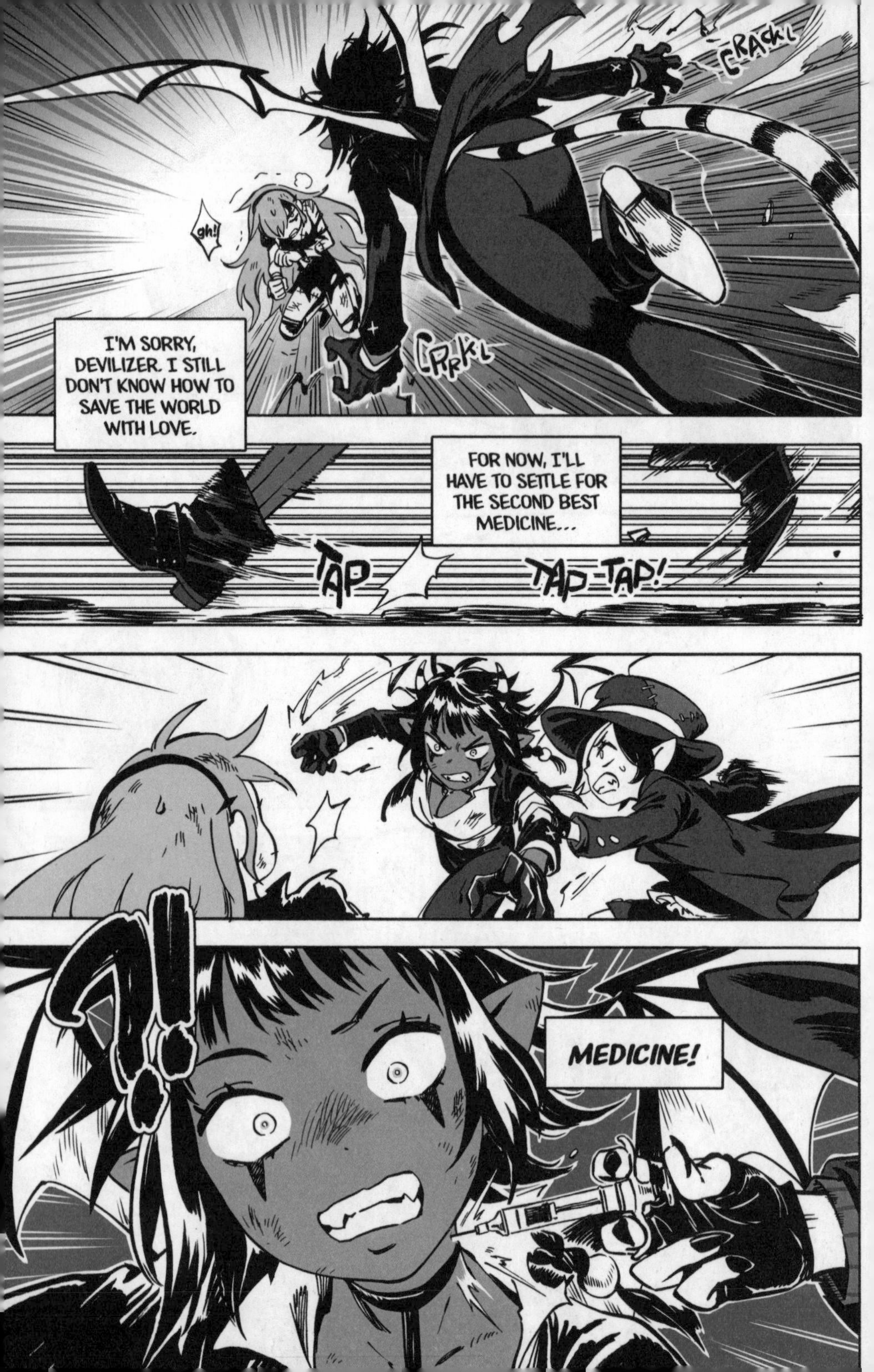
CRACKL
gh!
I'M SORRY, DEVILIZER. I STILL DON'T KNOW HOW TO SAVE THE WORLD WITH LOVE.
CRRKL
FOR NOW, I'LL HAVE TO SETTLE FOR THE SECOND BEST MEDICINE...
TAP
TAP TAP!
MEDICINE!

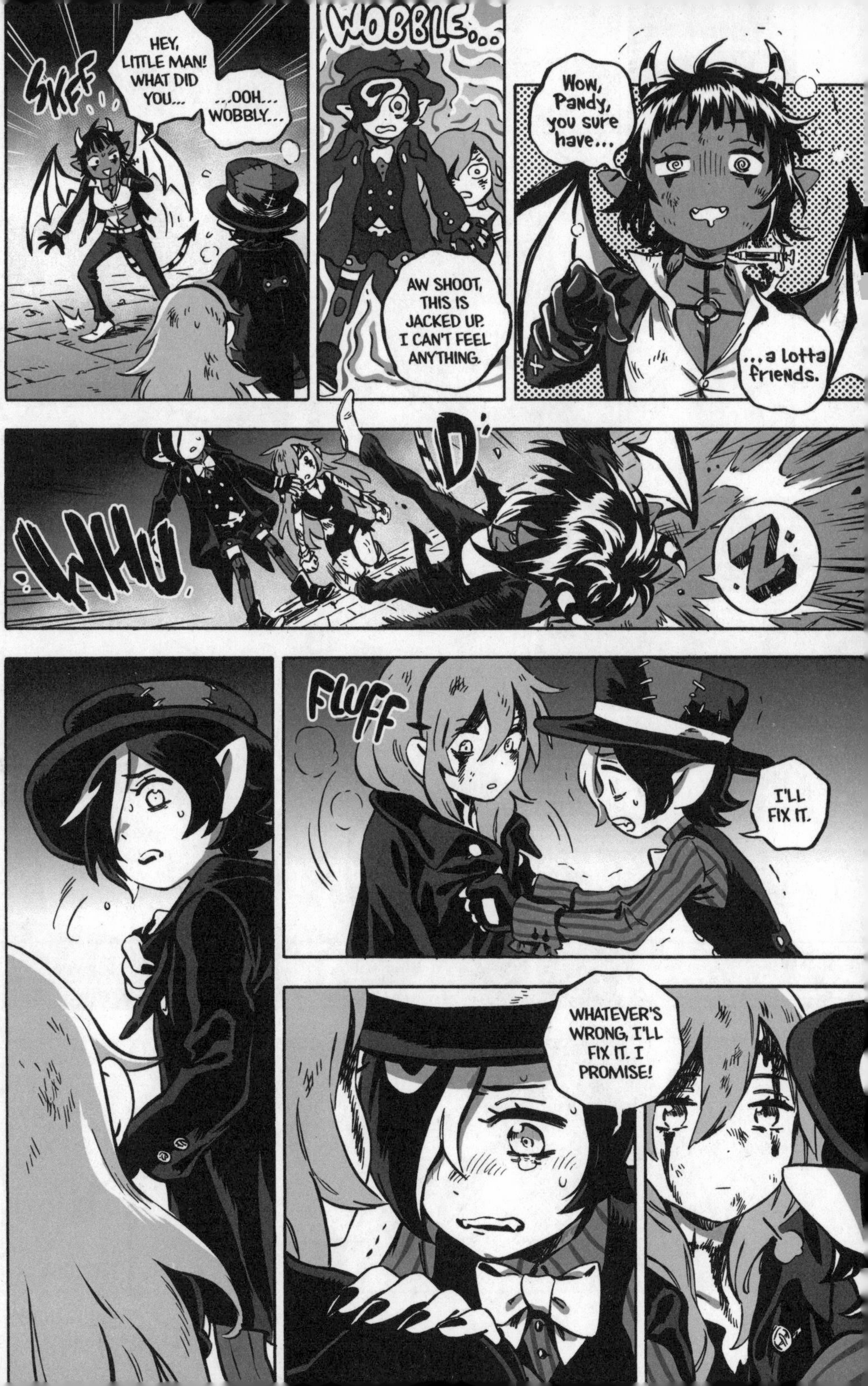
SKFF
HEY, LITTLE MAN! WHAT DID YOU...
...OOH... WOBBLY...
WOBBLE...
AW SHOOT, THIS IS JACKED UP. I CAN'T FEEL ANYTHING.
Wow, Pandy, you sure have...
...a lotta friends.
WHU
D
Z
FLUFF
I'LL FIX IT.
WHATEVER'S WRONG, I'LL FIX IT. I PROMISE!

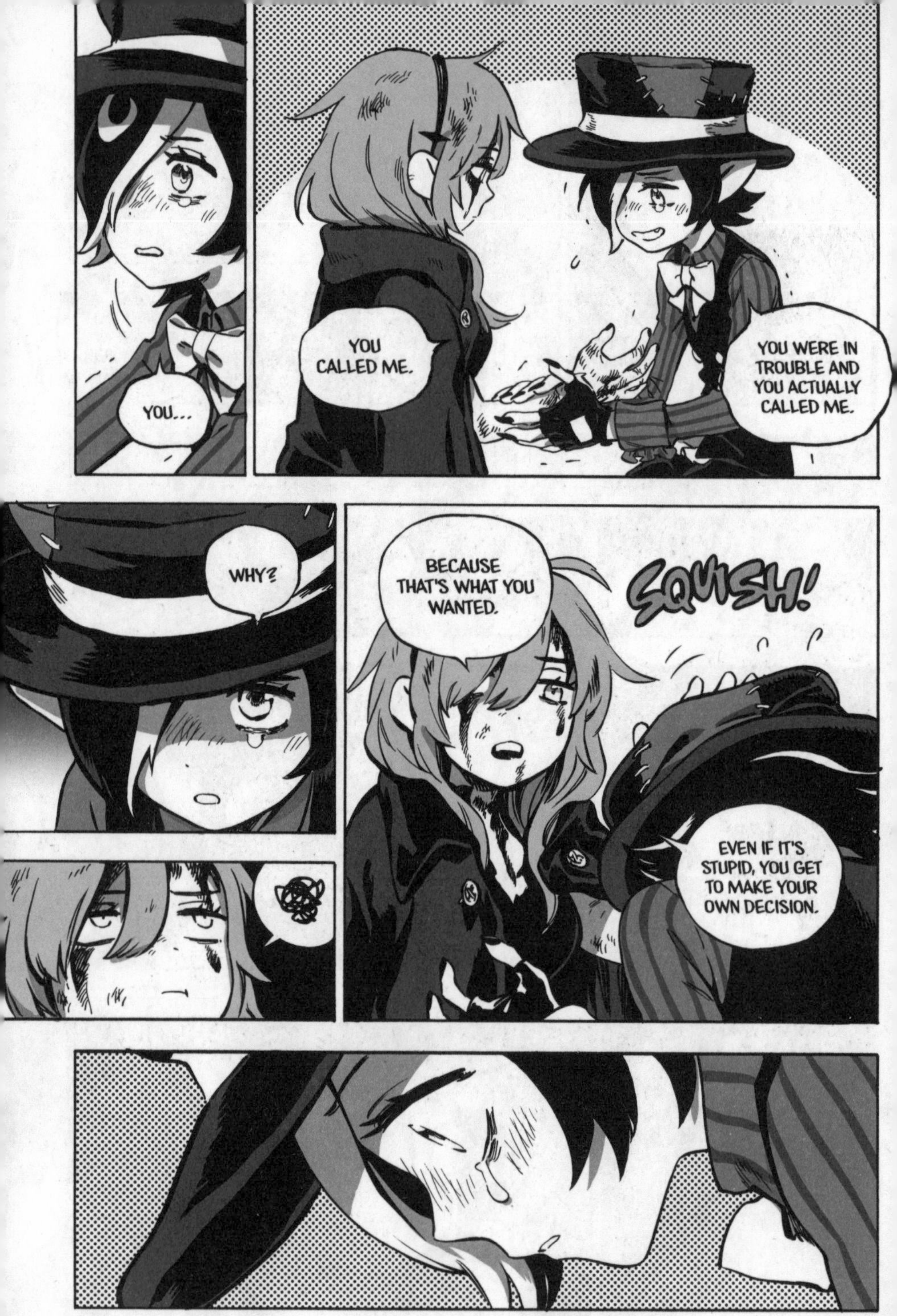
YOU...
YOU CALLED ME.
YOU WERE IN TROUBLE AND YOU ACTUALLY CALLED ME.
WHY?
BECAUSE THAT'S WHAT YOU WANTED.
SQUISH!
EVEN IF IT'S STUPID, YOU GET TO MAKE YOUR OWN DECISION.

S-STUPID...? I GUESS IT WAS, HUH?

I DON'T KNOW WHAT I THOUGHT I WAS GOING TO DO, REALLY. I JUST WANTED TO PROTECT YOU *SOMEHOW.*

SNIFFLE

I BROUGHT STUFF FOR EMERGENCY SURGERY JUST IN CASE... BUT I DIDN'T THINK I WOULD USE IT LIKE *THIS...*

BRR...

WAIT... WHO IS THAT LADY, ANYWAY? WHAT EVEN HAPPENED?

Z..Z

Z.Z.Z...

IS CLARENCE—

RIGHT HERE.

gasp!

HWOOO

OOO

I JUST GOT OFF THE PHONE WITH YAHGIE. HE'S HEADED TO RICKET'S PLACE.

LET'S LIMP OUR WAY OVER THERE BEFORE ANYTHING ELSE CRAPPY HAPPENS.

SPURT

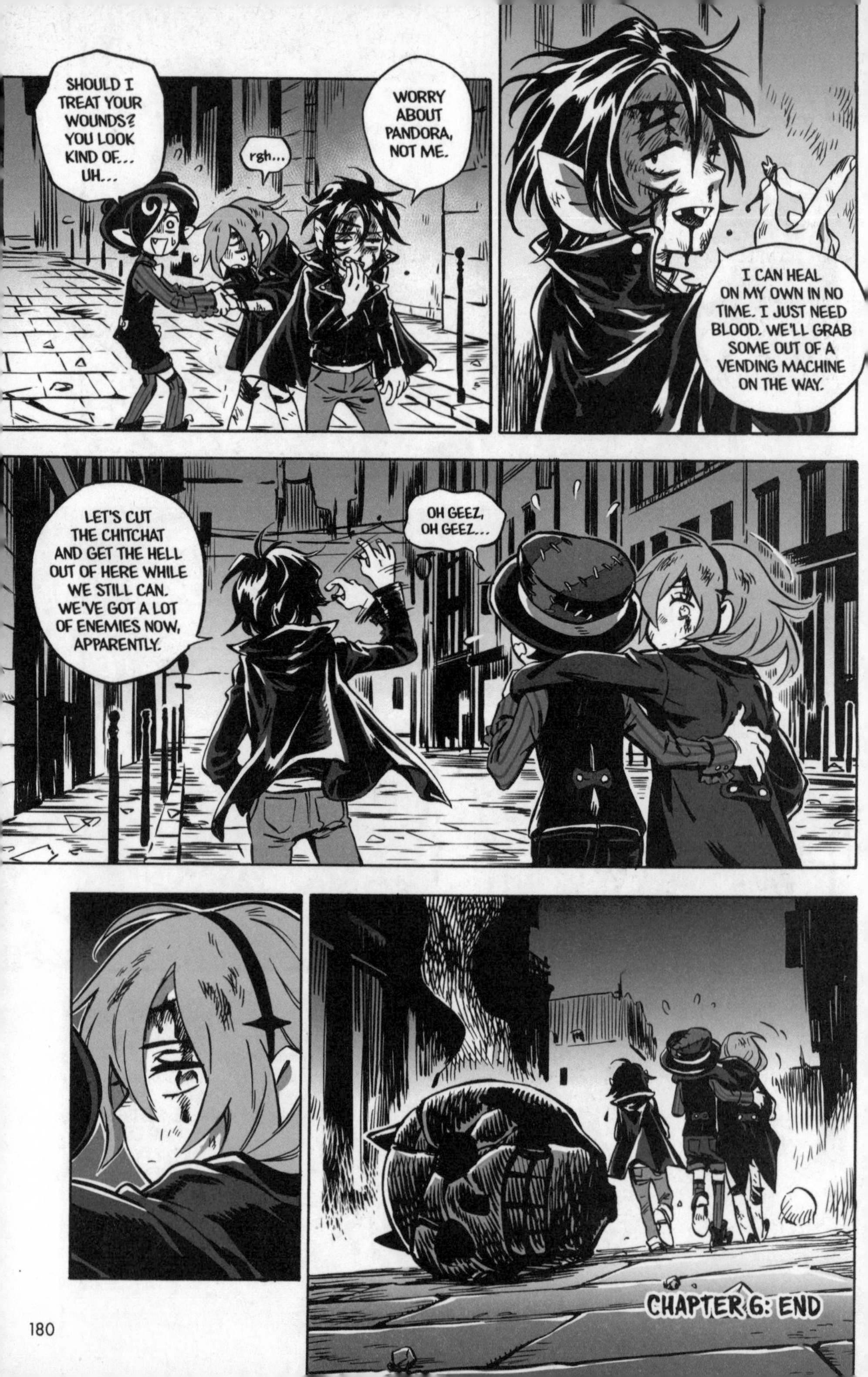
SHOULD I TREAT YOUR WOUNDS? YOU LOOK KIND OF... UH...
rgh...
WORRY ABOUT PANDORA, NOT ME.
I CAN HEAL ON MY OWN IN NO TIME. I JUST NEED BLOOD. WE'LL GRAB SOME OUT OF A VENDING MACHINE ON THE WAY.
LET'S CUT THE CHITCHAT AND GET THE HELL OUT OF HERE WHILE WE STILL CAN. WE'VE GOT A LOT OF ENEMIES NOW, APPARENTLY.
OH GEEZ, OH GEEZ...
CHAPTER 6: END

WHAT DID THE VILLAINS DO NEXT?

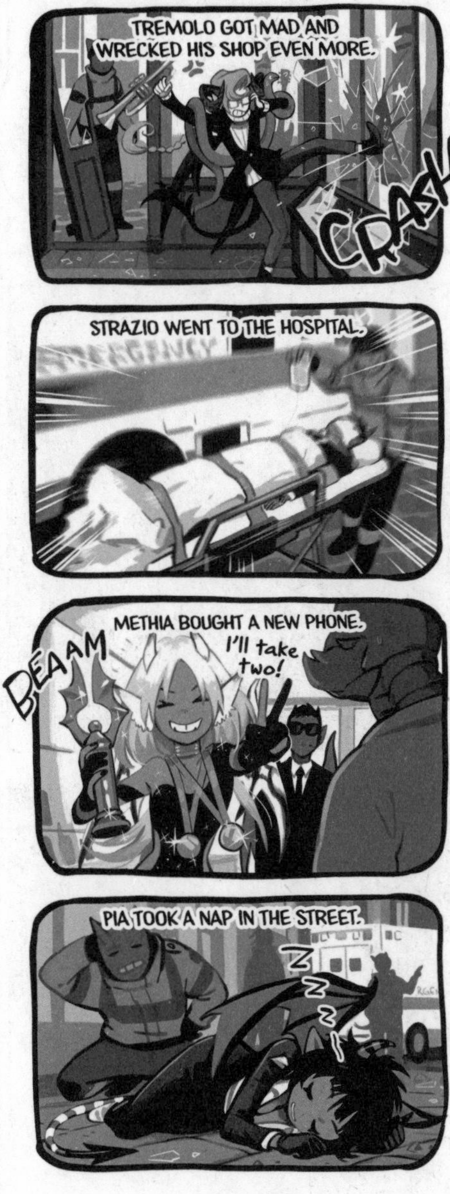
TREMOLO GOT MAD AND WRECKED HIS SHOP EVEN MORE.
CRASH
STRAZIO WENT TO THE HOSPITAL.
METHIA BOUGHT A NEW PHONE.
BEAAM
I'll take two!
PIA TOOK A NAP IN THE STREET.
Z Z Z

POPULAR GIRLS

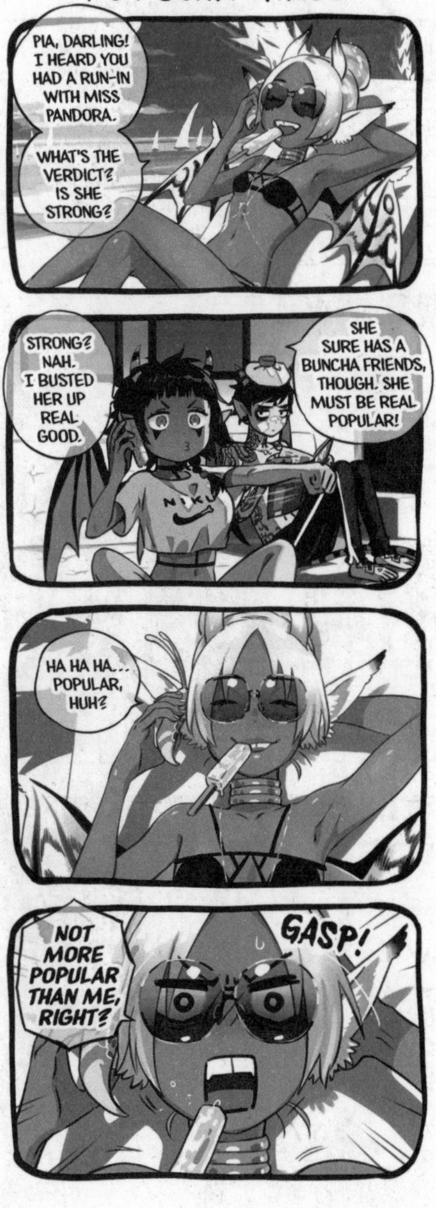
PIA, DARLING! I HEARD YOU HAD A RUN-IN WITH MISS PANDORA.
WHAT'S THE VERDICT? IS SHE STRONG?
STRONG? NAH. I BUSTED HER UP REAL GOOD.
SHE SURE HAS A BUNCHA FRIENDS, THOUGH. SHE MUST BE REAL POPULAR!
HA HA HA... POPULAR, HUH?
NOT MORE POPULAR THAN ME, RIGHT?
GASP!

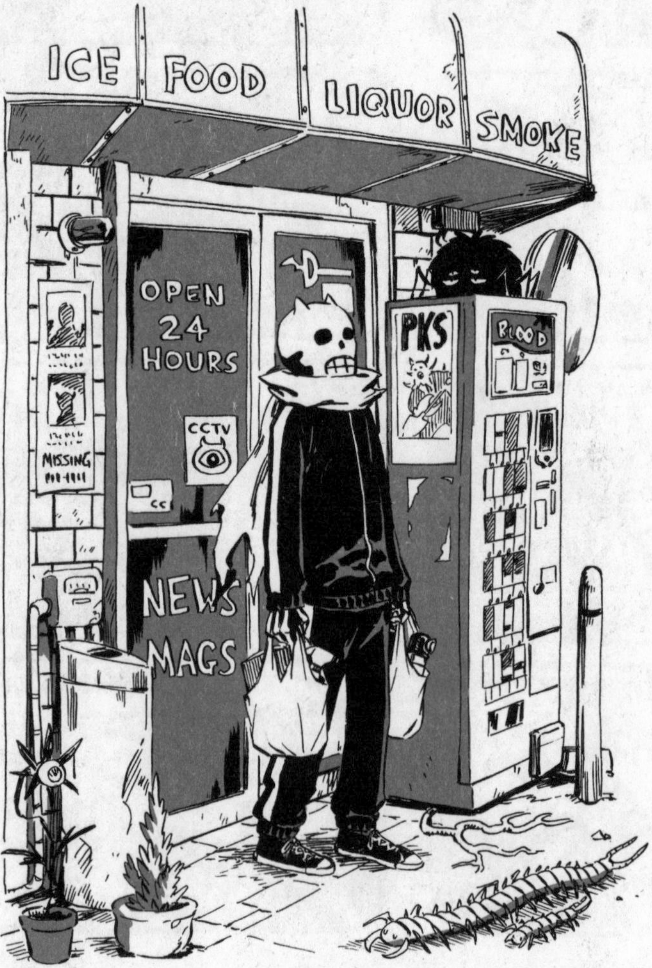
ICE
FOOD
LIQUOR
SMOKE
OPEN 24 HOURS
CCTV
MISSING
NEWS
MAGS
PKS
BLOOD

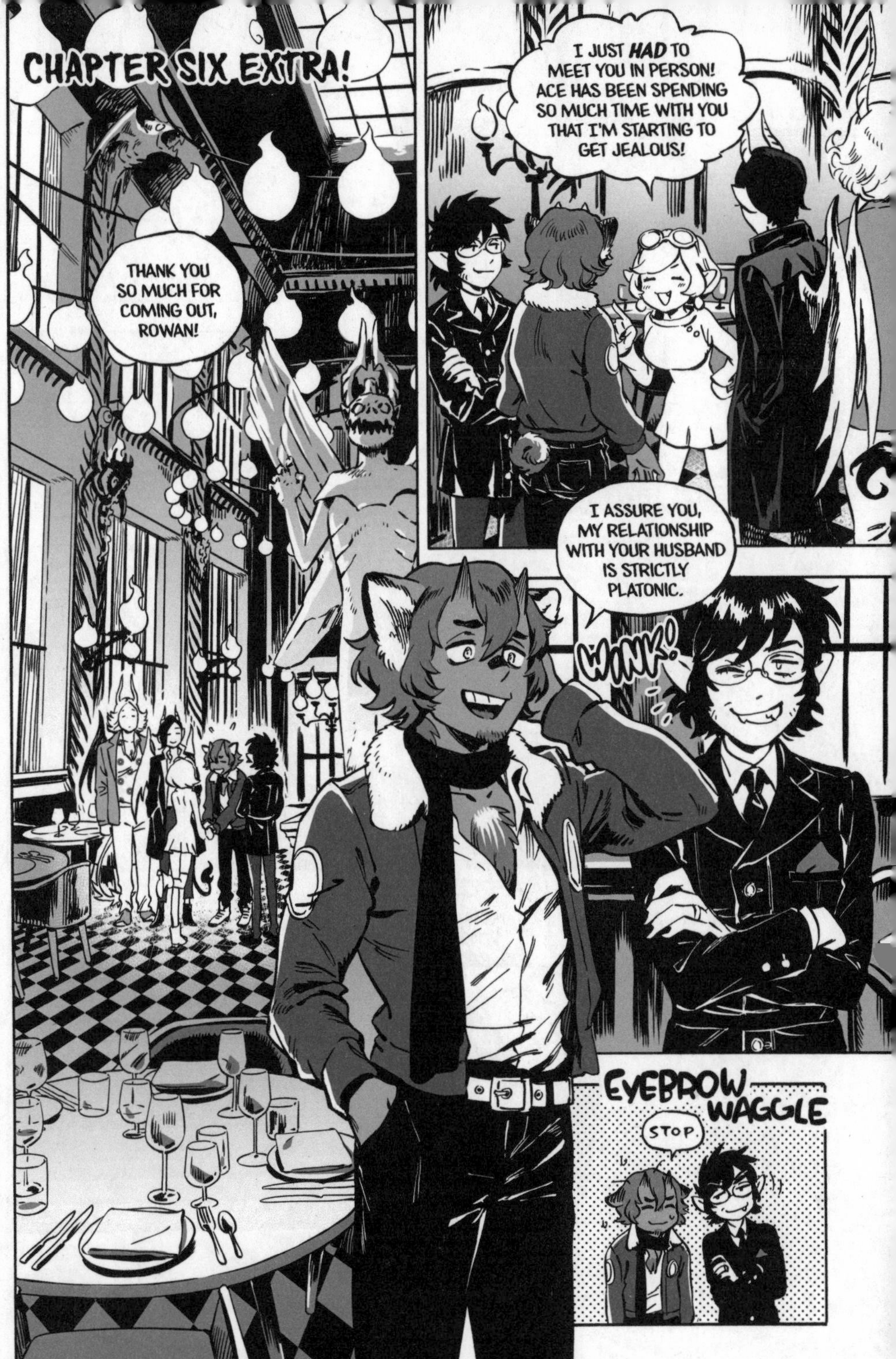
CHAPTER SIX EXTRA!
THANK YOU SO MUCH FOR COMING OUT, ROWAN!
I JUST **HAD** TO MEET YOU IN PERSON! ACE HAS BEEN SPENDING SO MUCH TIME WITH YOU THAT I'M STARTING TO GET JEALOUS!
I ASSURE YOU, MY RELATIONSHIP WITH YOUR HUSBAND IS STRICTLY PLATONIC.
WINK!
EYEBROW WAGGLE
STOP.

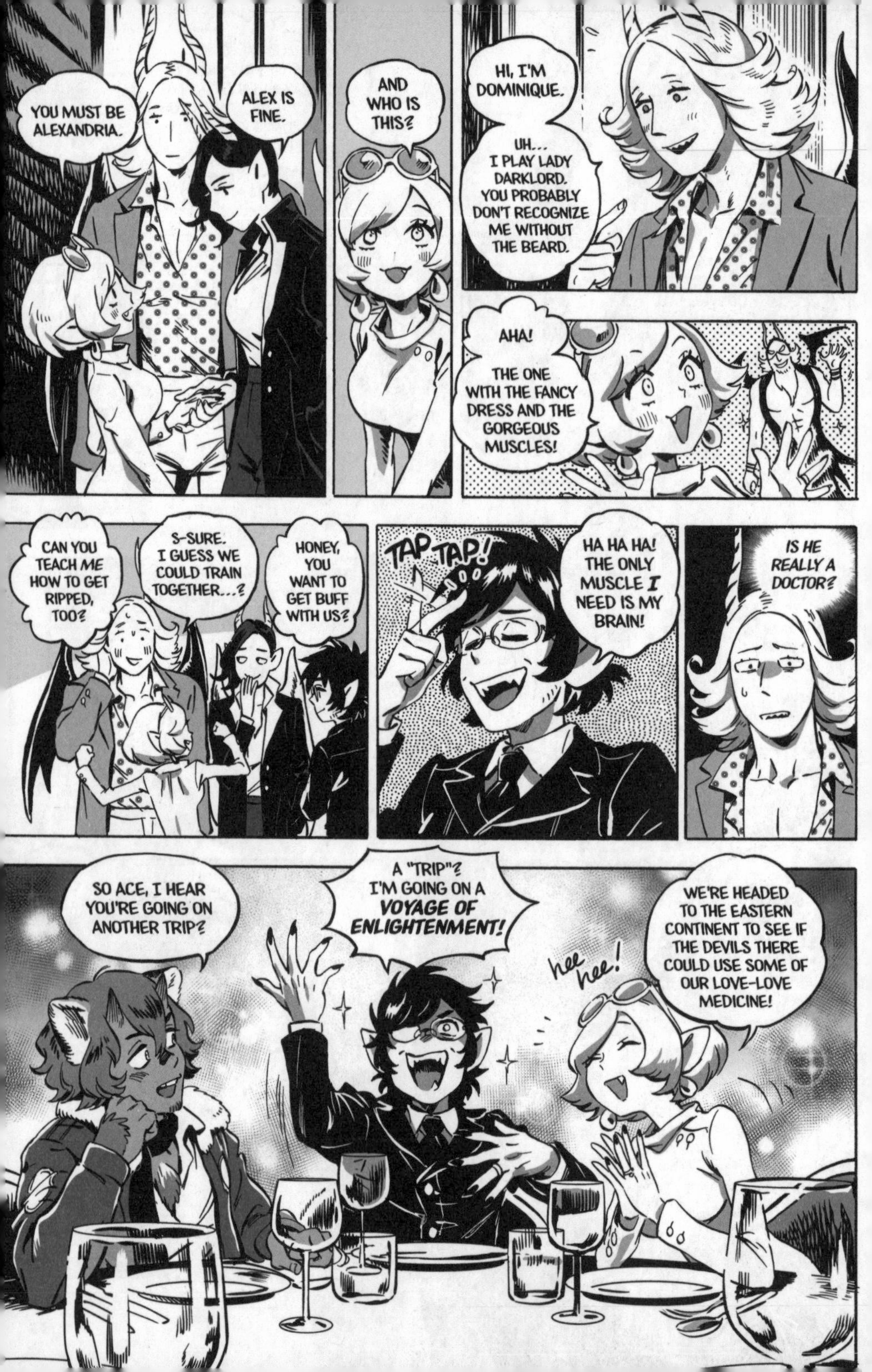
YOU MUST BE ALEXANDRIA.
ALEX IS FINE.
AND WHO IS THIS?
HI, I'M DOMINIQUE.
UH... I PLAY LADY DARKLORD. YOU PROBABLY DON'T RECOGNIZE ME WITHOUT THE BEARD.
AHA!
THE ONE WITH THE FANCY DRESS AND THE GORGEOUS MUSCLES!
CAN YOU TEACH ME HOW TO GET RIPPED, TOO?
S-SURE. I GUESS WE COULD TRAIN TOGETHER...?
HONEY, YOU WANT TO GET BUFF WITH US?
TAP TAP!
HA HA HA! THE ONLY MUSCLE I NEED IS MY BRAIN!
IS HE REALLY A DOCTOR?
SO ACE, I HEAR YOU'RE GOING ON ANOTHER TRIP?
A "TRIP"? I'M GOING ON A VOYAGE OF ENLIGHTENMENT!
hee hee!
WE'RE HEADED TO THE EASTERN CONTINENT TO SEE IF THE DEVILS THERE COULD USE SOME OF OUR LOVE-LOVE MEDICINE!

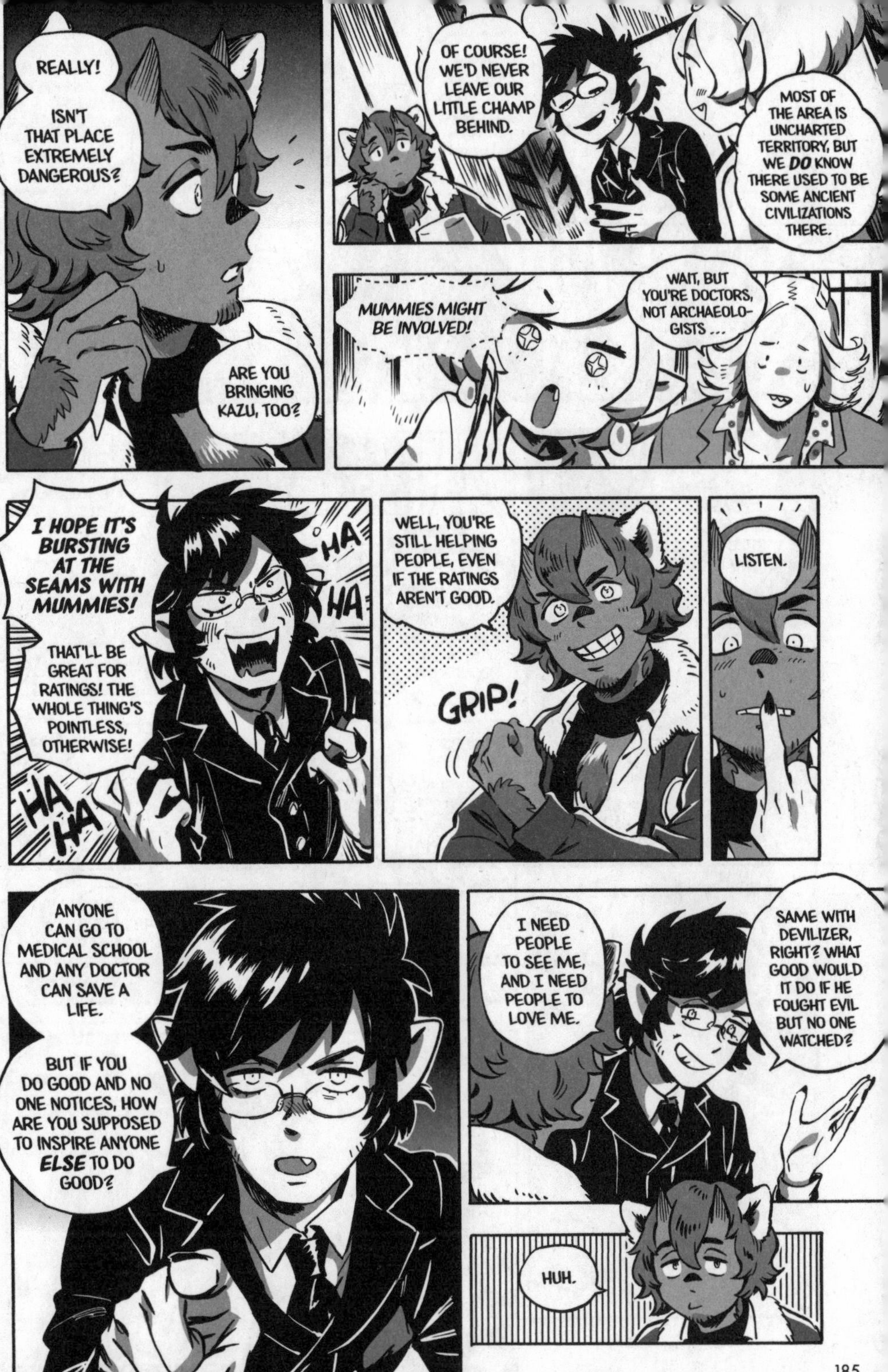
REALLY!
ISN'T THAT PLACE EXTREMELY DANGEROUS?
ARE YOU BRINGING KAZU, TOO?
OF COURSE! WE'D NEVER LEAVE OUR LITTLE CHAMP BEHIND.
MOST OF THE AREA IS UNCHARTED TERRITORY, BUT WE DO KNOW THERE USED TO BE SOME ANCIENT CIVILIZATIONS THERE.
MUMMIES MIGHT BE INVOLVED!
WAIT, BUT YOU'RE DOCTORS, NOT ARCHAEOLO-GISTS ...
I HOPE IT'S BURSTING AT THE SEAMS WITH MUMMIES!
HA HA
THAT'LL BE GREAT FOR RATINGS! THE WHOLE THING'S POINTLESS, OTHERWISE!
HA HA
WELL, YOU'RE STILL HELPING PEOPLE, EVEN IF THE RATINGS AREN'T GOOD.
GRIP!
LISTEN.
ANYONE CAN GO TO MEDICAL SCHOOL AND ANY DOCTOR CAN SAVE A LIFE.
BUT IF YOU DO GOOD AND NO ONE NOTICES, HOW ARE YOU SUPPOSED TO INSPIRE ANYONE ELSE TO DO GOOD?
I NEED PEOPLE TO SEE ME, AND I NEED PEOPLE TO LOVE ME.
SAME WITH DEVILIZER, RIGHT? WHAT GOOD WOULD IT DO IF HE FOUGHT EVIL BUT NO ONE WATCHED?
HUH.

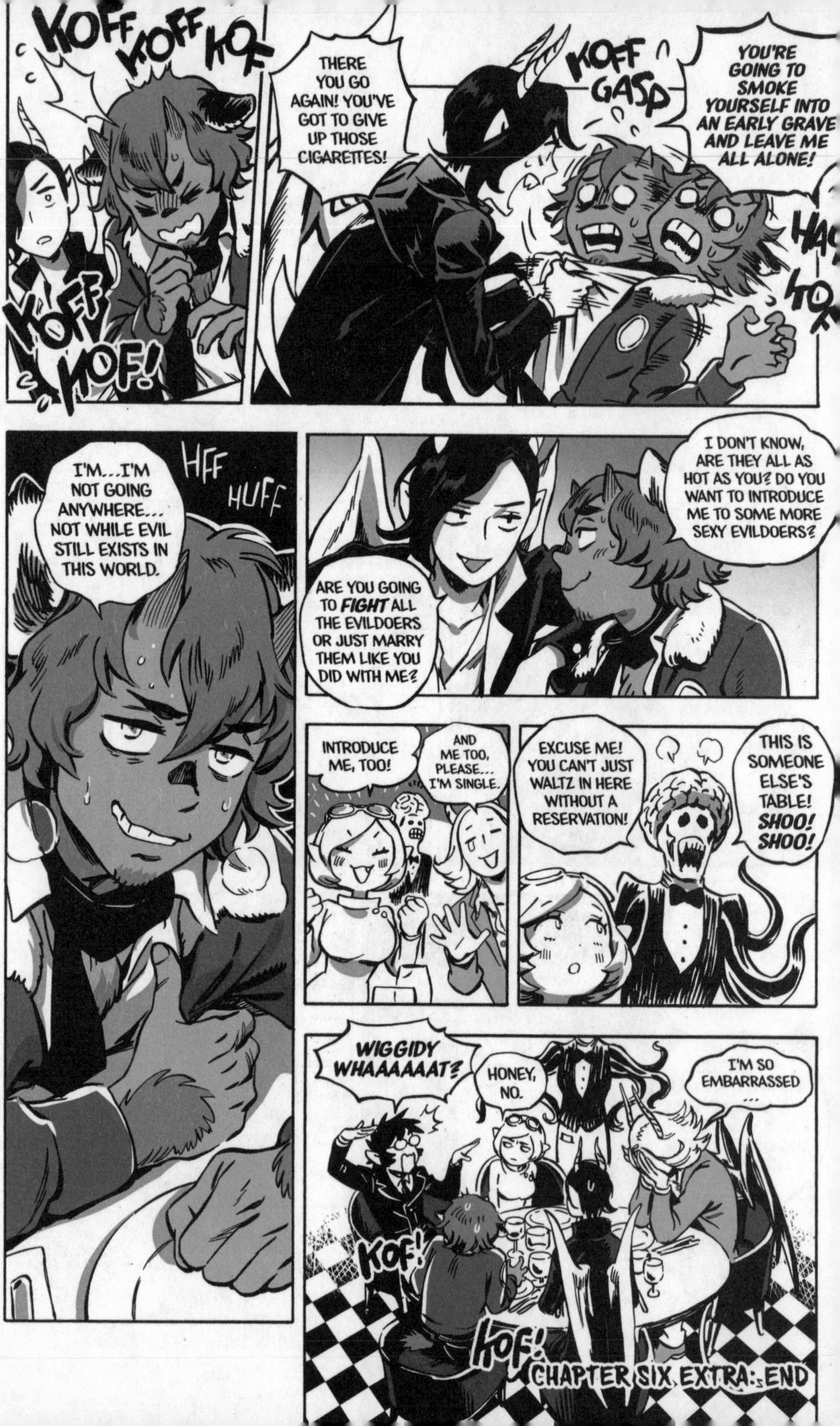
KOFF KOFF KOF
KOFF KOF!
THERE YOU GO AGAIN! YOU'VE GOT TO GIVE UP THOSE CIGARETTES!
KOFF GASP
YOU'RE GOING TO SMOKE YOURSELF INTO AN EARLY GRAVE AND LEAVE ME ALL ALONE!
I'M...I'M NOT GOING ANYWHERE... NOT WHILE EVIL STILL EXISTS IN THIS WORLD.
HFF
HUFF
ARE YOU GOING TO FIGHT ALL THE EVILDOERS OR JUST MARRY THEM LIKE YOU DID WITH ME?
I DON'T KNOW, ARE THEY ALL AS HOT AS YOU? DO YOU WANT TO INTRODUCE ME TO SOME MORE SEXY EVILDOERS?
INTRODUCE ME, TOO!
AND ME TOO, PLEASE... I'M SINGLE.
EXCUSE ME! YOU CAN'T JUST WALTZ IN HERE WITHOUT A RESERVATION!
THIS IS SOMEONE ELSE'S TABLE! SHOO! SHOO!
WIGGIDY WHAAAAAAT?
HONEY, NO.
I'M SO EMBARRASSED ...
KOF!
KOF!
CHAPTER SIX EXTRA: END

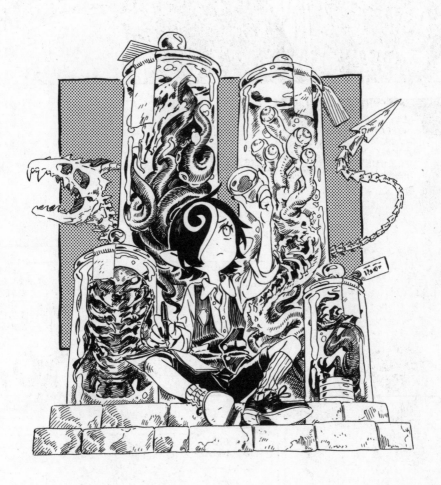

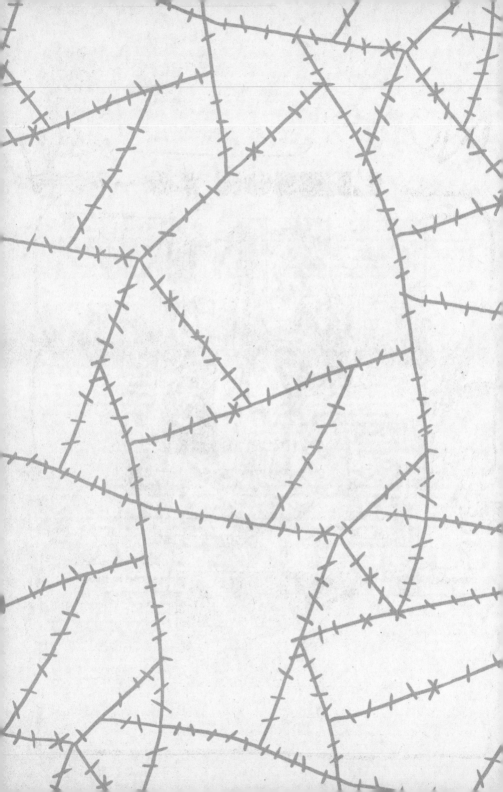

BIKKURI NOTES!

WELCOME TO SOCIAL STUDIES!
TODAY WE'RE GOING TO BE TALKING ABOUT SPORTS!
OF COURSE, SINCE I'M PLANTED IN A ***POT***, THE ONLY SPORT I CAN PLAY IS CHESS. DON'T YOU DARE TELL ME THAT CHESS IS A "GAME." IF BASKETBALL IS A SPORT AND YOU CAN "PLAY A GAME OF BASKETBALL," THEN THE SAME APPLIES TO CHESS!

WE'LL ALSO BE TALKING ABOUT ORGANIZED CRIME TODAY. THAT'S LIKE SPORTS, RIGHT?

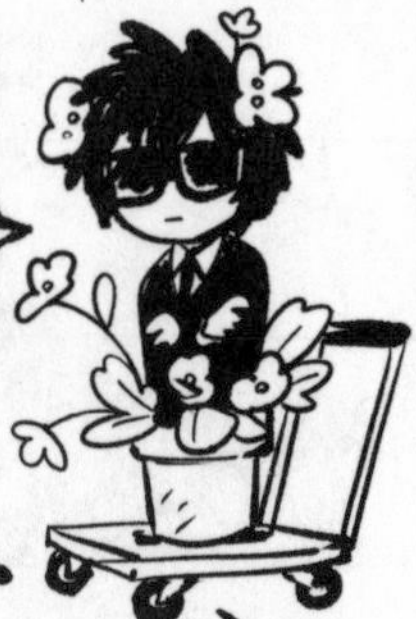

LESSON #4

UNIFORMS

The Scarlet Crown uniforms are quite nice, but they can pull that off, because their school only has daemons attending it. We considered having some sort of uniform at Hemlock Heart, but even something as simple as a cardigan couldn't be worn by every type of devil. We also considered having a patch that students could wear on an article of clothing of their choice, but even that got too complicated. As of now, students can wear whatever they like as long as it doesn't make Elliot scream.

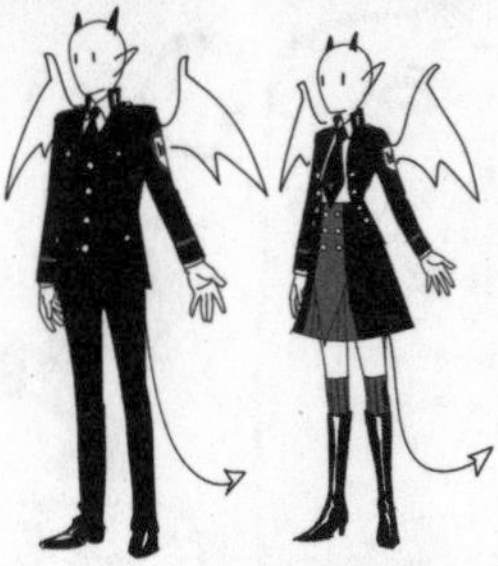

SCHOOL ANTHEM

I thought Scarlet Crown Academy's school anthem was pretty gratuitous, but then I found out that it was written by a famous composer! That's like having a guy cook food for the guy who cooks you food! I'll never know how it feels to be rich...

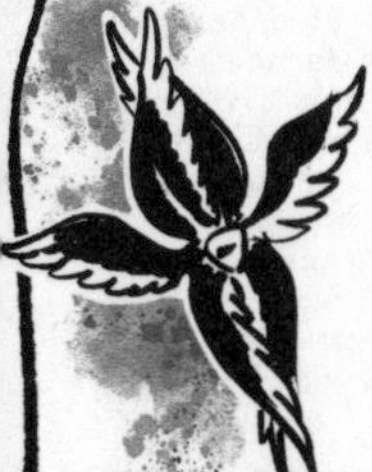

ZOMA-GORAMOSS

The Zoma-Goramoss have a very old, very advanced civilization. In recent history the rest of devil society has caught up with them, but in the past they had medicine and technology that the average dirt-licking devil could only dream of. These days, they get along with other devils well enough, but they haven't integrated into city life whatsoever. Their high-altitude cities are off-limits to outsiders, so any exchanges, cultural or otherwise, are always made on their terms.

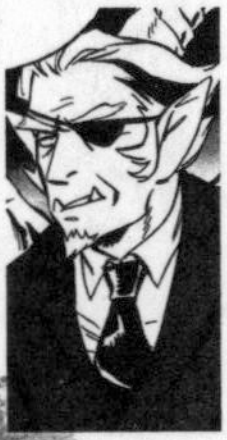

GREGORIO

Gregorio Orthrus Grambleclaus is the principal of Scarlet Crown Academy. He's as old as dirt! Actually, daemons are very hearty creatures and they tend to have good health insurance, so it's quite common for them to live over 100 years. Even so, I don't have such high expectations for Elliot. He'll probably see a scary bug and die of shock before he even hits 50.

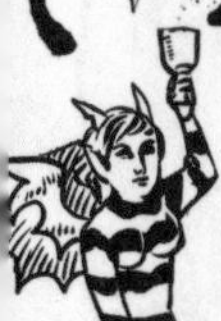

THE HISTORY OF EGGSCRAM

Modern devils participate in the Zoma-Goramoss hatching ritual because it's fun. Sure, we could just play Eggscram with a ball, but what would be the point? Although we don't commune with the Zomas much, we still form a bond through Eggscram. It's the passion of our people that makes the egg hatch, after all.

However, it wasn't always like that. In the past, the Zomas were often revered as gods by less developed civilizations, who were dazzled by their imposing presence and advanced technology. Although the Zomas would often provide "blessings" in the form of medicine or other necessities, they could essentially coerce other devils to participate in Eggscram through fear. It's a bit of an ugly, sometimes bloody history, but modern devils have to put all sorts of things like that behind them if they want to get along in a mixed society.

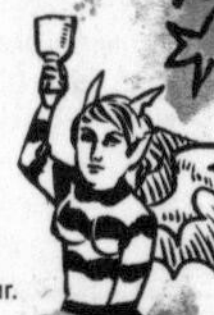

DRAGON POWER!

Dragons are strong! Dragons can fly! Dragons can spit fire! They have cool, durable scales, too! Dragons are considered "Class S" devils, which puts them at the top of the charts, right there with daemons. Actually, they're considered SX Class for their fire-breathing abilities. Bottom line is, I need a dragon girlfriend to carry me everywhere, please.

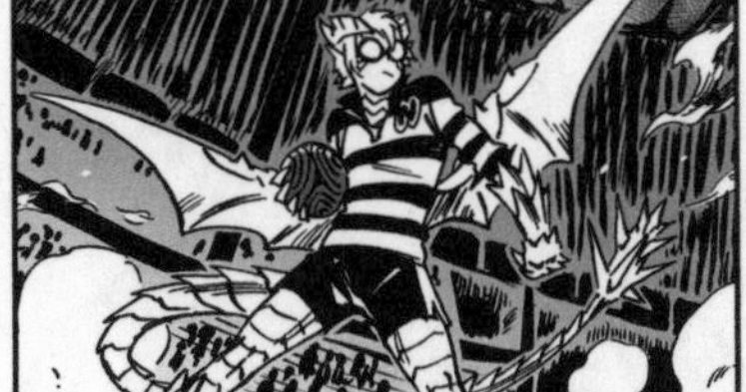

DRAGONS IN SOCIETY

So, if dragons are so awesome, why aren't they calling the shots everywhere? Well, that's because they're more into hands-on work and less into cushy office jobs. Dragons are relentlessly hard workers and they aren't afraid to get their hands dirty. Of course, there are exceptions to the rule with every devil type, but dragons tend to work better alone, at their own (often blistering) pace.

CLASS SYSTEM BASICS

City-dwelling devils are divided into classes based on their physical and communicative functionality. Since our modern society was primarily formed by daemons, classification is more or less based on their physiology. Classes are technically categorical rather than explicitly discriminatory, but thanks to daemons writing the rules, it ends up feeling like a hierarchy with them at the top.

HIGH SCHOOL EGGSCRAM MATCHES

Eggscram is about passion and emotion and growth, so it's the perfect sport for high schoolers to play. In fact, the Zomas usually prefer high school players to the more seasoned adult teams. The adult teams mostly exist for "emergency" matches, when high schoolers can't answer the call. Requesting a professional team is considered a very conservative approach to hatching an egg, but some nervous parents don't want to take any chances.

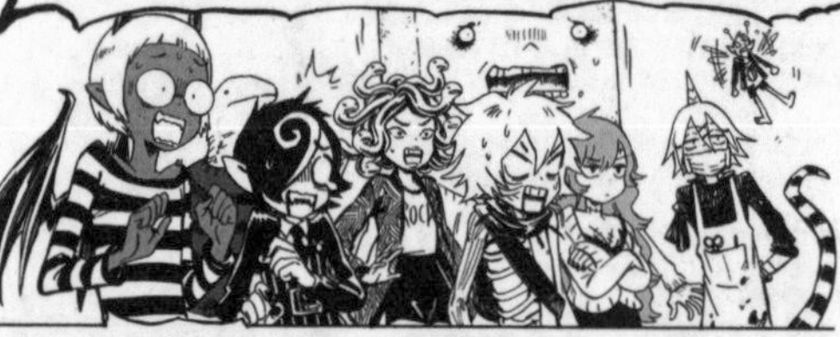

NURIKABE

Walton may complain a lot, but he's actually a very hard worker. As you might guess by looking at his tiny legs, nurikabe aren't used to moving around much. In fact, they will sometimes spend months, or even years, standing perfectly still, like a normal wall. They live for a long time, so they can afford to be patient, but I do wonder if they'll find their niche in city life. Although Walton's attitude certainly isn't doing him any favors, I can see why he might feel the need to assert himself.

PROFESSOR CEPHALLI

Cephalli is a respected scholar from the deep sea who teaches our Subaquatic Social Studies course. After exchanging some correspondence with Elliot, he became interested in the concept behind his school and agreed to teach a course to spread awareness about undersea life to land dwellers. A lot of his class consists of aquatic or semi-aquatic devils, but rather than looking for an easy "A," many of them are simply finding new ways to connect to their roots to learn how to bridge the gap between land and sea dwellers.

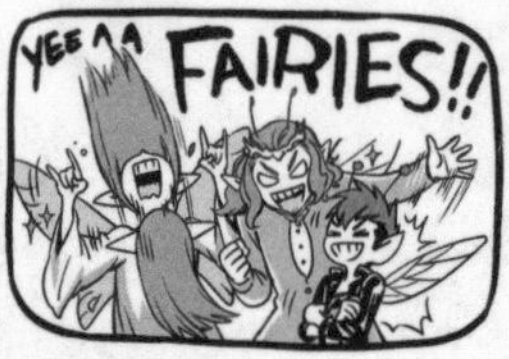
YEE^^A
FAIRIES!!

Despite their diminutive size, fairies have integrated fairly well into modern devil society. They have a reputation for being clever and they're invaluable when it comes to intricate work. Although the city isn't exactly built to "their scale," it's easy enough to get fairy-sized electronics that plug into regular-sized computers with an adapter. Since they take up so little space, finding a nice plot of land is also quite affordable for them.

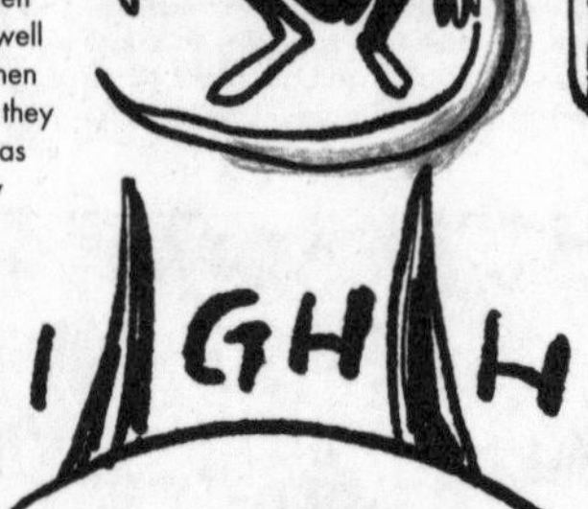
$A=\pi r^2$
$v=\frac{1}{3}\pi r^2 h$
$x\sqrt{3}$

LIZARDMEN

I know that their name is inherently sexist, but what do you want me to do about it? For the record, their women are called "female lizardmen" not "lizardwomen." If you try to explain this issue to a lizardman, they won't even get it. That's not to say that lizardmen are unintelligent, just that they don't do well with philosophical and social issues. When it comes to math and science, however, they really excel. In other words, they're just as unlikely to be the life of the party as any other mathematician.

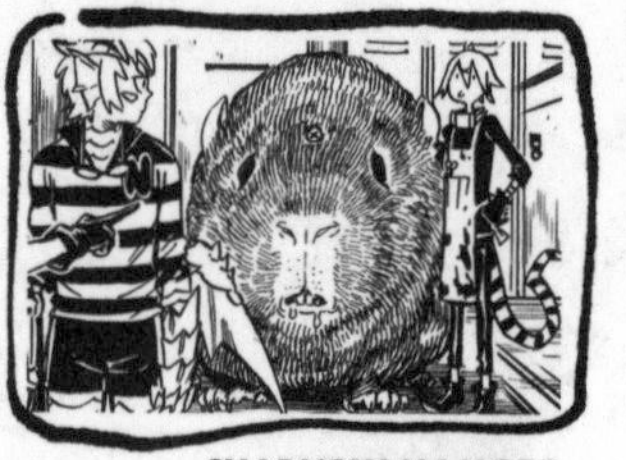

CHARLIE YAMAMOTO

I received a memo from the principal this morning, encouraging me to talk about your cool and popular classmate, Charlie, who has definitely engaged in lots of charming antics that you have all forgotten for some reason. Oh, wait... I received a memo from the principal just now that says you're supposed to forget about your uncool and unpopular classmate, Charlie, who did not engage in any charming antics and absolutely did not exist.

RICKET

Please be nice to Ricket. She's the only daemon in the school and she's really small and weird. I don't know what she went through with the Drama Club, but I do know that they are petty and loud and insufferable. Yes, yes, it's incredibly unprofessional for a teacher to trash talk a group of students, but they literally hiss and bite.

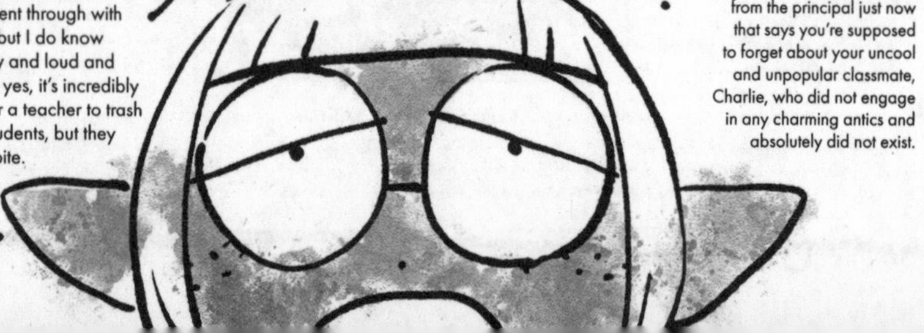
SIIGHHH...

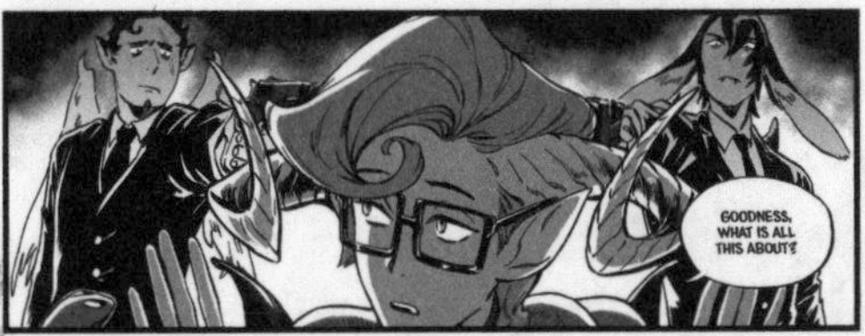
GOODNESS, WHAT IS ALL THIS ABOUT?

THE MOB

Although they aren't the only organized crime syndicate in the world, when devils mention "the mob," the image of a sharply dressed daemon usually comes to mind. Umbra City was originally a daemon settlement and the mob as we know it today already existed by the time other devils started to populate the city. In a sense, you might even consider the mob an important part of daemon culture.

NICODEMUS MESMER

Commonly known as "Miracle Nic," this guy is famous for his weird late-night TV commercials. Evidently, he's a doctor who can perform miracles, but the details of his actual work are pretty scarce. In one particular commercial, he had a family of "happy customers" give a testimonial. They looked absolutely haunted. "He's the real deal. He's the real deal," the father muttered in a raspy whisper.

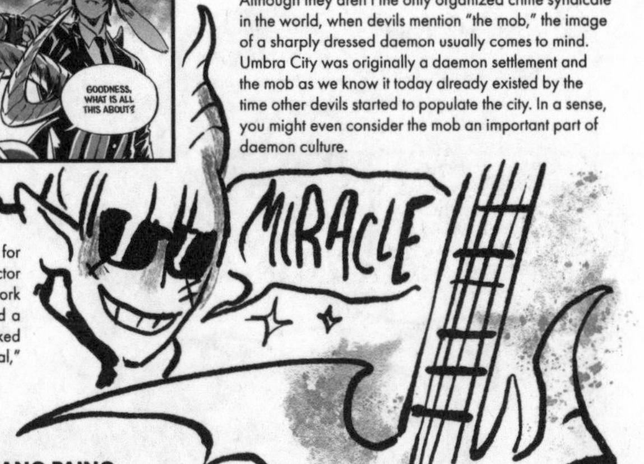
MIRACLE

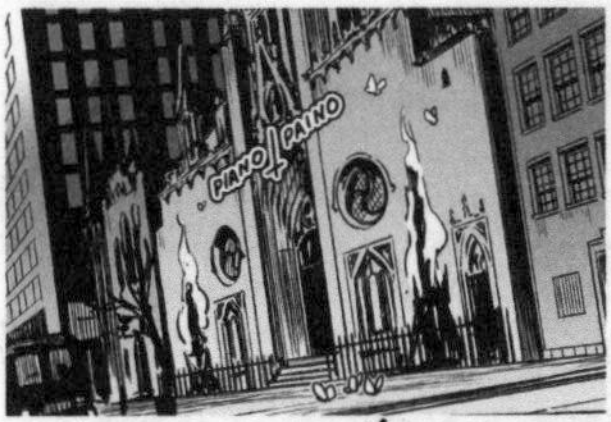
PIANO PAINO

PIANO PAINO

Like many places in the city, this isn't a "daemon-exclusive" joint, but non-daemons tend to get turned away at the door. Also, daemons, you need to stop acting like you invented jazz!

TALKING GUITAR

I had a talking guitar when I was a kid. You pressed a button on it and it said "Let's rock!" Nothing scary about that. However, the thought of technology becoming advanced enough to create a fully sentient guitar is mildly disturbing. The idea of devils becoming guitars through some insane breeding program is the stuff of nightmares, though.

MOTHS

Aren't moths cute?

They're fluffy and friendly and harmless, so they make great pets! Well, not the street moths. Those make a huge mess and they smell weird. Thankfully, those undesirable traits have been bred out of domesticated moths.

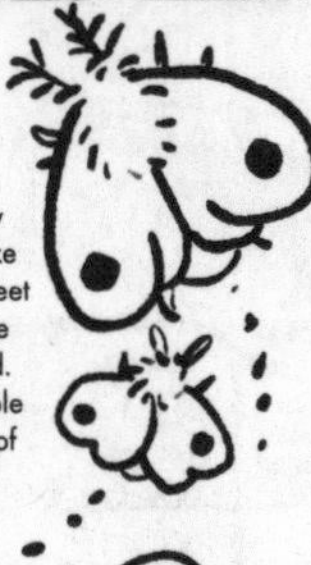

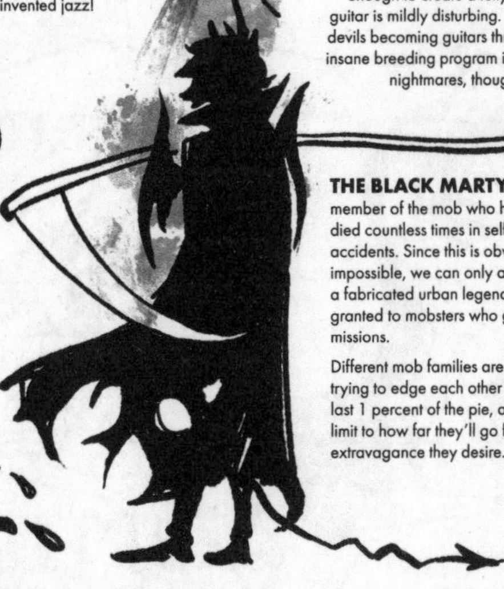

THE BLACK MARTYR is a member of the mob who has evidently died countless times in self-induced accidents. Since this is obviously impossible, we can only assume that it's a fabricated urban legend and a title granted to mobsters who go on suicide missions.

Different mob families are always trying to edge each other out for that last 1 percent of the pie, and there's no limit to how far they'll go for whatever extravagance they desire.

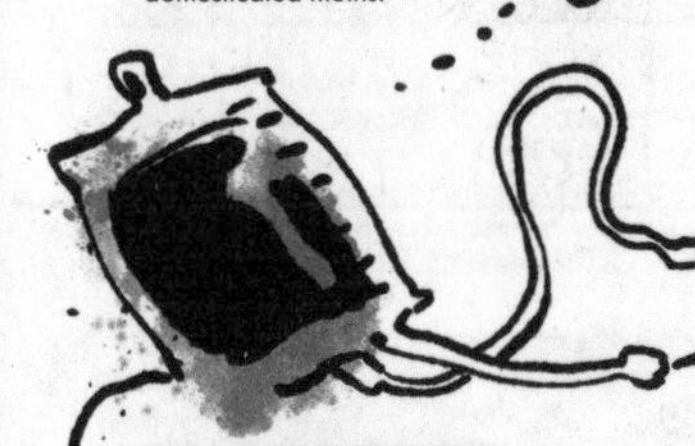

NOSFERATU CUISINE

Although I'm sure you've gone over this in your culinary enculturation class, let me do a quick rundown on bloodsucker eating habits.

- Only blood provides sustenance to nosferatu. It does not have to be devil blood, but that is preferred.
- If a nosferatu eats anything else, their body will not treat it as food. It will be expelled undigested. They absorb blood very quickly, so the other parts tend to be purged in short order.
- Through careful experimentation, nosferatu have found foods and methods of cooking that they can indulge in, so long as blood is a primary component in the dish.
- It takes a long time for a nosferatu to build tolerance for "regular" cuisine, even with blood as a primary component. Since the process tends to end in illness and vomiting, a nosferatu must be committed to train his stomach.
- Because of the harsh requirements of bloodsucker cuisine, there are relatively few nosferatu chefs.
- Nosferatu cuisine is a "new age" movement, celebrating a love of food and an integration into a mixed-devil society. Furthermore, some modern bloodsuckers are "straight edge," meaning that they never drink blood fresh from the source.
- More traditional bloodsuckers turn their nose up at the practice.

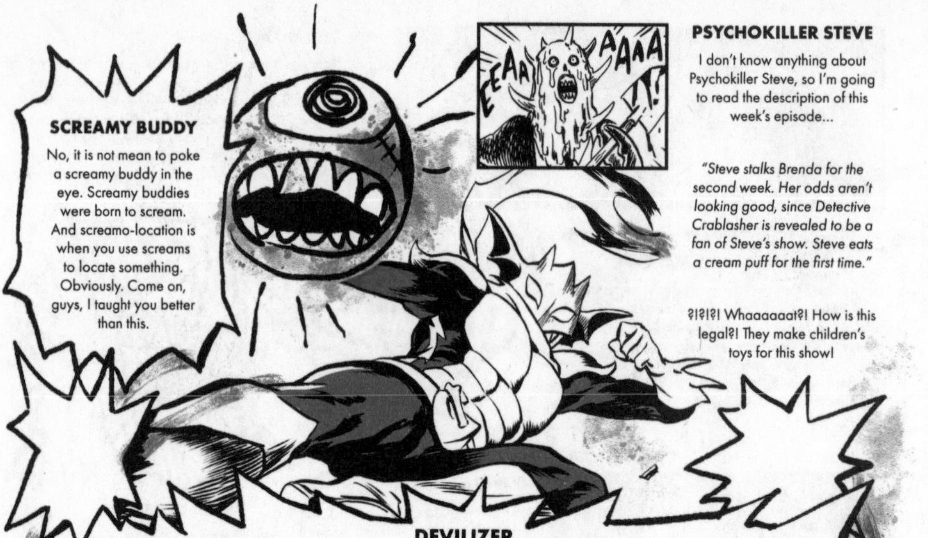

EEAAA
AAAA

SCREAMY BUDDY

No, it is not mean to poke a screamy buddy in the eye. Screamy buddies were born to scream. And screamo-location is when you use screams to locate something. Obviously. Come on, guys, I taught you better than this.

PSYCHOKILLER STEVE

I don't know anything about Psychokiller Steve, so I'm going to read the description of this week's episode...

"Steve stalks Brenda for the second week. Her odds aren't looking good, since Detective Crablasher is revealed to be a fan of Steve's show. Steve eats a cream puff for the first time."

?!?!?! Whaaaaaat?! How is this legal?! They make children's toys for this show!

DEVILIZER

Devilizer ran for several years and was immensely popular, but ended suddenly when the lead actor, Rowan Redhorn, passed away. The end of the show is a sort of collective trauma for a lot of young viewers. No statement was made after Rowan's death, and no attempts were made to continue the show or create a spinoff. It brought on a shift away from superhero and sci-fi programming, so now we get absolutely depraved reality TV like *Psychokiller Steve*, I guess!?

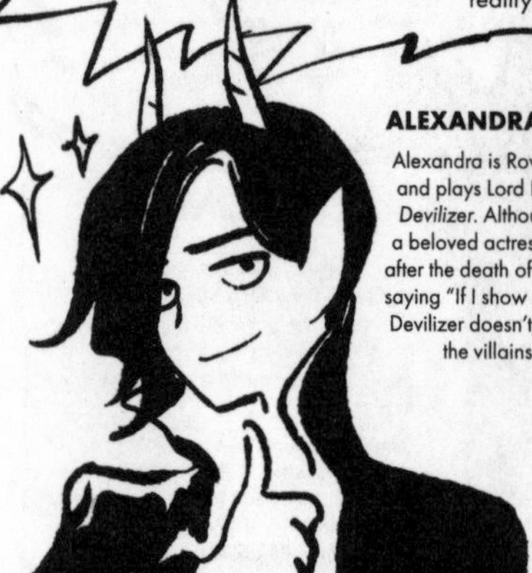

ALEXANDRA KNIGHT

Alexandra is Rowan's widow and plays Lord Darklady on *Devilizer*. Although she was a beloved actress, she retired after the death of her husband, saying "If I show up again and Devilizer doesn't, it'll look like the villains won."

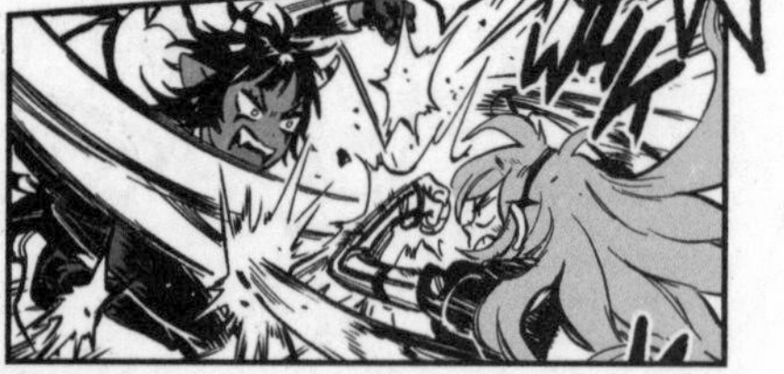

WHAK

STREET FIGHTS Although street murders are not encouraged, most police officers don't like to get involved, so they're not likely to do anything until after a crime is committed. So, if a bunch of maniacs are fighting in the street, the police are likely to start whistling nonchalantly and turn the other way. It's not exactly fair to say that they're all paid off by the mob, but as a general rule, it's smart to leave daemons in suits alone.

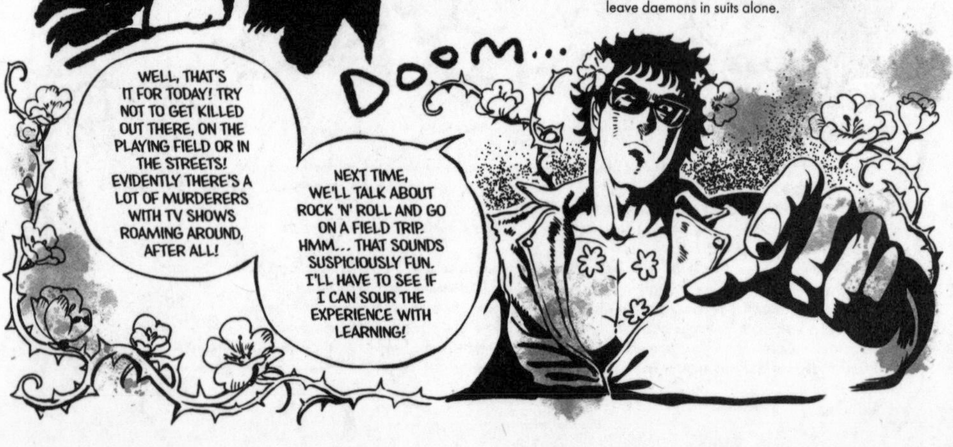

WELL, THAT'S IT FOR TODAY! TRY NOT TO GET KILLED OUT THERE, ON THE PLAYING FIELD OR IN THE STREETS! EVIDENTLY THERE'S A LOT OF MURDERERS WITH TV SHOWS ROAMING AROUND, AFTER ALL!
NEXT TIME, WE'LL TALK ABOUT ROCK 'N' ROLL AND GO ON A FIELD TRIP. HMM... THAT SOUNDS SUSPICIOUSLY FUN. I'LL HAVE TO SEE IF I CAN SOUR THE EXPERIENCE WITH LEARNING!
DOOM...

CAST
BIOS

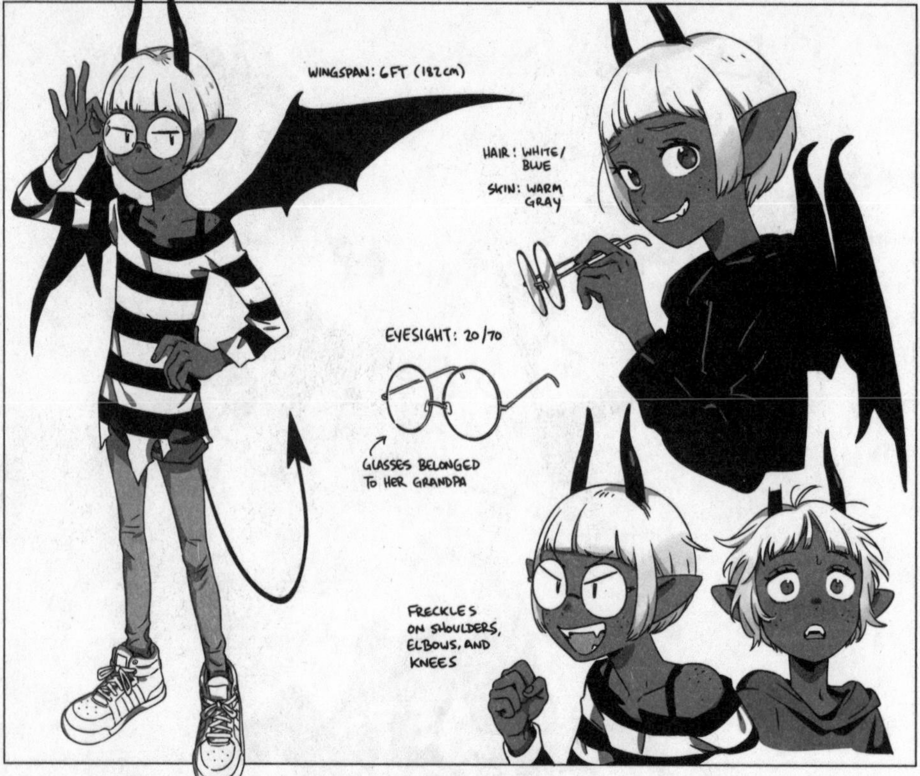
WINGSPAN: 6FT (182cm)
HAIR: WHITE/ BLUE
SKIN: WARM GRAY
EYESIGHT: 20/70
GLASSES BELONGED TO HER GRANDPA
FRECKLES ON SHOULDERS, ELBOWS, AND KNEES

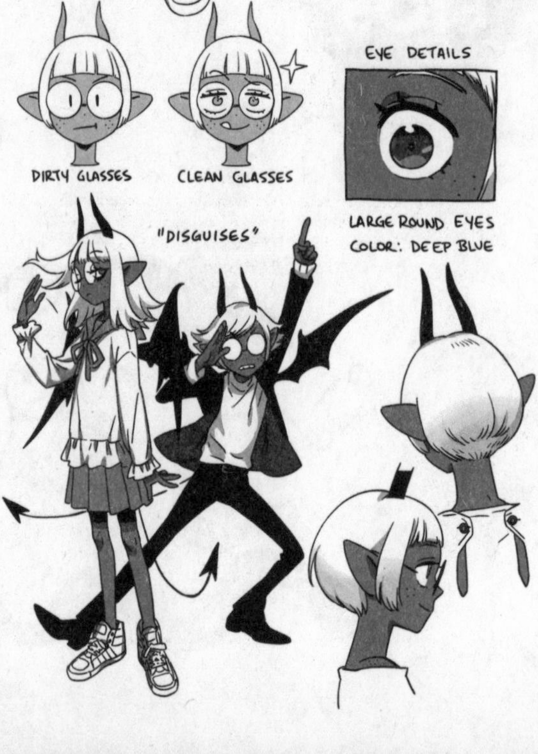
DIRTY GLASSES
CLEAN GLASSES
EYE DETAILS
LARGE ROUND EYES
COLOR: DEEP BLUE
"DISGUISES"

RICKET PANTANO

Devil Type: Daemon
Birthday: Feb. 29
Age: 14
Height: 5'7" (170 cm)
Occupation: High school freshman
Likes: Creating characters, being a prince
Dislikes: The wrong kind of drama
Fav. Food: Flan
Fun Facts:
- Since people tend to ignore her, her disguises are very effective
- She's an expert at stage combat
- She's looking for her princess

CREATOR'S NOTES:

Rem: It's hard to look at Ricket and not see myself at that age.
Bikkuri: Ricket is pretty awful sometimes, but it's easy to forgive her, since she's so unfortunate.

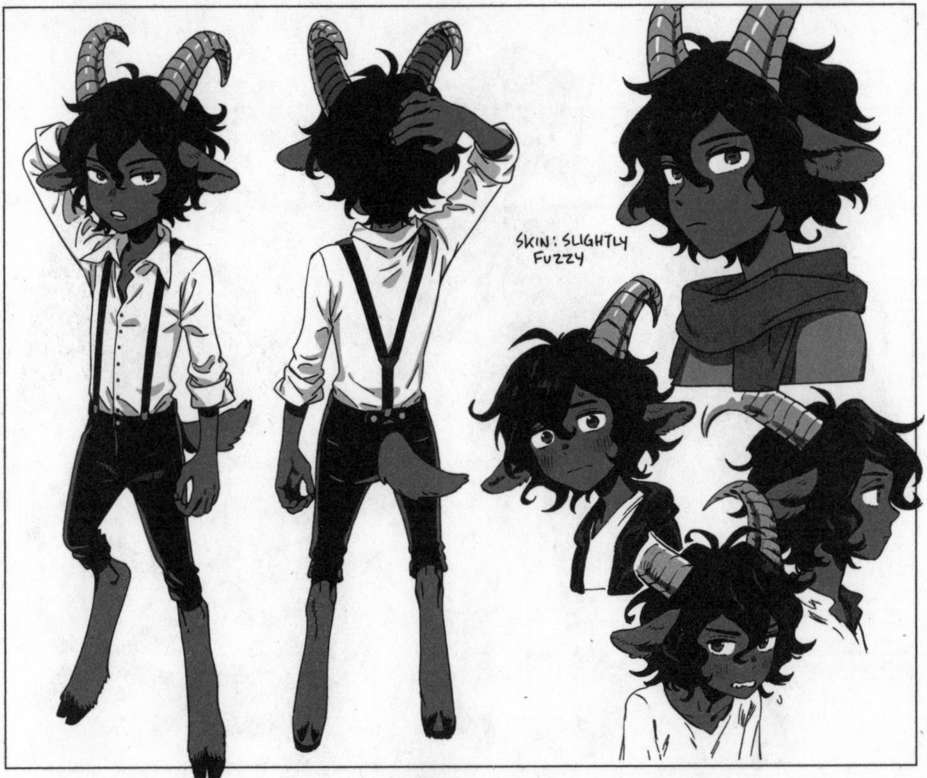
SKIN: SLIGHTLY
FUZZY

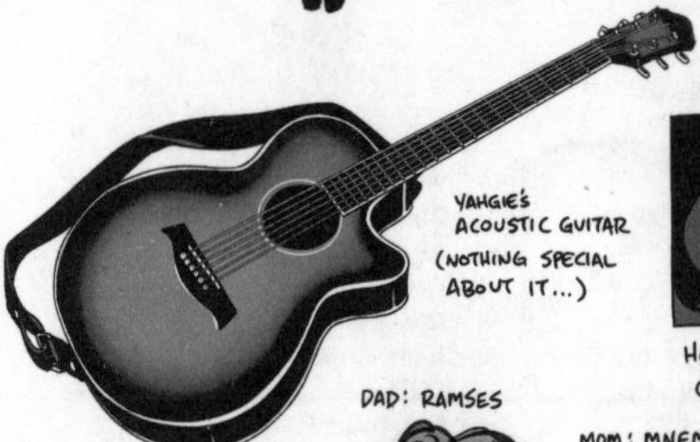
YAHGIE'S
ACOUSTIC GUITAR
(NOTHING SPECIAL
ABOUT IT...)

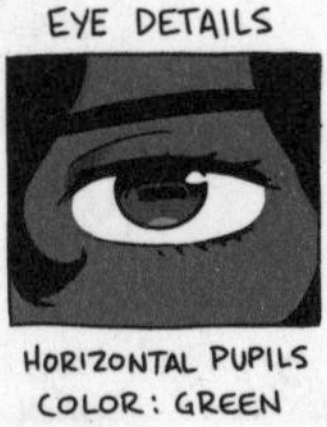
EYE DETAILS
HORIZONTAL PUPILS
COLOR: GREEN

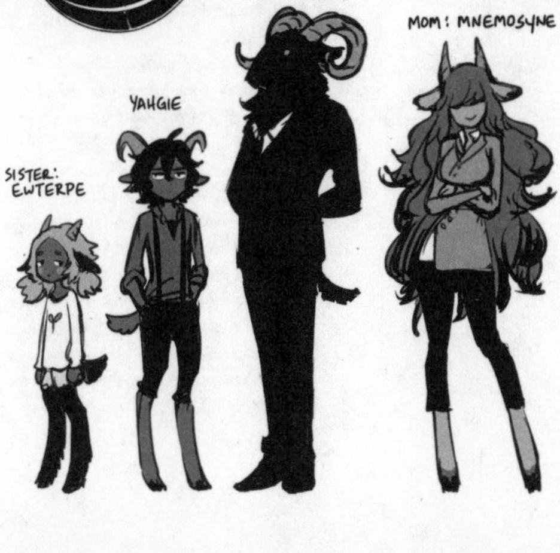
DAD: RAMSES
MOM: MNEMOSYNE
YAHGIE
SISTER:
EWTERPE

YAHGIE CABRA

Devil Type: Satyr
Birthday: Nov. 1
Age: 15
Height: 5'3" (160 cm)
Occupation: High school freshman
Likes: Looking cool, ninjas (secretly)
Dislikes: Lame people/Kazu
Fav. Food: Anything Clarence cooks, as long as it's vegan
Fun Facts:
- Genius-level guitarist/garbage-level lyricist
- Suffers from game show-related PTSD
- Can easily climb vertical surfaces

CREATOR'S NOTES:

Rem: I hope that our readers can always laugh at Yahgie like I do, and not just be disappointed in him.
Bikkuri: Yahgie has a lot of room to grow, but it would be a betrayal of his character if he really pulled his life together. A lot of characters in *Devil's Candy* are stupid in different ways, but Yahgie is unique in how aggressively stupid he is.

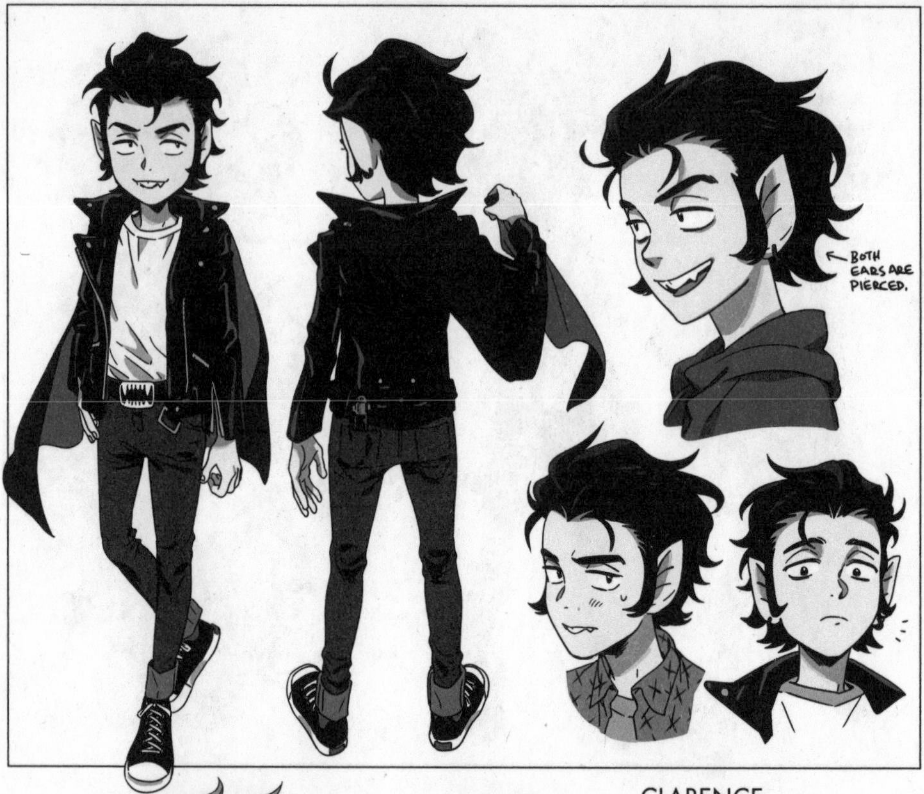
BOTH EARS ARE PIERCED.

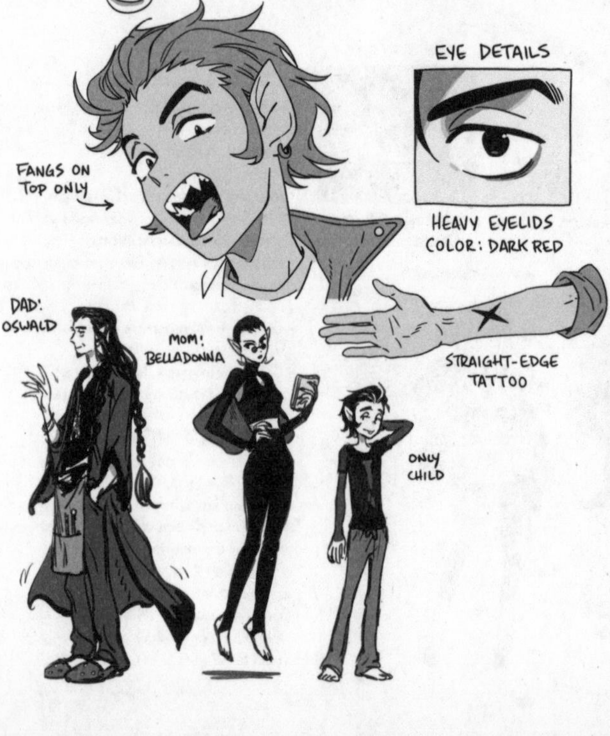
EYE DETAILS
FANGS ON TOP ONLY
HEAVY EYELIDS
COLOR: DARK RED
STRAIGHT-EDGE TATTOO
DAD: OSWALD
MOM: BELLADONNA
ONLY CHILD

CLARENCE REGULUS NOSOPHOROS

Devil Type: Nosferatu
Birthday: Feb. 14
Age: 14
Height: 5'5" (165 cm)
Occupation: High school freshman
Likes: Cooking, leather jackets
Dislikes: Uppity people, dishonesty
Fav. Food: Pumpkin ramen
Fun Facts:
- He's a great listener
- He plays pizzicato on double bass
- He won't drink blood straight from the source

CREATOR'S NOTES:

Rem: I love Clarence a lot and whenever someone tells me they like him I'm so touched! Thank you for noticing him!
Bikkuri: There's a lot to explore in terms of what it means to be a bloodsucker in modern society, so I think it takes some time to truly understand what makes Clarence tick.

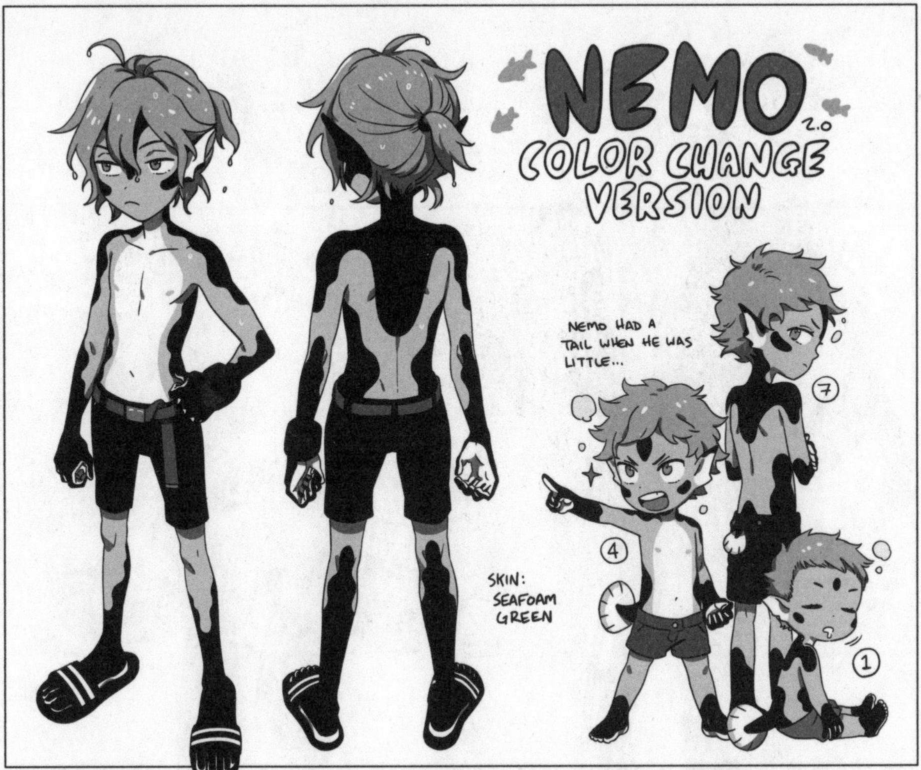
NEMO 2.0
COLOR CHANGE VERSION
NEMO HAD A TAIL WHEN HE WAS LITTLE...
7
4
1
SKIN: SEAFOAM GREEN

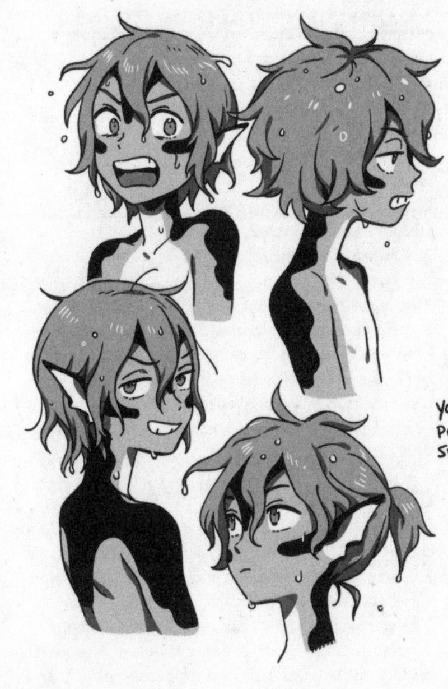

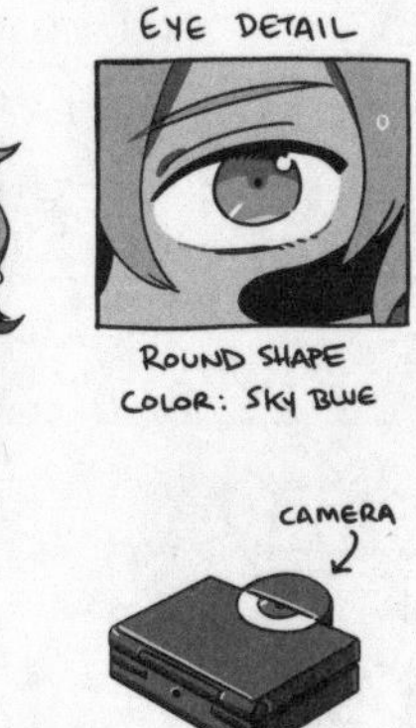
EYE DETAIL
ROUND SHAPE
COLOR: SKY BLUE
CAMERA
YOKAIDO POCKET GAME SYSTEM

FACTS ABOUT NEMO MUSTERMAN

- Half Grindylow, half some invisible creature.

- Nemo's skin turns transparent when it's dry.

- His respiratory system is similar to what you'd see in an amphibian, like a frog or salamander. Cutaneous respiration allows him to breathe easily underwater, but wearing too much clothing makes him feel out of breath.

- His skin and hair glow under black light, whether he's wet or dry.

- His ears are always visible, but you usually can't see them under his shaggy hair.

- He likes to sleep underwater.

- His skin isn't slimy or slippery, but it is kinda sensitive and he chafes easily. (More reason not to wear tons of clothing.)

- The cold doesn't bother him as much as everyone else, but he's not cold-blooded.

- He eats a lot of seafood.

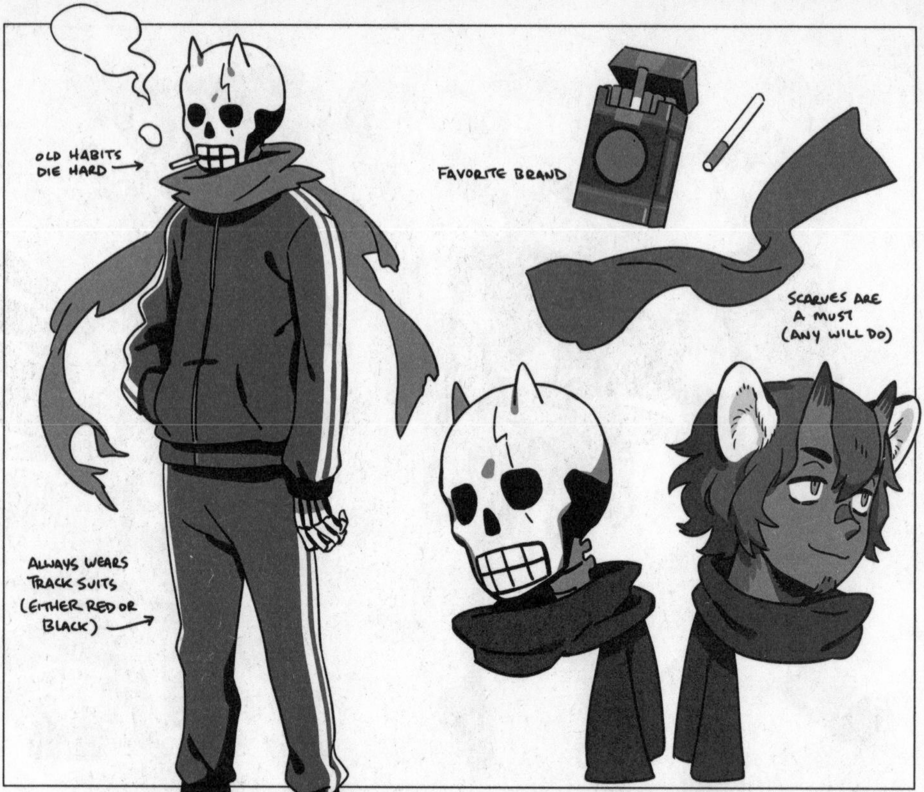
OLD HABITS
DIE HARD
FAVORITE BRAND
SCARVES ARE
A MUST
(ANY WILL DO)
ALWAYS WEARS
TRACK SUITS
(EITHER RED OR
BLACK)

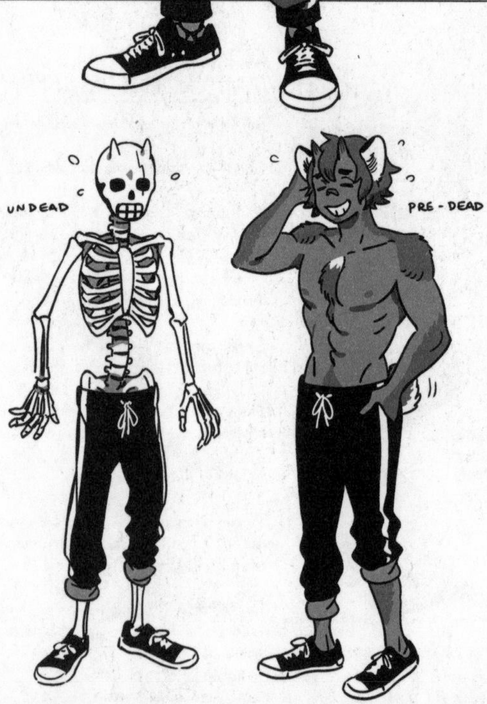
UNDEAD
PRE-DEAD

ROWAN REDHORN

UD#: 61427

A.K.A. "SKELETON NINJA SENSEI" OR "MR. 61"

Devil Type: Kobold
Birthday: Aug. 25
Age: 40 (+3 years of being dead)
Height: 5'6" (168 cm)
Occupation: Physical education and self-defense teacher
Likes: Kids, martial arts, smoking
Dislikes: Feeling useless, smoking
Fav Food: Cockatrice game pie
Fun Facts:
- Since skeletons give up their names when they die, only Pandora knows his true identity
- No one knows what unfinished business is keeping him in the realm of the living, but he was drawn to Hemlock Heart for some reason
- Kazu's parents still keep in touch with his widow
- He's extremely flammable

CREATOR'S NOTES:

Rem: Skeleton Ninja Sensei was my first *Devil's Candy* character. While in college I had a wild dream about a Day of the Dead skeleton in a tracksuit and a zombie nurse, and the rest is history!

Bikkuri: Skeleton Ninja Sensei isn't a ninja after all! Initially, I was going to wait longer before revealing his identity, but we had a chance for a good payoff, so I went all-in.

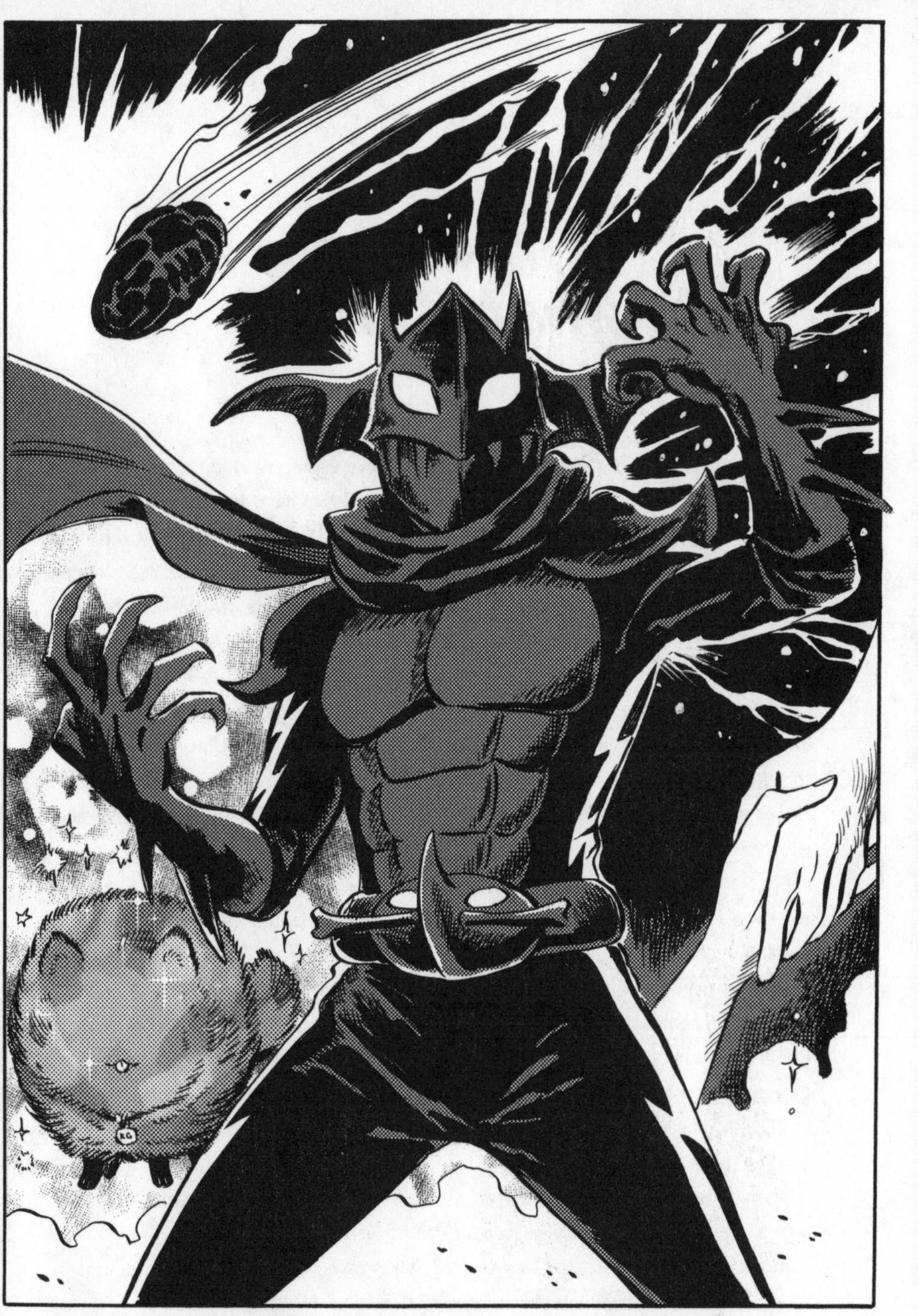

SHORT STORY: DEVILIZER EPISODE 1

You Are
What You Eat

Deep in the deepest of deep space—beyond the galaxy, the super galaxy and far into the Gala Gala Galaxy—there dwelled the dying planet of Darknazar 66. "Dying" is perhaps a kind way to put it, for in truth the planet was being killed—or rather, *executed*—by the Federation of Space Justice. Charged with countless acts of space crimes against space civilizations and gross misuse of universe-threatening space science, Darknazar 66 had received several warnings before a super-ion weapon of mass destruction was deployed against their world.

Their world-king had gazed into the abyss of forbidden science and danced deeper and deeper into its depths, seduced by the power it provided his planet. Unwilling to abandon this dark technology, the king hoped to fight and destroy the Federation of Space Justice. However, as Darknazar's core split into pieces, its oceans boiled away and its skies filled with fire, it was clear that his rebellion would not end in victory.

For better or worse, the king had planned for such a defeat, and in the final moments of his world, that plan was being carried out by two scientists huddled near a pulsating black mass in a tube. The king himself was a bloody heap in the corner of the lab, murdered by none other than the scientists tasked with preserving his legacy.

The pair had thought themselves physicists, rather than murderers, but desperate times had driven them to madness. Or perhaps they were mad to begin with; they *had* committed their lives to dangerous and forbidden sciences, after all. In the dying moments of the planet, who could say if they had been corrupted by a twisted world or if their world had been corrupted by *them*?

At any rate, they blamed their current state on their world-king and refused to give him a throne to sit upon in the strange new future they were creating.

Although Darknazar 66 itself was doomed, if things went according to plan, its essence would be preserved thanks to the strange black mass before them, hidden away in their rapidly collapsing lab. Known as the Psychoarc Planisorb, it was intended to absorb and condense every element of Darknazar 66 into its core, then depart for a new planet, shooting across the cosmos like a meteor. It would absorb not only biological matter, but sociological and philosophical concepts as well. Once it crashed on a faraway planet, it would release all the Darknazarian Elements contained within and transform the world into a new Darknazar.

Although it was too late for the inhabitants of Darknazar, the device could house one Darknazarian, who alone would be the herald of their legacy. That was intended to be the world-king, but the pair of scientists had decided they were better suited to be lord and lady of their new world. Although the device was only designed for one, they were unwilling to sacrifice each other and decided that a new world would not be worth seeing if they couldn't see it together. So, with this act of love and selfishness, they held hands and pressed the button to activate the Psychoarc Planisorb, instantly reducing their burning world to nothing but a tiny, lonely sphere in a seemingly endless sea of stars.

Many, many space miles away—on a much more familiar planet, in a much more familiar city, filled with much more familiar devils—a young kobold named Chip Brisket took his glamdogg, Kiggy, for a walk. Glamdoggs were a rare sight in the city—or to be more specific, a rare sight anywhere. The gentle and noble beasts were highly coveted as pets, but extremely difficult to acquire. This was partially because they were quite picky about their owners and prone to sometimes fatal fits of depression. If an owner's love for their glamdogg were to fade, then the glamdogg's body would wither away. If their owner's love for them was pure, then they would become more and more glamorous.

Chip's glamdogg was extremely glamorous. Its silky soft fur was so plush that all of its features, save its tiny black feet, were buried in a beautiful, multicolored ball of fluff. This was thanks to the fact that Chip had no living relatives, no friends, no significant other, and no particular hobbies. All he had in his life was work, love for his glamdogg, and uncertainty about the future. Both his job and his glamdogg had been more or less inherited from his grandfather. Having no direction in life, Chip followed in his grandfather's footsteps and became a police officer after he passed away. "That's what Kiggy would want," he thought, making wild assumptions about the animal's feelings. Regardless, Kiggy was quite happy and seemed to want to share that happiness with Chip. Every morning, Chip awoke to its little black paws sitting on his chest as it chirped quietly, almost like a tiny bird.

Chip gave no outward impression that he suffered from ennui. His ears and tiny tail were well-trimmed, he was in excellent shape, and he was both handsome and fairly well-spoken. Despite his lack of passion for his profession, he passed his aptitude tests with flying colors.

He was even convinced, for a time, that he would be a good police officer.

His hostile work environment soon eliminated all of those hopes.

The hostility was not directed at Chip himself, nor did it come from his fellow officers. Rather, it came entirely from the chief of police and was directed entirely at devils who had committed traffic violations. This may sound insignificant, but the amount of fury that the chief had for traffic violators was enough to make everyone at the station uneasy. He would bring in the offenders himself and drag them into his office by the ear, tail, or tentacle. What followed was pure terror; banging, screaming, begging for mercy. No one knew what the chief was doing and no one had the courage to ask. Some officers even brought earplugs to spare themselves from both the screams and the equally awkward silence that followed.

Chip wondered if perhaps the chief had lost a family member to a traffic accident and was taking out his inconsolable rage on the world. "Maybe I should try reaching out to him," he thought. This, of course, was never going to happen, partially thanks to the chief's strange behavior toward the police officers.

"Do you think I'm smart?" he would often ask.

"Sure, chief. You're a smart guy."

"Yeah, but do you think I'm smarter than I was last week?"

"I, uh...I wouldn't know, chief."

Then the chief would click his tongue and walk away in a huff. Not very approachable.

All of this stress, which could not possibly be rationalized or dealt with, was swallowed into the soft fur of Kiggy as Chip cuddled him each night. Taking Kiggy for a walk also put Chip at ease. In this case, that was to his detriment. Perhaps because he was happy to be walking his glamdogg, and perhaps because he was desensitized to screaming thanks to the chief, Chip failed to notice the flocks of devils running away from the park and yelling at the top of their lungs. It wasn't until the sky turned an eerie purple that he noticed anything was wrong, and by then it was far too late to run from the large black mass hurtling toward the ground like a meteor. Chip grabbed Kiggy and held him in his arms protectively, because he did indeed love his glamdogg, and despite being an uninspired police officer, in his heart he still longed to protect others.

Chip was plagued by a strange dream. For someone else it might have been amusing, but for him it was quite stressful. It was a nightmare about Kiggy's name-choosing ceremony.

Glamdoggs were not named by their owners, but rather, chose their own names by being placed on a large mat with the alphabet written on it. When the real Kiggy—

not Dream-Kiggy—chose its name, it walked over the letter "K," then spun around and chirped again and again on the letter "G." As a result, the name on its birth certificate was "Kgggggggggggggggggggggggggggggggggggggggggggggggggggggggggggggggggggggggg."

Dream-Kiggy, however, was a very naughty glamdogg. He chose a profane and extremely inappropriate name for himself. Horrified, Chip entreated him to try again. Each new name that Dream-Kiggy chose was more lewd than the last. It was as nightmarish as a dream about glamdogg names could possibly be.

Chip awoke as he always did, with Kiggy's paws resting on his chest. Relieved that both the profane naming ceremony and strange falling object seemed to have been nothing more than his imagination, he clutched Kiggy ever tighter. Alas, Kiggy had already left this world. All that was left was ash and two charred, disembodied little paws.

Yet rather than being swallowed by anguish, Chip was seized with fear, for it seemed that something strange and terrible had happened to his own body as well. The clawlike hands that clutched the ashen Kiggy were hardly recognizable as his own. He scrambled up with a start, examining his body in confusion and panic. He was covered in what seemed to be leather, accented by pieces of thick shell on his chest and shoulders. His head was the wrong shape entirely. It felt hard, like a helmet, but spiky and oddly shaped, jutting out in unusual directions.

Under normal circumstances, one would think that he had simply been outfitted with some sort of odd costume, but Chip felt an overwhelming and deeply unsettling lack of self within the "clothes" that he wore. He removed his hands from the "helmet," fearing that it might come undone, leaving only an empty void where his head should be. Within this living suit of armor that had become his body, Chip could feel only one thing: rushing, burning blood. There was a fire flowing like a river through every inch of the emptiness inside him. It hissed maddeningly, like the whisper of a thousand voices. Unable to silence them, he could do little but listen to their call.

Justice

Justice

Justice

Chip was shaken from his daze by the sound of sobbing. Searching for its source, he saw that he had awoken in some sort of hellscape. He never could have guessed that it was simply the park, transformed. There were no signs of life anywhere in sight and a sort of strange black ooze could be found all over the barren ground. Upon closer inspection, the "ooze" seemed be a living creature—or rather, many living creatures. Like tiny worms, they stretched themselves up towards the hazy purple sky. Some of them seemed to have little white teeth shining amidst their ichor, but Chip could not be troubled with such details at the time.

Following the crying, like a siren song, he made his way to a massive crater in the ground. Within it was the black mass that had fallen from the sky, and a pure-white figure huddled beside it. The mass itself seemed to consist of a countless number of the black worms that littered the former park. They threaded together tightly into larger, belt-like pieces that wrapped around each other to form a sort of orb. The figure, from which the sobbing came, was daemon-like in appearance, with horns and wings. Their pale skin seemed to glow faintly, and their long white hair shimmered as if moonlight were dancing upon it. Gazing at the sky, Chip saw only darkness, with no such silver illumination to speak of.

There was something tender and tragic about the figure, but Chip couldn't help but notice that their physique was quite imposing. Their silky hair cascaded over broad shoulders and their muscular arms led to long, daggerlike claws. It was as if they were carved out of marble, their creator unsure if they were sculpting a goddess of the moon or a god of war.

Momentarily transfixed, Chip noticed that the figure was clutching a hand, pale and immaculate like their own, reaching out from the orb-like mass. Although Chip could not even begin to decipher this scene, there was something about it that made his burning blood run cold. Suddenly fearing that the creature would turn their gaze toward him, Chip fled from the crater as quickly as his unfamiliar feet could carry him.

It was to Chip's great surprise that he had not been transported to some sort of terrifying afterlife. In fact, as soon as he fled the park, he found the city he lived in to be almost exactly as he left it. The park itself had been covered in what appeared to be a purple dome that he had unknowingly passed through the walls of when he fled. The hazy, dark sky that he had gazed upon was simply its ceiling, blocking out the light of the natural world. Chip was in no state to hypothesize about what had occurred, but he did immediately notice that his emergence from the dome caused great alarm among the curious and frightened devils surrounding it. As Chip stepped out, a bold onlooker tried to walk in, only to find himself violently thrown to the ground. It was another mystery that there was no time to solve.

As he walked the streets in a daze, Chip realized that he was unwittingly making his way to the police station where he worked. This in itself was not especially odd, but the motivation behind his actions perplexed him. It was not that he was searching for a familiar place, but rather that he was being *propelled* to the location. His burning blood pulsed hotter and hotter, pushing his strange new body forward. As he drew closer to the station, however, he came to an understanding. He was answering the call of the blood, whispering, now screaming, in his ears.

Justice

Justice

Justice

The station was in an uproar when Chip entered, which was no surprise considering that a massive purple dome had suddenly appeared in the middle of the city.

Perhaps it was fear, or shock, or something else, but the other officers did not halt Chip's advance to the chief's office. Although the door was locked, he tore the doorknob clean off and walked inside without a second thought.

The chief, an unusually large goblin with greenish flesh packed into a blue uniform, was licking his fingers, which were covered in something juicy. His office was strewn with the corpses of traffic offenders, their heads sawed open and their brains removed.

"Why?" Chip demanded, coldly. The chief dared not resist his interrogation.

"I'm gonna be smart, that's why! I'm gonna eat all these brains and then solve all the crossword puzzles! I'll get smarter and smarter, and then I'll figure out how to rig the lottery and get rich! All I gotta do is keep eating brains!"

"Eating the brains of criminals didn't make you smart, it just made you a criminal!" Chip boomed, surprised at himself. The voice that came out of the strange helmet head was unrecognizable as his own.

The chief drew his gun, but it was far too late. Chip delivered a swift chop to his head, neatly exposing the portion of his brain that wasn't thrown to the wall along with the top of his skull. The chief gurgled for a moment, a sorry excuse for last words, then slumped over, sliding gracelessly from his chair to the floor.

Chip paused. Was this the justice he was seeking? It *felt* like the right thing to do, but as he gazed upon the chaos of the room, it also felt like he had only added one more corpse to the pile. He could not return the brains to the traffic offenders, after all. Had he really been brought here by the power that seized him, or had he actually wanted to kill the chief on his own? These ponderings, resembling rational thought, began to awaken Chip from his daze. No longer an instrument of some blind force of justice, Chip was unsure where to go. Perhaps jail would be his home now. He had committed murder, after all. He walked from the chief's office slowly, hands raised.

All eyes in the station were glued to him.

"Are you...some kinda superhero?" a werewolf police officer asked. It was Yams

Dougherty. Chip didn't care for him much, but he didn't seem like such a bad guy.

"I'm a beast. I hunger only for justice."

Did I really just say that!? I mean, it's true, but in context it makes me sound even more like a superhero. I'm just a very confused murderer!

"What's your name?" asked Bourbon McDermott, a yeti officer. Chip didn't care much for him either, mostly because his personal hygiene wasn't so great.

My name?

Chip's mind was in a strange place. Thinking about superheroes reminded him of a TV show he enjoyed called *Eggmaster Gorgos*. It was not about a superhero, but the protagonist had a young son who read comic books. His favorite comic book hero was a character named Devilizer. Devilizer didn't decapitate corrupt police chiefs and his mental health was not nearly as uncertain as Chip's right now, but there was no time to think of something clever.

"Devilizer," Chip said, unwilling to reveal his true identity (if he even existed anymore).

Attempting to escape the station before he had to answer any more questions, Chip marched out the door, hoping that the stunned silence he left behind would buy him enough time to escape to his apartment. Although the police officers remained frozen in place, Chip found himself suddenly lethargic. He hobbled down the street at a snail's pace, his burning blood now scarcely room temperature. Or perhaps whatever mysterious power that propelled him before had already been spent and he would dry up on the sidewalk like a dead fish. At any rate, even as his body failed him, he was happy that he would die with his mind intact. The fog of fury and justice had left his head and a sort of euphoria seemed to creep into his skull.

This moment of peace was soon interrupted by the strangest sight Chip had ever seen, even at the end of an extraordinarily strange day.

Before him stood some sort of monster. It was certainly nothing like any devil Chip knew of. It was tall and bulky and shaped like a picnic basket. Large, white, angry-looking eyes peeked from inside, along with various, cartoonishly oversized foods. The creature had four arms bursting from the sides of the basket, each of them holding a pair of scissors. Its thin but muscular legs peeked out from the basket as well, adorned with scandalously short athletic shorts and stylish running shoes.

Like any normal anyone would, Chip hoped he could avoid this logic-defying monstrosity, but it seemed that it had come specifically to meet him. Blocking the entire sidewalk, it stood in Chip's way. Even though its face (if it even had one) was all but hidden, the angry look in its shining white eyes made it clear that it was looking for a fight.

"You belong with us!" the basket monster screeched. Chip wasn't sure what kind of voice a scissor-wielding basket should have, but it definitely wasn't this. Other than the obvious, there was something deeply unnatural about this creature. Something ominous and loathsome. It wasn't what it had (its food looked rather delicious, actually), but what it was lacking. There was an intangible element that all devils possessed that was absent in this creature.

"I am a Cultural Ambassador!" it said, proudly. "I represent the world of Darknazar 66. Soon, this world shall be Darknazar as well!"

Boy, he sure doesn't make any sense.

"My name is Gracoorus! Short for Grandma's-Cooking-Running-With-Scissors! I am the combined essence of two Darknazarian cultural concepts! Grandma's cooking...and running with scissors!"

"We have those here, too." Chip said weakly.

The monster was furious. It ran at Chip with its scissors flailing. It really was as dangerous as your mother told you. Pierced by one of the hateful utensils, Chip bled profusely onto the sidewalk.

Ah, I must have a body in here after all. I'm too tired to fight back...too tired to run. I'll be with you soon, sweet Kiggy.

The monster dropped two pairs of its scissors and lifted Chip up, stuffing him into its giant basket.

"You'll be one with us now! You'll see! You'll see!" it mumbled, as if it somehow had food in its mouth. This strange and grotesque scene was suddenly interrupted by rapid gunfire, striking the basket monster and sending sparks flying everywhere.

"You put Devilizer down!" yelled Bourbon McDermott. Every officer in the station (except one guy named Friendo Biscuitson) came to Chip's aid. Although it was blatantly against policy, they blasted the basket monster in the back with bullets again and again to save their new favorite superhero.

"We're tired of being such crappy cops!" cried Yams Dougherty. "We got our justice back!"

The monster turned around furiously. Perhaps too furiously, as he accidently flung Chip onto the pavement in the process.

"You aliens ain't gonna take our city!" It was Friendo Biscuitson! He'd come after all, he just didn't run as fast as the other guys!

Aliens? Is that what they were? He said he was from Darknazar 66. Maybe that orb was their UFO and they came here to conquer our planet...

Chip wasn't the type to shoot first and ask questions later, so he wasn't ready to make a judgment call on whatever cosmic struggle was occurring. However, he did know one thing...

They killed Kiggy. They killed a poor, innocent creature and probably everyone else in that park. If they're allowed to continue, even more glamdoggs could die.

Chip's blood on the sidewalk began to boil. If you listened to its hissing closely enough, you might even make out a word:

Justice

Ah, there's that fire again.

Chip rose from the ground and thrust his open hand toward the sky. Cheering, the police irresponsibly fired their weapons into the air. The blood was more than a whisper now, it was a scream.

"Howl! Burning Blood!" Chip cried aloud. He flew at the basket monster like a tornado of claws and vengeance.

There was a bit of a logistical issue involved in attacking a creature with such a strange shape. Would harming the food harm it? Was it actually a smaller creature inside the basket, or was the basket itself like flesh? Faced with these impossible questions, Chip simply tore the arms off of the monster. All of its strength and all of its courage melted in an instant, for true justice is both swift and certain. The creature fled in terror, spewing blood and spilling grandma's cooking all over the sidewalk. To its credit, the running shoes it wore weren't just for show, and it was well beyond Chip's reach in no time at all.

Acting quickly, Chip wrenched a pair of scissors from one of its disembodied hands and launched them at the creature's muscular legs. It fell hard and fast. Dashing after it like a lightning bolt, Chip grabbed the handle of the basket and turned the creature around to face him.

"If you want grandma's cooking, you can find it on this world. As for running with scissors...you can take that to the afterlife with you!"

With that said, Chip drove his claws into the creature's big, silly-looking eyes again and again until its screams were no more. Whatever was inside the basket bubbled and oozed until there was nothing left except the little black worms that Chip had seen in the park. Upon closer inspection, they did have mouths, which they used for one tiny, final wail, before they melted into nothingness.

Like a cymbal crashing in his face, Chip was struck with a powerful vision. Countless grandmothers from an unknown place and time, cooking for their loved ones. Children running with scissors, for whatever foolish reason they do that. If they were aliens, they didn't look so different from the inhabitants of this world. Were they finally free now?

Chip felt an immeasurable wave of relief wash over him. His armored breastplate began to crack and his helmet soon followed. He could feel his own kobold body beneath it. He could feel the hairs on his arm standing on end. Whatever the armored suit had taken, it was giving back. He was alive after all.

Once again fearing that his identity would be revealed, Chip made a swift retreat. The police officers were distracted by all the food on the ground.

"You gotta try this!" said some idiot. "Tastes just like grandma used to make!"

In the newly dubbed Darknazar Park, a daemonic figure stretched out their muscular arms as a beautiful black gown slithered up their naked body, hugging it tightly. As they donned a white mask, a razor-toothed smile spread across their face.

"This justice of which you speak is a puzzle to me, Devilizer...for you have stolen it from its rightful place, here in my heart. Yet I do not despair, for I know it will taste all the sweeter when I seize it back...from your cold, dead body."

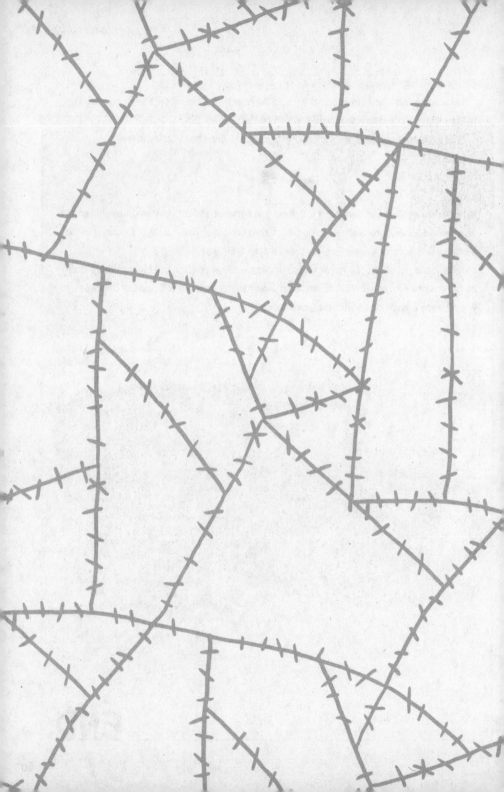

BONUS CHAPTER: DEVIL'S DAY TRIP

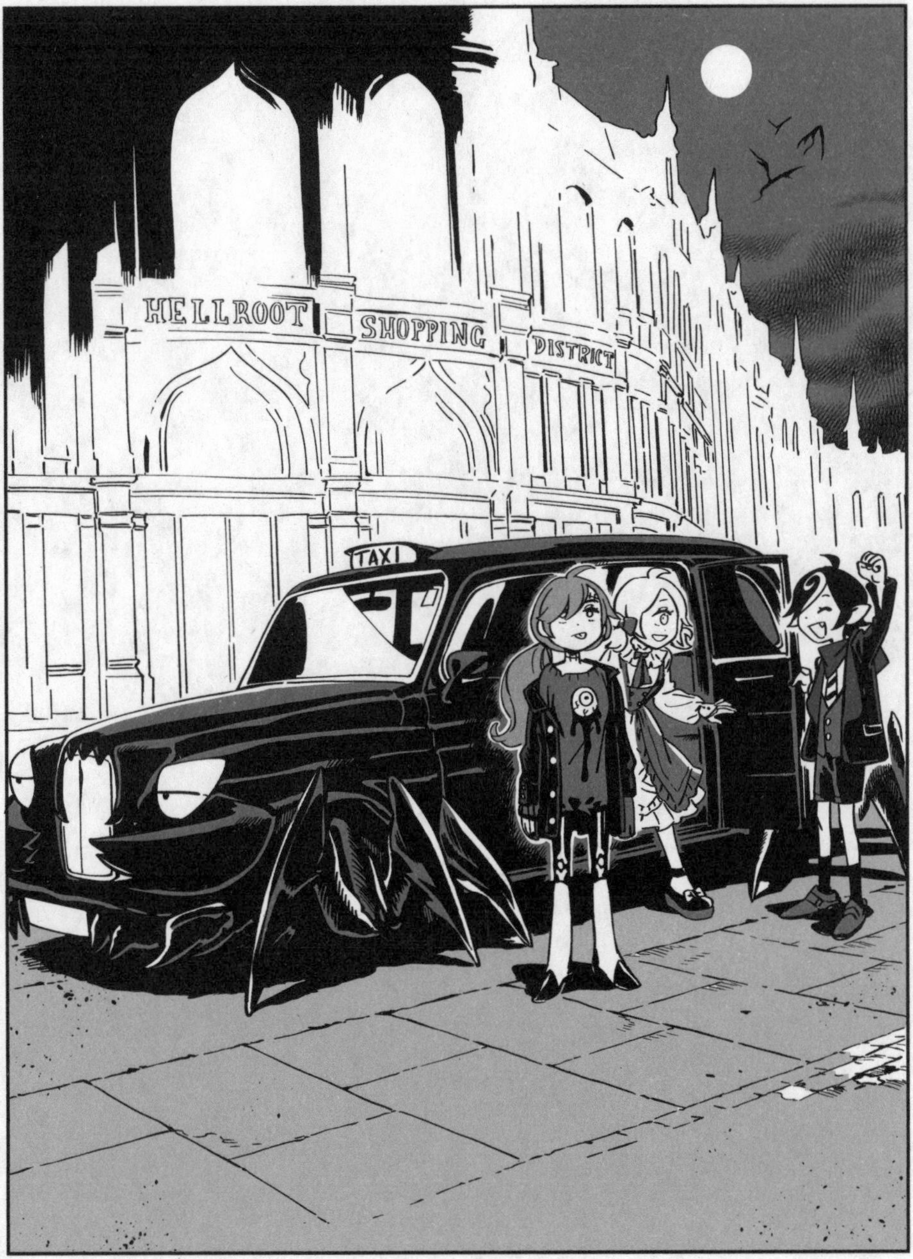
HELLROOT
SHOPPING
DISTRICT
TAXI

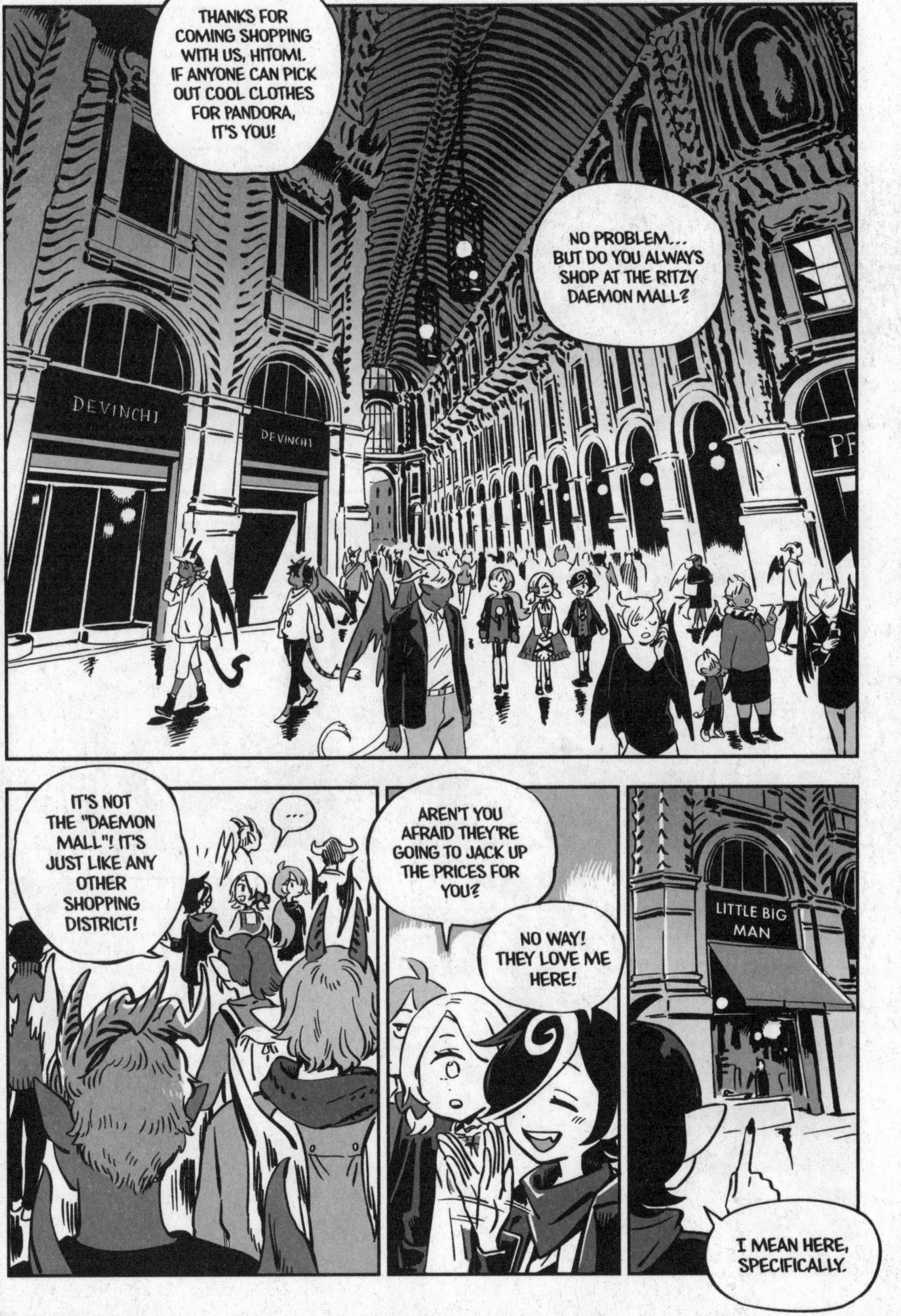
THANKS FOR COMING SHOPPING WITH US, HITOMI. IF ANYONE CAN PICK OUT COOL CLOTHES FOR PANDORA, IT'S YOU!
NO PROBLEM... BUT DO YOU ALWAYS SHOP AT THE RITZY DAEMON MALL?
DEVINCHI
DEVINCHI
IT'S NOT THE "DAEMON MALL"! IT'S JUST LIKE ANY OTHER SHOPPING DISTRICT!
...
AREN'T YOU AFRAID THEY'RE GOING TO JACK UP THE PRICES FOR YOU?
NO WAY! THEY LOVE ME HERE!
LITTLE BIG MAN
I MEAN HERE, SPECIFICALLY.

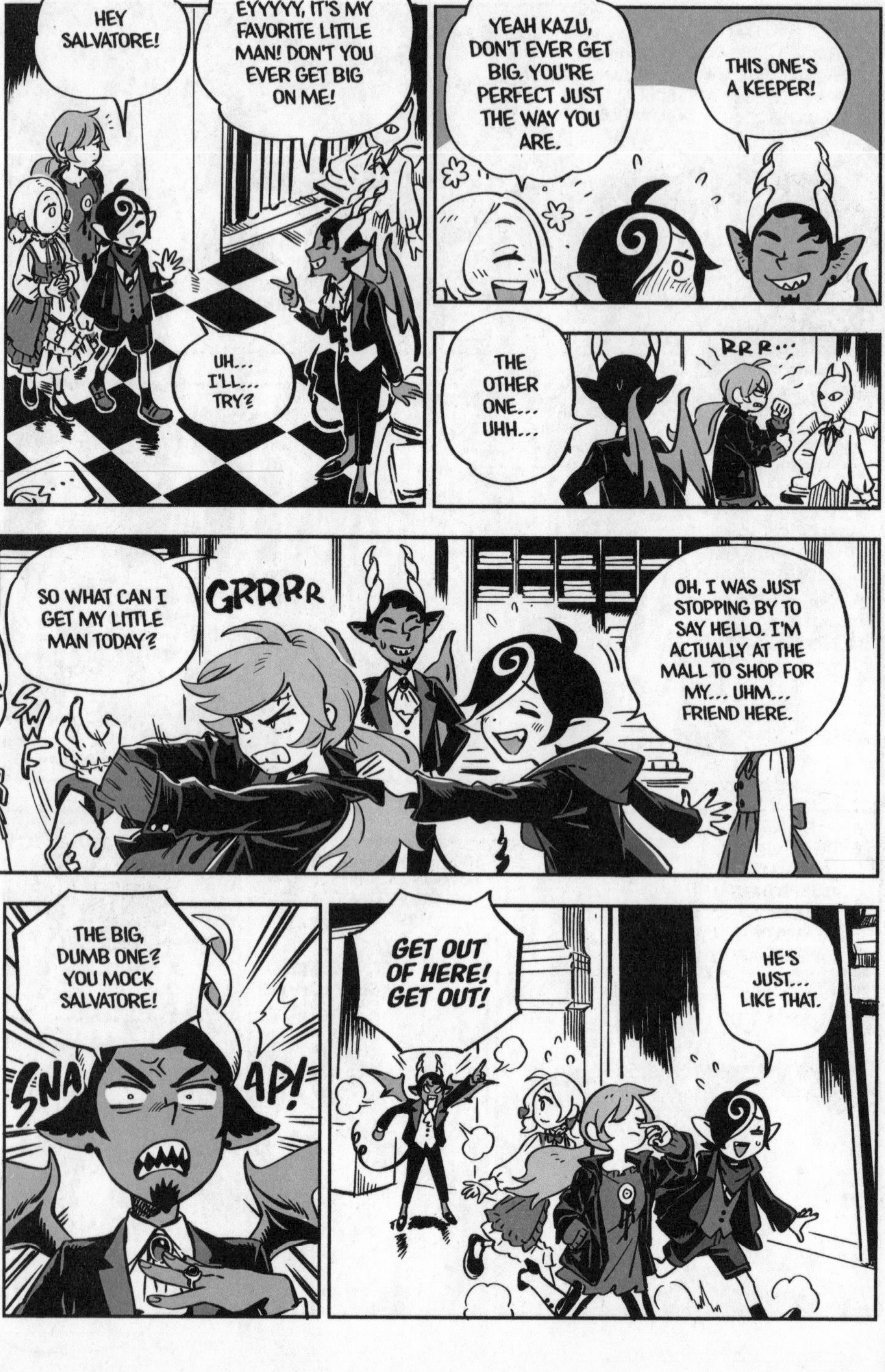
HEY SALVATORE!
EYYYYY, IT'S MY FAVORITE LITTLE MAN! DON'T YOU EVER GET BIG ON ME!
UH... I'LL... TRY?
YEAH KAZU, DON'T EVER GET BIG. YOU'RE PERFECT JUST THE WAY YOU ARE.
THIS ONE'S A KEEPER!
THE OTHER ONE... UHH...
RRR...
SO WHAT CAN I GET MY LITTLE MAN TODAY?
GRRRR
SWF
OH, I WAS JUST STOPPING BY TO SAY HELLO. I'M ACTUALLY AT THE MALL TO SHOP FOR MY... UHM... FRIEND HERE.
THE BIG, DUMB ONE? YOU MOCK SALVATORE!
SNAP!
GET OUT OF HERE! GET OUT!
HE'S JUST... LIKE THAT.

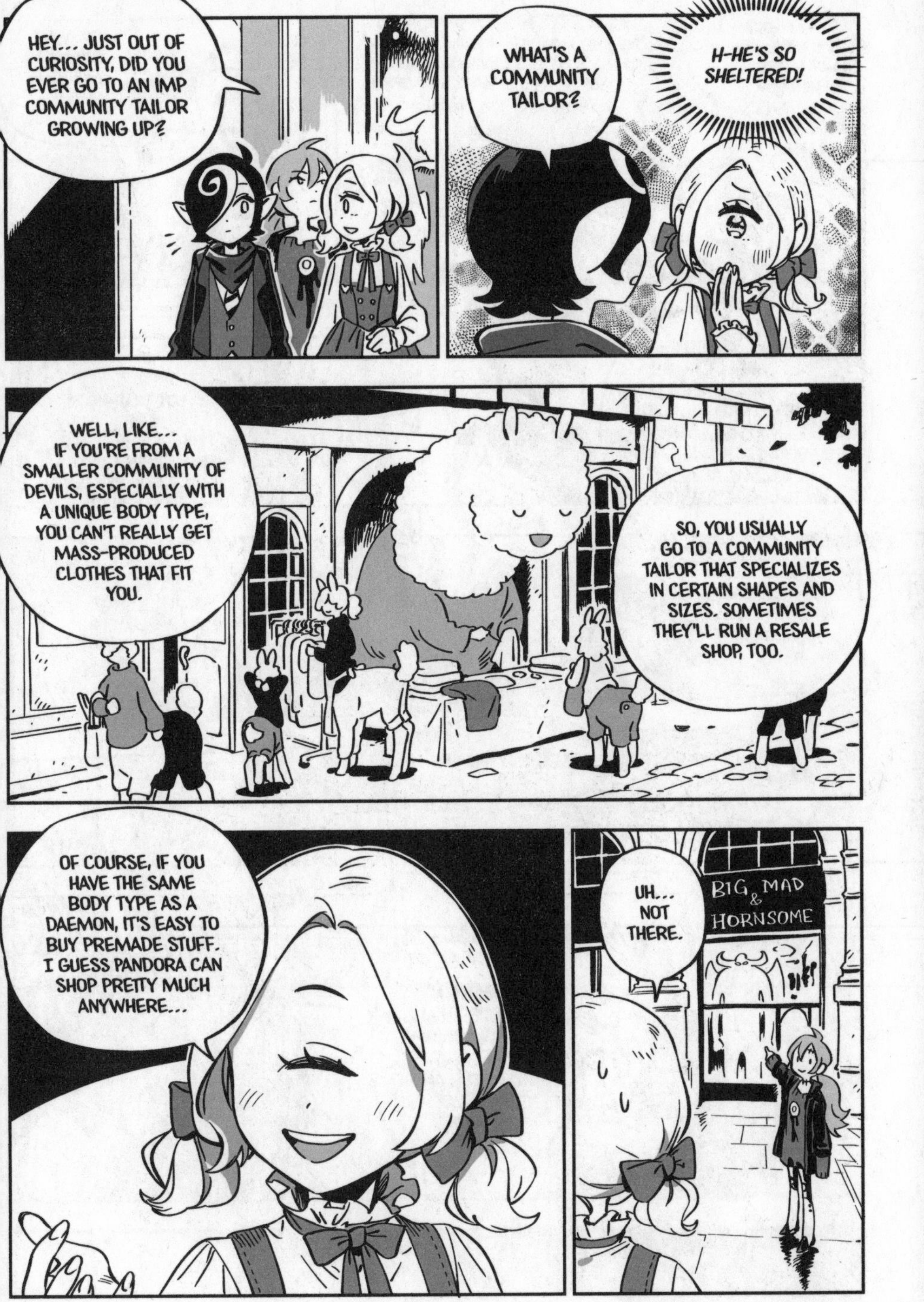
HEY... JUST OUT OF CURIOSITY, DID YOU EVER GO TO AN IMP COMMUNITY TAILOR GROWING UP?
WHAT'S A COMMUNITY TAILOR?
H-HE'S SO SHELTERED!
WELL, LIKE... IF YOU'RE FROM A SMALLER COMMUNITY OF DEVILS, ESPECIALLY WITH A UNIQUE BODY TYPE, YOU CAN'T REALLY GET MASS-PRODUCED CLOTHES THAT FIT YOU.
SO, YOU USUALLY GO TO A COMMUNITY TAILOR THAT SPECIALIZES IN CERTAIN SHAPES AND SIZES. SOMETIMES THEY'LL RUN A RESALE SHOP, TOO.
OF COURSE, IF YOU HAVE THE SAME BODY TYPE AS A DAEMON, IT'S EASY TO BUY PREMADE STUFF. I GUESS PANDORA CAN SHOP PRETTY MUCH ANYWHERE...
UH... NOT THERE.
BIG & MAD
HORNSOME

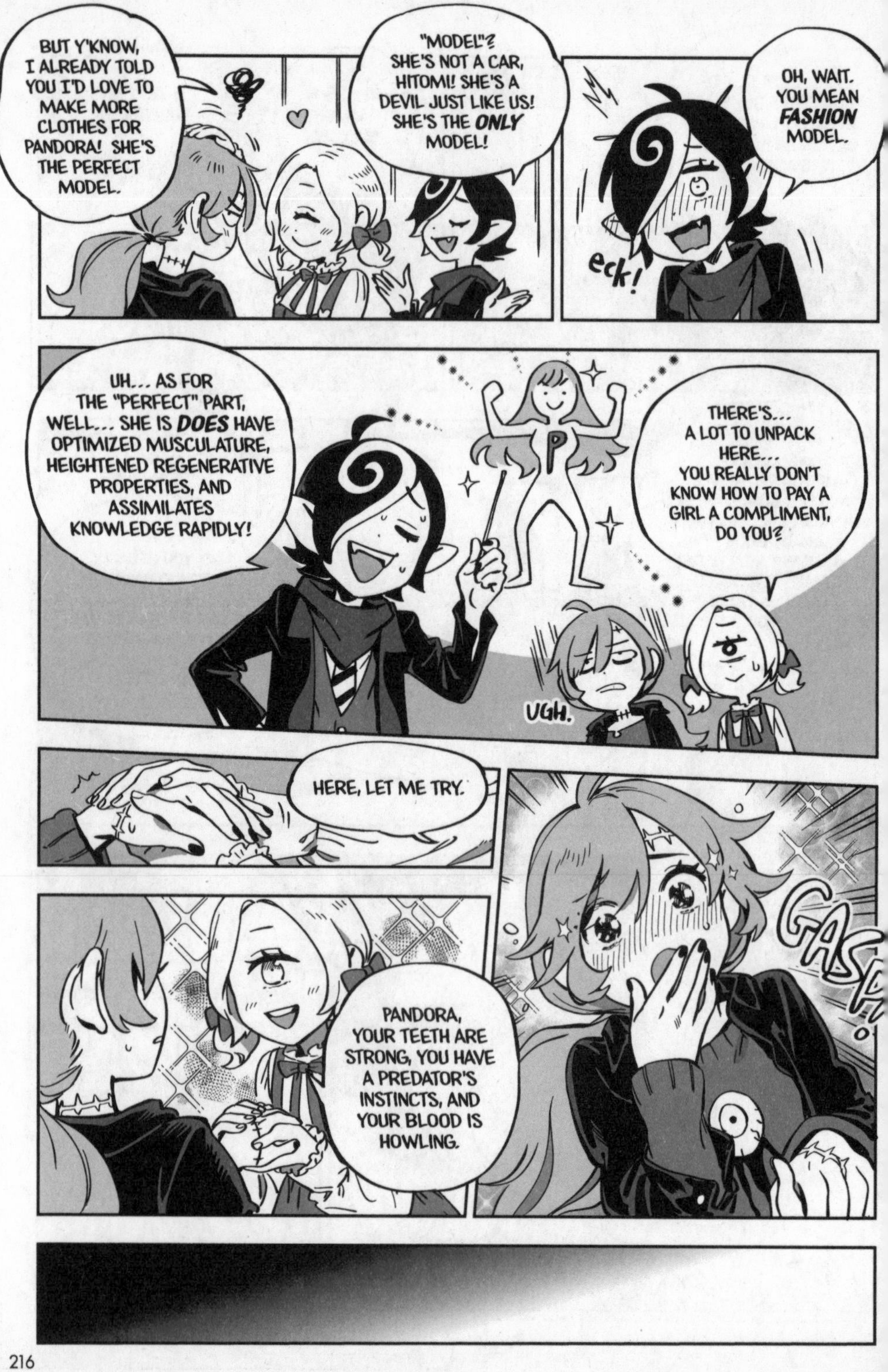
BUT Y'KNOW, I ALREADY TOLD YOU I'D LOVE TO MAKE MORE CLOTHES FOR PANDORA! SHE'S THE PERFECT MODEL.
"MODEL"? SHE'S NOT A CAR, HITOMI! SHE'S A DEVIL JUST LIKE US! SHE'S THE ONLY MODEL!
OH, WAIT. YOU MEAN FASHION MODEL.
eck!
UH... AS FOR THE "PERFECT" PART, WELL... SHE IS DOES HAVE OPTIMIZED MUSCULATURE, HEIGHTENED REGENERATIVE PROPERTIES, AND ASSIMILATES KNOWLEDGE RAPIDLY!
P
THERE'S... A LOT TO UNPACK HERE... YOU REALLY DON'T KNOW HOW TO PAY A GIRL A COMPLIMENT, DO YOU?
UGH.
HERE, LET ME TRY.
PANDORA, YOUR TEETH ARE STRONG, YOU HAVE A PREDATOR'S INSTINCTS, AND YOUR BLOOD IS HOWLING.
GASP!

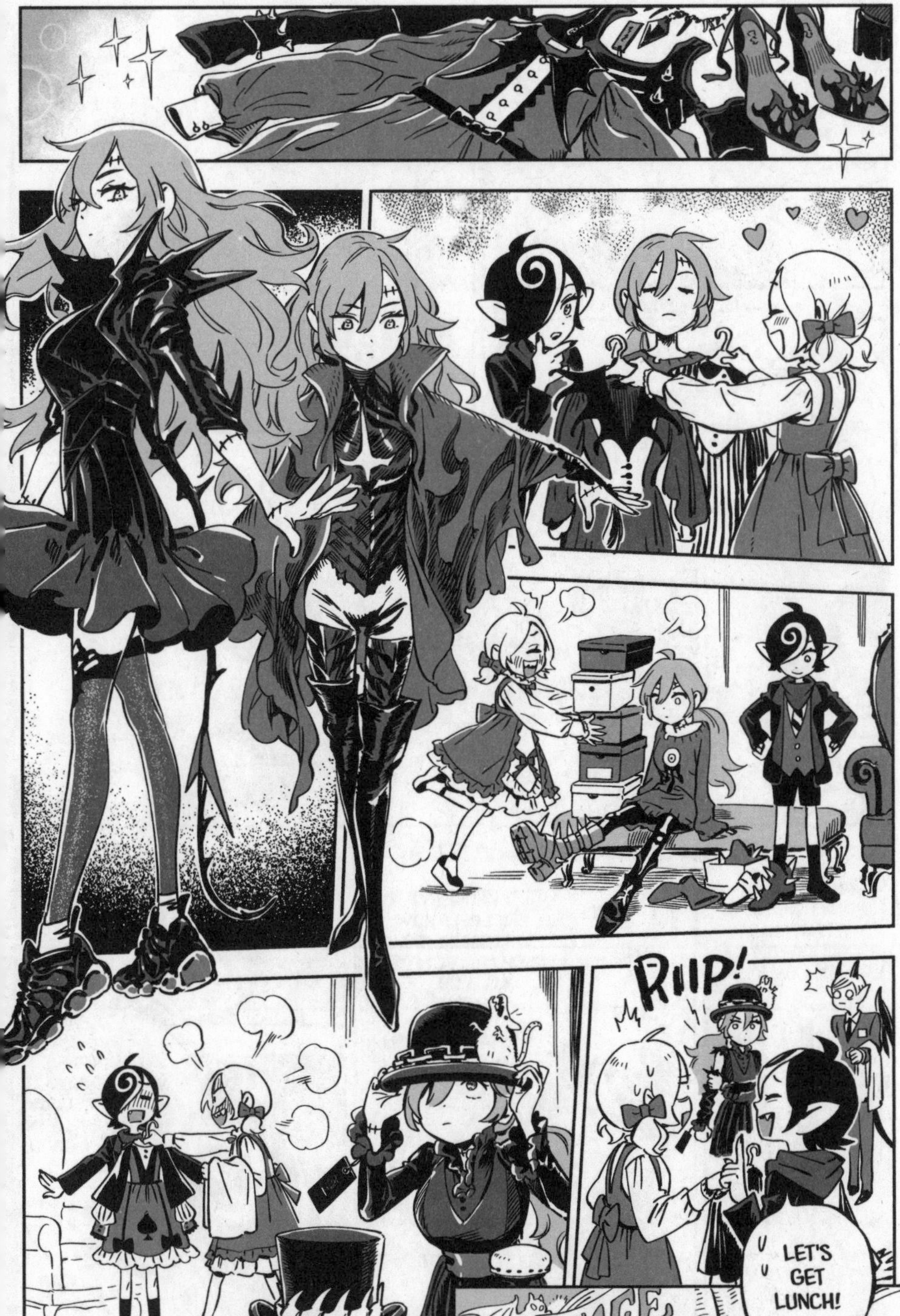

RIIP!
LET'S GET LUNCH!
CAFE

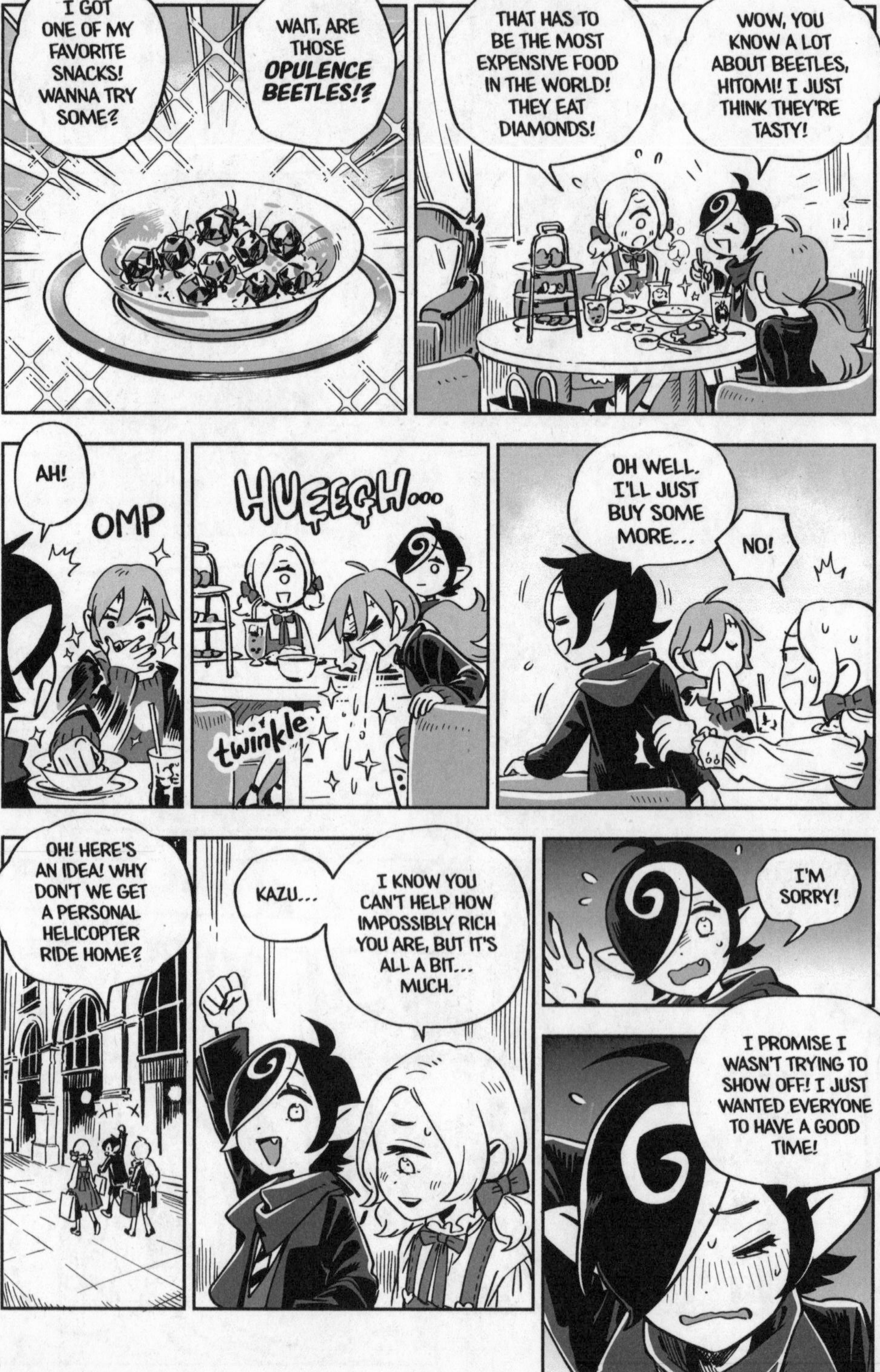
I GOT ONE OF MY FAVORITE SNACKS! WANNA TRY SOME?
WAIT, ARE THOSE OPULENCE BEETLES!?
THAT HAS TO BE THE MOST EXPENSIVE FOOD IN THE WORLD! THEY EAT DIAMONDS!
WOW, YOU KNOW A LOT ABOUT BEETLES, HITOMI! I JUST THINK THEY'RE TASTY!
AH!
OMP
HUEEGH...
twinkle
OH WELL. I'LL JUST BUY SOME MORE...
NO!
OH! HERE'S AN IDEA! WHY DON'T WE GET A PERSONAL HELICOPTER RIDE HOME?
KAZU...
I KNOW YOU CAN'T HELP HOW IMPOSSIBLY RICH YOU ARE, BUT IT'S ALL A BIT... MUCH.
I'M SORRY!
I PROMISE I WASN'T TRYING TO SHOW OFF! I JUST WANTED EVERYONE TO HAVE A GOOD TIME!

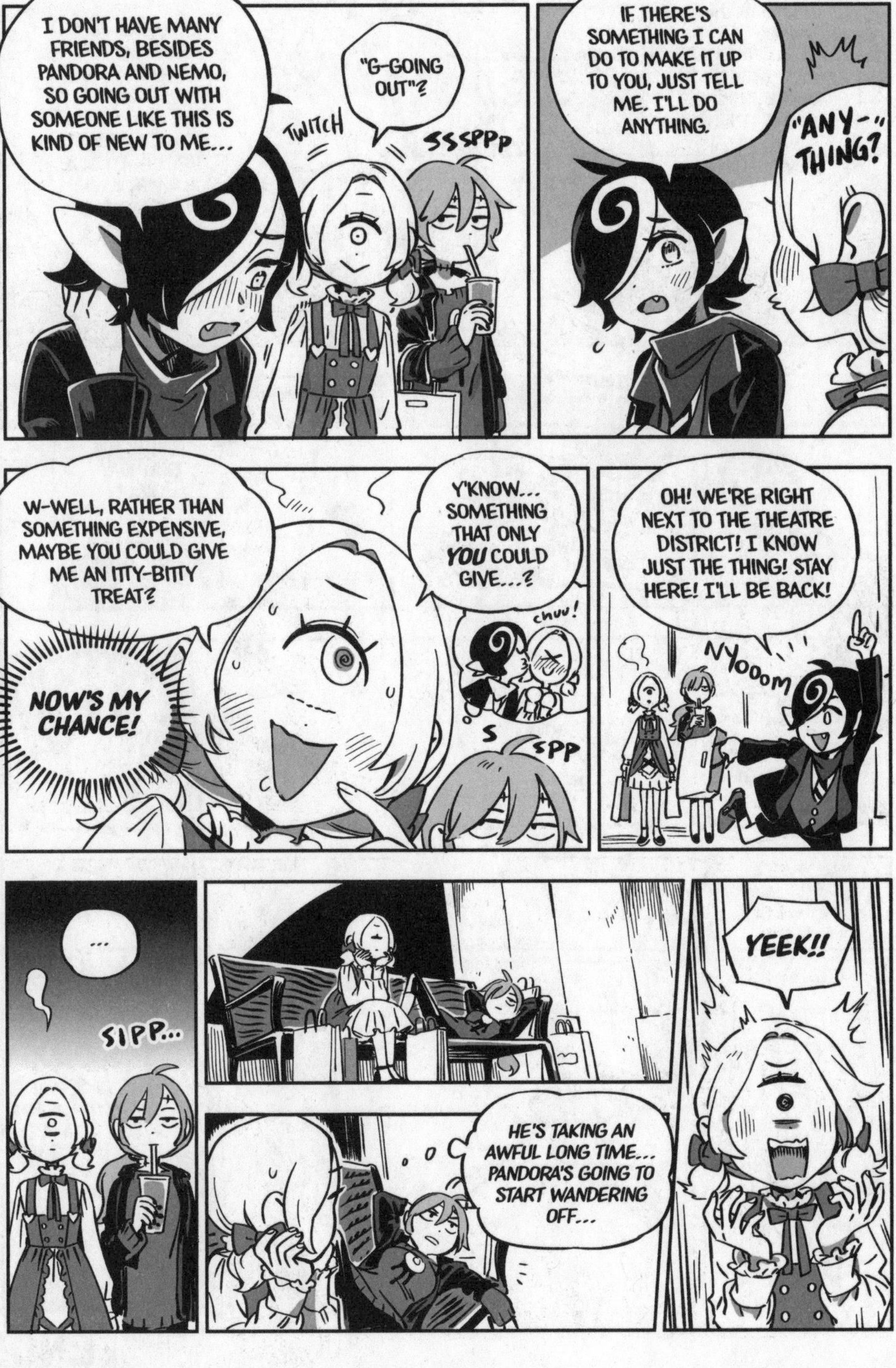
I DON'T HAVE MANY FRIENDS, BESIDES PANDORA AND NEMO, SO GOING OUT WITH SOMEONE LIKE THIS IS KIND OF NEW TO ME...
"G-GOING OUT"?
TWITCH
SSSPPP
IF THERE'S SOMETHING I CAN DO TO MAKE IT UP TO YOU, JUST TELL ME. I'LL DO ANYTHING.
"ANY-" THING?
W-WELL, RATHER THAN SOMETHING EXPENSIVE, MAYBE YOU COULD GIVE ME AN ITTY-BITTY TREAT?
NOW'S MY CHANCE!
Y'KNOW... SOMETHING THAT ONLY YOU COULD GIVE...?
chuu!
S SPP
OH! WE'RE RIGHT NEXT TO THE THEATRE DISTRICT! I KNOW JUST THE THING! STAY HERE! I'LL BE BACK!
NYOOOM
...
SIPP...
HE'S TAKING AN AWFUL LONG TIME... PANDORA'S GOING TO START WANDERING OFF...
YEEK!!

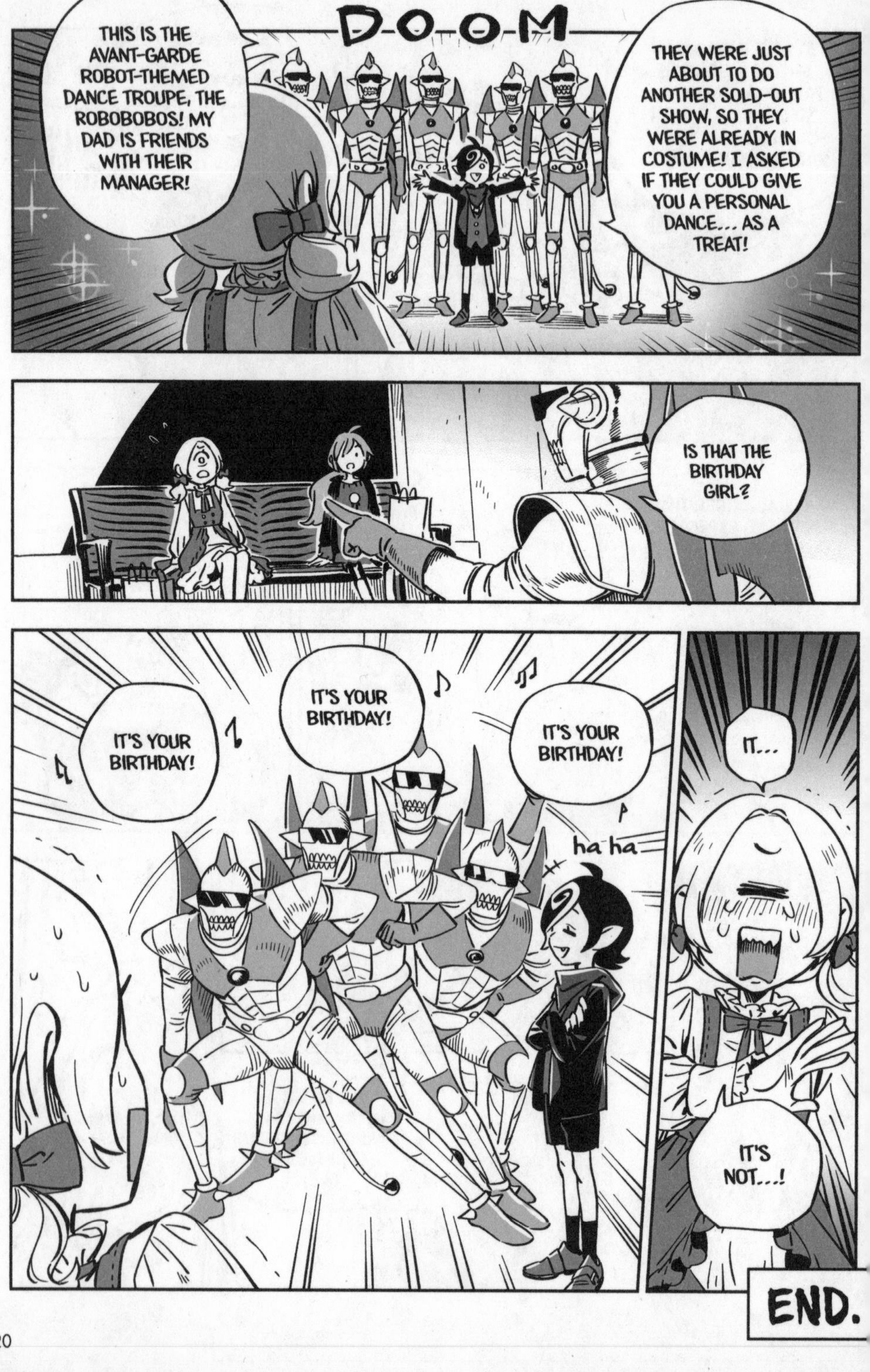
DOOM
THIS IS THE AVANT-GARDE ROBOT-THEMED DANCE TROUPE, THE ROBOBOBOS! MY DAD IS FRIENDS WITH THEIR MANAGER!
THEY WERE JUST ABOUT TO DO ANOTHER SOLD-OUT SHOW, SO THEY WERE ALREADY IN COSTUME! I ASKED IF THEY COULD GIVE YOU A PERSONAL DANCE... AS A TREAT!
IS THAT THE BIRTHDAY GIRL?
IT'S YOUR BIRTHDAY!
IT'S YOUR BIRTHDAY!
IT'S YOUR BIRTHDAY!
ha ha
IT...
IT'S NOT...!
END.

DEVIL'S CANDY

CONTINUES IN
VOLUME 3

BIKKURI

Bikkuri is a prolific manga adapter, voice actor, and scriptwriter who has worked on popular anime series such as *One Piece* and *Ghost in the Shell*. Frequently collaborating with Rem, including their winning entry for Kodansha's *Morning International Manga Competition*, he will keep writing until the grave takes him.

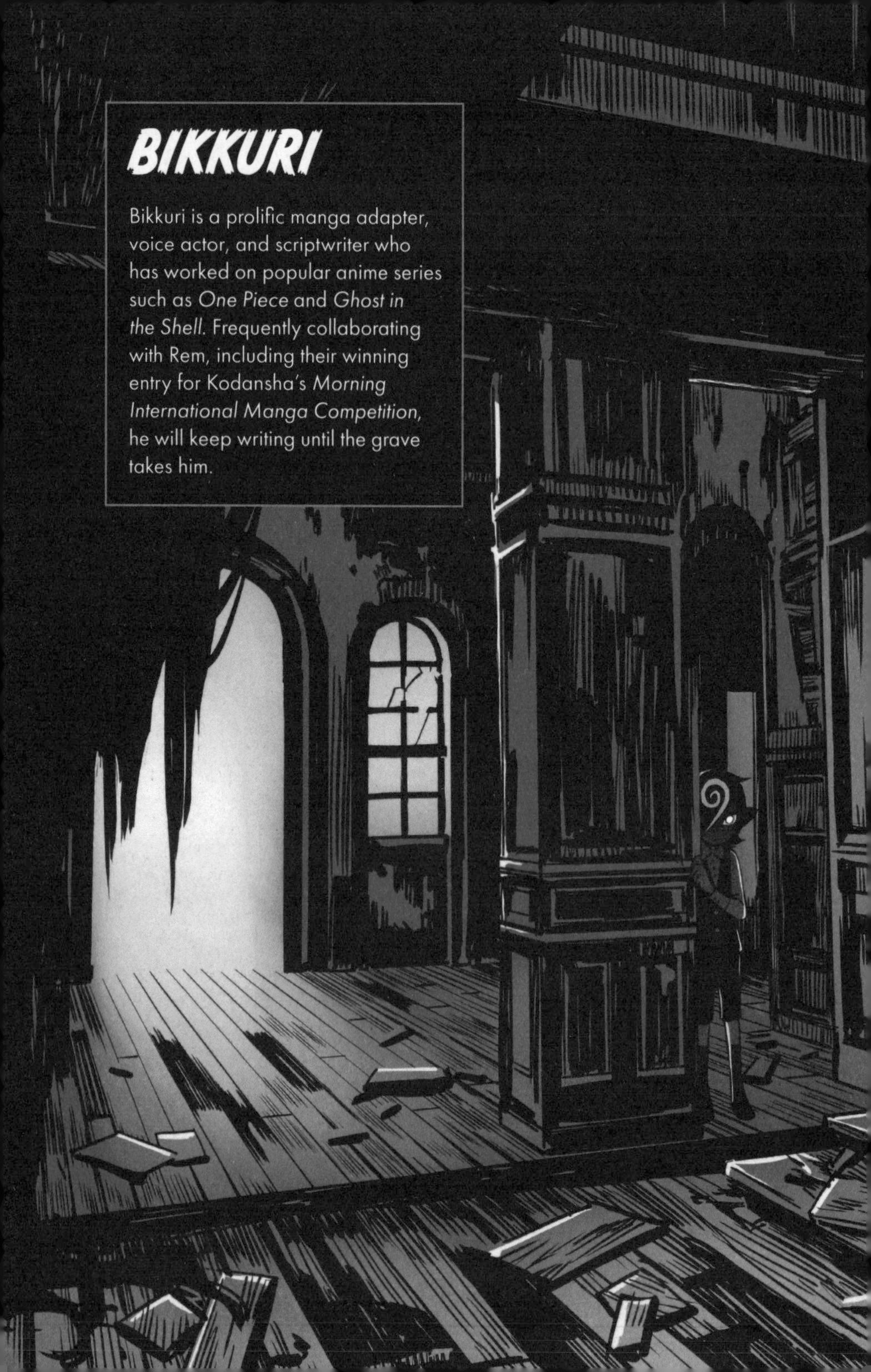

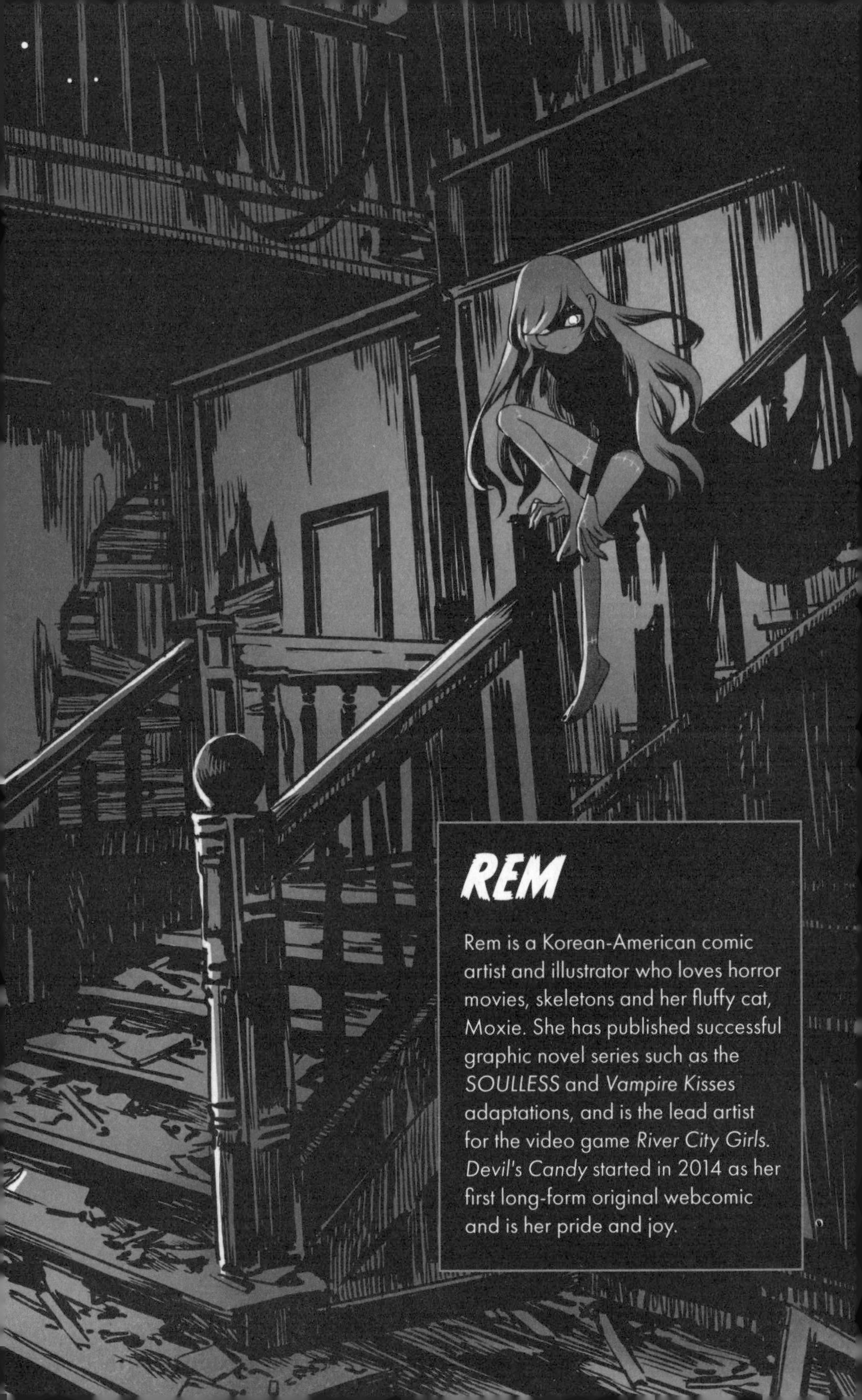

REM

Rem is a Korean-American comic artist and illustrator who loves horror movies, skeletons and her fluffy cat, Moxie. She has published successful graphic novel series such as the *SOULLESS* and *Vampire Kisses* adaptations, and is the lead artist for the video game *River City Girls*. *Devil's Candy* started in 2014 as her first long-form original webcomic and is her pride and joy.

VOLUME 2
VIZ ORIGINALS EDITION

STORY BY BIKKURI
ART BY REM

LETTERING ✗ Erika Milligan
DESIGN ✗ VIZ Media
COPY EDITOR ✗ Justin Hoeger
EDITORIAL ASSISTANT ✗ Luka M.
EDITOR ✗ Fawn Lau

Copyright © 2014-2022 Rem (Priscilla Hamby), Bikkuri (Clint Bickham)

Printed in Canada

Published by VIZ Media, LLC
P.O. Box 77010
San Francisco, CA 94107

10 9 8 7 6 5 4 3 2 1
First printing, July 2022

viz.com